THE
ELECTRIC
LIFE

Also by Sven Birkerts:

AN ARTIFICIAL WILDERNESS (1987)

THE ELECTRIC LIFE

ESSAYS

ON

Modern Poetry

SVEN

BIRKERTS

William Morrow and Company, Inc.

NEW YORK

Copyright © 1989 by Sven Birkerts

Most of these essays appeared in the following periodicals:

Ploughshares, The Boston Review, Pequod, Margin, The Iowa Review, The Agni Review, The Boston Phoenix, Sulfur, Parnassus, The Nation, The New Republic, Partisan Review, The Boston Globe, The Threepenny Review.

Essays in *The Electric Life*, some under different titles, were first published as follows: "The Poet in an Age of Distraction" in *Ploughshares*, Vol. 10, No. 1 (1984); "When Lightning Strikes," *The Boston Review*, April 1985; "The Rage of Caliban," *Pequod*, No. 22 (1987); " 'Poetry' and 'Politics,' " *Margin*, Autumn 1987; " 'The Whitsun Weddings': A Commemorative Reading," *The Boston Review*, Spring 1988; "Craig Raine's 'In the Kalahari Desert,' " *Ploughshares*, Vol. 13, No. 4 (1988); "Marianne Moore's 'Poetry,'" *The Iowa Review*, Vol. 17, No. 3 (1987); "James Wright's 'Hammock': A Sounding," *The Agni Review*, No. 21 (1984); "Robert Lowell I," *The Boston Review*, October 1987; "Robert Lowell II," *The Boston Phoenix*, April 17, 1987; "Paul Blackburn," *Sulfur*, No. 16 (1986); "May Swenson," *Parnassus*, 1985; "Adrienne Rich," *The Nation*, June 7, 1986; "Frank Bidart," *The Boston Phoenix*, December 6, 1983; "John Ashbery," *Sulfur*, No. 19 (1987); "Modern Sequences," *Parnassus*, Fall/Winter 1984; "Derek Walcott," *The New Republic*, January 23, 1984; "Melissa Green/Patricia Storace," *Parnassus*, 1988; "Brad Leithauser," *The Boston Review*, May 1982; "Jorie Graham I," *The Boston Review*, September 1983; "Jorie Graham II," *The Village Voice, VLS*, June 1987; "Amy Clampitt/Christopher Jane Corkery," *Partisan Review*, No. 1 (1986); "Alice Fulton," *The Boston Review*, December 1986; "Baron Wormser," *The Boston Globe*, March 24, 1985; "Christopher Middleton/Samuel Menashe," *Partisan Review*, No. 4 (1987); "Gary Snyder," *Sulfur*, No. 19 (1987); "Paul Muldoon/Tony Harrison/Christopher Logue," *Partisan Review*, No. 3 (1988); "Irish Poets," *The Boston Globe*, August 17, 1986; "Rainer Maria Rilke," *The Threepenny Review*, Fall 1988; "Gunnar Ekelöf/Tomas Tranströmer," *Parnassus*, Fall 1983; "Boris Pasternak," *Parnassus*, Spring 1987; "Czeslaw Milosz," *The Agni Review*, No. 19 (1983); "Zbigniew Herbert," *Sulfur*, No. 15 (1986); "Adam Zagajewski," *The Threepenny Review*, Summer 1986; "Octavio Paz," *The New Republic*, March 14, 1988.

All rights reserved. No part of this book may be reproduced or utilized in any form or by any means, electronic or mechanical, including photocopying, recording or by any information storage and retrieval system, without permission in writing from the Publisher. Inquiries should be addressed to Permissions Department, William Morrow and Compnay, Inc., 105 Madison Ave., New York, N.Y. 10016.

Library of Congress Cataloging-in-Publication Data

Birkerts, Sven.
The electric life : essays on modern poetry / Sven Birkerts.
p. cm.
Bibliography: p.
Includes index.
ISBN 0-688-07861-3
1. Poetry, Modern—20th century—History and criticism.
I. Title.
PN1271.B55 1989
809.1'04—dc19
88-27543
CIP

Printed in the United States of America

First Edition

1 2 3 4 5 6 7 8 9 10

BOOK DESIGN BY MARIA EPES

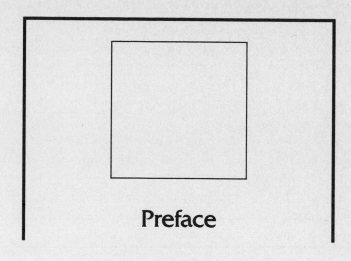

Preface

I take my title and my epigraph from a high-sounding and full-throttle passage in Shelley's *A Defence of Poetry*. Shelley's claims are so far at odds with the popular conception of the poet's position (assuming that the general population even gives the matter a thought) that the reader might think I'm being perverse in citing them. Not so. Or, rather, no more so than Shelley himself; for surely he knew how things stood between the poet and the general public. The relationship has not changed that much in the century and a half since the *Defence* was penned.

I begin with those noble words because in one very important sense they are true. If we believe that our inner being, our consciousness, is constituted through language—and I have yet to hear a persuasive argument that it isn't—then the poet, as the most intent and concentrated user of language, occupies a very privileged position. Not socially, to be sure—but existentially. Then he is not so much an entertainer as an explorer.

This, simply put, is the belief that underlies these various essays and that welds their various occasions of origin into what I hope is a single occasion of presentation.

The pieces have been grouped under four headings. In pondering this arrangement, I found that it marked out certain of the critic's functions—or levels of engagement—quite neatly.

First, a set of general essays: my attempts to address the kinds of questions that occur to everyone who spends time reading poetry seriously. There are questions—many questions—about language, about the nature of creativity, about the place of poetry in a world riven by political and social unrest.

Following the general essays are a handful of "close readings." Close attention is directed at a few chosen densities of language—the intuitions and speculations of the first section are put to the test.

Next, a series of assessments of English-language poets, most of them contemporary practitioners. While these essays don't pretend to do full justice to the energetic and pluralistic poetry "scene," they do sample with some catholicity.

Finally, I include a group of essays on poets in translation. I have serious reservations about reading poetry outside one's area of linguistic competence, but curiosity and desire—I wanted some kind of contact with these legendary individuals—carried the day. Though I would say that I consider all of these pieces as approaches and ventures ("essays" in the original sense of the word), those in the final section are emphatically so. Maybe that accounts for the special fondness with which I regard them.

I would like to thank a number of editors and friends: Sharon Dunn, Askold Melnyczuk, Thomas Frick, Tom Sleigh, William Corbett, John Ferguson, Ann Hulbert, Wendy Lesser, Leon Wieseltier, Elizabeth Pochoda, Howard Norman, Kit Rachlis, Clayton Eshleman, Mary Karr,

Herb Leibowitz, Margaret Ann Roth, Seamus Heaney, Joseph Brodsky, Maria Guarnaschelli, and of course my family and Lynn, my long-suffering wife. Also, a most loving welcome to Mara Sophia, who arrived even as the proofs were being corrected.

—SVEN BIRKERTS

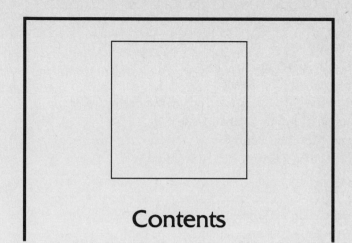

Contents

It is impossible to read the compositions of the most celebrated writers of the present day without being startled with the electric life which burns within their words. They measure the circumference and sound the depths of human nature with a comprehensive and all-penetrating spirit, and they are themselves perhaps the most sincerely astonished at its manifestations; for it is less their spirit than the spirit of the age. Poets are the hierophants of an unapprehended inspiration; the mirrors of the gigantic shadows which futurity casts upon the present; the words which express what they understand not; the trumpets which sing to battle, and feel not what they inspire; the influence which is moved not, but moves. Poets are the unacknowledged legislators of the world.

—SHELLEY, *A Defence of Poetry*

THE
ELECTRIC
LIFE

PART I:

APPROACHES

Hamann's Bone

The Poet in an Age
of Distraction

When Lightning Strikes

The Rage of Caliban

"Poetry" and "Politics"

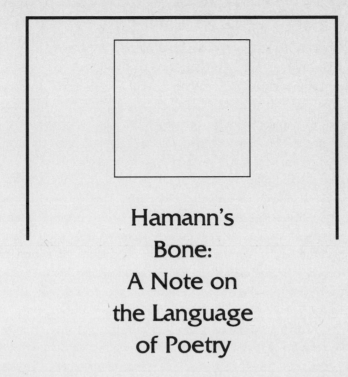

Hamann's
Bone:
A Note on
the Language
of Poetry

T he title of this prefatory piece is odd enough to require a bit of explanation. Surficially speaking, there is
no great mystery. I was once reading an account of the German phi-
losopher/language mystic J. G. Hamann, and came upon the following
quotation from the man's correspondence: "Language is the bone upon
which I have been gnawing all my life." I liked the ring of that—
enough to copy the words into a notebook. I felt that they registered a
truth about my own thinking process. Basically, that whatever subject I
happen to be meditating upon, in the end I always find myself back up
against the problem of language; back, that is, to the fact that all
analysis of human expression comes to a dead end before the mystery

of language and its relation to consciousness. This is not to say that I am, like Hamann, a language mystic, but the reader of these essays will see that my approach to poetry is deeply colored by certain views—or biases, if you will—about both the importance and the unknowability of human language behavior. The observations that follow, which are not meant as a contribution to linguistic science, may give some sense of the spirit with which I approach poetry.

All verbal communication, written as well as spoken, involves a marriage of two elements—sound and sense. This is basic, like saying that all material entities exist in both space and time, but it's a good place to start. Indeed, we can quickly refine upon the premise by saying that all verbal communication is comprised of sound *become* sense. Whether it was a pressing collective need for sense that originally organized sound (out of a recognition, say, that it was a valuable shorthand for gesture), or whether sound coalesced out of some imperative of its own to *make* sense, is not certain. But the fact remains that the two elements are almost indissolubly bound in language. I say "almost" because there are moments—moments that I experience most intensely while reading lyric poetry—when the two seem to come apart. I recognize with a shock that these are sounds that are parading before me as meanings and emotions; I realize how thin the wall between meaning and music can get.

"Ontogeny recapitulates phylogeny," runs Haeckel's famous dictum—the growth of the individual tells the tale of the species. Behind the bougainvillea of its syllables this is a satisfyingly concise—and staggering!—formulation. Whatever its usefulness for the biological sciences, however, it cannot clear up for us the mystery of the origin of language in man. We cannot derive its beginnings in the species by studying its development in the child. For what the child comes into and appropriates, the species had once—maybe many times—to create for itself. Still, there may be a few things to be learned from looking close to home.

To begin with, the child's acquisition of language seems to depend on the gradual particularization of certain sound combinations out of an otherwise undifferentiated—and probably pleasure-producing—

babble. (The etymology of "babble," which is closely linked to that of "baby," reveals an onomatopoetic origin; Skeat gives the primary meaning of the word as "to keep saying *ba, ba*." The relation of "babble" to "Babel," the biblical site of the scattering of tongues, is only that of a suggestive homonym.) Mastery comes for the child with a growing awareness that certain combinations produce results, that they give some leverage over people in an "out there," and that they are often associated with important objects. Again, whether it's the growth of consciousness that prompts these identifications or the identifications that bring about the growth is hard to say. Most likely the processes are mutually reinforcing. But two things are incontestable: that sounds are vitally bound up with the child's emerging self-identity, and that meanings come at the heel of mutterings.

The child eventually forsakes his self-created languages—if that's how we choose to understand babbling—for the lingua franca. It's obviously the utilitarian thing to do. But what about the earliest speakers? How did our ancestors work out the first consensual word(s)? Remember, too, Lévi-Strauss's insistence that language could not have originated piecemeal, that the coining of a single word already implies the idea of the whole language. Would those inventors have been driven to the deed by need, or joy, or terror. . . ? We can imagine, on the one hand, some sort of decision process, a purposeful putting together of heads; but the events may also have been as spontaneous and inevitable as the first copulation. For that matter, we don't even know if prelinguistic man passed his days in mute silence or in a condition of incessant "infantile" babbling. Nor could we say, if it *was* babbling, that it was without subjective differentiation: Each sound-maker might have been refining his own private idiom.

But language did emerge. Certain sounds fell into combination with certain other sounds (choose your own *Ur*-locale) and were accepted as indicating, referring to, or possibly even *incarnating* the objects and actions of the surrounding world. How *was* consensus achieved? Was there, even within tribal confines, a struggle among competing idiolects? And how quickly were these speakers able to use their word for "tree" without requiring the presence of the specific tree as collateral? Would there have been a prolonged period during

Hamann's Bone

which the sound was held to be an immediate attribute of its object—its sonic aura, as it were? Which was the greater evolutionary stride, naming the object or being able to use that name meaningfully when the object was not in sight?*

I imagine a rough-sounding, highly generalized communication among the first speakers. But at the same time, I wonder about the subjective conditions—what speaking and hearing *felt* like. Is it excessively romantic to suppose that the earliest interchanges were charged with an intense numinous immediacy? What did it feel like to say the tree word then? It might just be preposterous for us to position ourselves on a psychic continuum with our ancestors, to assume that we are cut—inwardly—from the same essential cloth.

Everything about our private and collective systems of meaning is bound up with language—and we don't have a clue about its origins. This may mean, ultimately, that we don't have a clue about ourselves, either. Consider: All of our researches and interrogations are conducted through a medium that we don't even begin to comprehend! We can store elephantine encyclopedias on microchips, but we don't know by what process sound became a vehicle for sense, or just how our language and our selfhood are entwined.

Were the first bondings of sound fortuitous, or did they happen through some matching of a sound value to the perceived essential nature of a thing? Or, to press the question, could there have even *been* a perception of the essential nature of anything without the registry of sound? And what about sound values—are they relative, or somehow "fixed," connected with the primary organization of the psyche?

And what about those first words? Emerson once wrote, most suggestively, that "every word was once a poem." Maybe the earliest coinages were not so much contractual decisions made by tribal elders as "inspired" creations—each one different—by mankind's first artistic vanguard. If only we could establish with certainty what the first tribal languages were really like. But as these were in place long before

---

*I assume here that nouns preceded verbs, and that both nouns and verbs were in use long before the particularizing advantages of adjectives and adverbs were discovered. These forms may have evolved mainly to allow speakers to streamline an increasingly cumbersome word-hoard, one that required separate designations for variations in the surroundings.

Approaches

the development of writing, this can never happen. The myth, or writ, of Genesis—"And out of the ground the Lord God formed every beast of the field, and every fowl of the air; and brought them unto Adam to see what he would call them: and whatsoever Adam called every living creature, that was the name thereof"—is as good an account as any, especially if we replace the "Lord God" with our conception of the unconscious psyche. In doing so, however, we should consider the possibility that before language, the individual psyche was entirely "primary process," or unconscious. That, in other words, the first rudimentary separation between "conscious" and "unconscious" came with the leap into language.

Intriguing though these questions and hypotheses are, they are also, in one sense, beside the point—especially the question of whether the first sound combinations were accidental, expeditious, God given, or poetically created. And here we might look again at the child in its language acquisition stage. From a certain perspective it doesn't much matter whether the sounds learned by the child express the actual "essence" of their referent, or whether they are simply agreed-upon counters. The important thing is that the moment of acquisition, following the babble, represents a bonding of the sound to the untutored perception of the thing. The sound of the word "lake" will siphon up and contain the child's whole sensory experience of the entity *lake*. The experience will shape itself into the sound, pushing out to the perimeters of the word and filling them exactly. The sound will henceforth *signify*—it will never be a neutral, replaceable counter, no matter how arbitrary the original coinage.

The idea of a *moment* of acquisition is problematic. We cannot ourselves recall if there was, in fact, such a thing, and we do not stand to gain much by interrogating a three-year-old child. But it might be relevant now to cite Helen Keller's account of her linguistic breakthrough (which I discovered in Walker Percy's very pertinent essay "The Delta Factor"):

We walked down the path to the well-house, attracted by the fragrance of the honeysuckle with which it was covered. Someone was drawing water and my teacher placed my hand under the

---

Hamann's Bone

spout. As the cool stream gushed over one hand, she spelled into the other the word *water,* first slowly, then rapidly. I stood still, my whole attention fixed upon the motion of her fingers. Suddenly I felt a misty consciousness as of something forgotten—a thrill of returning thought; and somehow the mystery of language was revealed to me. I knew then that "w-a-t-e-r" meant the wonderful cool something that was flowing over my hand. That living word awakened my soul, gave it light, hope, joy, set it free!

What did language *feel* like to its speakers after the first words had been created and successfully exchanged? Did the world become a riot of saying? Was the word-sound for "stone" felt to inhabit the thing? Was the equivalence between word and object a deep one—did powerful sensation stream through the $=$ sign? Or did the sound drape over the thing every which way, fitting the boulder exactly while hanging slack over the shape of a mere rock? Ethnographic and anthropological theories—based, admittedly, on studies of surviving "primitive" societies—assert that a strong charge of the sacred accrued to certain words. A charge so strong, in fact, that certain words were proscribed. Language, it would seem, possessed a puissance that we cannot even begin to imagine. One of the many histories to be written is the history of the evaporation of the felt contents from our languages.

For there can be little doubt but that the subjective distance between the word and its object has been widening steadily from the time of the first speakers. Shelley gave this idea vivid expression in his *A Defence of Poetry:*

In the infancy of society every author is necessarily a poet, because language itself is poetry; and to be a poet is to apprehend the true and the beautiful, in a word, the good that exists in the relation, subsisting, first between existence and perception, and second between perception and expression. Every original language near to its source is in itself the chaos of a cyclic poem. . . .

Approaches

Or, to recall Emerson again—from his essay "The Poet"—"Language is fossilized poetry."

If every author was, in the infancy of society, a poet, then perhaps every poet in our leached-out time exerts his best energies toward the restoration of some of that lost potency to language. What was once a poetry of natural speech must now be struggled toward using every possible resource, every available tactic of defamiliarization and recontextualization. A persuasive magic must be worked before we can read "stone" or "tree" and register anything more than the faintest sense imprint. (Rilke: "Are we, perhaps, here just for saying House, Bridge, Fountain, Gate, Jug, Olive Tree, Window—?") Our whole linguistic apparatus has to be shaken before that fossil can be returned to life.

The poet does not, most likely, set himself this task consciously. No, he responds to an inner imperative (see my essay "When Lightning Strikes" in this volume) that will not let him be satisfied until his words have expressed a particular sensation, feeling, or thought at the most intense possible level. The more impoverished the inner resources of language (certainly there is no shortage of words), the more diffuse the voltage in the system, the more he must exert himself to electrify the utterance. Once, when the language was full of sap, it may have been possible to say, "My heart is as light as a bird," and thus to make poetry. Nowadays, in part because of the sheer proliferation of speech, in part because of media debasement (see "The Rage of Caliban"), every primary analogy has been worn down. The words just make us smile self-consciously. Isn't it true that we live at a greater distance from the primary nouns? Haven't the claims of modern experience so altered every stimulus-response ratio that we are in danger of losing the capacity of being affected by *any*thing? Or could it be that the inner nature of language itself is changing, that mankind's poetic stage (if that's what it was) was just part of the sweet linguistic childhood of the species?

Whatever the reasons for the change, the fact remains that neither denotative expression nor, with rare exceptions, straightforward metaphor suffice for poetry. Sense is no longer rich enough to pay its own way. For the poetic event to "happen," the constituent elements of

Hamann's Bone

sense—the sound units—have to make up the deficit. The poet must either make an unfamiliar music (like Auden's syntactically discordant "Sir, no man's enemy, forgiving all"), or else disturb expectation with inventive line breaks and enjambments and startling verbal juxtapositions ("Complacencies of the peignoir"). Or, what is perhaps most difficult, he must find a way to get the totality of sound to gesture. This means that he must find a sequence of sounds that can, when absorbed in tandem with the sense of the words, compensate for the lost evocative power of the words themselves. This is where poet and poetaster part company—the music of poetry cannot be simulated.

This gesturing (what R. P. Blackmur meant by his phrase "language as gesture") has profound, if often subliminal, effects upon the reader. Indeed, these effects may be the very foundation of the aesthetic experience. The word is pushed against the stream of common denotative usage, and with the liberation of its latent associative charge, its power is restored. In the process, the poet has brought us to the point at which we can feel sound coalescing into sense. We feel a deeply satisfying replenishment; the windows of the senses have been buffed back to transparency.

There is another way to think of this fusion of elements. Once again, we hark back, if not to the image of our primitive ancestor, then to that of the child who is just beginning to distinguish among sounds. With one or the other in mind, we can venture another interpretation of the sound-sense fusion. That is, that the sound component of the poem, considered in its totality as the "music," addresses the unconscious psyche, while the sense, abstracted from the music, represents the track followed by the conscious mind. At certain moments—and this cannot be counterfeited—in a phrase, or a line, or an extended passage, the sound might enact or counterpoint the sense so perfectly that the two inner operations are suddenly brought into contact. The full resonance of the poem moves through the whole psyche of the reader, creating an elating sense of expansion. This effect may have much less to do with the ostensible subject or "message" than with the simple fact of the congruence. And this might explain, in part, why some of the very greatest poems in our language (see "On a Stanza by John Keats") are not *about* very much at all. They are beautiful because they flash their gleam in the direction of our origins, and because they set up harmonic vibrations between our instinctual and our rational beings. Reading a great poem may not make us understand anything more clearly. It may, however, effect a psychic reconciliation that allows us to *be* more vividly, if only for a short time.

An analogy. I am walking down the street right after a rain shower. I notice the glimmering droplets suspended in intervals on the branch of a bush. I am suddenly startled by both the delicate beauty of the sight *and*—at the same time—by the abstract recognition of immutable physical law. The simultaneous perception is an epiphany. A line of poetry can affect me in the same way: I respond to the rightness of the verbal expression, and, because of that rightness, I suddenly grasp that the whole is welded together out of bits of sound. That organizations of sound *mean*—this is no less miraculous than the existence of physical laws. And both recognitions point in the direction of the first and last mystery, the mystery that saturates the sacred writings of all cultures—that there is such a thing as being at all. This is ultimately what stirs me so when I read about a darkling thrush, or bare ruined choirs, or the mellow fruitfulness of autumn. Nowhere else do we get so close to language or to ourselves as in poetry.

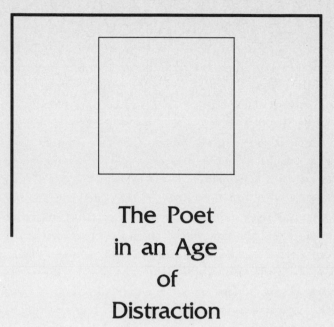

The Poet
in an Age
of
Distraction

The cultivation of poetry is never more to be desired than at periods when, from an excess of the selfish and calculating principle, the accumulation of the materials of external life exceed the quantity of the power of assimilating them to the internal laws of human nature. The body has become too unwieldy for that which animates it.

—SHELLEY

L ike the Royal Family, poetry wears titular tiaras that recall its former great estate but wields no power. Auden said that it "makes nothing happen" and he was right, though presumably he was talking about the poetry of recent centuries and not about the grand performances of Homer, Virgil, Dante, and Milton, which shaped and directed the imagination of Western man and die-stamped his languages permanently. Illusions about that kind of effectuality have, of course, long since disappeared. Poetry is now largely a face-saving operation, with poets pulling their bitterness inside out and preening themselves on their own uselessness.

But the poets are not that much to blame. From generation to generation they have done their duty by the word, deepening and furthering the idiom of their time. It's the idiom itself, bound as it is to social and historical experience, that has become bloodless. If poets appear irrelevant now it is because great abstract historical changes have relocated all of the power centers. The race is busily standardizing itself and turning its attention outward; sciences, technologies, and the mass processing of information are the order of the day. Truth, for the time being, is what can be measured, calculated, or found on some instrument. The imago is defined by our collective fantasies of control and efficiency. And the inner life is given its due only when the strain of imbalance sends a crack zigzagging through the outer shell. Psychiatrists flourish in the rich northern suburbs of our cities.

A great distractedness has settled over the West. Outwardly we may be as vigorous and purposeful as ever, but inwardly the static crackles. Every morning the world is laid before us in column inches and we take an anxious sniff. In the hours of light we master the unspeakable threat—but in the dark the faced-off missiles gleam like fangs. And we know that for the first time in history there is no place to hide, a piece of knowledge that the organism cannot endure. Either it finds a god to be friendly with, or else it interposes static between itself and the facts.

The poet today works in the face of this distractedness. There is nothing less likely to capture the public attention than the little web of words he would make. If we construct a scheme of social evolution, the poet is its dodo bird. Yet he persists in his making. And this is something miraculous. Decades ago, Robert Graves wrote: "At the age of sixty-five I am still amused at the paradox of poetry's continuance in the present stage of civilization." Amusement is arch—amazement would be more apropos. That "phrase" has only exacerbated its worst tendencies since.

Why *do* poets continue to write? Why keep playing if it's such a mug's game? Some, no doubt, simply fail to understand the situation. And willful perversity is not to be discounted in others. There is a part of human nature that delights in absurd, fruitless endeavor—the martyr impulse has tenacious roots. Nor is the poet immune to the redemptive fantasy: He sees the world transformed by the secret force of words. His longings are not confined by the small space of his operation. And when he reads the Bible, he takes special satisfaction from the phrase "the last shall be first," for in his mind there is a picture of humanity making an about-face. He sees himself with a raised baton.

But there is another, better reason why poets go on turning their lines. Useless or not, poetry is the most concentrated implementation of full consciousness possible. I say "full" consciousness. Undoubtedly the specialized concentration of mathematician or physicist exceeds that of the poet—but unidirectionally. The poet, in bringing the undivided strength of his being to bear upon the mysterious scrim of language, engages in the most profound general—that is, human—cognition. As Mandelstam wrote: "The spectacle of a mathematician who, without seeming to think about it, produces the square of some ten-digit number, fills us with a certain astonishment. But too often we fail to see that the poet raises a phenomenon to its tenth power, and the modest exterior often deceives us with regard to the monstrously condensed reality contained within."

Poetry, for the poet, is largely its own reward. As a dancer delights in the dance and the fisherman in the physics of his perfect cast, so the poet takes the highest pleasure in finding in himself those glowing points at which his language and his being fuse together. Something of this pleasure survives in the artifact, the poem, which is passed along as a gift to the reader. But the economy of the spirit is no different than the fiscal economy: Goods must be kept in motion. The distractedness of the world is most bitter for the poet. His superb recognitions go unremarked—his gift stays wrapped on the mantle.

Poetic composition is the most profound exercise of full human consciousness. Language and consciousness, though not identical, are coextensive. There is no higher grade of consciousness without language, and vice versa. The poem is the most concentrated and refined possible use of language. For once the words are freed of the burden of having to inform, and permitted to sound. Poetry is to customary usage as Sunday is to the rest of the work week. Aside from the beautiful

---

The Poet in an Age of Distraction

chatter of love between mother and child, or lover and lover, lyric poetry is the only wholly gratuitous use of language. As such it is an image of freedom.

The poet works with language—it is his material. But he does not work with it as a sculptor works with stone, or a painter with pigment and canvas. The poet *is* his material. The sculptor chips down his stone with mallet and chisel. The poem is a sonic sculpture that grows into shape like a living organism. The sounds have been molded into words, and words *mean*. There is a binding tension between sound as sound and sound as meaning. Words issue from the linguistically volatile psyche of the poet and come to life in the well of the ear. Ultimately they press upon the susceptible psyche of their auditor. The transaction that we call the experience of poetry always takes place between one being and another. The energy circulates from privacy to privacy. Far-flung though they may be in space and time, the poet and his reader are, for the duration of the experience, adjacent souls with permeable boundaries. Language can render the inward experience so persuasively that the space/time axis yields. Poetry has no larger "public" function—its limits are set. Poetry readings may be good advertising, but they cannot alter the monogamous character of the real event. In poetry, as in love, two is company, three is always a crowd.

Materialistic in our biases, we distribute value along a hierarchy of size and palpability. We scarcely reckon what cannot be seen. An object in space is always more real than a thought in a mind, a large object more real than a small one. We have not yet caught up with the implications of our much-vaunted science, which has achieved its most dramatic effects by prying apart the invisible atom.

We are confused, too, about the differing nature of inner and outer, and we tend to transfer our habits regarding the latter to the former. A poem is small on the page—it is therefore somehow frivolous when compared to the grand objective presence of a shopping mall. A curtain of glass culled from mere sand has automatic precedence over a sonnet culled from the energy field of the psyche.

Is it really such an amusing thought: that a cycle of sonnets may have as much general value as a municipal edifice? Bear in mind that there are four dimensions, and that what poetry appears to lose by not extending into space, it recaptures by reaching into time. The lines of Shakespeare and Milton gleam in the mind like rows of freshly cobbled bricks, while the actual bricks of their day have been rubbed back to dust. This may be a cliché, but it is not an idle one.

Ours is a material age, preferring the outer scape over the inner, and favoring space over time. The poet, in the perversity of his disposition, works in language and attempts to subvert time: He arranges imperishable (because immaterial) signs into patterns. He, too, loves space, but he feels its pathos more deeply than most. And though he can do nothing to forestall change and erosion, he can excerpt and preserve certain aspects of his inner experience by making a pattern of words. His words may endure long after everything that occasioned them is gone. The poet is a self-seeking mortal like everyone else, and this is not the consolation that it is sometimes made to seem. But it is something. And the poet, like any artist, operates according to the principle that something is better than nothing.

A poem is a construction in inner space (the concept is figurative). Language is to inner space as light is to material space: Just as we can see only where there is light, so we can grasp the inner life only where there are words. Language is, as Wilhelm von Humboldt put it, "the organ of our inner being."

Who has not stared into the mirror and felt the distance growing between the eye and its reflection? Who has not, in the same way, stared at a word and felt the shiver of anxiety as the sign and its meaning came apart—the letters suddenly as strange as the image on the glass? Said Karl Kraus: "The closer a look we take at a word, the greater the distance from which it looks back." Language and consciousness *are* coextensive, but we cannot say how. We can say nothing about either without both. Archimedes offered to move the world if someone could show him a place to stand. There is no place to stand.

Here is the poet's arena, where word and world and self have their unfathomable joinery. It is not surprising that poets are half-mad.

*   *   *

The Poet in an Age of Distraction

Whatever the origin of language in man—whether it was a gift from God, or else evolved through use from a set of arbitrarily invented signs—the fact remains that it *is* the organ of our inner being. Even if it was at origin an arbitrary collocation of signs, it is arbitrary no longer. For as nature abhors a vacuum, human nature abhors an empty sign. We have over time filled these sounds and letter shapes with all of our human essence. Now when we use them, they shine that essence back at us.

The poet, as the most conscientious user of language, sets himself the task of distilling from language this essence. He achieves this by freeing words from their menial tasks. By subtracting from the sign its primary designating function, he discloses what is left: the dense and subtle accretions of spirit. The word "bucket" in a poem is not the same that we find in the command "Get me the bucket." The latter indicates a functional object. The former, contextualized in a poem, is first a specific sound-shape, and second a suggestive emblem. Sprung from its task of indicating, the word becomes a bundle of personal and communal associations.

A poem is above all else a language event. It uses language and is at the same time a lens turned upon language. Time and again while reading poetry we have the sensation that if it were possible, figuratively speaking, to turn our heads quickly enough, we might catch a glimpse of our unmasked essential selves. Impossible, of course, but poetry knowingly aspires to the impossible—language becoming essence, essence becoming language. The best poetry approaches this fusion asymptotically.

Mallarmé dreamed of a pure verbal music, a poetry that would strip all designatory meaning from words—a piece of whimsy. Poetry cannot but build itself up from the tension between meaning and sound. Indeed, conventional kinds of meaning—as in "What is this poem about?"—are generally pretext. They provide a rudimentary structure, a stage upon which language can perform its striptease, discarding its designatory veils. To the extent that we are profound, our language is profound, for we have made it. When we experience that language intimately, touching the layers of emotion behind the sign, the deepest and most ancient elements of the psyche are activated.

"Meanings" and "messages" are as nothing in the face of this chthonic vibration.

The energy is in the language, not in the poem. The poem is a reactor, an optimum-efficiency system. The better the system, the more directly it makes language release its mysterious quanta.

Consider Shakespeare's Sonnet 42:

That time of year thou mayst in me behold
When yellow leaves, or none, or few, do hang
Upon those boughs which shake against the cold,
Bare ruin'd choirs, where late the sweet birds sang.
In me thou see'st the twilight of such day
As after sunset fadeth in the west,
Which by and by black night doth take away,
Death's second self that seals up all the rest.
In me thou see'st the glowing of such fire,
That on the ashes of his youth doth lie,
As the death-bed whereon it must expire
Consumed with that which it was nourish'd by.
   This thou perceiv'st, which makes thy love more strong,
   To love that well, which thou must leave ere long.

We cannot say that the sonnet contains any novel or complex idea. No, it is a simple conceit: I am aging, the fact that you will lose me must intensify your love. The content and our response are in no way commensurate. We can say that certain intricate figurations of sound account for part of our pleasure, and that the archetypal satisfactions of measure contribute further. But even in combination these elements cannot explain fully our reaction. There remains an elusive, floating x factor, and this must be sought in the precincts of language itself.

The sonnet, like any poem, is a retarding action, a brake applied to the consciousness of the reader. It slows us down so that we may encounter language at its ideal natural gait. And it is this encounter, in attentiveness, that is profound. For it affirms the connection between our language and our inner being and shows the capacity that language has to echo the external world to us. We race through the first line and a half of the sonnet, outpacing the words, riding the wave/trough of the iambs, until, on a slight, unexpected modulation—"or none, or few"—we are brought up short. And with this checking motion we are put off balance just enough to be startled by the beauty of the common word "hang"—its open vowel, its fibrous, stemlike guttural. "Hang" suddenly discloses a depth and rightness that we had always somehow overlooked. And with this minor revelation comes a sense of intensified connection between the word and the outer world—which we feel as an inexplicable intensification of self. Shakespeare's great gift is that, having initiated this intensification, he is also able to prolong it. Line after line the language quickens us, and the feeling of connectedness sustains itself. There is no higher, or ulterior, meaning, just the keen registration of experience in words delivering some proof we seem to need of a continuum between the material and immaterial.

We speak with language. And language itself speaks. How can this be? To speak is to convey contents. How can language be said to convey *its* contents if it is the conveyor itself? It can "speak" only if it is understood to be something more than a means. Which is precisely the point. As I said before: We have loaded the rifts ourselves. We have saturated language, our means of communication, with our private and collective being. And now, language simultaneously conveys and *is*. This paradoxical fact is what allows poetry to exist. Its genuine riches come not from the meaning that the poem conveys, but from the sense of limitlessness that the reader gets from words in combination. The designatory function of "hang," for instance, is promptly completed. The feeling of limitlessness comes when we realize that the word does not close or terminate at that. Holding its echo in the ear, we move through ever-widening circles. Mandelstam, who felt so deeply this "being" of words, wrote:

> In pronouncing the word "sun" we are, as it were, undertaking an enormous journey to which we are so accustomed that we travel in our sleep. What distinguishes poetry from automatic speech is that it rouses and shakes us into wakefulness in the middle of a word. Then it turns out that the word is much longer than we

thought, and we remember that to speak means to be forever on the road.

—*Conversation About Dante*

Poets are more or less unanimous in affirming that true poetry cannot be produced by conscious craft, however skillful. Indeed, conscious craft, appears to have little influence upon getting "the best words" into "the best order" (Coleridge). But if we excise the conscious or controlled elements from our account of the poetic process, what are we left with? The Muse, inspiration, the unconscious, "the ear"? Of these possibilities, the unconscious seems most useful—if nothing else, it conforms to the terminology of the psychologist. Poets, however, tend to be reluctant to locate the seat of their creativity in something called the unconscious—as if they were thereby robbing their art of its mystery and consigning it to the care of the empiricist. But this is a petulant gesture. To say that poetic creativity is rooted in the unconscious does not demystify poetry. If anything, it enlarges the mystery of the unconscious.

Poetry and the unconscious—a fan of questions slowly opens.

What is the linguistic structure of the unconscious? Or is that a contradiction in terms? If, as I asserted earlier, language and consciousness are coextensive, where does the *un*conscious fit in?

Simple answers are not forthcoming. For one thing, we have no reliable way to think about the unconscious. We know it through its effects; we hypothesize it to account for phenomena in the psyche that are otherwise inexplicable—in the same way that astrophysicists postulate black holes. Second, the psyche is not some Gaul that we divide into clear territories. There is no line where the conscious mind suddenly stops and the unconscious begins, no abrupt blank space where words disintegrate. Words themselves are as motile as mercury. If their outer contours are more or less fixed, their inner substance is chaotic. As Owen Barfield wrote: "The full meanings of words are flashing, iridescent shapes like flames—ever-flickering vestiges of the slowly evolving consciousness beneath them."

It makes more sense to think of a liminal area of some kind, a

The Poet in an Age of Distraction

"field" that is all impulse and energy at one end, and that becomes—if we imagine moving through it—increasingly organized in terms of sound and sense. All clear, conscious utterance, then, would be crystallized out of a ceaseless, fertile babble.

Finished hexameters do not march in stately procession out of the unconscious and onto the page. Most poetic composition involves the active collaboration of hinting unconscious and heeding craft. Still, there are occasional eruptions. Poets do speak of "hearing voices" and "taking dictation." We have to grant that the movement of energy out of the psyche and over the language threshold can be sudden and tremendous. It can make a poet believe that the gods are visiting. Randall Jarrell found a metaphor in the natural order: "A good poet is someone who manages, in a lifetime of standing out in thunderstorms, to be struck by lightning five or six times." The flashing bolt is, of course internal, as are the storms. Whether great or even "good" poetry depends upon these kinds of happy accidents is another question.

Proust elaborated a distinction between voluntary and involuntary memory—only the latter, he held, could present us with the true experience of the past. The essences of the past are hidden, stored in stray details, and we have no certainty that we will find them. But if and when the encounter does take place, a hidden order is disclosed behind the surface flow of hours and days. The mysterious excavation of content from time is possible only when time is felt as duration, that is, when the unconscious abstracts experience from linear time. Or, more accurately, we might say that the unconscious registers only duration, and that these discharges of the authentic past are, like inspiration, sudden rushes of unconscious energy through the standing wickets of reason. Proust's madeleine epiphany is a highly dramatic example of this. In fact, all moments in which we grasp our lives as pattern and continuity belong to time as duration.

Poetry, as language in quest of essence, also partakes of duration. Stepping into the circle of words, we step away from the circle of the clock face. We read the lines in the present, the now, but with every passing moment we are cut more completely away from that present.

As we immerse ourselves in the poem, the visual and acoustic surface of the words disappears into meaning:

> . . . music heard so deeply
> That it is not heard at all, but you are the music
> While the music lasts.
>
> —T. S. ELIOT

And the more complete this disappearance, the more profound the duration sense. For meaning and the construct of linear time are in contradiction: To be sensible of the one is to be proportionately insensible of the other. Finishing even the shortest poem, we are taken aback, startled to see what a slight grapevine it has been. While reading we move in a realm where the coverings of the words have fallen away—they shuttle through us as directed energy. Looking up from the page we feel the collision of kinds of time.

But who will deny that the great days of poetry are past, or are passing? Well over half a century ago, Ezra Pound read and summarized the invisible headlines:

> The age demanded an image
> Of its accelerated grimace,
> Something for the modern stage,
> Not, at any rate, an Attic grace;
>
> Not, not certainly, the obscure reveries
> Of the inward gaze;
> Better mendacities
> Than the classics in paraphrase!
>
> The "age demanded" chiefly a mold in plaster,
> Made with no loss of time,
> A prose kinema, not, not assuredly, alabaster
> Or the "sculpture" of rhyme.
>
> —from *Hugh Selwyn Mauberley*

The Poet in an Age of Distraction

The species is moving away from its immemorial ways of being. The pattern and pace of individual and generational life have been irrevocably altered. As the changes obliterate more and more of the communal memory, the poet's kind of cognition—which depends upon the saturation of language by culture, by human tradition—becomes increasingly peripheral. And even if the poet continues, his public will be winnowed. Other "kinds" of poetry will prosper, the fashionable, the agitated, the aggressively contemporary. But the poetry that comes from language, that is language looking at itself, will become one of the esoteric mysteries.

This is a complex tragedy, and the loss of the experience of poetry is only a small part of it. The less tangible aspect—both a cause and a consequence—is the erosion of the "felt" bond between language and the world it represents to us. Poetry depends upon this bond and functions to intensify it. I don't mean to suggest that there is a cable that will one day snap. No, a more appropriate image would be that of a map on which areas once explored and charted begin to blur their boundaries and lose their shape, until, one after another, they are re-marked *terra incognita*. More and more of the intricacies of private experience are falling out of the reach of natural language—and our distinction as a species is in part founded upon our ability to register these. I feel a gulf opening between outer and inner worlds—and language is less and less able to secure the connection. Useful as it is for some things, the new terminology of psychology will not be able to make up the lack.

Is this too dramatic, too pessimistic? Is it not possible that the great technological/material spurt will prove to be just that, that we will once again snap out of our distractedness and find ourselves face to face with our unknowable existence—the overwhelming *fact* of it—that the claims of the spirit will again assert themselves? If there ever were such a turnaround, it would force a movement back toward a language that comprehended the depths of the psyche's experience. Only in such a circumstance would the poet stand to recoup some of his ancient prestige. Then it would be clearer that it is by way of poetry that language secures its deeper "real" life, and that it has always been the task of the poet to make sure that there is bullion to back the currency that we pass so casually from hand to hand.

Approaches

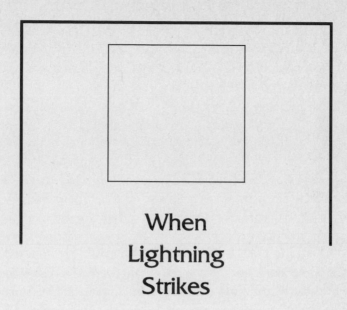

When
Lightning
Strikes

It was 1952, I was 44, and I thought I was done. I was living alone in a biggish house in Edmonds, Washington. I had been reading—and re-reading—not Yeats, but Raleigh and Sir John Davies. I had been teaching the five-beat line for weeks—I knew quite a bit about it, but write it myself?—no: so I felt myself a fraud.

Suddenly, in the early evening, the poem "The Dance" started, and finished itself in a very short time—say thirty minutes, maybe in the greater part of an hour, it was all done. I felt, I knew, I had hit it. I walked around, and I wept; and I knelt down—I always do after I've written what I know is a good piece. But at the same time I had, as God is my witness, the actual sense of a Presence—as if Yeats himself were in that room. The experience was in a way terrifying, for it lasted at least half an hour. That house, I repeat, was charged with a psychic presence: the very walls seemed to shimmer. I wept for joy.

—THEODORE ROETHKE

He [the poet] is going to all that trouble, not in order to communicate with anyone, but to gain relief from acute discomfort. And when the words are arranged in the right way . . . he may experience a moment of exhaustion, of appeasement, of absolution, and of something very near annihilation which is in itself indescribable.

—T. S. ELIOT

. . . there is a certain domineering note, or tune, that is going through one's mind. It's a very strange thing. I say tune; I can just as well say noise. In either case, whatever it is, *it's not just exactly a tune, a musical hum. For this hum has a certain psychological overlay. It's an extremely grey area . . . It's a certain frequency, so to speak, in which you operate and which, at times, you change.*

—JOSEPH BRODSKY

F or all of the differences in the kinds of poetry that are written, and for all the temperamental diversity among its practitioners, there is one point on which nearly everyone agrees: that a poem cannot be thought or willed onto the page. Valéry posed the question in *The Art of Poetry:* "Is it impossible, given time, care, skill, and desire, to proceed in an orderly way to arrive at poetry?" The answer from the chorus of poets is: Yes, impossible.

This does not mean that poetry can be produced without these elements, just that they do not suffice. In combination they may yield a readable verse, a neat line, some artifact of the kind that proliferates as never before in magazines and collections—but they will not yield poetry. Whatever else we may say about it, poetry has its origin in the unknown. At least some small part of any true poem must come to the poet as a gift, an unpremeditated spark from outside the circle of volition. This may be a word, a line, a scrap of rhythm. Slight it may be, but like the extended finger in Michelangelo's great fresco, it brings to life what would otherwise remain inert.

If poetry could be produced through a simple collaboration of skill and good wishes, we would long since have been inundated with the stuff. Or would we? Possibly much of the prestige that has always attracted people to the vocation derives from its mysteriousness, from the fact that, like love, it cannot be planned, controlled, or legislated. If one could make a poem the way one makes a rug or a table, would so many people burn in their secret selves to be poets? It's unlikely. They burn to be poets (or artists of some stamp) because they sense that creativity represents an inward power.

All poetry originates in a gift, but the circumstance, magnitude, and intensity of the experience will vary from poet to poet and from case to case. We may think of Rilke pacing the battlements of the Schloss Duino, quivering like a lightning rod when the first lines of the *Elegies* were dictated, as if from the turbulent sky overhead. But we must not forget the Rilke of the earlier "thing poems," working with the patience of an Old World artisan at the task of seeing. Creative inspiration is rarely scripted by David Lean—the mad-eyed Zhivago scribbling in front of a dripping taper is a figment of popular fancy. We would be more likely to encounter a demure creature sitting by an electric desk lamp or, these days, tinkering with the words arrayed on an illuminated screen. But this does not diminish the mystery, which still must exist, whatever the packaging. The difference between Rilke's ecstasy at Duino and another poet's thrill at the unexpected arrival of a line is quantitative, not qualitative.

Before we investigate the process of poetic creativity, we must clearly separate its two aspects. However merged they may at times feel to the poet, the volitional, conscious activity is very different from that which eludes the will. The Irish poet Seamus Heaney has given one sort of explication:

> Frost put it this way: "A poem begins as a lump in the throat, a homesickness, a lovesickness. It finds the thought and the thought finds the words." As far as I'm concerned, technique is more vitally connected with that first activity where the "lump in the throat" finds "the thought" than with "the thought" finding "the words." The first epiphany involves the divining, vatic, oracular function; the second, the making, crafting function.

Heaney's distinction is also acknowledged in the Greek and Latin etymologies of the word "poet." In Athens, poet meant "maker"; the Romans called him *vates:* "oracle."

The world of the ancients, though geographically smaller than ours, was not only felt to be vaster, but was everywhere shadowed and deepened by a sense of the terrestrial unknown. World conceptions were neither as materialist nor as functionalist as those we proclaim. The ancients believed, among other things, that the Muse was the source of poetry. Homer's "sing, goddess" and "tell me, Muse" were literal petitions, not formulaic niceties. Inspiration was the taking-into-oneself of an outer-dwelling spirit—the word roots clearly show this—which the poet could try to assist through an act of "in-vocation" or calling in. If the poet was blessed with any talent, it was for being a medium, a hospitable receptor. As Plato tells us in the *Ion:*

> . . . the poet is a light and winged and holy thing, and there is no invention in him until he has been inspired and is out of his senses, and the mind is no longer in him: when he is not in this state, he is powerless and unable to utter his oracles.

Once again we encounter the idea of the oracle. At first glance, these words do not square with the Greek designation of poet as maker, but the contradiction is only terminological. The implication of Plato's description is that the poet does not invent out of himself, but that he constructs with building materials obtained elsewhere.

Some variant in the belief in the Muse, in inspiration from without, survived for centuries, outlasting the pagan belief in a pantheon of gods, and coexisting with the consolidated Christian faith. Indeed, even in our century at least two esteemed poets—Robert Graves and John Berryman—pledged their fealty to the Muse; both insisted that their pledge was not metaphoric. We smile. But is this really so different from other poets claiming God as their source, or the spirits of the departed speaking through a Ouija board, or the so-called genius of the language itself? The creative current can be so unexpected and foreign, so different in feel from the lulling sway of the quotidian, that the poet naturally—and maybe modestly—hesitates to locate its source inside himself.

(Speculating along these lines, the psychologist Julian Jaynes has suggested that the early poets actually *did* hear a voice from within, but that the voice did not originate in an exterior spirit realm—it was caused by powerful emanations from the right side of the brain. Jaynes argues in *The Origin of Consciousness in the Breakdown of the Bicameral Mind* that our insistent cultivation of the analytic/deductive left brain has resulted in the gradual atrophy of the partner hemisphere. Neurological research may yet enlighten us as to the real identity of the Muse.)

It is impossible to trace the changing conceptions of poetic creativity with any linear or sequential neatness. Poets have always lived at an angle—to their milieu, to its prevalent beliefs, even to their fellow poets. Only the line of idiosyncrasy is constant. Nevertheless, we can generalize that by the late eighteenth century—at least in Europe—the poets' own conception had altered somewhat. There was a significant inward displacement of the creative focus. From Coleridge, Shelley, and Wordsworth we hear little about the Muse, and a great deal about the Imagination.

The Romantics believed that a faculty of untold resource and power had been implanted in each human being. Those in whom this Imagination was especially volatile became creators. Those who could not create could at least respond to its call in the works of others. This Imagination was not, in the last analysis, any less obscure or mysterious than the personal Muse, nor could it be summoned to action any more reliably. As Shelley wrote in a celebrated passage of his *A Defence of Poetry:*

> Poetry is not like reasoning, a power to be exerted according to the determination of the will. A man cannot say, "I will compose poetry." The greatest poet even cannot say it; for the mind in creation is as a fading coal which some invisible influence, like an inconstant wind, awakens to transitory brightness; this power arises from within, like the color which fades and changes as it is developed, and the conscious portions of our nature are unprophetic either of its approach or its departure.

How similar, finally, are Shelley's words to Plato's; the difference lies entirely in Shelley's phrase "this power arises from within." (Shelley in fact translated the *Ion.*)

We tend to think of history as a progression, and to assume that the latest explanation is always the most comprehensive and correct. And with the advent in our century of the psychological sciences, we think about poetic creativity in new terms. Instead of thinking of the imagination as the sovereign organ of creation, we call upon the id or unconscious, and in so doing we make tacit reference to a complex and sophisticated model of psychic functioning. Undeniably this represents a kind of advance, a step toward the demystification of the unknown;

but we must be careful to remind ourselves that this new conception is not yet an explanation. If we look closely at poetic process we will see that the appeal to the unconscious reduces the enigma of creativity only slightly. True, the focus is again shifted. Instead of Shelley's "inconstant wind" and "invisible influence," we speak of energies generated by an individual psyche, energies that have specific determinants in the emotional history of that psyche. But can we say, really, what an emotion is, or according to what pattern or influence these energies organize themselves? To say that poetry has its roots in the unconscious does not end the search—it starts it.

The unconscious is not a spatial entity—it is not some inner California transected by seismic faults and manifesting strange behavior. Though we do get a static image from the old three-part division—ego, id, and superego—Freud and his followers have all insisted that the psyche is a dynamic whole, a forcefield that can be no more located than could the pagan or Christian soul.

The unconscious represents a significant part of this forcefield. It enlists our instincts and drives—to that extent it can be called biological, but its changing contours enclose a bewildering system of non-biological functions. In no way can it be considered simply as a battery or storage facility for primal energies. Indeed, part of the problem we face is in determining how broadly or narrowly we wish to construe its operations.

In the broadest, most inclusive sense, the unconscious comprises everything that we are not conscious of at a given moment: At any time, therefore, it embraces virtually all of our psychic contents. Obviously this is not a serviceable definition. We need some scheme that will account for more and less available materials. I may not be thinking about yesterday's meeting, but my impressions or memories are more readily brought to consciousness than are images from the family vacation of fifteen years ago (though I may, with patience and concentration, be able to reconstitute much of that event). What's more, it seems that we are not equipped to store our whole experience for ready—that is, *willed*—recall. There are certain sensations and details from that vacation that no effort can recover. Yet, for all that, they are not necessarily lost forever. I may have what is now called a Proustian experience, an unexpected triggering of associations, whereby some part of that forgotten past is suddenly restored to me. Evidently we preserve things in logically ordered *and* associative patterns, but these might not even intersect.

This description is still simplistic. Clearly we also have contents that are not merely stray or elusive, but which have been blocked from consciousness. According to Freud, our Oedipal trauma actually *creates* an unconscious; it brings into being a protective complex of repressive energies. Our murderous feelings, and our horror at having those feelings, are blocked from awareness and made unavailable. They do not disappear.

Once the repressive dynamic has been instituted, any excessive feeling or undesirable memory may be similarly suppressed. But these materials are, in a sense, the most "real" and most vital parts of ourselves, and though they are blocked, they are hardly inactive. No, they intrude constantly upon our well-governed lives: in dreams, fantasies, memory pangs, slips of the tongue. Miraculously enough, some members of our tribe are endowed with the ability to grasp and shape these real sensations—visually, musically, in body motions, in words. We recognize the shapes as beauty—they elicit powerful harmonic responses from us—and we honor the shaper as an artist, as one who can express what remains inchoate in us.

How does the poet gain access to this hidden life? What determines the unconscious extrusions that find their way into poetry? In what manner are they given form? Does the poet exert any control over his creative activity, or is he as passive as Plato's "winged and holy thing"?

Freud believed that the psyche was a closed system, that every psychic event had a cause, and that, as in every closed system, the governing principle was one of dynamic equilibrium. Accumulated pressures needed to be dislodged and redistributed. When this did not happen, the system started to break down: Neurosis and psychosis might ensue. Freud believed, though, that the unconscious was linguistically permeated, and that a talking cure was possible. Through speech—words—one could locate the problem, and through recognition and expression it could often be resolved.

Keeping in mind Freud's model, let us recall Randall Jarrell's maxim. "A good poet," wrote Jarrell, "is someone who manages, in a lifetime of standing out in thunderstorms, to be struck by lightning five or six times." The metaphor is a memorable inversion, for of course the lightning is internal, as are the storms. What we really get is the image of the unconscious as a thermal system that periodically builds up a massive energy charge that it then releases. Jarrell's numerical specificity—that the good poet is struck *five* or *six* times—suggests either that there are few such discharges in a poet's life, or that not every discharge can be successfully turned to account. And, indeed, he is curiously on the mark, at least with respect to "good" poets. How much *do* we preserve from any but the very greatest—is it ever more than just a handful of lyrics? As for the greats, we can only guess what determined the frequency of storms for them. Were they really better poets, or were they just very good poets far more often? What would we think of Shakespeare if we had only five or six sonnets to go by?

Jarrell's aphorism once again underscores the poet's passivity before the sources of his art. It also brings us, via a circuitous route, to Marcel Proust's ideas about memory. Strongly influenced by the philosophy of Henri Bergson, Proust articulated—and, in his masterpiece, demonstrated—the distinction between "voluntary" and "involuntary" memory. Whatever could be recovered consciously, through volition, belonged in the first category. That which defied the reason and the will—which possessed, as it were, a will of its own—composed the second. For Proust, only the *mémoire involontaire* could generate the real materials of art, those sensations that are intact within us and that have not been bleached by the conscious mind. However, it was no use attempting any kind of salvage operation; those sensations would yield themselves only in epiphanic moments. Such a moment came for Proust when he dipped his madeleine in the teacup; the taste restored to him the hitherto lost feeling of a whole epoch of his childhood. It led, ultimately, to his monumental re-creation of lost time. His celebration of the epiphany (James Joyce was another such celebrant) is remarkably similar to what we find in the testimonies of poets—only the scale is different. What a poet might experience as a line, Proust experienced as an encompassing architectural vision.

If the mainspring of poetic creativity cannot be activated by will or desire, and if we speak of the unconscious (or the involuntary memory) as exercising something like independent volition, how then do we begin to explain its dynamic? Do we imagine that the unconscious is in some way actually composing poetry, that it sends the poet a clue so that its product may be brought into the light? Certainly many poets, like Proust, speak as if their activity were not so much creation as the discovery of something already shaped and intact. And when a poet does suddenly take down a complete line—with the intuitive certainty that it's correct—where is this line coming from? In what way does the unconscious have language?

Whatever we venture at this point will be tentative. The unconscious is a pullulating field of material and energy that is, by definition, not available to the conscious self. There is forgotten material, repressed material, and there is the agency of repression, of which we are likewise unaware. We could not say that there is any linguistic shape to the unconscious, or that language is in any way *stored* or *held* in its field. But it does seem that there is a high degree of permeability, almost as if words and sounds made up, in their totality, an equivalent field. This may be because we process such a large part of our experience through language. Our words, whatever their origin, are not neutral counters. We charge them with our deepest emotions and our most intimate associations. The unconscious may not *have* language, but language, in a sense, is imbued with much of our unconscious. Freud recognized this permeability and founded his psychoanalysis upon it. We may not be able to say precisely how language and psyche interact, but there is little doubt that they share a most intricate connection.

I would like to approach the question of poetic creativity backward—that is, from the point of view of the reader engaging a finished product. When we read a poem deeply, attentively, when we experience its language and rhythms, we find that we lose sight of the words themselves. Their surface, their sign appearance, falls away, and we are

When Lightning Strikes

left with specific emotions and sensations (often images). Our reading has, in effect, carried us past language. The poem functions, finally, to bind these emotions and sensations into some kind of figure, to produce out of the variety of means a nonlinguistic harmonic resonance. When we look back at the black marks on the page, it is with a certain detached astonishment. How could *they* have combined to make such a feeling in us?

Could we not imagine a similar process working in the other direction? Just as the poem carried us past words and toward a specific organization of psychic sensation, might it not be that a similarly specific sensation in the psyche of the poet attracted and organized just those words and rhythms? Does an invariable and determined configuration of psychic material precede composition? Are the "gifts" experienced by the poet just the first protrusions of something that demands to be excavated in its entirety?

These are crucial and far-reaching questions. And others follow in their wake. We have to ask, for instance, whether the realized poem, the "great" poem, could have been written differently. Very differently, that is. Everyone, of course, can think of cases of great poets altering or excising their lines. But were these changes not likewise dictated by the pressure of an established inner configuration—was this shape not the template for the final "right" decision? Really this is a resurrection of the ancient free-will/determinism debate. Is creativity—the very emblem of free will—determined? What would free will in creativity be? When a poet brings two sounds, or two words, together, is he inventing the combination, or is he merely recognizing a rightness of valence, a rightness already prescribed by a determined internal pressure? Is there any ultimate freedom of choosing that is not a betrayal or evasion of the exact dictates of impulse?

The Russian poetess Marina Tsvetaeva wrote:

I obey something which sounds constantly within me but not uniformly, sometimes indicating, sometimes commanding. When it indicates, I argue; when it commands, I obey.

The thing that commands is a primal, invariable, unfailing and irreplaceable line, *essence appearing as a line of verse*. . . . The thing that indicates is an aural path to the poem: I hear a melody, but not words. The words I have to find.

More to the left—more to the right, higher—lower, faster—slower, extend—break off: these are the exact indications of my ear, or of something *to* my ear. All my writing is only listening.

Her countryman and contemporary Osip Mandelstam put it with even more concision:

The poem is alive through an inner image, that resounding mold of form, which anticipates the written poem. Not a single word has appeared, but the poem already resounds. What resounds is the inner image; what touches it is the poet's aural sense.

To judge from these accounts, the unconscious psyche has something very definite to transmit, and the poem is not finished until that something has registered its "invariable" verbal print. We might think of it as a process of exorcism working through phonic and rhythmic equivalents. The word is more apt than it may at first seem. Nadezhda Mandelstam, the poet's wife, has left us a vivid account of Mandelstam's attempts to "brush off" and "escape from" the insistent and irritating hum that would start in his ears when a poem was ready to be written.

Such a view of poetic creativity has implications that fly in the face of much that is currently proposed by poststructuralist and reader-response schools of interpretation. Both advance their claims based upon an assumption of linguistic indeterminacy. Deconstructionists, like Jacques Derrida, view writing as a system of differences—every text, indeed every word, secures its provisional status in relation to every absent possibility. Signifiers signify in every direction; determinate meaning is nonexistent; the reader does not so much read as *rewrite* the text. And Roland Barthes, thinking along similar lines, defined a "healthy" sign as one that declares its arbitrariness and refuses emblematic fixity. Moreover, reader-response critics insist that authorial intentions are unknowable and irrelevant—what matters is the ways in which a work is scripted by its recipient. As Terry Eagleton has written (in *Literary Theory*): "There is no clear division for post-structuralism between 'criticism' and 'creation': both modes are subsumed into 'writing' as such."

But if we regard creative composition as a response by an artist to an explicit and determining psychic pressure, and if a poet has, in fact, assembled phonic and rhythmic equivalents in accordance with an invariable inner directive, then the poststructuralist position collapses—for if it doesn't, literature must. Both views subvert the primacy of the conscious and intending authorial ego, but where the poststructuralists take this as sanctioning the erasure of the author, I would argue that it must force our attention onto the unconscious. The poem has, in fact, the most determinate reality; its arrangements are anything but arbitrary. Our task as readers is to appropriate the text with the assumption that there is a specific meaning. Whether or not we can ever verify this—and the author may not be the best judge—is beside the point.

In responding in this way to a poem/text, we are, in a sense, buttressing certain age-old assumptions: that language is adequate for expressing even the subtlest human meanings, and that literature secures its social value precisely because it is the best means of conveying and preserving the complex life of sensibility. The nonlinguistic sensations that a poem (or any other work of literature) finally organizes in a reader, and the prelinguistic sensations or forces that instigate the poem, may or may not be similar. We have no way of proving the case either way. But the belief that they are kindred is the main impetus for the activities of both parties.

It is one thing to think of the unconscious spewing forth language, quite another to think of a poet listening for finished lines, lines that in many cases are already metrically patterned. Are there different kinds of pressure, different paths of release? Why is everyone not a poet? Are poets made or born? Every question is like a plant putting out its radial stalks.

It would seem that certain individuals demonstrate from an early age a special susceptibility to language, to words and their sounds, just as others might to music, or numbers and combinations, or colors. Genetic inheritance may be influential, as may be chance. It is the attraction, often described as love, that is recalled. Here, for example, is Dylan Thomas:

> . . . I wanted to write poetry in the beginning because I had fallen in love with words. . . . What the words stood for, symbolized, or meant, was of very secondary importance; what mattered was the sound of them as I heard them for the first time on the lips of the remote and incomprehensible grownups who seemed, for some reason, to be living in my world. . . .

Seamus Heaney has expressed himself similarly:

> I called myself *incertus,* uncertain, a shy soul fretting, and all that. I was in love with words themselves, had no sense of a poem as a whole structure, and no experience of how the successful achievement of a poem could be a stepping stone in your life. . . . Maybe it began very early, when my mother used to recite lists of affixes and suffixes, and Latin roots with their English meanings. . . . Maybe it began with the exotic listing on the wireless dial: Stuttgart, Leipzig, Oslo, Hilversum . . .

The obvious surmise is that such a feeling will lead the young inamorato to books, that exposure will lead in turn to imitation, imitation to the absorption of craft, and so on. The sense of a vocation is usually there long before the poet has anything compelling to say. It is there as a desire, a willingness to stand in thunderstorms.

Writers are perhaps permeated by language to a greater degree, or depth, than others—they have invested their being more fully in it. But they have also absorbed the conventions of their craft. If a gift line comes out in an iambic pentameter, it is probably not because the psyche naturally arranges its material in formal rhythmic sequence (though some have argued that it does, that forms and meters evolved because of their particular structural affinity to inner experience). More likely it is because the structural possibilities have been taken in along with the language and exist as combinatory options at that threshold where impulse galvanizes language. In terms of this learning and absorbing, the poet makes himself, but the love that guides it is given, not made. Try as we might to explain this love—as Muse, Imagination, psyche, or neural firing—its mystery abides. The ancient belief that the poet was the chosen instrument of the gods may not, when put into modern dress, be so absurd.

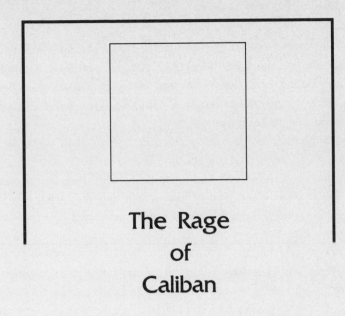

The Rage
of
Caliban

W e can analyze and theorize to our heart's content, but we will get nowhere near to understanding the crisis of poetry in our time until we face up to the enormous fact of the media. For nothing in recent history has so altered our relation to language, and hence to ourselves, as has the proliferation of information and entertainment technologies—and our acquiescence to them. The contours of social and private reality have been redrawn entirely since the decade of the 1950's. But the process has been subtle. There has been little recognition of change overall, and almost none with regard to the language arts. The critical assessment of poetry has continued unaffected, with the terms and procedures of the postwar period, the legacy of the mightily influential New Criticism, still in place. And though there has been some accommodation of Continental styles like structuralism, deconstruction, and hermeneutics, no one has yet demanded a reappraisal of the whole enterprise from the vantage point of the late millennium.

The problem is far greater, and more diffuse, than what an essay can hope to address. The media alteration of our culture is a *total* phenomenon; the web that we negotiate is being rewoven around us even as we move. A fixed post of observation is not to be had. I don't, therefore, feel obliged to apologize for the provisional character of the observations that follow.

Let me begin with a rough definition of my key term: "media." The word, as I will use it, represents the aggregate of those devices and processes whereby images and sounds (the component elements of information and entertainment) are disseminated. This is somewhat more narrow than the definition held by Marshall McLuhan, who saw a medium as, ultimately, anything that served to extend the reach of one of the human senses. But the arena is big enough as it is. The designation conferred by popular usage will suffice. When we think of "media," we think of radio, television, magazines and newspapers, and, increasingly, of sibling technologies like cassette recorders. Computers, of course, have their place in all of this, especially the "home" variety, which not only store, process, and regurgitate information, but which have made a whole industry out of home entertainment.

Walter Skeat gives us a consise Latin etymology for "medium"—"the midst, also a means"—which brings us right up against an illuminating paradox: that that which is the *means* of bringing something before us—a sound or an image—also stands in the midst. The means, in other words, plants itself between us and the original thing or event. When the TV screen presents us with the image of a man, the image and the medium that carries it are interposed between our presence and his. His presence is *media*ted; it is not imm*media*te. Is there a problem? The devil's advocate would say there is not. Without the image, he would argue, there is no perception of the man at all. With the image, by means of it, a geographical distance has been bridged. We have been given X's pseudo-presence, and something is better than nothing. Besides, he might point out, if we want immediate human presence we have only to step out into the street.

Were it all so simple, there would be no argument or problem. We would have our direct sensory experience of reality and we would have a fascinating array of sounds and images—a vicarious reality—to supplement it. Indeed, we would be living in violation of the old saw that says we can't have our cake and eat it. But that optimistic position collapses as soon as we realize that the two worlds—perceived reality and the media world—are not merely adjacent, but interact and have determining effect on each other. This is easy enough to establish in one direction: The media obviously draws most of its contents from the world at large. But what about the reverse? Does the media exert a reciprocal force upon the world, upon the people who rely on it? Is this force in some way changing the way we perceive? Specifically: Does exposure to, or use of, a particular medium affect us only for the duration of our involvement, or do we undergo a lasting change, however slight? Is our contact with the image of the man on the screen limited to what we observe and think about it, or has our psychically complex relation to the human presence been somehow altered? If we believe that it has—and I do—then we have to ask about the nature of the effect and about how that gets reinforced by thousands of hours of watching. Obviously, we are in a swampy terrain. Where empirical evidence cannot be found, intuition will have to serve.

The easiest way to suggest the nature of the change—to catch a glimpse of the skyline of the new city—is through personal reference. To begin with, I remember quite clearly a conversation I had with one of my grandmothers. This was many years ago. We were sitting together on the couch watching a news report on the *Apollo 11* mission. My grandmother remarked, as much with righteousness as with incomprehension and awe, that in her day the automobile had not yet been invented. Staring at her, I had one of my adolescent epiphanies. "You mean—" And I began to interrogate her, my flesh and blood, this ancient woman whom I suddenly saw as having ascended into the present out of some primeval ooze. Not only, it turned out, had she

The Rage of Caliban

lived her childhood in a world without automobiles (the word itself has an antique status), but she had also been without radio, telephone, television . . . Her presence there, next to the distended images of moon-walking astronauts, tells one part of the story.

My own memories of childhood have some bearing here as well. I was born in 1951, and though television was on the market at the time, it had not yet entrenched itself in the public life. Our family did not buy a set until about 1959. I can, therefore, understand the reminiscences of friends now in their forties. I, too, recall sitting on the living room rug and listening to *The Lone Ranger* on the radio. I still remember the vivid landscapes that I conjured for myself out of mere voices and sound effects.

Interestingly enough, it was my Old World grandparents who bought the first television I ever watched. We would often visit with them on Sundays, and I have dim—puzzlingly dim, really—memories of watching *Amos 'n' Andy, Yancy Derringer,* and *Have Gun Will Travel.* The impression I retain from those old radio shows is much stronger than what remains from those first viewings. The most obvious surmise might just be the best: Our own imaginings are more lasting for us than the fruits of someone else's. At any rate, before I was ten my parents bought a set (it was Christmas Eve—we all gathered to watch Ozzie and Harriet, who were celebrating their own Christmas) and I became a late-joining member of a now-historic generation: the first to have come of age in the era of television.

My point is quite rudimentary: I can look back to my own childhood and find a world interrupted—and brightened—by nothing more than a handful of radio programs, and that I now see around me a culture in which a great many homes have not only the most sophisticated TV sets, but also videocassette recorders, stereo systems, computers programmed for electronic games, and so on. And now our statisticians report that the average television-watching time *per household* in this country is in excess of seven hours a day. I get the image of a net with ever-tightening meshes. When I was a child, that net existed, but the apertures were wide and a great deal of unmediated reality slipped through. Television was a thing in the world, and it presented sounds and pictures from the world, but it was still possible to sidestep its influence. (I speak of television here, but I have in mind the full panoply of media technologies.) Now the mesh is quite fine. There are as many TV sets as people, and the development of satellite transmission and cable hookups ensures that anyone inclined to watch will have a vast array of choices. VCR equipment, priced for mass consumption, allows for storage, as well as almost unlimited access through cassette rental. People speak with straight faces of building "libraries" of videotapes. And as the options continue to increase and to attract consumers, more and more reality-hours (or however we wish to designate media-free time) are sacrificed. I sometimes imagine a world in which the meshes will have closed up completely—instead of a net, there will be an undulant fabric, a seamless visual and auditory fantasy of the world, in the presence of which the majority of the population will be dozing.

The real pioneer in the field of media study was, of course, Marshall McLuhan. His revolutionist's impatience with facts and sequential argumentation ultimately handicapped his cause—the impression persists that he was a colorful crackpot—but his fundamental insights cannot be ignored. He was, among other things, the first to appreciate the magnitude of the change wrought by the electronic media. He recognized that it was not a peripheral cultural event, but the central, transformative one. And McLuhan's mind was capable of a kind of historical dissociation that enabled him to conceptualize the development from an entirely new perspective.

In McLuhan's view, our modern transition to electronic media was a watershed event, analogous in impact to the introduction in the sixteenth-century of print technology. Where the latter altered the human "sense ratio" from its oral/aural tribal organization into a visual/linear one (which flavored abstract thinking and paved the way for Descartes, the Enlightenment, and Newtonian science), the former, though very much a product of science, was destined to restore us to the primacy of the oral/aural mode. The electronic mesh, with its instantaneity and its deep reliance on the spoken, rather than written, word would, in time, turn the world into a "global village." The return would not be, to be sure, to an original innocence, but McLuhan was remarkably sanguine: The transformation was seen as a desirable evolutionary advance. What strikes me as a futuristic nightmare is conveyed in his writings with a chatty nonchalance.

McLuhan's key insight—which is, as we shall see, intimately linked to the "global village" vision—has a beautiful obviousness about it. Our media, he states, are extensions of our senses and bodily attributes. The wheel is an extension of the foot, the telephone of the voice, and so on. In *Understanding Media,* he presents an ingenious, and quite poetic, picture of the whole of human history as a sequence of enlargements and refinements upon the biological endowment. McLuhan's most fascinating and far-reaching hypothesis, however, is as follows: The electronic media, taken together, represent an externalized nervous system. All at once it becomes clear what he is leading to—that mankind is in the midst of a process of de-individuation, that it is rapidly making itself into a single organism. When the electronic externalization is complete, everybody will be hooked up to everybody else; information will flash through the network constantly, as through one body. There will be no purpose to individual—that is to say, isolated—existence. While McLuhan does not spell this out in so many words, his premises lead inescapably in this direction. Our technology, and our deep impulse to surmount obstacles of space and time, are combining to submerge individual consciousness into an electronic collectivity.

Two decades have passed since McLuhan proposed his theses. Social and technological changes have essentially vindicated him. And while we have not yet fashioned ourselves into a single protoplasmic entity, the machinery for doing so is more or less in place. The process may even be underway. Think of it: When McLuhan wrote, the electronics revolution was in its infancy. He was speaking out of the era of Telstar and Univac. The microchip, floppy disk, home computer, VCR—these were nonexistent. Each innovation has further implemented that nervous system.

I wish that McLuhan had pushed his speculations and prognostications further. He was clearly fascinated by the larger social implications of the process, but he did not pay much heed to the impact on the individual human psyche. In what ways does this macroscopic reorganization affect the man in the street? How is human nature changing? How readily will that human nature accede to its dissolution into a larger whole?

With respect to these and similar questions, a closer examination of television would have been essential. For television is the prime catalytic agent, at once most representative and most pernicious. If electronic communications technologies suggest, in their aggregate, an externalized nervous system, then television may be seen as an externalization of consciousness itself. A paralyzing thought! But ponder it carefully. Understand that when you sit in front of the TV watching a program, you have turned the wattage of your own consciousness down in order to permit the other emanations to enter. You have replaced a part of yourself with *it*. We all acknowledge our passivity— we call it being entertained. Fine. But now imagine that at a given prime-time hour some eighty million of your fellow citizens have likewise turned down their inner wattage and are soaking in the same imagery and words. If we hypothesize that a nation has a consciousness—if only in the sense of a sum total of its constituent consciousnesses—could we not say that between 8 and 9 P.M. on a given evening the greater part of that national (collective) consciousness is occupied by a single set of images? In which case we could argue that even if there were *not* such a thing as a national consciousness, there is now. A quotation from Yeats fits nicely here. "Is there," he asked, "a nation-wide multiform reverie, every mind passing through streams of suggestion, and the streams acting upon one another, no matter how distant the mind, how dumb the lips?" The words have a ring of prophecy.

I admit, there is something exaggerated in what I am saying. Human diversity does exist, and our ability to reject stimuli is not negligible. But the fact is that the technology for unitary experience already exists, and it's not impossible to imagine a situation in which every living American would be staring with complete absorption at a single image—at which moment that image would be the surrogate consciousness of a quarter of a billion people. (I write this just a few days

The Rage of Caliban

after the 1986 Super Bowl. Estimates put the viewer audience at 120 million. Small wonder, then, that thirty seconds of advertising time cost as much as the GNP of a small African country.)

I have not lost sight of my original topic—the impact of the media revolution upon the practice and reception of poetry—but certain large-scale hypotheses need to be made before I can address it directly. As I intend to hew to a McLuhanesque line, at least for parts of my argument, these hypotheses have to do with what I perceive to be the missing elements of his analysis. That is, with the ways in which the growing media presence is changing our psychic organization. These have, I hope to suggest, a great bearing not just upon language and literature, but upon all serious cultural production. As the definition of media is elusive, I will center my questioning on television; as the most consequential of the media, it brings the topography of change into the clearest relief.

To begin with, we need to make a firm distinction between the form of the medium and its contents. The effects of programs on their audience interest me far less than the long-term influence of watching. Does the process modify the psyche? If so, how? As there do not seem to be very many reliable studies (I imagine that it's all but impossible to find a control group untainted by exposure), my approach will remain conjectural. The situation being what it is, however, we can hardly wait for science to tell us what to think.

The most obvious effects of television are the ones that educators and critics have been warning us about from the start. Namely, that prolonged watching encourages passivity and erodes the attention span. What could be more obvious? One turns the thing on, generally, to get surrogate companionship or to escape. It is certainly easier to take in a stream of images and spoken words than it is to decipher stationary lines of print. Escape is a psychic necessity, I won't deny it, but this form is particularly insidious. First, because it is always there, exerting the pressure of possibility. Second, because it is socially sanctioned, in many milieus even encouraged. Third, and most important, because its contents and process effectively displace consciousness with a manufactured product that resembles consciousness, and it is consequently very difficult to grasp the extent of one's own abdication. As I said, we need disengagement—otherwise we wouldn't sleep as much as we do—but excessive withdrawal deadens the whole range of human reflexes. Our senses, somatic and psychic, are honed through use, through active interchange with others. Projected images cannot stand in for reality, but the watcher lets them do just that. And as the reflexes and senses get dulled, the world outside comes to seem a rather vague and undifferentiated place. Its images don't change quickly enough; the pace feels too slow. The watcher hastens home to the entertainment center.

HARPER'S INDEX: Rank of watching television among activities people look forward to during the day: 1.

I am reminded here of Coleridge's important distinction between "Imagination" and "Fancy," the first being construed as an active power, the second, which "has no counters to play with but fixities and definites," an idle condition that brings nothing new into the world. Television, it would seem, is not only an inferior form of "Fancy" but a degradation of it. For even the play element—the arrangement of "counters"—is taken away; the watcher has nothing to do but absorb the manifestations of someone else's Fancy (TV programming seldom partakes of imagination). And here Freud's warning about the compensatory nature of Fancy (or "phantasy") might be noted: "Phantasies . . . are the immediate mental precursors of the distressing symptoms complained of by our patients." What would the doctor have thought about the objectification and collectivization of phantasy that is television?

Concern about the erosion of the attention spans of children was voiced back in the lithic days of TV, at a time when there were only a few networks and a handful of viewing choices. The fear was that children would be seduced by the glitter and excitement of cartoons and action shows, and that their attention habits would crystalize accordingly. Who can say how those first watchers made their way into adulthood? But a recent survey of American teachers by the Mark Clements Research Group shows us what the increased dosages of latter decades have brought:

> The PARADE/Clements survey asked a series of questions about how the time students spend viewing television has changed their ability to learn. Teachers overwhelmingly said students now expected to be "entertained in the classroom." They thought their students had "shorter attention spans" and found them "more responsive to visual methods of teaching." PARADE asked teachers to write in any other effects they thought important, and a sampling of these responses runs from the expected—"study less," "read less," "less physically fit"—to more profound impacts of television. "Poor listening skills," wrote a sixth-grade teacher from Utah. Many teachers described problems of "passivity," "lack of imagination," "expectations of easy solutions to problems." "Creates uncertainty about reality," said a high school teacher from Virginia. Most of the teachers surveyed said they had changed their teaching methods in response to television's impact. They use more audiovisual equipment in their classrooms and plan "more compact" lesson presentations. Some even have taken on a "flamboyant acting style," while others have tried to relate classroom work to specific television programs.
> —*Parade* magazine, December 1, 1985

These students are the beneficiaries of the new technologies. They manifest not only the impact of the medium and its contents, but also the first of the intensifications introduced by the remote-control panel. This new *de rigueur* apparatus has inaugurated a new mode of "collage" watching, which has as its fortunately unattainable goal the simultaneous consumption of all programming. If the old generic sitcom was felt to threaten the attention span, imagine the kinds of effects that incessant spot-checking of dozens of channels will have.

Vincent Canby, in an article entitled "The New Pop Movies: Made for Fidgety Viewers," gives us a glimpse of the malleability of the audience psyche. Citing a previous article by Sally Bedell Smith, who declares that owing to "a shortened attention span . . . more and more viewers are responding favorably to television programming that emphasizes the visual and diminishes plot and characterization," Canby writes:

> That these viewers—the channel-hoppers—also buy tickets to movie theaters has not been lost on Hollywood producers. The result: the production of an increasing number of films with built-in remote-control units, that is, with narrative structures that have an effect of making one movie seem like a collection of highlights from several. Eliminated, as far as possible, are exposition and any boring passages of the sort that would, in a television show, prompt a viewer to switch to another channel.

As it is the dollar of the mass consumer that fuels the American economy, the danger is that the whole culture and entertainment industry will follow suit (much as teachers have tailored their class instruction to the debilitated attention spans of their students), thus hastening the end of all serious—certainly all difficult—presentation.

This aspect of television—that it turns everything into entertainment—has been taken up at some length in Neil Postman's *Amusing Ourselves to Death: Public Discourse in the Age of Show Business*. Postman sees TV not as a suddenly arrived marvel, but as the apotheosis of a development that began with the invention of the telegraph:

> Telegraphy gave a form of legitimacy to the idea of context-free information; that is, to the idea that the value of information need not be tied to any function it may serve in social and political decision-making and action, but may attach merely to its novelty, interest, and curiosity.

The displacements wrought by "tele-" technology in the graphic (print-oriented) culture are compounded in the visual sphere. Television thoroughly destroys any remnants of temporal or geographic context, pushing forth instead its own creation, a universalized *now* that admits every possible combination and juxtaposition of elements. And I don't just mean the coexistence on different channels of cartoons and cooking programs. There is, in addition—and especially—that incessant and surrealistic melding of elements on every separate channel: The disaster footage on the news report yields instantly to the idiotic bleating of the detergent commercial, and so on. We've all marveled, I'm sure, at the facial plasticity of the news anchor—the "talking head"—who at one moment is expressing grave, adult concern at some incidence of human suffering, and who is, not thirty seconds later, exchanging schoolboy quips with weatherman. Any harshness that may result from these collisions of affect is eradicated by the cosmetic fluidity of the medium. We can't stand back enough to let the contrast reach us—the old visual stimulus is simply replaced by the new, and we batten on to it. Sensing our powerlessness, we relent; this is, we say, the way television is. But is it not increasingly the way *we* are?

Again, is this uncentered flow of fragments something that affects us only so long as we are in its presence? Is it only while we are watching that we see all things under the aspect of "interesting" or "entertaining?" (Let me remind the reader that these are not just attributes of TV. I recently saw a cover of *People* magazine—which itself could not exist without the "personality" pool created by TV—that listed "The 10 Most Interesting People of 1985," and that managed to get both Madonna and Joseph Mengele onto its roster.) Isn't there a strong possibility that the incessant bombardment of disconnected imagery, with no reference to any implicit scale of value, attenuates not just our intellectual but our moral attention span as well? The only hierarchy that television admits is that of time. Where a half-hour news program is forced to give us headlines from South Africa in a minute or less, the commercial advertiser who is willing to spend the money can fill up an equivalent slot with the image of a singing cat. To suggest that human suffering is somehow insulted is to be, in our jaded and cynical culture, a spoilsport.

As always, it is the children and adolescents who are at greatest risk. And what is most threatened, along with the ability, or inclination, to pay attention, is the grasp of what to pay attention *to*. Which comes down, in the end, to a grasp of what is real and what is not. Here is an account by Jerzy Kosinski of an experiment he once conducted; though his sample is a small one, the findings are ominous enough:

> During the years when I was teaching, I invited several seven- to ten-year-old children into a very large classroom where two very large video monitors were installed, one on the left side and one on the right side of the blackboard. TV cameras were also placed on either side of the room. I sat before the blackboard, telling a story. Suddenly, an intruder from outside rushed into the room— prearranged, of course—and started arguing with me, pushing and hitting me. The cameras began filming the incident, and the fracas appeared on both screens of the monitors, clearly visible to all the children. Where did the kids look? At the event (the attacker and me), or at the screen? According to the video record of a third camera, which filmed the students' reactions, the majority seldom looked at the actual incident in the center of the room. Instead, they turned toward the screens which were placed above eye-level and therefore easier to see than the real event. Later, when we talked about it, many of the children explained that they could see the attack better on the screens. After all, they pointed out, they could see close-ups of the attacker and me, his hand on my face, his expressions—all the details they wanted—without being frightened by "the real thing" (or by the necessity of becoming involved).

Kosinski's students did not seem to understand that the presence of the event on the monitors did not cancel the actuality of the real clash. Afraid of what was happening in front of them, they turned to stare at the screen, at which point they were able to assimilate it as entertainment. While this is not conclusive evidence, it does invite us to consider whether the television habit might not undermine the authority of the real in the child's psyche. The boundary between 3-D and 2-D was here crossed with unnerving ease.

*   *   *

The Rage of Caliban

Television could exist, theoretically, without viewers, but it could not exist without enormous financial investment. In capitalist America, the process is, at least on the surface, simple. Corporate advertising underwrites programming. The dollar follows the viewer. It is axiomatic, therefore, that the networks will do whatever is necessary to capture and hold the attention of the viewer. For the sponsor's nightmare image is of a yawning watcher with a remote-control panel in his mitt. To prevent the yawn, to still the finger before it hits the button— these are the highest imperatives. Every sensational topic is explored and drained of surprise: infidelity, wife beating, drug and alcohol abuse, child molesting, AIDS . . . No place, person, or event is exempt so long as it can generate its quantum of interest. What results is a gradual depletion within the viewer of any remaining sense of mystery about the unknown. All of a sudden we are faced with the specter of a finite world, a world no longer felt to be an inexhaustible hoard of images. And from this follows a loss of interest in the future. We become convinced that nothing new can happen.

What we have to realize is that we are not being assaulted or invaded by some brute foreign entity, that the pervasiveness and influence of TV and our other media have to do with their familiarity. We assimilate them without protest. No one even blinks at the strangeness of it all—that these images appear to burgeon out of nothing. Television was able to pass so effortlessly into our cultural life because it functions as an objectified, stand-in consciousness. We feel that we know it, that it is, in a sense, us. I'm not talking about contents so much here as about the medium itself. I have written elsewhere about how this curious identification is secured (see "Television: The Medium in the Mass Age" in An Artificial Wilderness). There is, for one thing, what might be called the electronic bedding effect: Behind the images on the screen is a vast and ramified system, a technological network that is at the same time a bureaucratically dense human network—we therefore feel ourselves in the presence of an inchoate, but superior, intelligence. And our participation—our watching—is confirmed and enhanced by the knowledge that a large portion of our fellow humans are likewise engaged.

The more people we believe to be sharing the experience with us, the more power and prestige we confer upon that unidentified presence. Yes, presence. For though television is, strictly speaking, a technology, we project presence upon it. The reflex is ancient and animistic. And, indeed, it's far easier to invest this moving, speaking thing with authoritative consciousness than it was for early worshipers to believe that their god was alive in some carved fetish. The fluent, quickly elided imagery that passes across this enormous retina both suggests our own inner processes—as if these were our dreams and reveries highlighted and enlarged—and makes us feel as though we are being looked at, addressed, somehow *known*. Television critic Mark Crispin Miller caught this paradox and its implications in the title of his essay "Big Brother Is You, Watching."

The underlying issue here is one of authority. When we read a book, the page faces us in silence. We transform its ciphers into inward sequences, fleshing out thoughts, observations, and descriptions from our inner store of experience. If we defer to anything, it's to the *author*-ity of the conception—that is, to the invisible author. We may feel that he is superior to us in intuition and expression, but we seldom deify him. The continuous presence of television, however, is manufactured by a complex collaboration. We feel no trace of individual presence behind its changing images; rather, there is the implicit authority of consensus. Television is humanlike, but superior. It does not make mistakes (hence the great fascination with "bloopers" and outtakes)—we do. Insofar as we identify the medium as a consciousness or project presence upon it, we also confer a trans-human power. For we have identified it as the voice of the country at large, and it acquires the right-thinking infallibility that only gods and powerful politicians can claim. True, we comment freely on the idiocy of programs and ad segments, but the subliminal authority goes unchallenged—it is backed by the statistical presence of millions.

For several years now I have been teaching a writing course for freshmen at Harvard. My students are, for the most part, bright and hardworking, just as one might expect. But I find myself making certain observations semester after semester. First, that their range of literary

---

The Rage of Caliban

and historical reference is appallingly narrow. Most don't read unless they have to. Reading, for them, is not a natural reflex; it is an acquired taste. They listen to music, go to movies, and watch TV. The kind of information that they receive and store has little to do with historical and cultural contexts—they are overwhelmed by the sustained presentation of a *now*. Their minds move laterally, over surfaces, not into depths.

I find, in addition, clear traces of media exposure in their writing. Most of them are glib on the page, but very few are able to worry a point until they discover the complexities underneath. Many papers move episodically, taking up one point after another without striving for connective links. "Also" is the most commonly used transition device; it serves to introduce a new series, much as "And now, this . . ." supplies subject transitions on TV. I'm not arguing that their products resemble TV shows in any way (though a case could be made, beginning with the fact that most of their words are now assembled on computer screens), but I am suggesting that these minds have absorbed thousands of hours of prime-time programming, and that this is bound to have had effects in the cognitive realm. These are especially evident in those students who confess to having an uneasy relationship with the printed word.

My most alarming insight—the one that triggered in me the impulse to write this essay—came during a particular class discussion. I was talking about language, etymology, and the ways in which a poet's use of language differs from that of other users. I observed that all of us, however subliminally, have a charged feeling for certain primary words, and that each of these words represents an original "breakthrough" experience. There was perhaps a moment, I said, when the word-sound "tree" first fused meaningfully with our perception of the branched and bark-covered entity in front of us. At this point I noticed that a number of hands had gone up. One after the next they nodded and confirmed me: Yes, they knew what I was getting at. They could remember Big Bird on *Sesame Street* bringing them the images and names of the things in their world. Further questioning seemed to confirm it: A substantial portion of their language acquisition had been by way of television. They had not learned the names of many of the things in the so-called real world; they had learned the names of the images of those things. We can't even begin to assess the deeper psychic implications of that information. Clearly, though, the felt contents of their language are different than those of even their immediate forebears. It's as if a whole generation, knowing no better, had turned from the sunlight and had gone back into Plato's cave.

In what ways, then, is our relation to language likely to be affected by a habituation to the electronic media? An impossibly broad question, really. Could we say, at any point in our history, what our collective relation to language is? Is it something that we relate *to,* or is it something that we *are?* Is language the totality of what is being written and spoken at a given time, or are its parameters determined by the usages of the dominant social class? The difficulties of definition are almost insurmountable. But again, there may be some value in declaring general intuitions within a context of commonsense definition.

To begin with, our usage—the ways in which language is written and spoken at home, in school, in public life—is getting structurally simpler. That is to say, impoverished. The possibilities for subtlety and discrimination are diminishing. The system of rules and possibilities— what Saussure called *langue*—is, of course, unchanged. But actual usage, the concretizations that we find within the system—the *parole*—are being steadily modified. This is not to be attributed only to the atrophy of the average attention span. It also has to do with the fact that simplified usage (and with it a modest, self-effacing diction) is presented by the media as the desirable norm. We are reminded at every turn that this is the appropriate linguistic mode for our time. When, on occasion, a character on TV is given a large vocabulary and a more complex way of speaking, we are asked—usually by the laugh track—to mock him for his pretensions, to find in his manner something odd or suspect.

The explanation is simple enough. Television is scripted to the intelligence, habits, and interests of the viewing mass. A program cannot hope to attain high Nielsen ratings if it overshoots by too much the lowest-common-denominator mentality. But the influence, sadly, is not confined just to this sector. For these shows are, owing to the seduc-

The Rage of Caliban

tions of the form itself, enjoyed by the whole population. Through Skinnerian repetition, tastes and responses are lowered in the direction of that denominator. And the reflexes are subtly implanted and strengthened. As on television, so in life: Anything that sounds like a complex sentence or a subordinate clause gets a nervous snicker and a raised eyebrow.

The determining factors behind this leveling of language are many, and they are more intricate than what I can indicate here. For example, not only are more and more people watching increasing amounts of TV, but they are also engaging proportionately less with the printed word. To gain a deeper understanding of the changes taking place, we would have to study not only how the psyche absorbs the television influence, but also how it absorbs and processes print.

Postman makes a case for print as a superior paradigm for public discourse. He cites, for instance, the tremendous popular interest in the Lincoln-Douglas debates in the late 1850's. Auditors, he relates, were required to sit still for hours at a stretch. A ninety-minute turn at the podium was common, and lengthy rebuttals were expected. What's more, the oratory itself was ornate and intricate. Sentences of Jamesian periodicity, packed with clauses and subtle reverses, combined verbal ambitiousness with a spirit of play. And the audience members, by all accounts, were delighted, not just by the spectacle, but by the linguistic to-and-fro. They followed as the fine points were teased out, and rated performances with applause and foot stomping. They were able to do this because they were trained in the written word, and were fully capable of following a sequential argumentation, however stylized. Literacy rates in colonial and postcolonial America were estimated to be among the highest in the world.

Postman contrasts this with the inanities of political debate in our time—which is no longer aimed at an actual audience, but at a video camera and recorder, and an invisible, restless consumer. His worries about the democratic integrity of our political life are not unfounded. The language base has obviously shifted—shrunk, even. The changes in public discourse reflect a recognition by politicians of the altered desires and capabilities of the constituency.

Some would argue, I'm sure, that the change is for the better, that

Approaches

a simple, unadorned speech is preferable to a Byzantine rhetoric, and the contention would have some merit. Clear and forceful expression—if that's what it is—has much to recommend it, and the pretentiousness and deceit that can invade more stylized usages are obviously undesirable. But how great is the difference here between simple vigor and the primerlike utterances that we make to children? We have to be very careful that we don't make a virtue out of a limitation. And if the standard fare on TV is any indication, vigor and directness are in short supply.

The real point is quite basic. Language has always served a double function: to communicate information *and* to mirror, or give expression to, our inner lives, to those feelings, intuitions, and judgments that are not readily accessible to our five senses. Our language, especially now that the adjunct languages of science and mathematics have been refined, is more than adequate to the first. It is the second function that suffers when the linguistic resources are limited. What can no longer be communicated are the fine nuances of subjective being. In the simplification of utterance, subtle distinctions begin to vanish. As we speak, so we are. Language and inwardness are coterminous. If we refuse to plumb the ambiguities, the numberless shadings of our thoughts and feelings—if our tools are no longer fit for the task— then we begin to sacrifice portions of our separate identities. We come closer to that abstract least common denominator, which is precisely where the herd mentality begins. This is the greatest single danger posed by television—it relentlessly addresses and gives social validation to the most obvious and least individuated part of ourselves.

I come back to the original question: What has been the effect of the media, especially television, upon poetry, the most verbally centered of the arts? There are two perspectives from which to consider the matter. According to the first, poetry is an elite art that has always stood apart from the larger disturbances of popular culture. If we believe this, then we would also have to say that poetry has little connection with the language habits of the tribe. To say this, of course, is to imply that it plays no significant role, directly or indirectly, in the world at large, that it is nothing but a superior parlor amusement. Whatever the

The Rage of Caliban

public may believe, I don't think that many poets would agree to this. Most would say, I suspect, that their practice exerts a vital, if inconspicuous, influence on the language of the whole culture, that pressure applied to the tip of the pyramid passes eventually to the base.

The second perspective, implied by this image, is that the poetic art is organically bound to the speech idioms of the time. Wordsworth declared this in his preface to the *Lyrical Ballads,* and Eliot, Frost, and Williams are just a few of the practitioners who have affirmed it in our century. The organic metaphor is more sophisticated and inclusive than that of the pyramid, for the transfer of influence is held to work in both directions. The poet takes his words and rhythms from the speech of his time; he transforms and quickens them in his work, returning to his readers the expression of their own inwardness. This may sound romantic and high flown, but the ambitions of poets have never been modest.

Robert Frost gave a particularly vivid expression to the poet's reliance on the vernacular of his time and place. In a letter to John T. Bartlett, he wrote:

> A sentence is a sound in itself on which other sounds called words may be strung. . . . The sentence-sounds are very definite entities. (This is no literary mysticism I am preaching.) They are as definite as words. It is not impossible that they could be collected in a book though I don't see at present on what system they would be catalogued.
>
> They are apprehended by the ear. They are gathered by the ear from the vernacular and brought into books. Many of them are already familiar to us in books. I think no writer invents them. The most original writer only catches them fresh from talk, where they grow spontaneously.

It must be obvious now where my argument is tending. In Frost's day, which was not all that long ago, the various sentence-sound patterns were there to be gathered. They were shaped by regional speech, social class, occupation, and so on. Variety and distinctiveness were merely the reflection of the profusion of natural experience in a locale.

Approaches

But now we would have to say that that profusion has given way to homogeneity. The media linkup is complete, and at every second a standardized idiom is rubbing away the idiosyncrasies and burrs from our speech. Television, of course, is the main agent of offense. Its whole thrust is to tear down difference and distinction and to submerge all trace of dialect in a fabricated nonregionalese. As the medium saturates the culture, American speech—and with it the living patterns that were one of the principal resources of poetry—starts to become a single, processed entity, a complex organism in a state of devolution.

What does the poet, especially the young, media-infected poet, have to draw upon apart from this new lingua franca? What is he to do if every attempt at departure from the homogenized norm sounds arch, mannered, or pretentious? Add to this the fact that the poet needs to believe that he is writing for his culture, his peers and compatriots. How can he address his time and get a hearing without resorting to the familiar blanched sounds and leveled cadences? Only the subject matter is variable—but even here the possibilities are limited, for not everything will "play."

I was recently reading through a thick anniversary issue of *Antaeus,* one of our most serious and literate journals. I did not have to look past the *B*'s of the alphabet to start finding examples of the depleted kind of poetry that I'm talking about—it is epidemic. Here are just three sample passages:

Sunday. Nothing to do.
Weeds, stumps drift by, gusts jump on the river.
The water's high, the soft banks barely hold it,
sun comes and goes through the haze,
too early for the spectacular, pink fire of the cherry,
and in me I hear Jeff say
his mother and her mother needed each other so much
they died three weeks apart, in me
my mother cries bitterly for the love she needs.
                                    —from "Gratitude" by STEPHEN BERG

It was boring going up the mountain,
my companions speaking of ponderosa
pines and midsummer snow
on Mt. Baldy. My legs didn't hurt,
I just preferred that bar in Wrightwood,
halfway to the valley, where beer
helped the talk into surprise
and the pool balls clinked
and there was no obligation to beauty.

—from "In the San Bernardinos"
by STEPHEN DUNN

Walking home, I see the last ice
Of winter crusting the yards, and here
The pale, twisted limbs of a doll left out
When children stopped playing. And
Went indoors, and the first, soft snows
Came down in the air like stilled speech.
The houses pass on both sides of me. Each
With an aunt who is ill, or with a father
Who has become, at this age, a secret
Even he cannot know, and who waits to be
Told what it is, or how it's story,
Without him, can go on. At home,
I drop a cube of ice into a glass
Of clear ouzo, and swallow, and see
Nothing amusing in the way the leaves
Have held onto their branches all winter.

—from "Ice" by LARRY LEVIS

One could, obviously, cull examples to defend any bias one had a
mind to. But I'm convinced that a careful reading of recent journal and
book publications would confirm that the kind of flat, anecdotal, first-
person lyric that I cite here is the dominant poetic mode of our time.
Optimists maintain that what is happening is a full-scale reclamation of
domestic experience, that these poets are, collectively, the heirs of the

confessional liberation initiated by Lowell, Plath, and others, and that their trajectory represents a healthy rebound from the obscure formalities of high modernism. This ignores, however, the most obvious feature of this poetry: its absolute linguistic and rhythmic poverty. It is very nearly prose, and not even interesting or arresting prose. Poetry like this simply could not exist—and be considered poetry—in a vital linguistic milieu. Whatever else we deem poetry to be, we cannot deny that it represents an intensification, or heightening, of common speech. If these examples are considered in this light, we come to only one conclusion: that common speech has lost its last residues of vigor. As for placing the blame—I urge that we take a hard, unblinking look at the electronic web that we are drawing ever more tightly around ourselves.

I cannot conclude this with the stately and satisfying capitals QED. It is obvious that I have slighted a good many poetic modes, and that the connections that I attempt to draw between the media and language are undemonstrable. But as I noted at the beginning, I have tried to trace the skein of an intuition, nothing more. Let me conclude, therefore, not with an argument, but with an image of our bafflement.

In his preface to *The Picture of Dorian Gray,* Oscar Wilde wrote: "The nineteenth century dislike of Realism is the rage of Caliban seeing his own face in the glass. The nineteenth century dislike of Romanticism is the rage of Caliban not seeing his own face in the glass." I would bring this up to date by saying that the glass—our language—no longer returns *any* image to poor Caliban. He has pushed his ancient rage aside and has submitted to the narcotic of distraction. But that rage will one day return and erupt—perhaps in a deed of self-destruction—for it is in the nature of things that a Caliban cannot become an Ariel.

The Rage of Caliban

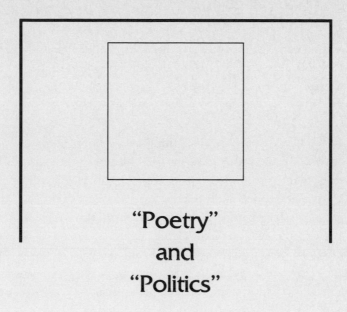

"Poetry"
and
"Politics"

T he poetry/politics debate began when Plato booted the poet from his ideal Republic, maybe even sooner; it will go on so long as there is language. For the classicist-formalist temperament will never stop insisting that art is an *order* apart from the world, with laws of its own. And the opposition will forever maintain that *all* human endeavor, art included, is implicitly political. The poet Carolyn Forché has given concise summation of this latter, "romantic" position in her essay "El Salvador: An Aide-Mémoire" (in an anthology entitled *Poetry and Politics,* edited by Richard Jones):

All language . . . is political; vision is always ideologically charged; perceptions are shaped a priori by our assumptions and sensibility is formed by a consciousness at once social, historical and aesthetic. There is no such thing as nonpolitical poetry.

To say that there is "no such thing as nonpolitical poetry," however, is not quite the same as saying that all poetry is political. It is a question of emphasis. And the assertion that all language is political, much as I like the sound of it, is very nearly meaningless. The moment that you make all language political, you strip the designation of its particularizing power. It's like saying that all men are brothers— they're not; they're finally more *not* brothers than brothers. What's more, if all language is political, then some language will necessarily be *more* political, at which point the hierarchy that was thrown out the front door has come back in through the window.

Forché's good friend Terrence Des Pres has hit upon this sad truth in his essay "Poetry and Politics," which was written for a symposium held at Northwestern University in 1984—a convocation grandly called "The Writer in Our World" (the proceedings have been published as a book of that title). Des Pres begins his piece by rehearsing the terrifying facts about our present planetary situation: "If global violence is on the rise and, up ahead at no great distance, we see ourselves mocked and unnerved by the nuclear option . . . then I presume that we turn where we can for sustenance, and that some of us take poetry seriously in exactly this way—as a spiritual resource from which we gather fortitude and nourishment." So far, so good. I doubt whether anyone who values literature—or their own spiritual sanity— would disagree.

But then Des Pres makes a most interesting observation:

To a degree, to a surprising degree, we turn *elsewhere,* not foremost or finally to poets of our own country, but to poets from abroad and mainly from cultures threatened by imperial takeover. We forgo the pleasures of native voice and endure the indignity of translation in order to come upon an authority seldom apparent among the 4,000 or so poets now publishing or the 50,000 poems-per-year that flood our literary magazines.

Speaking for myself, and for most of the people I know who read poetry seriously, he's right. We do not look to our poets, even the best of them, for clues about how to live in the face of Fear (capital *F:* the fear that makes all else in our well-appointed lives meaningless, that is, for our mad age, the alpha and omega of political reality). When the spirit feels the clutch of that fear, the hand reaches for Milosz, Mandelstam, Celan, Montale, Akhmatova, Zbigniew Herbert, Heaney, Brodsky . . .

Why? The reasons are, for the most part, obvious. Indeed, Milosz discussed precisely this poetic authenticity in his Norton Lectures a few years back (available from Harvard University Press as *The Witness of Poetry*). Speaking about Polish poetry, but in effect poetry from all oppressed or embattled nations, Milosz proposed that mortal danger restores to the word the potency that heedless usage has stripped away; that under the tightening of the totalitarian screw, language becomes the spirit's last arena of freedom. American readers, I believe, look to this poetry because they sense, even through the veil of translation, that words have been mobilized for their noblest truth-telling ends, and that expression has been won through the ordeals of experience—all too often through extreme suffering.

No question, the difference between kinds of poetry—ours and theirs—is immense. Maybe George Steiner was right when he remarked that what's bad for a nation is good for literature. Still, however much we love literature, we are not about to start wishing hardship upon the citizenry of the free West.

Milosz was primarily interested in accounting for the various ways in which crisis renews poetry. Reading him we can learn some of the reasons why the poetry of the oppressed serves as a resource for the American reader. But it may be just as interesting to look at the situation from the other side. What is it about our culture that inhibits, or even *pro*hibits, the production of sustaining—let's say it: *political*—poetry?

"Poetry" and "Politics"

I'm talking now about a *tradition* of political poetry. I will not dispute that we have any number of poets who write with deep political awareness—think of Levine, Rich, Ginsberg, Levertov, Forché herself . . . but somehow, their voices remain culturally marginal; they command authority only for the partisan coterie. Why should this be?

I can think of a number of possible explanations. The first is so obvious that it all but defies precise formulation. Namely, that in terms of historical suffering—I mean invasion, bombardment, starvation, deportation, genocide, totalitarian oppression—America is a tyro. Our national experience, Vietnam included, has always been, for the majority of the population, one of action at a distance. We are recent; we lack generational sediment. What historical rhythm we have established does not include the shared memory of disaster, certainly not in this century. We have not been cursed with the calamities that, for better or worse, bind individuals across lines of caste, class, and family. We have known nothing like what the Poles experienced under the Nazi occupation, or the Russians under Stalin, or the Irish under the enduring British yoke. In America, the sufferings of individuals, whether of Vietnam veterans or the socially disinherited (now known as the underclass), have remained just that; and for that reason they have gone largely unrecognized. This is not because we lack the capacity for empathy. It's that we have no *collective* reference for grief, terror, and privation. Private wounds elicit no larger public resonance: The individual's history has nothing in common with the tribal history.

If we are, as a nation, without collective historical awareness, we are also without any possible means for remedying that. A collective sense of *anything* is impossible without a shared public forum, some means through which disparate voices can address, or confront, one another. How else can a people recognize itself as such? But America is just too big, its constituents too widely dispersed. The closest thing we have to a public forum is television. And this is a devastating irony, for television only simulates the sharing of experience. In reality, it alienates and privatizes, drives each of us deeper into a disconnected solitude. Television is monologue posing as dialogue; the participatory illusion ultimately works to atrophy rather than strengthen the human bond.

Approaches

Media theorist John Maguire has captured the dilemma quite accurately. I quote from his correspondence:

Dan Rather is in a public space. Everyone is watching him. I say something rude; it has no effect on him *or* on those watching and listening to him. The society is telling me that public space is Dan Rather's . . . and I am excluded. Integrating this message as I grow up, when in public I am tongue-tied, don't have opinions, would never heckle or snicker, and certainly never cheer or clap. Maybe I might roll my eyes if I silently disagreed with something . . . more than that would be overstepping my bounds. What right have I got to make my opinions public? I'm a watcher, not a sayer.

Result: a society in which, when you walk on the street and say something in public, you get no echo, no feedback, no resonance. Those who can still act and speak freely have their skill and confidence undercut when the audience is so awfully, artificially and comfortably silent. Democracy declines, of course, when hardly anyone is willing to speak and when speech is no longer understood as possibly moral action.

The effects of this media creation, this false public space, on all discourse are insidious. Poetry, as the most linguistically concentrated of all arts, suffers especially. For poetry does not just combine the available words from the dictionary into persuasive patterns. No, it uses language; it draws its life from the rhythms and usages of the time—from the speech of the people. Poetry is built up, as Robert Frost long ago pointed out, upon an archive of available sentence-sounds. These are the fundamental rhythmic patterns that underlie all of our spoken communication. In a culture where these are various and vigorous—Elizabethan England, for example—poetry is more apt to flourish; certainly it is more likely to engage a readership. The question, then, concerns the relation of the poet's idiom to what Pound called "the speech of the tribe." What *is* the speech of our tribe? The truth, I fear, is that in our day it is the ubiquitous, homogenized, nonregional prattle that we hear on television. It saturates the available airspace—you cannot avoid it if you try. And how, pray, is the poet to draw from *that*? How is he to make a poetry that is as necessary and nourishing as bread, that can speak of real circumstance and of meaningful human response?

The words themselves have not changed—they look and sound much as they always have. The problem is that they *mean* less. Both speaker and listener are removed, abstracted from, the primary conditions in which language is rooted. Our lives are, in a very real sense, mediated. And the more we bathe in the light of the cathode-ray tube, the greater grows the gulf between the word and its referent reality. We can talk *about* things, but we find it extraordinarily difficult to *express* things. The same holds true for politics. We can discuss political matters—and we do so as perhaps never before—but our poetry cannot embody political vision. Because such a vision must arise out of the direct, heartfelt recognition that our lot is joined with everyone else's. *That,* and not ideology, is the origin of a living political poetry. That is what our Eastern European bretheren are able to provide.

Linguistic authenticity is the very quality that we revere in the work of a poet like Seamus Heaney. Though his lines are seldom political in any overt sense, they retain an implicit—I would even say organic—sense of communal connectedness. The language has specific gravity; it is adequate to the felt reality of life in a world of severe natural and social conditions; it is aware of ancestral bonds and local, tribal, responsibilities. Heaney convinces me that these implicit linguistic recognitions can often transmit a more vital political meaning than can more obviously topical kinds of address.

I will make a heretical contention: that the most innocuous of Heaney's rural lyrics ultimately offers more political sustenance than the passionately "aware" lines of a poet like Forché. In saying this, I do not mean in any way to undermine the courage and enterprise of Ms. Forché. I simply want to show the extent to which the problem is one of linguistic culture and not poetics.

Here, first, is Heaney's poem "The Peninsula":

When you have nothing more to say, just drive
For a day all round the peninsula.

The sky is tall as over a runway,
The land without marks so you will not arrive

But pass through, though always skirting landfall.
At dusk, horizons drink down sea and hill,
The ploughed field swallows the whitewashed gable
And you're in the dark again. Now recall

The glazed foreshore and silhouetted log,
That rock where breakers shredded into rags,
The leggy birds stilted on their own legs,
Islands riding themselves out into the fog

And drive back home, still with nothing to say
Except that now you will uncode all landscapes
By this: things founded clean on their own shapes,
Water and ground in their extremity.

Now, the last passage of Forché's "Ourselves or Nothing," a poem
dedicated to Terrence Des Pres:

In the mass graves, a woman's hand
caged in the ribs of her child,
a single stone in Spain beneath olives,
in Germany the silent windy fields,
in the Soviet Union where the snow
is scarred with wire, in Salvador
where the blood will never soak
into the ground, everywhere and always
go after that which is lost.
There is a cyclone fence between
ourselves and the slaughter and behind it
we hover in a calm protected world like
netted fish, exactly like netted fish.
It is either the beginning or the end
of the world, and the choice is ourselves
or nothing.

"Poetry" and "Politics"

I realize that it's not fair to compare a complete poem with an excerpt. My excuse is that I'm not so much interested in contrasting *poems* as I am in looking at two very different ways of using language.

The Forché passage is very much about global political reality, and it takes the large view. Spain, Germany, the Soviet Union, and El Salvador are all invoked, as are the emblematic images of mother-and-child, snow, barbed wire, blood and earth. The poem concludes with a strongly stated plea. Forché asks that we admit both complicity and ultimate responsibility. The final lines echo, perhaps intentionally, Auden's well-known ending to "September 1, 1939": "We must love one another or die."

So many pressing truths about our world have been stated—how is it that I remain as unaffected as I do? My first impulse is to fault myself, my own empathic failure. I am one of Forché's netted fish, hovering "in a calm protected world." I recognize the references, feel the accusatory bite of "mass graves" and blood that will "never soak into the ground." But the fact is, finally, that the language of the poem keeps me out. It is *about* politics; it does not express or embody the primary humanity that is the origin of all social contract. The phrases have been debased by newscasters. Passionate utterance has come perilously close to rhetoric. Her "silent windy fields" and snow "scarred with wire" engage nothing in me—the words have long since been leached of their referential reality.

In the late-night hour, haunted by anxieties and fears, I would much sooner turn for strength—not solace—to "The Peninsula." While the poem does not address the source of my unease in the way that Forché's does, and though it does not point out the necessary moral response, it manages in its quiet way to bring certain universal human priorities into alignment. "The Peninsula" is about the private struggle for equilibrium, about finding a true relation between an *out there* (in this case the natural world) and an *in here*. When we reach the penultimate line, with its lovely "things founded clean on their own shapes," we register the rare sensation of things converging with the words for things. This is a poem about the poet's mission. And that affirmation, the rightness of its expression, reaches me in a way that the injunction to choose "ourselves or nothing" does not. Heaney's poem reveals to me that we are connected across distances by language. It tears a hole in that netting that Forché has taken such pains to wrap me in. When I compare the two experiences, I feel inclined to reverse her pronouncement that "all language . . . is political," and to assert instead that all politics is language. Politics is, after all, that process whereby we transcend our self-enclosed condition; language is the tool that we have evolved for accomplishing this.

Part II:

Readings

Note:
Close
Reading

Close reading, as I understand it, is really nothing more than paying attention to a text. The difficulties are not in the conception, but in the doing. To close-read a poem is, in part, to create a receptivity, a silence, in yourself so that the work can leave an impression. Just as you cannot race past a painting in a museum and call that "seeing" the art, so you cannot move your eyes rapidly over the words of a poem and imagine that you have "read" it. If "rapid" and "rape" are not etymologically cognate, they ought to be.

As we glance at, look at, and finally *see* a painting, so do we read, hear, and only then *experience* a poem. Each stage represents a deepening involvement with the work in question. To *see* a painting or to *experience* a poem is not, of course, to be done with it. Quite the contrary: It is to have brought the interaction to a level of mattering. Only from that level can the created thing begin to influence, or change, your life.

Close reading, then, is a preliminary action, a way of getting from A to B, from reading to hearing. Close reading does not guarantee experiencing, but experiencing will certainly not happen without hearing. For a poem, whatever else it is, is also a verbal construction, a massing of sounds and rhythms in the auditory arena. Meaning is only part of what a poem is about. The other part is about poetry—or language—itself. That is, about how meaning is made. There is no poem worth anything that is not also to some significant degree an aesthetics, a disciplined marveling at the ways in which language impinges upon the psyche.

The goal of close reading might be stated as follows: to hear the language of the poem as intensely as the poet heard it in the process of composition, and to feel its rhythms, and hesitations and pauses, not just in the ear but in the whole body. The only talent required is a talent for focus and deceleration. To read poetry as it is meant to be read, you must push your way through the shallow-field perceptual mode that modern life makes habitual. The operation is not nearly as simple as it sounds. The eye has been taught to speed across word clusters. The sound in the ear, which lags behind the eye, is usually a noise, like the garbling that comes when tape gets dragged across the magnetic heads. That garble has to be slowed. First to normal speech tempo, then by half again. Otherwise the intricacy that the poet "listened" into his lines will remain unavailable.

The harder it is for you to slow down, the more you need to be rescued from the twentieth century; the more you *need* poetry.

The rest of this section is made up of five close readings: of poems by John Keats, Philip Larkin, Craig Raine, Marianne Moore, and James Wright. Each reading ends up highlighting a different aspect of poetry. My analysis of a stanza of "To Autumn" features mainly sound values—how do they combine to make that music that we recognize as beauty? The essay on Larkin's "The Whitsun Weddings" examines the poet's development of a narrative and his cunning manipulation of the first-person voice. The Raine reading, by contrast, focuses on the arrangement of dissociated images. The approach to Marianne Moore's "Poetry" asserts that her decision to revise the poem may have been an expression of aesthetic self-hatred. Finally, the "sounding" of James Wright's "Hammock" poem is an effort to extract the maximum resonance from a short and simple-seeming lyric.

Note: Close Reading

Season of mists and mellow fruitfulness,
    Close bosom-friend of the maturing sun;
Conspiring with him how to load and bless
    With fruit the vines that round the thatch-eves run;
To bend with apples the moss'd cottage-trees,
    And fill all fruit with ripeness to the core;
        To swell the gourd, and plump the hazel shells
    With a sweet kernel; to set budding more,
And still more, later flowers for the bees,
Until they think warm days will never cease,
        For Summer has o'er-brimm'd their clammy cells.

                        —from "To Autumn"

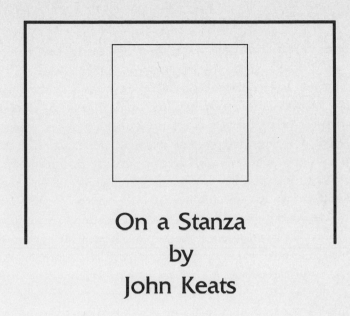

On a Stanza
by
John Keats

Somehow a stubble plain looks warm—in the same way that some pictures look warm—
this struck me so much in my Sunday's walk that I composed upon it.

—Keats, letter to J. H. Reynolds

"Distance is the soul of beauty," wrote Simone Weil. Though it is by no means the only gnomic aphorism on the subject (Dostoevsky: "Beauty will save the world." André Breton: "Beauty will be convulsive or it will not be at all." Keats: "Beauty is truth, truth beauty . . ."), it remains for me the most tantalizing. The first time I encountered it, I felt instinctively that it was true; that is, it gave shape to a feeling that had long been inchoate in me. At the same time, however, I could not unravel it into any kind of explanation. The formulation seemed to retain a distance of its own, a subtle paradox at the core. For I find that whatever strikes me as beautiful manifests not distance but nearness, a quality of transparent immediacy; I feel that I am confronting something that I've always known. How can that "nearness" be squared with "distance"?

So long as I persisted in regarding Weil's words in the abstract, I remained baffled. It was only recently, when I tried to discover for myself why a certain poem was beautiful, that I began to understand. What Weil was addressing was the paradox at the heart of the aesthetic encounter. When we are stirred by beauty in a particular work of art, what we experience is the inward abolition of distance. It is only when we try to put our finger on the source of the sensation, when we try to *explain* the beauty, that the horizons are reversed. At that moment the near becomes the far, much as it does when we try to fathom our own reflection in the mirror: The more intently we look, the stranger becomes the object of our scrutiny.

I set myself what seemed at first a simple task: to say why Keats's "To Autumn" was beautiful. The poem has always been one of my personal touchstones. Whenever I feel the occupational contamination of "words, words, words . . ." I look to its three stanzas for the rightness that restores faith. Nor am I alone. Generations of readers have singled out this last ode for special praise. I have seen it cited many times as the most perfect poem in the language. A more suitable test case for beauty, it seems, would be hard to find.

Before starting in on my own, I took a quick tour through the writings of certain estimable critics and scholars. I wanted to get a taste for the kinds of approaches that had been adopted in the past, and also to make sure that I did not belabor anything that was old hat. In a few sittings I learned more than a mortal should know about Keats's strategies of "stationing," his deployment of harvest imagery, his secularism, his debt to Milton and Shakespeare, and so on. I found much that was fussy, and just as much that was fascinating. But in all of the pages I read, I found nothing that helped me to understand why the immediate encounter with the words on the page is so thrilling, why the melody of the thing lives on in the mind, or how it is that the sensations are carried from line to line with an almost supernatural rightness. The beauty of the poem was in every case assumed; no one tried to account for it. I had to wonder: Is beauty that has been made out of words impervious to other words? Or is there an etiquette that I remain ignorant of—that one does not bring up certain matters? I left the library with a heady feeling of exploratory license.

Osip Mandelstam once wrote: "Where there is amenability to paraphrase, there the sheets have never been rumpled, there poetry, so to speak, has never spent the night." I let these words guide my first steps. For anyone can see at a glance that "To Autumn" resists summary. It rests on no clearly delineated narrative, and carries no capsule message. And while there *is* sense in the poem, it is not the primary source of our response. But neither is that response, as with some poems, a matter of startling, unexpected imagery or metaphoric enlargement/reversal. We do not see the world as we have never seen it before. Rather, we are presented with an array of familiar, if heightened, sensations. Clearly, then, the magic must have to do with the interactions of sense and verbal music, with the rhythmic orchestrations and the intensifications that result.

I am convinced that the beauty of the ode is to be sought with the fine cross hairs of sound and sense, that it inheres in the subtlest details and is sustained from breath to breath—that generalizations will serve for nothing. We experience such a rapid succession of perfectly managed sensory magnifications that we are, in a strange way, brought face to face with the evolutionary mystery of language. The absolute rightness of the sound combinations forces us to a powerful unconscious recognition: that sound is the primal clay out of which all meaning has been sculpted.

I intend here to give a fanatically (and phonetically) close reading of the first stanza of "To Autumn." To work through any more than a stanza with as highly ground a lens would be tiresome to the reader and to some extent redundant. Certain readers may object to the procedure, claiming that the effects I find are too fantastic, that I am amplifying phonic detail out of all proportion, and that my findings are not part of the intended experience of the poem. Let me defend myself (briefly) in advance.

First of all, I believe that when we read a poem we absorb and process a great deal more than we are consciously aware of, and that it

On a Stanza by John Keats

is precisely those cues that we pick up at the threshold—that we hear and feel but do not overtly take note of—that combine to give us the aesthetic surge. A passage strikes us as a perfect expression, but we cannot quite say why. Indeed, I wonder if this might not account for some of the mystery of beauty: that we confront an order or pattern that is opaque to the conscious monitors but perfectly transparent to the preconscious, or unconscious. Maybe Simone Weil's "distance" is really referring to a gap between parts of the psyche. In which case, perhaps the feeling of beauty depends upon a tension—or charge— born of an opposition within one's own psyche.

My second defense is so rudimentary that it could easily be over-looked. That is, given Keats's poetic endowment—the evidence of which is, of course, the poetry itself—what we might perceive as a hairsplitting discrimination was perfectly conspicuous to him. Let's not forget that we read poetry in the odd hour, as amateurs; Keats pressed his lines into place with the full intensity of his being. When a poet is composing, the value of every sound is magnified a thousandfold. His radar is attuned to frequencies that we are not even aware of. (Yeats characterized this rapt state beautifully: "Like a long-legged fly upon the stream / His mind moves upon silence.") I would argue, therefore, not only that *(a)* if you find it, it's probably there, but also *(b)* however much you find, there is sure to be more. Poetry will not disclose its secrets so long as we impose a ceiling upon its resonance and refer-ence. The poet does not use language as we do when we write a letter or a report. It is present to him when he composes as a totality of possibilities—the slightest pressure at any point sends waves through the entire system. To limit the associational field is to hobble the response.

Season of mists and mellow fruitfulness,
    Close bosom-friend of the maturing sun;
Conspiring with him how to load and bless
    With fruit the vines that round the thatch-eves run;

The governing sensation of the full stanza, which is most tellingly enacted in its last four lines, is of active ripening—of nature swelling all living things with her ichor—and overflow. Keats's description is as straightforward as could be, and the lines are crowded with nouns and active, richly suggestive verbs. The presentation proceeds from the un-bounded vista of the invocation through a series of increasingly par-ticular close-ups, to culminate in the minute cells of the honeycombs. We do not have to dig past the surface to get at the delights of the sound—they are there to be scooped right off the page. And just as we can enjoy the play of colors in one of Monet's haystacks—with no deeper understanding of his struggle to balance off the objective inter-actions of light and matter on the retina with the limitations of inter-mittent perception—so we may respond to the sonorities and the abundance of carefully arranged detail while remaining oblivious, at least consciously, of the underlying intricacies.

Literature is full of picturesque renderings of the natural world. But with "To Autumn" we are well beyond the picturesque. In these lines the words do not merely designate or connote—they take on a gestural life so explicit that they temporarily displace the world to which they refer. They do so by replacing it with a self-sufficient language world, where things are not only named and arranged, but into which are incorporated deep suggestions about the working of physical process. The mystery of it—that language should be capable of so much—defies explanation and analysis. At best, we can note some of the more conspicuous instances of this functioning.

"Season of mists . . ." Mists, as we know from our science primers, result from the condensation and evaporation of ground moisture, the very same moisture that is taken up by the capillary roots of trees and plants and that eventually fleshes out the cells of the fruits. The sun, which from our Ptolemaic perspective rises up as if out of the earth itself, creates the mist by hastening evaporation and subse-quently "burns" it away. This process, recalled for us in the poem by the nouns "mist" and "sun," is fully enacted on a phonetic level. Here we get our first evidence of the ode's deeper linguistic rightness.

Observe, first, what the mouth must do to vocalize the line: "Sea-son of mists and mel-low fruit-ful-ness." The lips widen and stretch to make the initial *ee* sound in "Season," contract the same position to pronounce "mists," and contract it yet again, just slightly, to form the syllable "mel-." If we think of these contractions as representing diminishing circumferences—as, say, cross sections of a funnel—then with the small *o* of "-low" and the *oo* of "fruit-" (which cannot be made without a pouting protrusion of the lips and an even smaller aperture) we have come to the narrowed apex. This would not necessarily be significant in itself, but when we consider the unstated physical process—the moisture being siphoned out of the soil and into the fruit through the myriad fine roots, the push against gravity—then these lip movements become instrumental.

But this is not all. There is also a simultaneous *lingual* event. For in order to enunciate cleanly the words "mel-low fruit-ful-ness," the tip of the tongue must sketch out the shape of a fruit. Try the sounds slowly and expressively. Notice how the tongue ticks off points along a circumference. Isn't there a distinct impression of rondure? The event is further complicated, and its resonance deepened, by the fact that the sounds we are making signify so directly: "mel" (the Latin root for "honey"), "fruit," and "ful(l)ness." We have spoken only one line, but we have already abetted the ripening process and have tasted the contours of a small, sweet fruit.

One of the first things we notice about the opening lines of the stanza are the many sibilants. These function in several ways. First, their purposeful positioning virtually forces us to create what might be called an associational field. We screen them differently than we would in other contexts. When we hear on the newscast, for example, that there are "early morning mists in low-lying areas," we do not feel free to conjure with the sounds; we know that they are being used in a strictly denotational mode. The situation is obviously different when it is Keats writing: "Season of mists and mellow fruitfulness." And there is more involved than just placement and rhythmic emphasis. We assume an intentional pressure: The sounds were mobilized because they were the best possible equivalents for the desired sensation.

The proximity of the *s* sounds in the first three words—there are four—encourages us to associate the sibilance with mist. This is not that unnatural, in any event: The *s* holds latent suggestions of moisture (if only because rain makes a hissing sound), which a context like this would immediately activate. But there is also a very subtle and effective sensory crossing that takes place once we know the poem. For just as the sense of the first two lines allows us to make a link between the *s* sounds and the mists, so in the fourth and fifth lines the battery of *t*'s ("thatch-eves" and "cottage-trees") invites us to connect the *t* sound with the hard opacity of the actual trees. Pictographically, of course, the shape of the letters encourages such a leap—the sinuosity of the *s* corresponding with the undulant movement of the vapors, and the *t* resembling a branched tree. Once this association has been subliminally registered, we can find in the word "mists" both a phonic and a visual representation of cloudy exhalations swirling about the branches of an orchard tree. And once we make such an association, needless to say, we are drawn into the poem in a profound way.

> Close bosom-friend of the maturing sun;
> Conspiring

The deliberate profusion of sibilants also creates an unmistakable hiss in the opening lines. This gathers momentum through the first two lines and is not released until we encounter the perfectly situated participle "conspiring." The word works on us both etymologically and through the sound itself. To "conspire" means, literally, to breathe together. We get a sense of complicity, of mutual exhalation, of dampness of exhalation (mist represents nothing so much as breath vapor), and, as I will discuss later, sexual activity. At the same time, the word discharges completely the hiss that has gathered in the preceding lines. The vertical thrust of "spire"—which suggests with a single stroke that the sun has moved up in the sky—compresses an otherwise gradual event: The mist is burned off in the space of a syllable. We might observe, too, that "close," "bosom," and "conspiring" all keep the solar emblem *o* near the mist-suggesting *s*—with the pitched *i* of "spire" that connection is sundered.

A series of slight syllables follows the break: "-ing," "with," "him," "how," and "to." We can almost imagine that Keats is drawing out a slender vine or branch, tapering it to slightness before attaching the round and dense-feeling "load." The line is a beautiful illustration of the relative gravity of word sounds. The weighted—but distinctly lighter—sound of the monosyllable "bless," positioned as it is after "load," figures in the ear the supple movement of a laden vine and gives us the aural equivalent of a diminishing bob.

> load and bless
> With fruit the vines that round the thatch-eves run;

The enjambment of "bless/With" further accentuates the down and up motion, and the appreciably lighter *oo* of "fruit" continues the upward arc, even as the placement of the noun in a passive construction finally connects it to the vine. The syntactical inversion of the rest of the line echoes the preceding "load and bless/With fruit." Both phrases require an extension of the breath and thereby render more palpable our sense of elongated curling vines.

This fourth line is pivotal. With "vines" and "thatch-eves," we cross for the first time from the all-inclusive apostrophe of autumn into a particular kind of landscape. Helen Vendler has worked out the full topography of the poem in *The Odes of John Keats*—I can add nothing to her discoveries. But I would underscore the importance of the transition. Just as the stanza narrows down from a vast environment to the "cells" of the honeycombs, so too does it move us from a diffuse seasonal mistiness into a realm of highly tactile particulars: "thatch-eves," "moss'd cottage-trees," and "hazel shells" . . .

> To bend with apples the moss'd cottage-trees,
>   And fill all fruit with ripeness to the core;
>   To swell the gourd, and plump the hazel shells
>   With a sweet kernel;

The central lines of the stanza are dominated by sensuous detail. I have already proposed that the clustered *t*'s call to mind the actual density of an orchard. The impression is further solidified by the incidence of strong stresses at the end of the line: *"moss'd cottage-trees."* And the numerous vowel and consonant doublings add to the effect— *pp, ss, tt, ee,* and *ll* twice in a mere eleven words—as if nature's prodigality extended to the alphabet itself. Nor is their impact strictly

---

visual. An alerted ear—and what ear can fail to be quickened by a poem like this?—finds the subliminal stutter in words like "apples" and "cottage." Again, it is the associational field that imparts significance to these normally incidental combinations.

And fill all fruit with ripeness to the core;

Here, at last, the iambic pentameter resolves. And with wonderful effect. The harmonic regularity of nature is at last disclosed. The very filling of the fruit conforms to the eternal paradigm. The line both denotes and enacts measure. Nor is it accidental, I think, that the first evenly cadenced line should sit at the very center of the stanza, at its "core," as it were. For as I observed at the outset, the dominant action in these eleven lines is one of gradual overflow. This line, then, as the midpoint, marks the perfect peak of ripeness. The liquid has filled its container to the limit; the next five lines will send it brimming over.

To swell the gourd, and plump the hazel shells
With a sweet kernel;

If *s*'s can be said to invoke mists, and *t*'s trees, then what are we to make of the loading of *l*'s in these central lines—"fill," "all," "swell," "plump," "hazel," and "shells"? Pronouncing the sixth and seventh lines with exaggerated care, we quickly discover how intricately mingled are the *l*'s and the other consonants, especially the *r*'s. It is the consonantal weave that keeps the tongue dancing without rest along the roof of the mouth, an activity that, when wedded to the sense, gives us the suggestion of a great many fruits burgeoning simultaneously. Especially effective is the placement of the exquisitely plosive "plump"—we feel as though things are bursting on every side of us.

It is worth noting here, too, the subtle reversal that Keats has devised. Where "fill all fruit with ripeness to the core" describes an inward movement, as though ripening were a process beginning at the surface and continuing toward the center, the remaining actions of the stanza are all outward: swelling, plumping, and o'er-brimming. Again, this underscores the importance of the sixth line. We can view it, if we choose, as the node of a chiasmus (X) figure. Lines 1–5 *in*-still the fruit with moisture; lines 7–11 move out from the center and culminate in a *dis*-tilling activity.

One curious element in the middle part of this stanza is Keats's repetition of the word "fruit." This is in addition to his use of "fruit-fulness" in the first line. In both instances, the general term is followed by cited particulars, either "apples" or "the gourd" and "the hazel shells." The oscillation between the general and the specific (the whole ode, it seems, proposes a landscape that is neither entirely typified nor altogether singular) allows the universality of cyclic return to play against concretely sensuous detail. The repetition of "fruit" prevents us from immersing ourselves in an unequivocally particular setting. What's more, the word sends us back to the original denominations and commands of Genesis ("Let the earth bring forth grass, the herb yielding seed, and the fruit tree yielding fruit after his kind . . ."; "Be fruitful, and multiply . . ." and so on). I would not like to stress this connection too strongly, however, for the order apostrophized in "To Autumn" is secular, not Edenic. The biblical echo points back to time-less harmonies, but it does not invite us to consider "Man's first diso-bedience."

Before turning to the final lines of the stanza, we might remark one more interesting subtlety. Keats has, in the sixth line, disassembled the signal word "fruitfulness," scattering its components: "And *fill* all *fruit* with rip*eness*. . . ." We pick this up subliminally, unaware that part of our pleasure in the line comes from this all-but-imperceptible echo. The weft is tightened; the evenly cadenced core of the stanza touches us with what feels like perfect inevitability.

> to set budding more,
> And still more, later flowers for the bees,
> Until they think warm days will never cease,
> For Summer has o'er-brimm'd their clammy cells.

The most remarkable event in the stanza as a whole is Keats's flawlessly executed enactment of the physical sensation of overflow. The cluster of strong accents—"And *still more, later*"—instigates a rising tension. The near regularity of the penultimate line cannot quite appease the ear. It inspires, instead, a precarious suggestion of arrest; we feel the tense convexity with which liquid holds shape just before spilling over. And then comes the midline impact of "o'er-brimm'd," a word that both describes and encodes the action. The three unaccented syllables preceding "-brim-" ensure that the emphasis will fall upon the instant at which convexity yields.

A number of critics have connected the feeling of surfeit generated by the stanza with Keats's decision to adopt an eleven-line (instead of ten-line) stanza. The added quantity has obvious effects on the reader, and Keats has made the most of these. By giving the penultimate line acceleration and rising pitch—"cease" pitches forward like the crest of a wave—he has made it all but impossible for us to take our natural pause. We are driven on to complete the stanza, to extend our exhalation past the normal limit. We feel the expenditure with our whole pneumatic apparatus, even as we murmur the three sets of doubled *m*'s—"Summer," "o'er-brimm'd," and "clammy"—mimicking the languorous vibration of satiated bees.

The sexual suggestion of these last lines cannot be passed over. If we listen to the whole stanza and follow its rhythmic progression, we cannot but register the climactic moment that comes with "cease" (who was it who called the orgasm "a little death"?), and the echoing contraction of "-brimm'd." Though Keats may not have orchestrated his lines with such an end in mind—consciously, at least—a reader has to be wearing earplugs to be unaware of it. Nor is it just a question of rhythmic emphasis. The honey hoarded by the bees (never named, but conjured up early on by the "mel-" of "mellow") is substantially akin to the "honey of generation" in Yeats's "Among School Children." For that matter, doesn't the entire stanza combine its images of swelling fruits and rising liquids under the aspect of its opening conceit—that the "conspiring" earth and sun are the intimate begetters of all that lives (in which case "Close bosom-friend" is something more than platonic in its suggestion)? Nor should we forget that the thrice-named "fruit" is itself seed. Not just fecundity, but procreative fervor underlies the imagery and sensation of this stanza.

*　　*　　*

On a Stanza by John Keats

As I said at the outset, I'm not going to work my way dutifully through the complete ode. My purpose is not to advocate any new interpretation. Neither am I under the illusion that this stitch-by-stitch approach will tell us anything about the "meaning" of the work. As far as I'm concerned, there is in this case no meaning extrinsic to the obvious sense of the words on the page. I do hope, however, that the close reading of a single stanza will emphasize that its aesthetic effect—our perception of beauty, if you will—derives largely from a complex series of sound and sense interactions, many of which are apt to elude us as we read. And that, further, our experience of beauty may well have something to do with the gap, or *distance,* between what we are aware of perceiving and what we pick up subliminally.

Two questions remain. First, let us suppose that we have un- covered a great many of these inconspicuous interactions. Have we then, by eliminating much of the distance between conscious and un- conscious perception, somehow slackened the mainspring of beauty? Can we, in other words, pick a poem apart so completely that under- standing supplants astonishment? I would say not, for the simple rea- son that our psyches are not structured in such a way that we can both read in a participatory manner *and* at the same time reflect upon the ways in which that involvement has been achieved. The very workings that we uncover through an operation of willed dissociation—like the ones that I have just pointed out—function, when we read, to keep us fixed inside the language circuit. And if we do, through one of those unaccountable psychic switches, find ourselves staring at the cause of a particular poetic effect, our response might very well be enhanced. For what we recognize at such a moment is the preternatural fitness of language for the transmission of subtleties of perception.

The second question is complex and cannot be fully dealt with here. Namely, to what extent was the poet aware of, and responsible for, the felicities that I have been extracting from his work? Or, to put it another way, can we legitimately locate effects that the poet was not in some way aware of and intending? As I said earlier, we must always keep in mind that the poet's aural endowment is probably greater than ours—though *how much* greater is impossible to gauge. How we an- swer the question of intention, however, will depend upon what we believe about the process of poetic composition. If we believe that it is consciously governed, willed, dependent on the taking of infinite pains—a nonsensical view, in my opinion—then the poet's own awareness matters greatly. If he did not intend *x,* then *x* does not exist.

As soon as we allow the unconscious a role in creativity, on the other hand, the reader is given a great deal of license. For then it is not a case of the poet's inventing lines, but rather of his finding sounds and rhythms in accordance with the promptings of the deeper psyche. The poet does not rest with a line until he has released a specific inner pressure. Or, to put it another way, the pressure looks to the language for its release. It magnetizes and attracts certain elements from the phonic spectrum and sets them into combinations. The poet presides over this process—in a sense he is *its* instrument—working toward that feeling of "rightness" which is his ultimate standard. Needless to say, he very often might not know why he brings two sounds together. When we turn up the most uncanny effects in his lines, therefore, we have every reason to believe that his deeper "Muse" put them there, even if *he* did not.

On a Stanza by John Keats

THE WHITSUN WEDDINGS

That Whitsun, I was late getting away:
   Not till about
One-twenty on the sunlit Saturday
Did my three-quarters-empty train pull out,
All windows down, all cushions hot, all sense
Of being in a hurry gone. We ran
Behind the backs of houses, crossed a street
Of blinding windscreens, smelt the fish-dock; thence
The river's level drifting breadth began,
Where sky and Lincolnshire and water meet.

All afternoon, through the tall heat that slept
   For miles inland,
A slow and stopping curve southwards we kept.
Wide farms went by, short-shadowed cattle, and
Canals with floatings of industrial froth;
A hothouse flashed uniquely: hedges dipped
And rose: and now and then a smell of grass
Displaced the reek of buttoned carriage-cloth
Until the next town, new and nondescript,
Approached with acres of dismantled cars.

At first, I didn't notice what a noise
   The weddings made
Each station that we stopped at: sun destroys
The interest of what's happening in the shade,
And down the long cool platforms whoops and skirls
I took for porters larking with the mails,
And went on reading. Once we started, though,
We passed them, grinning and pomaded, girls
In parodies of fashion, heels and veils,
All posed irresolutely, watching us go,

As if out on the end of an event
   Waving goodbye

Readings

To something that survived it. Struck, I leant
More promptly out next time, more curiously,
And saw it all again in different terms:
The fathers with broad belts under their suits
And seamy foreheads; mothers loud and fat;
An uncle shouting smut; and then the perms,
The nylon gloves and jewellery-substitutes,
The lemons, mauves, and olive-ochres that

Marked off the girls unreally from the rest.
   Yes, from cafés
And banquet-halls up yards, and bunting-dressed
Coach-party annexes, the wedding-days
Were coming to an end. All down the line
Fresh couples climbed aboard: the rest stood round;
The last confetti and advice were thrown,
And, as we moved, each face seemed to define
Just what it saw departing: children frowned
At something dull; fathers had never known

Success so huge and wholly farcical;
   The women shared
The secret like a happy funeral;
While girls, gripping their handbags tighter, stared
At a religious wounding. Free at last,
And loaded with the sum of all they saw,
We hurried towards London, shuffling gouts of steam.
Now fields were building-plots, and poplars cast
Long shadows over major roads, and for
Some fifty minutes, that in time would seem

Just long enough to settle hats and say
   I nearly died,
A dozen marriages got under way.
They watched the landscape, sitting side by side
—An Odeon went past, a cooling tower,

On a Stanza by John Keats

And someone running up to bowl—and none
Thought of the others they would never meet
Or how their lives would all contain this hour.
I thought of London spread out in the sun,
Its postal districts packed like squares of wheat:

There we were aimed. And as we raced across
    Bright knots of rail
Past standing Pullmans, walls of blackened moss
Came close, and it was nearly done, this frail
Travelling coincidence; and what it held
Stood ready to be loosed with all the power
That being changed can give. We slowed again,
And as the tightened brakes took hold, there swelled
A sense of falling, like an arrow-shower
Sent out of sight, somewhere becoming rain.

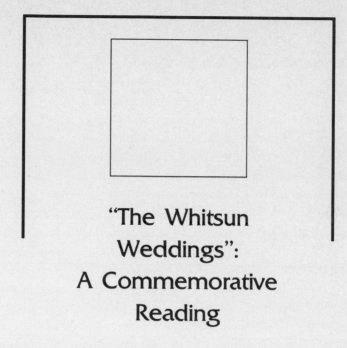

"The Whitsun Weddings": A Commemorative Reading

W hen Philip Larkin died in December of 1985, there was no big public fuss. No one rose up to proclaim that the English vessel now lies "emptied of its poetry," or anything of the kind. It was, in a sense, a victory for Larkin, for throughout his career he rebuffed attempts by others to attach epithets of greatness or importance to his person. Still, in those scattered precincts where poetry is read and loved, a keen feeling of loss persists. No more will that wonderfully expressionless countenance tease the press photographer; glum dyspepsia has lost its sovereign icon. As for the poetry, the Muse had, Larkin admitted, long ago ceased making any but the most perfunctory courtesy calls. But as the next-to-nothing of his output suddenly became the final nothing, we perhaps realized how much we had believed in the possibility of a creative resurgence. No more. That slimmest of *oeuvres* must now expand to fill the space that desire has carved. It must suffice—and it will.

Larkin's vision and his tone were in perfect alignment. I can't think of anyone who could put across an attitude, a stance—a *feeling* about life— so simply and yet so distinctively. He was the perfect moral realist; he understood the exactions of time and the quotidian, and the knowledge is there right away in the sound and the beat. Thumb through your Larkin for some of the perfectly thrown first lines: "Groping to bed after a piss"; "Home is so sad. It stays as it was left"; "Side by side, their faces blurred"; and so on. When a great musician plays, the music begins with the first note. The rhythm is not invented; it jumps free of the rib cage and fastens to the air. And when the tune—or poem—is over, we feel the effort of stepping back into time. For while inside the closed order of rhythm and sound—even if it has been telling us the worst—we have been relieved of our mortal burden. Reading Larkin's poems on psychic entropy and limitation, we feel strangely exalted.

Nowhere do we register this paradox more fully than in his long poem "The Whitsun Weddings." The work is not so much a characteristic expression of Larkin as it is an apotheosis. The full range of his voice is here, the splenetic tics as well as the melancholic lyricism. The narrative "I," the traveler, is at once detached, brooding, and penetratingly observant of his physical surroundings and the telltale markings and rituals of the English middle class. Moreover, as so often in Larkin's poetry, the reflections are not presented at the pitch of revelation; they mark, rather, the natural movements of a sensibility reconciled to its despair. Their drift is instantly familiar: They survey the blind ceremony of hope, projecting upon it the erosions of habituation and defeat; they glimpse the illusion of free will and promptly situate it within a larger context of fatal determinism. Compassionate though its music may be, the poem cannot quite conceal a certain grim satisfaction. One thinks of that old mocking epitaph: "As you are now, so I once was. As I am now, so you will be."

Larkin has a genius for hiding away his scaffold and his working tools. He strings together understated colloquial lines that engage the ear and yet almost never send it back to check the source of its pleasure. The work is, in fact, stringently formal. But it is never—unlike the art of Richard Wilbur or James Merrill—self-consciously so.

> That Whitsun, I was late getting away:
>   Not till about
> One-twenty on the sunlit Saturday
> Did my three-quarters-empty train pull out,
> All windows down, all cushions hot, all sense
> Of being in a hurry gone.

It's hard to believe that the eight 10-line stanzas are uniformly rhymed in an *a b a b c d e c d e* pattern, and that the lines themselves—except for the four-syllable second line—are very nearly always ten syllables and fall with some regularity into an iambic pentameter. The formality is discreet—subfusc, even—Larkin refuses to pounce on his rhymes, prefers instead a smoothly slipping enjambment. The abbreviated second line is not a quirk: It is the subtle catch at the beginning of every stanza that bumps the ear from its expectation and allows the whole to keep the flavor of a ruminative aside.

But far more impressive than Larkin's navigation of the wicket course of rhyme or syllable count is his implementation of a narrative strategy that is at once dynamically propulsive and casual seeming. This, more than any formal pyrotechnics, allows him to forge what appear to be idle observations into a thrilling tension. The highly synchronized interaction of thematic and technical strategies deserves close attention.

If the ultimate sensation that we derive from reading "The Whitsun Weddings" is one of physical—and existential—gravity, then part of the reason is that Larkin has given us a world that is at every moment obedient to the workings of natural law. The poet observes a Flaubertian rigor with respect to the world that is behind the words: After the one-twenty departure, the cattle are "short-shadowed"; by the time the train leaves the last platform, poplars are seen to "cast/Long shadows over major roads." The coordinates are drawn with geometrical precision. As the sun moves across the sky from east to west (or appears to), the train follows its "slow and stopping curve southwards." The registration of departure time, coupled with the observation in the sixth stanza that the last leg of the trip requires "some fifty minutes," impresses a further verisimilitude. The reader feels certain that the entire visual and temporal experience could be confirmed, that the sequence would be just as Larkin has depicted it: fish dock, river, canals with "floatings of industrial froth," and, later, Odeon, cooling tower, blackened walls . . .

The poem begins with highly specific impressions of surroundings, and it ends in the same way. In the middle stanzas, however, the awareness of landscape is displaced by a more general and meditative inventory of wedding parties. This has several effects. For one thing, it reinforces the psychological naturalism of the piece—for is this not exactly how we all travel, attuned to details during departure and arrival, dissipated into revery for much of the rest of the time? It also allows the speaker to touch that reflective depth which is unavailable to the agitated observer, and without which the last powerful thrust would be impossible. No less important, the passage from time-bound specificity into the timelessness of duration and back makes the poem a representation of the entire trip instead of an anthology of excerpted moments. Stanzas 3 through 6 compress time plausibly. This is essential, for the integrity and force of "The Whitsun Weddings" depend upon our impression that an entire process has been undergone.

Larkin begins the poem with departure, ends it with the "tightened brakes" of arrival; the journey is his frame. Within these bounds he has rendered a full movement of sensibility, tracing the complete history of an inner event. Initial obliviousness of the traveler is marked by the uninflected observations: "Wide farms went by, short-shadowed cattle, and / Canals with floatings of industrial froth." Then, encroaching awareness: "At first, I didn't notice . . ." (III, 1); "Once we started, though . . ." (III, 7); "Struck, I leant . . ." (IV, 3). The phenomenon of the weddings claims the speaker. He observes, focuses. The deeper and more abstract processing does not come until the two final stanzas— but it has been prepared masterfully. Indeed, Larkin's intuition here defines the boundary between skill and genuine artistry. Skill by itself could never have staged the shifts in point of view that bestow inevitability upon the final passage. Intuitive insight had to supervene.

From the very first stanza, Larkin has promoted a pronomial fluidity, allowing the "I" of the first line to become the "We" of the sixth;

the "We" is, in turn, almost transformed into the "it" of the train itself: "We ran / Behind the backs of houses, crossed a street." This carefully planned indeterminacy lets us absorb the first shift without a shock. For at the end of the third stanza, Larkin neatly flips the observing lens. All at once it is the people on the platform who are watching the train pull away:

> Once we started, though,
> We passed them, grinning and pomaded, girls
> In parodies of fashion, heels and veils,
> All posed irresolutely, watching us go,
>
> As if out on the end of an event
>   Waving goodbye
> To something that survived it.

The very next words, "Struck, I leant," return us to our original vantage. But then in stanza 5, the exchange of perspective is repeated, and extended:

> And, as we moved, each face seemed to define
> Just what it saw departing: children frowned
> At something dull; fathers had never known
>
> Success so huge and wholly farcical;
>   The women shared
> The secret like a happy funeral;
> While girls, gripping their handbags tighter, stared
> At a religious wounding.

The transition back, into the widened point of view of "we," is carried out beautifully—the "we" has now enfolded the couples as well:

> Free at last,
> And loaded with the sum of all they saw,
> We hurried towards London, shuffling gouts of steam.

How we read these reversals is important. If we believe that Larkin is using authorial prerogative to change the vantage, then the poem is diminished. If, on the other hand, we trust that the narrative "I" is making the

---

"The Whitsun Weddings"

switches himself, placing himself imaginatively in the position of the watchers left behind, then the ending achieves its full resonance. For the maneuver not only adds tension and interest to the narrative, but functions to prepare us for the quickly oscillating perspectives that bring the poem to a close. Everything depends upon the vibration set up between the subjective fantasies of the newlyweds and the *sub specie aeternitatis* wisdom—cynicism—of the "I." Our emotional response is more powerful if we feel that both perspectives are warring in a single consciousness.

The last two stanzas are cunningly woven: Larkin works the pronouns like a shuttle device. After the newlyweds have been absorbed into the "we" of all passengers, they are once again distinguished:

A dozen marriages got under way.
They watched the landscape, sitting side by side

A dozen marriages, each couple believing itself to have a unique destiny. Larkin creates a double tension, first between the hopeful couples and the superior understanding of the "I," secondly between the singular illusions of each separate couple and the generic state of illusion shared by all. Both are held together in the mobile imagination of the narrator, united through this curious negative:

—and none
Thought of the others they would never meet
Or how their lives would all contain this hour.

Then:

I thought of London spread out in the sun,
Its postal districts packed like squares of wheat:

There we were aimed.

"There we were aimed." With this, the newlyweds are again merged with the other travelers, the "I" included; they become a "frail / Travelling coincidence." The word "coincidence" carries both the etymological denotation of "happening together," and the connotative sense of the unforeseen. The latter is pivotal, invoking its opposite—destiny, fate—which, when linked to the concept of gravity, forms the magnetic core of the poem. The "I" has submerged itself once and for all in the first-person plural. This is a key stroke, since the unknown future and the fated decline, first attached to just the happy couples, are thereby universalized.

The final stanza of the poem is a *tour de force,* summoning together elements from the preceding stanzas and forging them into an image that simultaneously represents and releases tension. The shape of an arc, which has subtly presided over the first seven stanzas, is materialized into a bow, and the bow is bent and fired. The procedure is a delicate one. First, the sun has been traversing its westward arc, lengthening the shadows. The train, picking up speed after its final stop (the acceleration brings new energy into the poem), is completing its "curve southwards." In the seventh stanza we see "someone running up to bowl," an image that both implies the arc of the arm's backward sweep and, as an incomplete action, sets up an expectation of resolution.

The final stanza then gathers these hints into a conclusive emblem. The opening, "There we were aimed," provides the first suggestion. "Bright knots," taken in this context, touches off submerged associations with a knotted bowstring, and the otherwise innocent "Pullmans" adds a punning sense of bending. "Walls of blackened moss / Came close" concretizes tension, while individual words and phrases—"held," "ready to be loosed," and "power"—bring us the image of a drawn bow without explicitly naming it. There remains just the final excruciating shriek of the "tightened brakes." The rest is release, the dispersal of lives like so many arrows leaping off strings. A rush of sibilants underwrites the final transformation: The glorious shower of arrows alters, through the play on "shower," into the dreary rain to come. The journey begins and ends, but the arcing trajectory of lives reaches toward all of us through its invocation of the future. The participle "becoming" affirms that the laws of fate are as reliable as the laws of nature.

"The Whitsun Weddings"

IN THE KALAHARI DESERT

The sun rose like a tarnished
looking-glass to catch the sun

and flash His hot message
at the missionaries below—

Isabella and the Rev. Roger Price,
and the Helmores with a broken axle

left, two days behind, at Fever Ponds.
The wilderness was full of home:

a glinting beetle on its back
struggled like an orchestra

with Beethoven. The Hallé,
Isabella thought and hummed.

Makololo, their Zulu guide,
puzzled out the Bible, replacing

words he didn't know with Manchester.
Spikenard, alabaster, Leviticus,

were Manchester and Manchester.
His head reminded Mrs. Price

of her old pomander stuck with cloves,
forgotten in some pungent tallboy.

The dogs drank under the wagon
with a far away clip-clopping sound,

and Roger spat into the fire,
leaned back and watched his phlegm

like a Welsh rarebit
bubbling on the brands . . .

When Baby died, they sewed her
in a scrap of carpet and prayed,

Readings

with milk still darkening
Isabella's grubby button-through.

Makololo was sick next day
and still the Helmores didn't come.

The outspanned oxen moved away
at night in search of water,

were caught and goaded on
to Matabele water-hole—

nothing but a dark stain on the sand.
Makololo drank vinegar and died.

Back they turned for Fever Ponds
and found the Helmores on the way . . .

Until they got within a hundred yards,
the vultures bobbed and trampolined

around the bodies, then swirled
a mile above their heads

like scalded tea leaves.
The Prices buried everything—

all the tattered clothes and flesh,
Mrs. Helmore's bright chains of hair,

were wrapped in bits of calico
then given to the sliding sand.

"In the beginning was the Word"—
Roger read from Helmore's Bible

found open at St. John.
Isabella moved her lips,

"The Word was Manchester."
Shhh, shhh, the shovel said. Shhh . . .

"The Whitsun Weddings"

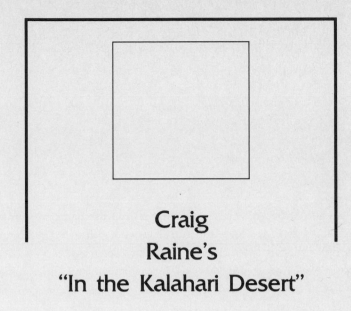

Craig
Raine's
"In the Kalahari Desert"

N ot so much written as spliced together bit by discrete bit, Craig Raine's "In the Kalahari Desert" unfolds before us like some campy newsreel. It plays off the genre clichés of missionary accounts—the broken axle, the heat, the vultures, the reading of requisite verses from the Good Book—against a precise and peculiar set of images, which propose, in the best "Martian" style, an unsettling estrangement of perception. The result is an artifact of compelling mysteriousness, which is at once a reflection on first and last things *and* a sly send-up of the conventions of such missionary chronicles.

Raine begins with a strategically distanced—no, *paradoxical*—simile:

The sun rose like a tarnished
looking-glass to catch the sun

and flash His hot message
at the missionaries below—

The effect is that from the very start we regard the narrative under the aspect of refraction. It is not the sun itself, but a looking glass reflecting the sun—a calculated intervention that ensures that everything that follows will be treated less as fact than as emblem, cipher, or metaphor. As the principal narrative characters are introduced, therefore, our tendency is to see them as cutout representative figures; we do not grant them individual particularity. Isabella, the Reverend Roger Price, and the Helmores—and later Makololo—they are the traditional players, known to us from a hundred feature films. The ascetic, austere reverend, his attractive, devoted wife, the foolish (because ignorant) Zulu guide—calling upon a racist cliché, we can almost see the whites of his superstitiously rolling eyes. . . .

The next lines, then, come as something of a shock:

The wilderness was full of home:

a glinting beetle on its back
struggled like an orchestra

with Beethoven.

Such virtuoso inventiveness to hold against the blandly familiar setup! We promptly register the visual rightness of the simile, but then we experience a recoil effect as we grasp its alienating implications. There are two ways of reading the sentence. As a supreme irony—in which case we translate: The wilderness was *not at all* full of home. Or else as an indication of the extent to which the psyche will search out traces of the familiar in a threatening environment.

But the image is *so* uncanny, its vehicle and tenor are so strikingly incommensurate, that we are unable to place ourselves within the narrative. Rather, we are forced to concentrate on the artifice of the poem, to ponder its constructedness. Instead of participating in the travails of the Price mission, we focus upon the spliced bits of information and sensory detail from which Raine is fashioning his account.

Makololo, their Zulu guide,
puzzled out the Bible, replacing

words he didn't know with Manchester.

Here Raine introduces what might be called the thematic core of his poem. Typically, though, he refuses the orchestral omen notes, playing instead for an effect at once wry and burlesque. The burlesque is in the image of incessant substitution; the wryness derives from Makololo's choice of the word "Manchester." The poor fellow doubtless found some association of grandeur there (perhaps he was prompted by the familiarity of the first syllable: "Man"). *Any* substitution would be absurd and incongruous, of course, but to pick the very city that Engels studied for his book on the working classes, the blackest of England's satanic mill towns . . . We will see, later, how Raine returns to this matter of linguistic confusion, amplifying and extending this initially comical note.

The next three images—Mrs. Price's likening of Makololo's head to "her old pomander stuck with cloves," the dogs drinking water "with a far away clip-clopping sound," and the good reverend watching his phlegm "like a Welsh rarebit / bubbling on the brands"—are all vividly sensory. They are, none of them, nearly as alien as the earlier image of the beetle on its back. Indeed, these three rather humble detailings, by moderating the strangeness of the opening, bring us momentarily closer to the lives of the people. We discern the lineaments of personality and sensibility. Mrs. Price's association gives us a strong sense of her fundamentally domestic orientation, while Roger Price's evident delight in his own bubbling phlegm suggests both a certain crudeness of character and a quality of narcissistic self-absorption.

Also, needless to say, we see in Mrs. Price's reflection the fundamental, if unconscious, racism that underlays so much of the missionary enterprise. One simply cannot liken another human being's head to "an old pomander stuck with cloves" unless one's perceptions derive from a radically dissociated sensibility. Raine does not touch upon the matter of racism again in the poem, but this single detail, carefully placed, sends its echoes outward.

The disasters of wilderness now befall the Prices:

When Baby died, they sewed her
in a scrap of carpet and prayed,

with milk still darkening
Isabella's grubby button-through.

We are startled to learn, so late in the narrative, that there *was* a baby. Our image of Mrs. Price is correspondingly altered. She becomes at once more human and vulnerable (her *grubby* button-through), and, in another way, more detached. To be sure, this latter impression comes about through Raine's mode of presenting material. The death of the baby is given in utterly uninflected tones; it takes up as much space as the description of the reverend's phlegm that directly preceded it. Thus, we tend to read the tragedy as one event among myriad others, as yet another of the implicit costs of bringing the Word. "It is God's will, dearest—we must not be deterred." The affectless reporting of the death, combined with the humble notation of the grubby button-through, underscores the matter-of-factness of the death, and hints at the bedrock faith that can permit such a quashing of expected emotion.

But as we read further, we see that Raine has in fact altered his time-frame entirely. The death of the baby is not to be read in a continuum with the preceding details. Those belong to the period of innocent and untested expectations. The death represents the first exaction of the real. From the sequence of peculiar close-ups we now move to a more detached narrative vantage. The death of the baby counts for as little as it does because the "action" has suddenly been telescoped. We hear now the straightforward voice of documentary. The unknown has given way to the inevitable:

> Makololo was sick next day
> and still the Helmores didn't come.
>
> The outspanned oxen moved away
> at night in search of water. . . .
>
> Makololo drank vinegar and died.

The Prices, bereft of their baby and their guide, turn back. They "found the Helmores on the way. . . ." The crucial word here is "found"—it alerts us to the situation before the sight of the bobbing and trampolining vultures. Not that the conventions would have us expect anything different . . . but Raine brings the truth home with a chillingly apt contrast of images, a contrast that, in a sense, replays the trajectory of the Prices' journey. The first image, that of the disgusting carrion-eaters at play, is suddenly displaced by a second—one of stark inevitability. The birds are "like scalded tea leaves." The Prices, too, have seen their zealous and unthinking presumption shattered by a merciless nature. The beetle is *not* an orchestra—it is a creature dying.

The Helmores are given their desert burial. Everything, "all the tattered clothes and flesh"—as though flesh and clothing really were equivalent, as if the body is, in truth, nothing more than a garment for the eternal soul.

> "In the beginning was the Word"—
> Roger read from Helmore's Bible
>
> found open at St. John
> Isabella moved her lips,

Craig Raine's "In the Kalahari Desert"

"The Word was Manchester."
Shhh, shhh, the shovel said. Shhh . . .

Raine concludes with an elegant fusion of tones and significations. The prophetic voice of St. John, which quite literally binds creation with the speech of God (the ultimate identifying of a signifier with its referent), is intercut with Isabella's surfacing recollection of poor Makololo. But what was at first quaint and humorous is now pure pathos. We think of the poor man dying for a cause he could not even begin to comprehend. There is a suggestion, too, of Isabella's private mutiny. At the very moment when she ought to be concentrating on the divine pronouncement, her thoughts depart, however inadvertently, in a more personal direction. Only the reverend's fierce will keeps the spirit of the blighted mission alive.

The final line—"Shhh, shhh, the shovel said. Shhh . . ."—reminds me of the end of Shelley's "Ozymandias": "The lone and level sands stretch far away." Except that where Shelley's scape is utterly pitiless, Raine sounds a more intimate, if no less ominous, note. The shovel passes its message softly, confidingly, like a mother cautioning a child. But the message is the same: The ephemeral human will be silenced by the eternal, spiritless sands. They have the proverbial last word.

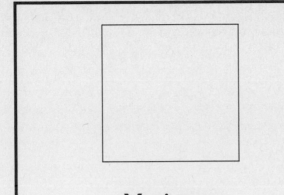

Marianne Moore's "Poetry": She Disliked It, She Did

Marianne Moore's decision to cut her well-known anthology piece "Poetry" down to an unremarkable three-liner bearing the same title has baffled readers and critics alike. Such a histrionic, exhibitionistic gesture—like a woman taking scissors and roughly shearing off an admired head of hair. (No sexism intended here—I'm referring to a celluloid archetype.) Clearly it was an act of some kind of loathing, a deed perpetrated against the self. My guess is that Moore wished to inflict a symbolic injury upon a sensibility that could produce poetry only of a certain kind. Never mind that it was a poetry that had won for her a near-universal adulation. It was as if she knew in her heart wherein lay the real soul of poetry—in the *genuine*—and she knew that her own work could never get there. The disfiguring truncation of one of her best-loved poems was her way of incising the recognition directly into the body of that work.

From the *Selected Poems* of 1935, as preserved in *The Complete Poems of Marianne Moore,* we can cull a rather interesting set of aesthetic statements:

> "Taller by the length of
>   a conversation of five hundred years than all
>   the others," there was one, whose tales
>   of what could never have been actual—
>
> were better than the haggish, uncompanionable drawl
>
> of certitude; his by-
>   play was more terrible in its effectiveness
>   than the fiercest frontal attack.
>   The staff, the bag, the feigned inconsequence
> of manner, best bespeak that weapon, self-protectiveness.
>   —from "In This Age of Hard Trying,
>   Nonchalance Is Good and"
>
> Prince Rupert's drop, paper muslin ghost,
>   white torch—"with power to say unkind
> things with kindness, and the most
>   irritating things in the midst of love and
>   tears," you invite destruction.
>   —from "Pedantic Literalist"
>
> There is a great amount of poetry in unconscious
>   fastidiousness. Certain Ming
>   products, imperial floor-coverings of coach
> wheel yellow, are well enough in their way but I have seen
>   something
>   that I like better—a

Readings

mere childish attempt to make an imperfectly bal-
    lasted animal stand up,
similar determination to make a pup
    eat his meat from the plate.
                —from "Critics and Connoisseurs"

        complexity is not a crime, but carry
it to the point of murkiness
    and nothing is plain. Complexity,
moreover, that has been committed to darkness, instead of

granting itself to be the pestilence that it is, moves all a-
    bout as if to bewilder us with the dismal
fallacy that insistence
    is the measure of achievement and that all
truth must be dark. Principally throat, sophistication is as it al-

ways has been—at the antipodes from the init-
    ial great truths.
                —from "In the Days of Prismatic Color"

Small dog, going over the lawn nipping the linen and saying
that you have a badger—remember Xenophon;
only rudimentary behavior is necessary to put us on the scent.
"A right good salvo of barks," a few strong wrinkles puckering
    the skin between the ears, is all we ask.
                —from "Picking and Choosing"

        —a collection of little objects—
sapphires set with emeralds, and pearls with a moonstone,
                              made fine
    with enamel in gray, yellow, and dragon-fly blue;
    a lemon, a pear

and three bunches of grapes tied with silver: your dress a
                          magnificent square
    cathedral tower of uniform
    and at the same time diverse appearance—a

Marianne Moore's "Poetry"

species of vertical vineyard rustling in the storm
    of conventional opinion. Are they weapons or scalpels?
       Whetted to brilliance
by the hard majesty of that sophistication which is superior to
                                 opportunity,
   these things are rich instruments with which to experiment.
    But why dissect destiny with instruments
      more highly specialized than components of
                        destiny itself?
                  —from "Those Various Scalpels"

Perceiving that in the masked ball
attitude, there is a hollowness
that beauty's light momentum can't redeem;
   since disproportionate satisfaction anywhere
   lacks a proportionate air,

he let us know without offense
by his hands' denunciatory
upheaval, that he despised the fashion
   of curing us with an ape—making it his care
   to smother us with fresh air.
               —from "Nothing Will Cure the Sick Lion
                      but to Eat an Ape"

I could go on citing passages. Indeed, I could argue—some probably have—that the whole of Moore's *oeuvre* is an aesthetics, a careful
establishing through example and commentary of both what is seemly
for human conduct and what is essential for true artistic expression. It
is the latter that interests me here, especially since Moore appears to
propose values that are at odds with her own poetic performance.

"Are they weapons or scalpels?" she asks of the hypertrophied
refinements of civilization. We may well ask the same about her own
lines. The first citation, from "In This Age of Hard Trying, Nonchalance Is Good and," would suggest weapons, but of a defensive, not
a first-strike, variety. Moore praises the power of indirection over the
"haggish, uncompanionable drawl / of certitude," but then she miti-

gates that praise somewhat by tracing the origin of that power back to "self-protectiveness" and revealing it, ultimately, as a by-product of vulnerability. But this is nothing more than the age-old view of art as compensation.

Weapons or scalpels? Scalpels they assuredly are not. For the scalpel is an instrument designed to cut through surfaces; its purpose is to get the user *inside*. And Moore's art is anything but interior. She is a taxonomist, a gleaner, a weaver. The most thrilling feature of her poetry is its attentiveness and deliberation—the way she ranges over the intricate surfaces of the material and textual worlds, drawing forth what she needs with an avian fastidiousness. Moore's poems are not written from within; they are appliquéd. She subjects what she has elicited from the near-infinite plenitude of the *out there* to the stringent ordering system of her syntax. She produces her effects through shocks of precision and shocks of juxtaposition. Our diffuse imaging of the world collides with her insistently accurate ordering of things. If she strikes an occasional depth, if she produces what appears to be a penetration, it is not by virtue of any probing action of her own. This comes about, rather, because we, as readers, are forced to make an inference out of certain bits of adjacent information. *We* make the sequences yield sense—*we* do the penetrating.

How odd it is, then, that Moore should on so many occasions adumbrate artistic values that her own craft belies. Reading over these quotations, we can abstract a clear preference for frankness over duplicity, simplicity over ornamentation and needless complexity, directness over sophistication, and "unconscious" naturalness over the straining for effect that is artifice. A preference, in short, for the genuine. But Moore's own poetry is nothing if not ironic and oblique. Her detailings are almost blindingly precise, but their accumulation produces a sly indirection. Moore is ornamental and deliberately disproportionate. When she inspects destiny, she does so with instruments more specialized than destiny itself. She is, herself, "principally throat"—and in this resides her idiosyncratic magic.

The tension between her beliefs—or, to use a Moore word, "preferences"—and her practice is immediately evident in these quoted passages. It manifests itself as a pervasive irony. Listen as she militates against complexity in a series of lines that are themselves semantically, syntactically, and prosodically complex:

> Complexity,
> moreover, that has been committed to darkness, instead of
>
> granting itself to be the pestilence that it is, moves all a-
>   bout as if to bewilder us with the dismal
> fallacy that insistence
>   is the measure of all achievement and that all
> truth must be dark.

What is this self-reflexive rhetorical stratagem but an effort to distance and disarm a truth that she is compelled to iterate?

There is a second, even more obvious sign of her tension, her peculiar entrapment between preference and practice. Moore relies heavily on displacement. She speaks with a domino held in front of her features. She assigns the burden of speaking the truth to some creature (a cat, for instance, in a poem I did not cite here—"The Monkeys"), or to some incorporated literary source, like Xenophon. When she does use her own voice, as in "Critics and Connoisseurs" or "Those Various Scalpels," the linguistic screen—complexity—is securely in place. For Moore could not turn her recognitions directly upon herself without thereby negating her sensibility and her poetic mode—the work could not survive.

And yet this is precisely what she has done in her one act of self-mutilation. She has pronounced her truth directly, in the first person, and the second version shows us what results when the poet abides by her own strictures. The piece might make more sense if it were called "My Poetry."

POETRY

> I, too, dislike it: there are things that are important beyond all
>   this fiddle.
>   Reading it, however, with a perfect contempt for it, one
>   discovers in

Readings

it after all, a place for the genuine.
    Hands that can grasp, eyes
    that can dilate, hair that can rise
        if it must, these things are important not because a

high-sounding interpretation can be put upon them but because
                          they are
useful. When they become so derivative as to become
                          unintelligible,
the same thing may be said for all of us, that we
    do not admire what
    we cannot understand: the bat
        holding on upside down or in quest of something to

eat, elephants pushing, a wild horse taking a roll, a tireless wolf
                          under
a tree, the immovable critic twitching his skin like a horse that
                    feels a flea, the base-
ball fan, the statistician—
    nor is it valid
        to discriminate against "business documents and

school-books"; all these phenomena are important. One must
                make a distinction
however: when dragged into prominence by half poets, the
                result is not poetry,
nor till the poets among us can be
    "literalists of
    the imagination"—above
        insolence and triviality and can present

for inspection, "imaginary gardens with real toads in them,"
                shall we have
it. In the meantime, if you demand on the one hand,
the raw material of poetry in
    all its rawness and
    that which is on the other hand
        genuine, you are interested in poetry.

Marianne Moore's "Poetry"

POETRY (REVISED)

I, too, dislike it.
    Reading it, however, with a perfect contempt for it, one dis-
                                                            covers in
    it, after all, a place for the genuine.

If the original version of "Poetry" was the symbolic site of Moore's aesthetic assault upon herself, then we may reasonably regard it as representing the poetic sensibility that a part of her despised.

The poem is, in fact, a kind of anthology of the attributes and techniques that readers have most cherished in Moore—the very ones that made her the revolutionist she was. The original is prosy, prosodically sprawling; it is syntactically complex, to the point of near unintelligibility in places; it shows off Moore's taxonomic fetish, her delight in drawing together creatures from the various phyla of the natural and human worlds ("a tireless wolf . . . the baseball fan"); it incorporates textual material from other sources (Tolstoy and A. H. Bullen on Yeats)—thereby sabotaging self-containment, and opening the poem out to the continuum of the printed word; it is rhetorically strategic, in the way that so many of her poems are, starting with a straightforward assertion, building and cantilevering sense outward until it almost evaporates (e.g., the sentence that begins, "When they become so derivative . . ."), then rounding to some clear assertion; it encloses, here more fully than elsewhere, an aesthetic formulation: a justification of what is now fashionably called framing.

The revised "Poetry" has eliminated everything but the prosiness.

A short poem that is a shaved-down version of a well-known longer poem is not the same thing as an independent short poem—that should be obvious. Moore's second "Poetry" cannot be read except against the original text. It makes no declaration of independence. Indeed, Moore saw fit to include the first "Poetry" in the notes to her *Complete Poems*. We are asked to read her gesture, to puzzle out her reasons for disapproving of the original.

There are two ways of looking at the matter—unless, of course, we ascribe her move to pure whimsy. If we think of the second version as a rewrite, then the poem has to be seen as a replacement, effectively canceling the first version. But then Moore would not have included it in her *Complete Poems* even as a note. More tellingly, the modifications made are not those of a rewrite, but an edit. She did not alter a single word. The words (most of them) have been struck out; only punctuation and spacing have been altered. We are compelled, therefore, to regard the second "Poetry" as an operation performed upon the first. A cut, an erasure—our choice of words here carries large implications, determines whether we regard her action as one of subliminal violence, or some mere agitated impatience. . . .

If the short poem *is* an edit, then what interpretation can we make? One benign possibility is that Moore recognized, as an editor might, a prolixity; she saw "Poetry" as verbose and she moved to rectify the matter. She made her cuts in a spirit of "Enough said!" But this does not get rid of the larger symbolic statement. For according to that criterion, the bulk of Moore's work is marred by a similar abundance. It is her very method: to harvest and arrange. Trim one detail and you are soon throwing everything out the window.

The other possibility, to which I incline, is that Moore was deliberately repudiating everything that followed the first two sentences. Not just verbal superfluity, but manner and tone as well. The word "genuine" is placed for maximum impact. Moore was henceforth connecting genuineness with simple, direct, unsophisticated utterance. She was establishing it as the primary moving force of all real poetry. So much the worse that she could not attain it in her own work.

At the core of the issue is irony. Moore's poetry—and her "Poetry"—is the apotheosis of ironic discourse. It belongs to "civilization" as opposed to "culture," which means, according to the Spenglerian definition I'm using, that it represents vital forces embalmed, order and intellection set above instinct and energy. All ironic usage implies self-consciousness on the part of the speaker. An ironic statement does not fully coincide with itself—it incorporates a play between what is said and the underlying intention, between utterance and implication, between the content and the means. The etymology of the word gives us,

---

Marianne Moore's "Poetry"

from the Greek, "dissimulation" and "feigning"; an ironist is one who "says less than he thinks or means" (Skeat). Irony is, to put it bluntly, the inverse of the genuine.

We have Moore's statements on the matter. Using the image of the "drop," or concealing cloth, in "Pedantic Literalist," she asserts in no uncertain terms that duplicity—seen here as the gulf between affect and true feeling—is seen as inviting "destruction." In "Nothing Will Cure the Sick Lion," she strikes against the "masked ball attitude." Examples could be multiplied. And while in neither case is she addressing irony *per se,* she might as well be. Irony, like duplicity, depends upon a distance between feeling and expression; the difference between them is merely one of degree.

Irony, then, is the opposite of the "unconscious fastidiousness" that Moore celebrates in the child's attempt to prop the faltering pet (children, of course, are notoriously incapable of dissimulation). It shares nothing in common with the dog's reaction, the "few strong wrinkles puckering the skin between the ears," that she fastens upon in "Picking and Choosing." In poem after poem, as it turns out, she aligns herself with the *naïfs,* simple creatures and beings that coincide with themselves, that bear no taint of self-consciousness.

We can change what we do, but we cannot really change what we are. Moore was imprisoned—by disposition, by sensibility—in a condition of ironic self-consciousness. She could fully comprehend its limitations, but she was powerless to achieve the poetic simplicity and force she admired. Consciousness moves along a unidirectional path— it can strive to evolve, but it cannot undo previous evolutionary attainments. Moore was stuck.

Moore was not, however, a two-face. She did not say one thing while meaning another. No, her distinctive irony was the product of a disjunction between means and ends. Her technique, which we can see as her effort to come to terms with the gap between her belief and her natural endowment, was to render up the mind's motion, its progress toward some realization or certainty—even though, *especially though,* that realization finally argued against the hesitant discursiveness of the process. Moore set out after simplicity along the only route she could take: that of complexity. She stalked unsophisticated truths in a sophisticated manner. She could not help herself. But when her eye beheld what her hand had done, she had to cry out against it. The mere tension between expression and content was not enough. One time, and one time only, she excised as superfluous the manneristic approach to truth and gave just the truth itself. The truth she gave—her recognition of the genuine—reflected directly on her deed. And vice versa: The deed was the warranty for the words.

Considered by itself, without the ghost-text of the original, the short version of "Poetry" is Moore's worst poem. We should be happy that she did not thereafter insist that *Dichtung* and *Wahrheit* are always the same thing. She continued to spin out her delightful and sublimely ironic poems for a good many years. Though she had cut off all of her beautiful hair, it did grow back again.

LYING IN A HAMMOCK AT WILLIAM DUFFY'S FARM IN PINE ISLAND, MINNESOTA

Over my head, I see the bronze butterfly,
Asleep on the black trunk,
Blowing like a leaf in green shadow.
Down the ravine behind the empty house,
The cowbells follow one another
Into the distances of the afternoon.
To my right,
In a field of sunlight between two pines,
The droppings of last year's horses
Blaze up into golden stones.
I lean back, as evening darkens and comes on.
A chicken hawk floats over, looking for home.
I have wasted my life.

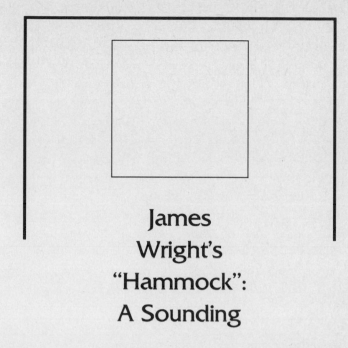

James Wright's "Hammock": A Sounding

H ere is a poem that could fit snugly on the back of a postcard. It is a poem, though, and not a postcard. And we read it, and read it again, and again—for reading poetry is, in part, a process of clearing rubble. The postcard we would read once, for its sentiment or information; then, if its reverse appealed to us, we might fasten it to the bulletin board with a pin. But here is a poem, and something else is happening, something that, if we open our gates to it, pulls us in past sentiment, past information.

We read it through. "I have wasted my life," declares the poet, the speaker, the voice. We read it through again, more carefully. Something has happened and we are not sure what. There has been little, if indeed anything, to prepare us for that statement. When we move our eyes back up to the first line, it is with some of the wary watchfulness of a crack detective. Either we have overlooked something, or else the poet has tossed us a red herring. We go back through the lines, combing the language, rhythm, and syntax for evidence that will support the last declaration. The procedure is wrongheaded, ultimately—a poem is not the site of a murder, but of the most delicate nativity—but through such attentiveness we do, at least, engage it at the level of linguistic nuance that poetry depends upon.

A successful poem—or a great poem, or a "realized" poem—is an inexhaustible repository of sonic and semantic events/interactions. When we read such a poem we cannot err on the side of attentiveness; no discrimination is too fine. This is not to say that the poet has *consciously* located subtle resonance: If all effects were conscious we could pull them out just as he put them in, and after a while we would have come to the end of it. But the language web extends past the shifting boundary of the field of the conscious, and the poem-making process depends as much upon associative marriages sanctified by a feeling of "rightness" as it does upon rational choice. And there is no limiting the effects produced by the unconscious interactions. They cannot be invalidated through any appeal to the poet's intention.

Lying in a Hammock at William Duffy's
Farm in Pine Island, Minnesota

We might begin by remarking the title, which is, at first sight, so long and unwieldy. Why didn't Wright just call his poem "Hammock," or "Lying in a Hammock"? Does it matter to us that the hammock was hung at William Duffy's farm, or that the farm was in Pine Island, Minnesota? No. We can only suppose that if the location does not matter to us, it did to the poet. And if we then suppose that the last line was hammered out in full seriousness (to decide otherwise is to render the poem irrelevant), then the titling confirms us. The precise location is given not to inform, but to memorialize a place and a time. The title is raised over the body of the poem like a marking stone: The scene that is described and enacted has assumed a great importance in the poet's life.

Readings

The title is important in another way as well. It signals to us that a tradition is being invoked. Opening my copy of Witter Bynner's collection of translations from the Chinese, *The Jade Mountain,* I find, quite serendipitously, a lyric ascribed to Hsü Hun:

Red leaves are fluttering down the twilight
Past this arbour where I take my wine;
Cloud-rifts are blowing toward Great Flower Mountain,
And a shower is crossing the Middle Ridge.
I can see trees colouring a distant wall.
I can hear the river seeking the sea,
As I the Imperial City tomorrow—
But I dream of woodsmen and fishermen.

—"Inscribed in the Inn at T'ung Gate
on an Autumn Trip to the Capital"

Wright has clearly learned something from the procedure of the Chinese lyricists—a swiftness, a lucent detailing that is at once casual and highly purposeful, a way of modulating from outer to inner worlds that implies a continuum even as it marks off the vastly disproportionate scale. Nor is he denying the influence. He is, if anything, paying homage. (The first poem in *The Branch Will Not Break*—from which "Lying in a Hammock" comes—is entitled "As I Step over a Puddle at the End of Winter, I Think of an Ancient Chinese Governor.") The movement of the poem, the abruptness of its final line—these will make a good deal more sense if we keep in mind not only the Eastern lyric tradition, but also the spiritual assumptions that underlie it.

For the Chinese poets—and the chronomancy of the *I Ching* depends upon this as well—every passing moment represented a unique configuration of higher forces, forces that passed through both subject and object (to use the Western concepts). A subject could, by heeding the momentary alignment of external details (or the fall of the yarrow stalks), catch a glimpse of his own spiritual location. Thus, the Chinese poet very often announced in his title the place and occasion of the poem. He would then limn with a few precise strokes the particulars of his setting, and conclude with a line or two giving the pitch of his feeling. Continuity between self and surroundings was implicit: De-

---

scription further characterized the feeling, while the feeling extended out into the landscape. "Lying in a Hammock" is, quite possibly, Wright's attempt to Americanize, or Midwesternize, elements of this tradition.

> Over my head, I see the bronze butterfly,
> Asleep on the black trunk,
> Blowing like a leaf in green shadow.

On the surface of it, these first three lines are straightforward enough—no oblique meanings or gnarled syntactic patches. The speaking voice has established a calm, descriptive tone. Repose is implicit, not least for the psychological reason that one does not remark details like the blowing of a butterfly when one is agitated or upset. A clear picture begins to emerge. Indeed, it is as though we were watching a painter at work. "Over my head"—the vertical axis is drawn; "the bronze butterfly" dabs in the first color, which, with the wide brushstroke of "black trunk" in the next line, is brightened by contrast. Nor is it only a contrast of colors; fragility and massive solidity are immediately put into opposition. "Green shadow" then softens the contrast of bronze and black through chromatic mediation. What's more, it brings dimension in, reminds us that we are not, in fact, looking at a simplified color composition. And as the impression of environment begins to take hold, we realize that it is by way of word-by-word widening of focus: A single butterfly is on a black trunk; the black trunk is bathed in green shadow. . . .

Color and scale apart, there are a few vital, though in some cases subliminal, linguistic effects to note. First, Wright is using the definite article, "the"—not "a"—with the butterfly. What we expect to, and perhaps do, read is the latter. The distinction seems minor, but it is not. With the definite article, as with the specificity of the title, the poet is preparing us for the "moment of truth." By saying "the," he has excerpted the moment of observation from temporal flow; he has weighted it. It is "the bronze butterfly" rather than "a bronze butterfly" because the perception represents the first step in what will be an unspoken internal movement—the beginning of a psychic dilation that will culminate in the words "I have wasted my life."

There are other details. For instance, the mimetic rightness of both the sound and positioning of "Asleep." "A-sleep" sketches in the ear the motion of a butterfly closing its wings. In addition, the sound of the word both suggests the whispery fragility of the insect and carries the hint of something sealed. The sticky *l* sound distinctly echoes its function in a word like "cling," where it contributes the phonic sense of adhesiveness. This is not arbitrary: The tongue has to adhere briefly to the roof of the mouth in order to make the sound.

So, we have *the* bronze butterfly *asleep* on the "black trunk." The latter is solidified by its strong double stress. (We may remark, too, a neighborly nod to Pound's famous "wet black bough.") Resting against that trunk, its wings closed, sealed, the butterfly not only *blows* like a leaf, it *looks* like one. That might be obvious. Less obvious is the back-and-forth motion that is set up by the reversed accents of "Asleep" (˘ ˘) and "Blowing" (˘ ˘); the rhythmic pacing tells us that there is the merest hint of a breeze. Last, we cannot ignore the heraldic significance of the butterfly. The poem is, after all, the record of an existential transformation. How natural that the glance should be arrested first by those folded bronze wings.

The reader will perhaps have detected an echo between Wright's "green shadow" and Andrew Marvell's "green shade." Certain questions are raised. I doubt whether a poet of Wright's sophistication could have combined those two words without recalling Marvell's pastoral. But does the combination represent anything more than a passing verbal homage? In other words, dare we go so far as to call it a literary allusion—that creature so assiduously hunted by the scholar and the degree candidate? Who can say? We certainly would have no trouble setting out a network of parallels: In "The Garden," the soul, in rapt contemplation, has cast "the Bodies vest aside" and has mounted up into the branches of a tree. Wright's "I" is, if not *in* a tree, at least attached by rope to a couple. And, as the last line manifests, his soul, too, has been contemplating itself intently.

We enter upon that thorny terrain that is somewhere between the fortuitous and the intentional. If Wright was aware, as he must have been, of Marvell's poem, to what extent did he allow that poem to contribute resonance to his? That is, did he consciously write "green

---

James Wright's "Hammock"

shadow" in order to secure an added layer of allusiveness, or was it merely a playful gesture? The question leads us to the heart of the issue—how much does the poet consciously control the process of composition, how much is he guided or controlled by unconscious impulses, and how much are we bringing to the poem that was neither consciously nor unconsciously available to him? In a case like this, where the odds are high that the poet was directly aware of the echo, we might venture the following: that some unconsciously perceived similarity between his impulse and Marvell's poem generated the words "green shadow"; that the poet recognized their appropriateness and decided to use them; that, insofar as there is a similarity between poems, it was initially unconscious and, therefore, unpremeditated; that "green shadow" does not, in the intentional, *Waste Land* sense, function as an allusion: It does not point to a body of meaning outside the poem.*

> Down the ravine behind the empty house,
> The cowbells follow one another
> Into the distances of the afternoon.

Observe how the stress distribution in "Down the ravine" (´ ˘ ˘ ´) neatly enacts the descending movement, while the even, plodding iambs of the next line (˘ ´ ˘ ´ ˘ ´) give us the frank, four-footed progress of the cows. "Into the distances of the afternoon" (´ ˘ ´ ˘ ˘ ˘ ˘ ˘ ´), with its long stretch of unaccented syllables, rounds out the effect. The cows have gradually wandered out of hearing; a long time has passed. A subtle play of stresses has done the work of condensing time. The march of iambs in the second line disintegrates in the third—just as clear sounds are broken up by distance. A half hour,

*Though Marvell's poem is the first to come to mind, it is not the only relevant text. A friend has called my attention to John Clare's "Valentine—To Mary," which, in its last stanza, has the following lines:

> The substance of our joys hath been
> Their flowers have faded long
> But memory keeps the shadow green
> And wakes this idle song

What if Wright went through the same unconscious/conscious process, only with the Clare lines entirely blocking out the Marvell? Would we not have to acknowledge that the ghost of that all-important word "memory" haunted Wright's lines? Of course, we can never be sure. Perhaps we should count ourselves fortunate.

Readings

maybe more, has elapsed. Our vestigial nature clock, activated by rhythm, tells us that. The condensation is further secured by the combined metonymy/synesthesia: Cowbells are made to stand for cows, and the cowbell sounds are transposed from the auditory into the spatial sequence. The result is an almost imperceptible blurring of the space/time distinction and an enhancement of the subjective sense of reverie.

Time compression is essential to the impact of the poem. The final line—"I have wasted my life"—can register only if we have been persuaded that a prolonged period of brooding, conscious or unconscious, has preceded it. If Wright had not compressed time in this way, if he had just noted in quick impressionistic strokes the butterfly, the bell sounds, and so on, and then made his announcement, the result would have been comical.

Time in poetry is very different from time in most prose and all spoken discourse. Entering the language circuit of a poem, we leave behind time perceived as succession and participate, instead, in time as duration. (Henri Bergson, whose writings directly influenced Proust's conception of the duration experience—as indissolubly linked to the workings of the involuntary memory—devoted volumes to explicating these two different time perceptions.) Shedding our customary orientation, however, is not immediately possible—it is part of the rubble-clearing operation that I spoke of. We have to relinquish the scheme of time expectancy by which we guide ourselves in our extraliterary commerce. Duration, simply put, is the subjective experience of time. It is felt time, time cut away from all measure, time lived without any reference to the *idea* of time: timelessness. Childhood, romantic love, sudden visitations of memory, and the crests of aesthetic experience all belong to the order of duration. All literature, insofar as it aims at the aesthetic, seeks to immerse us in duration. Where prose tends to work gradually, inveigling us from sentence to sentence, poetry, with its exponentially greater linguistic density, plunges us in immediately.

The duration experience is intimately bound up with the nature of language and with our ability, or need, to find infinite resonances in the interactions of sound and sense. The more deeply and directly we engage the words, the more the sense contents are freed from the shell

---

James Wright's "Hammock"

of the sign, the smaller is the breach between that cipher and our belief in its reality. As the eye through instantaneous inner transformation "hears," so does the ear indulge in a kind of "seeing." It does not merely receive sound: Working in concert with the other senses, it promptly attaches tactile, spatial, chromatic, and other associations to it. The sensory crossing that we can perform in a single line is remarkable; the evanescent "sightings" and "hearings" that happen at the threshold of our awareness are manifold. At one pole—reading the postcard, say—the eye moves quickly over words and picks up nothing but the sequence of designatory meanings. At the other pole, the awareness of reading a sign all but vanishes as the contents play upon the spume of our subjectivity. Our sense of a separate self disappears into this play; we forget that we are reading.

Poetry, through density, rhythm, and any number of concentrating devices, slows us down and, simultaneously, heightens our attentiveness. Words that we scarcely glance at in the morning paper become veritable combs of sensation. Poetry, wrote Mandelstam, "rouses and shakes us into wakefulness in the middle of a word. Then it turns out that the word is much longer than we thought, and we remember that to speak means to be forever on the road." This is a poet's capsule definition of duration, really. For to feel the word lengthening is also to abandon for a time the "objective" ordering grid that we are constantly superimposing upon our naked apprehension of the world.

> Down the ravine behind the empty house,
> The cowbells follow one another
> Into the distances of the afternoon.

Behind the sequential accounting of impressions, like the forest that we are constantly missing for the trees, is the timeless rustling of language. Three lines, eighteen words, but as we speak them slowly to ourselves we realize that there is no squaring the word count with the dilation of sensation—it will continue for as long as we permit. Opening onto the world, the words ultimately propose the boundlessness that belongs to their referent reality. And, truly, it *feels* as though we are taking forever to get through the syllables. "Down the ravine"— the two stresses (ˉ ˘ ˉ) crowd us with the impressions of slow, laboring animal life. We read through the whole next line under this retarding influence—it is stress-enforced. But as we work through "Into the distances of the afternoon," we are conscious of a sudden rhythmic liberation. "In-"changes the pitch. The heaviness is turned into lightness and transparency, the plodding sensations are undone, rendered into the abstraction of "distances." Eighteen words, but the psychic shift we go through is considerable. It contributes to our feeling that time has elapsed.

We are six lines into the poem and we have come to a lull. The music is diminuendo. Rhythmic liberation notwithstanding, we are conscious of a waning, a tapering-off that threatens to bear the contemplative voice into the realm of Morpheus. "Into the distances of the afternoon" has entirely attenuated the rhythmic tension. But just as we are about to join the speaker for a nap in the hammock, the poem jerks us back:

> To my right,
> In a field of sunlight between two pines,
> The droppings of last year's horses
> Blaze up into golden stones.

Three rapid-fire syllables ring out against the long pauses of the preceding line. The speaker has roused himself, and us, into a renewed, and changed, attentiveness. The switch ends—and thereby emphasizes—the lull that went before.

The sounds and stresses in the second line work topographically: The long open vowel of "field" is phonically wedged between the two *t* sounds—by proxy, as it were. In fact, it is the open "-ween"—the chime sound—that is wedged, but we automatically transfer the pictorial effect. We see the brightness of the field framed by the two pines. The shady darkness of the point of vantage is conveyed by implied contrast.

The quick succession of stresses in "last year's horses" has a double function. On the one hand, it hints at the dropping action of a horse; on the other, it tenses the ear to receive the full magnificence of "blaze," that brassy yellow verb. Note, though, that Wright does not speak of last year's droppings, but "last year's horses." The emphasis

---

James Wright's "Hammock"

shift is almost inconspicuous. But it tells us a great deal about the subliminal activity of the speaker. It tells us, for one thing, that he is preoccupied with change and irrevocability. His perception is the result of an instant inner association—from the sight of the droppings, to the recognition that they are old, to a summoning-up of horses that, in Heraclitean flux, are no longer the same. Implicit, of course, is the awareness that *he* is no longer the same either. In this light, "Blaze up into golden stones" carries an interesting double sense. Literally, it presents the gleaming of sunlight on dung. But the usage of "stones" is just curious enough—how can droppings blaze up into stones?—to prompt a metaphoric secondary reading. The stones can be understood to be grave markers or memorials—the glowing dung is all that remains to remind us of the horses as they were last year. We can more or less chart the unconscious drift of the reverie.

"Blaze up into golden stones" signals a surge of the psyche. It is the first direct metaphoric transformation in the poem and it has several effects. First, it introduces new energies and reorganizes the circuits. Until now the procedure has been one of notation. A change in linguistic pattern marks a change in the speaker: He has moved from passivity to activity; he is, imaginatively, at least, exerting himself upon his surroundings. Not dramatically, it's true, but the change of state is indicated. By shaking himself out of the self-containment of disinterested observation, he has taken the first—and for the poem, necessary—step toward self-assessment.

But there is an even more obvious function to the phrase. The metaphor, coupled with the directional "To my right," recalls the "I" to the reader and reminds him that the outward notations of the preceding lines have perhaps paralleled—or initiated—a psychic progression in the speaker. And, indeed, the "I" is now ready to claim the stage:

I lean back, as evening darkens and comes on.
A chicken hawk floats over, looking for home.
I have wasted my life.

There is a steady escalation of momentum in these final lines. The caesura moves from initial to medial, tightening the tension. At the same time, we feel a vertical impetus; literally, through the placement of a hawk, and phonically, through the release from the slow, drawn-out vowels of "evening darkens and comes on." We are still on an upward cant when the horizontal punch is delivered: "I have wasted my life."

The poem supplies an undeniable rhythmic satisfaction—it closes with an unambiguous, hard snap. Yet, as I read through, I find two patterns that are at first sight contradictory. If, focusing one way, we heed the larger units, the sentences as opposed to the lines, we experience a distinct loss of momentum. Three long sentences are followed by three short final sentences. It is almost as if the breath units have been arranged to mime the slowing of the hammock's sway. The arc dwindles as the recognition approaches. With the last line we reach inertia: The swinging stops. Sudden immobility fixes the revelation and closes the poem.

The second pattern, however, suggests a surfacing motion. The somnolent calm of the first six lines gives way to an accelerating surge. The tempo change initiated with "To my right" combines with the shortened sentences and the moving caesura to create the feeling of the sudden eruption of a long-suppressed emotion. "I have wasted my life" breaks clear of the surface described by the reticence of the preceding twelve lines. It pushes us out of the hitherto-closed circle and into a new direction.

Contradictory though the patterns may be, they can coexist within the poem. The image that comes to mind is of one of several tantalizing optical puzzles: the wine glass that yields the facing profiles, or the stairs that reverse direction at every blink of the eye. We cannot follow both through simultaneously; we cannot get both entropy and eruption in the same reading. But the fact that both are present confers an interesting dimensionality upon the poem. Every reading is shadowed by its rhythmic Other.

What, finally, is the *sense* of the poem? How are we to understand the shock of the last line? Is it intended to be a surprise slap, or has the poem been subtly tending toward that moment? The calm of the speaking voice, the observation of pastoral detail—these have hardly induced in us any existential foreboding. "Precisely!" might run the predictable argument. "Wright is saying that man—or, at least, the speaker—no longer belongs to that order. The poem is about being cast out from Eden."

Sensible as such an explanation might be, it misses the mark. The poem must account for itself from within its own bounded order. We cannot import an explanatory idea in order to make it "work"—the idea itself must be in the poem. We must be able to derive it directly from the verbal complex on the page.

I have wasted my life.

The conclusion cannot be taken as something separate from the body of the poem. It has not been tacked on—it is integral. We have to believe that the narrator's psyche is a continuum, that nothing will manifest itself that has not been somehow introduced or predicated. Even if the line represents a sudden eruption from the unconscious, an eruption unexpected even by the speaker, the disposition of the details and the rhythmic movement of the lines have to have forecast it. Otherwise we are forced to deal with the specter of psychic discontinuity and a conception that poetry is, in the last analysis, nihilistic: Anything can be said at any time.

If we assume a psychic integrity for the speaker—that is, if we accept that the unconscious processes *must* in some way impinge upon the immediate conscious operations (the observation and reporting of external detail)—then we can look for the former by way of the latter. We cannot, however, as good students of Dr. Freud, expect to find any kind of straightforward mirroring. What the speaker observes is not going to translate directly into an image of what is happening in the deeper vaults of his being. No, repression, censorship, and the distorting stratagems of the ego almost never allow for such a simple mapping.

Our only evidence, really, if we hold to the idea of a continuum, comes with the occasional disjunction, the differently weighted word or phrase that breaks the flow of neutral observation initiated in the first line. The first such instance occurs in line 4: "Down the ravine behind the empty house." "Empty" is not the natural adjective. The narration has thus far been confined to surfaces and value-free descriptions. "Large" or "yellow" would have been more in keeping with the pattern; "empty" opens a chink into the subjective, bearing a literal and an emotional sense.

"Last year's horses" is the next such divagation. I have already discussed how it reveals the deeper preoccupations of the speaker. Finally, and most tellingly, we have the penultimate line: "A chicken hawk floats over, looking for home." A psychologist would call "looking for home" a clear instance of projective identification. Three shifted emphases. Any one, taken by itself, could not support the conclusion. But as we know from geometry, three points determine a plane. And "empty," "last year's horses," and "looking for home," when plotted upon the rhythmic structure, give us enough for a flash perception of the inner dynamic.

At the beginning of this essay, I remarked that this kind of detective work is ultimately wrongheaded. It may yield up insights, but it also takes us away from what really matters in the poem: the voice. The clues might line up perfectly, but if the whole is not sustained in every syllable by the felt pressure of a human soul, the search has been utterly irrelevant. The detective, after assembling all of his evidence, gazes into the eyes of the suspect; in films, if not in real life, he finally goes by instinct. If the voice *is* there, if we do feel that soul, then everything else is secondary. That is, we do or do not register the impact of "I have wasted my life" depending upon our belief in the real presence of the speaker. If his sounds and cadences have convinced us, we will follow the jump and trust its necessity—whether we understand it fully or not.

The critic can say only so much. Try as he might, he can never establish to another reader's satisfaction that this intangible "voice" in fact exists. Interpretation and enumeration must finally yield to the mysterious suasions of subjective reality.

James Wright's "Hammock"

PART III:

The Critic's Work

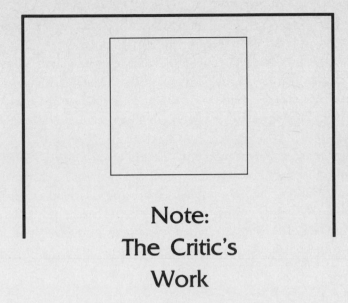

Note:
The Critic's
Work

T he pieces assembled here are, for the most part, pieces written on assignment, at the request of various editors. They represent the critic's honorable daily work. I would hope, though, that they represent something more—that each essay is an application or elaboration of the ideas introduced in Part I.

While these reviews do not pretend to be a complete mapping of the terrain of contemporary American (or English-language) poetry, they do cover a fairly extensive representative range. Here I was fortunate in the assignments that came my way: Many times they brought me face to face with a poet I might not have encountered, certainly not written about, in the normal course of things. Thus, at different times I found myself writing about poets as temperamentally diverse as May Swenson, Adrienne Rich, Frank Bidart, Paul Blackburn, Derek Walcott, John Ashbery, Gary Snyder, and Jorie Graham. Not, as I said, a complete mapping—but certainly a sounding of some of our varied registers.

I have prefaced this section with a fairly quick-moving guided tour of some of the more conspicuous approaches, or modes, that make up our "scene" at present. The categories are my own and the lists are meant to be suggestive rather than exhaustive. There is probably not a reader or poet alive who won't find something to quarrel with in my way of parceling things.

The Critic's Work

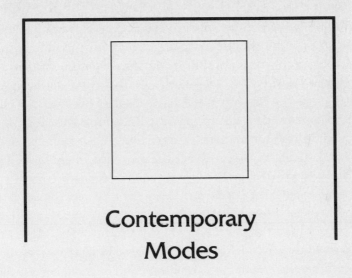

Contemporary
Modes

F or a long time I wanted to devise a taxonomy, a field
guide, a key that would make some sense of the developments of contemporary poetry, taking into account both the
available modes and the history of their antecedents. But no matter
how many charts I made, I could find no one arrangement that would
not be as misleading as it was instructive. For one thing, the different
approaches and trends that I isolated seldom allowed a clear marking
line to be drawn around them. Tendencies that were divergent at the
root nevertheless seemed to get their upper branches tangled. Nor
would poets remain still long enough to be tagged. They grew,

changed, and insisted upon availing themselves of what I'd deemed competing aesthetic strategies.

The plan for an authoritative guide was therefore scrapped. The charting impulse, however, remains. What's more, I still believe that some designating of this sort is not only possible, but necessary. There *are* identifiably distinct poetic modes out there. The edges may blur in places, and the players may move from one to another, but certain generalizations can be made. Generalizations that might help readers make sense of what appears at first—and second—glance to be a bewildering plurality of poetic styles.

But what perspective to choose? My first thought was to confine myself strictly to the modes deployed by practicing poets today. Such a breakdown of options, however, would be of little use without some historical grounding. Some. But how much? The prospects of infinite causal regress—the nightmare of any would-be scholar—loomed menacingly. I sought for expeditious compromises.

Let me begin with two very different—but ultimately not unrelated—preambles. One, an identification of the two deep-seated tendencies—or, to be grandiose, "world views"—underlying the cluttered surface of competing aesthetics. The other, a simplified tracking of modern developments along a temporal axis, a way of noting how A and B led to C and D.

Beneath or behind the various, and often opposing, camps and *isms* that make up the contemporary scene is a fundamental dispositional split among the users of language. We've all heard those provocative rhetorical gambits: "There are two kinds of people. . . ." I would propose one for poets as well. I would say—ignoring here the claims of other literary genres—that there are two kinds of poets: those for whom the world is prior to the word, and who use language to *depict* reality; and those for whom the world is only accessible through language, who use words to *create* reality. Poets who work *with* language, and poets who work *from* language.

This is, in effect, a division drawn between ways of encountering and defining reality. I venture it has existed since writers first began writing. For the purposes of this discussion, though, we can focus upon the parting of ways between T. S. Eliot and Ezra Pound, which would prove so fateful for the development of modern poetry.

In most surveys of the modern movement, we find the names of Eliot and Pound closely linked. It was Eliot, after all, who submitted his epochal collage-poem, *The Waste Land,* to Pound—his *miglior fab-bro*—for editing. What is less known is that the two masters came to hold what amount to opposite—indeed, *warring*—positions with re-gard to language. Donald Davie has put this most succinctly in his essay "Eliot and Pound: A Distinction":

> . . . as compared with Pound, Eliot presents himself as pre-emi-nently a rhetorician, a man who serves language, who waits for language to present him with its revelations; Pound by contrast would master language, instead of serving language he would make it serve—it must serve the shining and sounding world which continually throws up new forms which language must strain itself to register. Either all the forms of reality are hidden in language and will be revealed by language if only we trust it sufficiently; or else nature is inexhaustibly prodigal of new forms, for ever outrun-ning language, which must be repeatedly constrained to keep in the chase.

Now, this is not to say that all subsequent aesthetic developments fall squarely into one or another pocket. But the distinction does allow us to make a few clarifying generalizations. We can draw connecting dots from Pound to William Carlos Williams to Black Mountain, a genealogy commonly recognized. We can also link to this linguistic temperament most, if not all, species of polemical poetry (I will take this up later). The Eliotic temper, on the other hand, is discernible in Wallace Stevens, in much—but by no means *all*—formalist poetry, and, in a more extreme form, in the work of John Ashbery.

We hear a great deal these days of the battle between formalists and free-versifiers, but that opposition is trivial alongside this split of sensibilities. A poet may, in different stages of his career, write freely or formally—but no study or influence can do much to change this core orientation.

*   *   *

Contemporary Modes

En route to a picture of what Robert Pinsky has called "the situation of poetry," we might now hazard an encapsulated history. In the broadest metaphorical terms, American poetry since World War II has moved from equilibrium, through sudden upheaval, and is now sorting out the meaning of that upheaval. Or, to put a more dramatic spin on it: Poetry went from a postwar status quo into a period of revolution; since the mid-seventies we have experienced an uneasy period of reaction.

The dominant aesthetic of the postwar period was that of the Southern-agrarian New Critics. Poet-critics like John Crowe Ransom, Allen Tate, and Robert Penn Warren, promulgated an Eliotic ideal of formal, difficult, self-enclosed poetry and neutral, exacting, close-focus criticism. Both enterprises served the conservative, elitist ends of "the tradition." The early work of many of the leading younger poets— Roethke, Schwartz, Lowell, Berryman, and Jarrell—reflected these same values.

There were, of course, developments on other fronts: the Pound-Williams—inspired experimentation taking place at Black Mountain College; the prosodic agitations of the early Beats. But it took the larger cultural unrest of the sixties—civil rights protest, opposition to military involvement in Vietnam, the rock-and-roll explosion—to dislodge the ruling orthodoxy. When the time was right, the changes came with great rapidity. The poet figure was suddenly seen as the pioneer of the new consciousness. Allen Ginsberg wrote the galvanic *Howl;* New York poets like Frank O'Hara and John Ashbery brought the raw energies of urbanism and abstract expressionism into their work; Lowell, Berryman, and others shook off the constraints of their formalist masters and explored the possibilities of a directly personal poetry. Free verse, confession, surrealism, deep imagism—a dozen different modes were simultaneously in vogue. And for a time nothing looked as inhibited or limiting as the kinds of formal values that Ransom and Tate had advocated. As poet Alan Shapiro has put it in his essay "The New Formalism":

. . . in the Sixties and Seventies one often heard the argument that meter and rhyme are emotionally and psychologically repressive, and that a preference for closed forms goes hand in hand with a preference for closed, authoritarian societies. To Robert Bly, for instance, metrical composition reflected a "nostalgia for jails." What our technology—the product of a hyper-rational culture—was doing to the people of the third world our metrical techniques were doing to our own emotions, to our unconscious "rebellious energy," from which alone authentic art can spring.

But as everyone knows, the brave sixties ended, the war ended, Nixon resigned office . . . Very quickly everything that had seemed wild, anarchic, and full of possibility appeared exaggerated, naïve, and wrongheaded. The great reaction set in. In poetry this meant retrenchment, a large-scale abandonment of the more ecstatic expressive modes in favor of more circumspect and—yes—more formal approaches. The tear gas had hardly dissipated before there appeared a great many young poets who were not at all ashamed to be called "neo-" or "new" formalists. Their aesthetic is as good a place as any to begin this survey of currently viable poetic options.

Formalist/Neoformalist

Though formalist practice was overshadowed by the excitements of the sixties, it did not die out. Rather, it survived in the valley of its own saying, in the work of poets like Richard Wilbur, Anthony Hecht, May Swenson, Howard Nemerov, James Merrill, Elizabeth Bishop, and Donald Justice. Younger poets were not paying much attention. They busily worked the newly liberated autobiographical vein, finding what discipline they needed in attending to line breaks. So-called free verse was in its heyday.

A contrary pressure was steadily building, however. And the early 1980's saw a fairly dramatic upsurge of formal poetry written by poets near or under forty. There are, of course, different kinds and degrees of formalism. But within its broadest designation one might now name: Brad Leithauser, Mary Jo Salter, Gjertrud Schnackenberg, William Logan, Timothy Steele, Alfred Corn, J. D. McClatchy, Richard Kenney, Henri Cole, Vikram Seth, Dana Gioia, and—under an alternative definition—Alan Shapiro, Tom Sleigh, Melissa Green . . .

The difference I mark out within this list is quite important. For while there is a basic formalist disposition—manifesting itself in attention to metrical possibility, to rhyme, and tending to view the finished poem more as a crafted entity than as a statement of process—we can distinguish two divergent subtendencies.

First, there are those poets whose conception of form is dominated by some notion of gestalt. Their focus is upon the total effect of the container, the "wrought urn." Thus, they are more apt to work with difficult or ingenious metrical patterns, variable line lengths, and complex systems of internal and end rhyme. Their unit of composition is, in a sense, the stanza. They have been praised for virtuosity and attacked for slightness, for a mandarin disengagement from common experience. As Brad Leithauser wrote, in an essay entitled "The Confinement of Free Verse": "Prosody is a game played with the reader's legitimate expectations, and the more firmly these are established, the more fruitfully can the game's designer meet or upset them." A few short stanzas from the title poem of Timothy Steele's *Sapphics Against Anger* might fairly represent this kind of formalism. The diction is stylishly ironic, after the manner of Wilbur or Hecht; the message itself—a call for measure and restraint—could serve as a motto for this contingent:

> Better than rage is the post-dinner quiet,
> The sink's warm turbulence, the streaming platters,
> The suds rehearsing down the drain in spirals
>   In the last rinsing.
>
> For what is, after all, the good life save that
> Conducted thoughtfully, and what is passion
> If not the holiest of powers, sustaining
>   Only if mastered.

The other group of formalists—and many of its members cringe at any implied association with the mandarins—takes its main inspiration from the hammered and fired lines of Robert Lowell (early and late). They would restore compression and rhythmic urgency to the lyric. Their dominant unit of composition is the packed pentameter-based

---

The Critic's Work

line. The angle on subject matter, as we can see in these lines from Tom Sleigh's "Judas Waking," is anything but detached or ironic:

His name, his habits, burnt off like a foul gas,
Had left him all the warmth of bedclothes
And blankets, had left his eye untrammeled,
So as he looked, he felt the impartial

Nature of the room, the rocker, the hassock
With kapok poking out, the placid clock's
Glowing numbers. And outside too, darkness
Skating up the ice-glazed hill to the press

And melt of stars, he saw no harshness
In the glitter weighing down the pines, no kiss
Of betrayal hunting the moon's cheek, swollen
To such ripeness in the light-scrubbed pane

Surrealist/Symbolist

The members of this affinity group trace their heritage back to Baudelaire, Rimbaud, and the French symbolists, with a healthy tributary strain of surrealism incorporated on the way to the present. More immediate influences include the translated poetry of Neruda, Vallejo, Trakl, Tranströmer, and some others. The energetic and clashing juxtapositions found in certain Beat poets were also important.

These poets take an adversary position against standard social orders (they hold most formalists in contempt); their posture is often antiheroic. Most conspicuous in their work is the creation of startling effects through the use of uncanny images. Some of the poets in this small but energetic brotherhood—they do tend to be male—include Charles Simic, who draws heavily upon the folklore of his native Yugoslavia; Robert Bly, who has forged together the influences of Spanish, Swedish, and German modernism and the precepts of Jungian psychology; also James Tate, Bill Knott, Michael Burkard, Stephen Dobyns, Franz Wright, Tom Lux, Russell Edson, Mark Strand . . . These poets share a dark humor, an emphasis on visual elements, a reliance on anecdotal narrative structures. They have a strong kinship tie with the "Martian" poetry of Craig Raine and others in England. Here is Bill Knott's "The Stillborn (Domesticity #3)":

Eyelashes did their job:
they lengthened the afternoon,
like a dress hem.

Then that night the hem began to rise, in stages
revealing
scenes from my shameful life.

Those calves
up which the hem reproachfully rasped,
catching,
lingering over the ugh pictures
did belong to a woman

or were they mine—
I hid my eyes.
I wouldn't attend to
the walls either

endless walls, slowly
basted
with suicide.

The eyelashes did their job.
But I, who could neither sew
nor cook groped and groped those long legs
stubborn, afraid to look.

Post—Black Mountain

The poetry of this heteroclite group—which is sometimes con-fused with the poetry of the L=A=N=G=U=A=G=E poets (more because of personal affinities than aesthetics)—has strong blood-ties to the work of Pound, Williams, Charles Olson, and, later, Robert Creeley and Paul Blackburn. Creeley is now the living link. In his

---

The Critic's Work

poetry, and in that of kindred sensibilities like William Corbett, Tom Clark, Joe Brainard, John Wieners, Jonathan Williams, Robert Kelly, and Gary Snyder, we find a poetics based upon immediate perception; a clear, unadorned presentation of the image; an attention to daily, often humble, surroundings; a conception of the poem as a voiced entity, built up often out of the nuances and clashes of American speech idioms. William Corbett's "My Uncle" is a good example:

My uncle had a birthmark
a liver colored flame on his face.
Who knows where that came from.

I remember one photograph
from 40's Hollywood, my uncle
Leo Carillo and a woman
who was not my aunt for long
and who was not
the English Duchess my uncle could have married
during the war.

The rest is one Sunday afternoon
visit to a second floor apartment.
It smelled of cooking.
I was five or six
when he last spoke to me.
He wouldn't know me now
if he fell over me.

Polemical: Political/Feminist

This is not so much a group of poets in any sense as a particular consciousness, or sensibility, which uses poetry—formal or free—to serve what it perceives as a higher end: the liberation of oppressed peoples, the promotion of the claims of women, or the expression of outrage at the denial of those claims. The underlying assumption has been best expressed by poet Carolyn Forché in her essay "El Salvador: An Aide-Mémoire":

All language . . . is political; vision is always ideologically charged; perceptions are shaped a priori by our assumptions and sensibility is formed by a consciousness at once social, historical and aesthetic. There is no such thing as nonpolitical poetry.

The modes employed by the various poets of this stamp range widely, from the narrative tableaux that Forché favors to the more expressionistic assertions of Adrienne Rich. Among the many poets who belong—if only sometimes—to this camp, we can list Philip Levine, Amiri Baraka, Denise Levertov, Margaret Atwood, Allen Ginsberg, Olga Broumas, Jane Miller, Marge Piercy, June Jordan, Diane Wakoski, Judy Grahn . . . The group is so large and diverse that generalizations about technique are impossible. One can only state that artistic, or formal, claims are nearly always secondary for these poets, in the service of the "message."

"Letter From Prague, 1968–78" by Carolyn Forché:

It is winter again, those cold
globes of breath that shape
themselves into bodies. I am still
in prison having bowls of paste
for breakfast; I wake
to the bath of lights in the yard,
the violent shadow of a man running
as I should have run,
as I should have climbed, leaving
the moons of my fingers where
no one would find them.
It is ten years and hard
to believe even now that in
1968 I should have been
so stupid, touching my glass
to a soldier's saying *viva*
Dubcek, viva svoboda, viva
socialisme. At twenty-eight
I am old, recalling bottles
we filled with gasoline

corked with rags from our
mothers' dresses, and that slow
word *soviet* spoken on a stream
of spit. I could have
fallen in love. There were
plenty of women in the streets
calling *roses, roses;* I should
have given them money, taken
their petals to a room where
I might have dropped to a bed,
my eyes tongued open at morning.
To touch myself now, there is nothing.

We can here identify another, related poetic group—women poets who explore the experiences and mythologies of femaleness, but from a psychological rather than political perspective. Some write auto-biographical lyrics; others make use of an interiorized, mythic idiom. There is, to be sure, considerable crossover, with feminist poets writing nonpolemical verse and nonfeminists at times striking a political note. Some of the poets I have in mind include Sharon Olds, Patricia Storace, Louise Glück, Marie House, and Jane Shore.

L=A=N=G=U=A=G=E Poets

Two allied but different tendencies are represented by the L=A=N=G=U=A=G=E poets on the one hand, and by John Ashbery and his followers on the other. What is vital to note is that they have arrived at not dissimilar positions from very different points of origin.

Ashbery's work reflects, in part, the influence of the French symbolists and of Wallace Stevens and, no less important, the momentum toward self-referentiality that underlay abstract expressionist painting. The word is, in his poetry, partially severed from its designating function. Not completely, but enough to allow for the composition of un-nerving, ghostly texts in which meaning seems to wax and wane. Ashbery makes it his practice to render his subjects indeterminate, and to loosen referentiality by shifting pronouns and by initiating and aban-

doning narrative. His effects are different from those achieved by sur-
realist-inspired poets, who generate shocks through the juxtaposition
of sharply designated images. Nothing in Ashbery is sharply designated.
Some of the poets who have come under the Ashbery influence are
John Yau, David Lehman, and John Ash. His impact upon younger
talents is enormous, comparable to that of W. S. Merwin on the students of the late sixties.

Here are a few lines from Ashbery's "All and Some":

"Climate" isn't a sign but it could be
A by-product, an anonymous blue-collar suburb
In the great mildness that has taken over the air
With snapping cogs, deft reversals.
The blinded sun's got to answer for this
But meanwhile the housing's been built
And actually moved into, some of it.

The L=A=N=G=U=A=G=E poets, by contrast, trace their
roots—their spiritual roots, at least—back to Black Mountain. Except
that an important part of their program calls for the abandonment of
the speech-based poetics that were the rallying cry of the Williams-
Olson-Creeley "fathers." As spokesman Ron Silliman has written, apropos Robert Grenier and Barrett Watten's magazine *This 1:* ". . . it
was the particular contribution of *This,* in rejecting a speech-based
poetics and consciously raising the issue of reference, to suggest that
any new direction would require poets to look . . . at what a poem is
actually made of—not images, not voice, not characters or plot, all of
which appear on paper, or in one's mouth, only through the invocation
of a specific medium, language itself."

Paul Metcalf put the matter thus: "The LANGUAGE *[sic]* poets, as
one friend of mine described them, claim that 'the poem should have
no other reference than to other neighboring phrases, words & measures upon the very same page—a totally enclosed, hermetically
sealed, self-sustaining world. . . . They stuck their tongue out at content, and closed the outside world, or even their own inside worlds, off
from the center of their poems.'"

Poets often associated with the L=A=N=G=U=A=G=E group

The Critic's Work

include Clark Coolidge, Charles Bernstein, Michael Palmer, Susan Howe, Lyn Hejinian, Bob Perelman, Kit Robinson, and Bernadette Mayer. As may be expected, these poets are enormously diverse in their practice, covering the spectrum from relative accessibility to (so far as I can tell) unreadability. The opening lines of Charles Bernstein's "The Klupzy Girl" might suggest where midspectrum can be found:

> Poetry is like a swoon, with this difference:
> it brings you to your senses. Yet his
> parables are not singular. The smoke from
> the boat causes the men to joke. Not
> gymnastic: pyrotechnic. The continuousness
> of a smile—wry, perfume scented. No this
> would go fruity with all these changes
> around. Sense of variety: panic.

These, then—by my lights—are the major tendencies in contemporary American poetry. I realize that by searching out the more-defined subgroups, I have made no mention of the dominant group. I mean: the mainstream. But the problem should be obvious. There is no way to particularize a norm. Shall we define it as the mode of no mode, the point equidistant from the aesthetic groups I have named? No, that would probably be false—even though the poetry of the American mainstream can at times make use of any of their particular techniques. It can be formal, surreal, political, speech influenced, even (I suppose) self-referentially associative.

But this is saying nothing. The American mainstream represents in all its regional and temperamental variety the search for authentic subject matter and authentic voice. Poets who at times belong in this most democratic of categories include: James Dickey, Donald Hall, William Matthews, C. K. Williams, Dave Smith, Peter Davison, Ellen Voigt, David St. John, James Galvin, William Stafford, Jane Kenyon, Tess Gallagher, Galway Kinnell, Philip Booth, Wendell Berry . . .

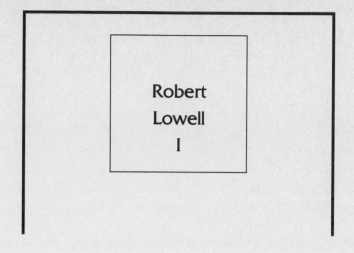

Robert
Lowell
I

It seems there's been something curiously twisted and against the grain about the world
poets of our generation have had to live in.

—ROBERT LOWELL to John Berryman, March 1959

T he concept of the generation is a curious one, if you
think about it. Strictly speaking, there's no such
thing—except, of course, in the family context. People are born, and
die, continuously. But just beneath that continuum we seem to register
mysterious magnetic fields of sensibility. I have in mind something
more than just shared experience—the sharing is of perception and
feeling. But what determines this, and how do people recognize it in
one another? Almost invariably we end up invoking that ectoplasmic
construct known as *Zeitgeist,* or "the spirit of the times."

If the generation business is confusing in the cultural present, it gets a good deal clearer in retrospect. Consider the case of a group of midcentury American poets: Elizabeth Bishop, Randall Jarrell, Delmore Schwartz, John Berryman, Theodore Roethke, and Robert Lowell. Not so long ago they were still among us, practicing their diversified craft. I meet people all the time who knew or studied with Lowell, Berryman, Bishop . . . But now these poets are gone and the sifting and sorting of contours has begun.

In recent years we've seen the publication of James Atlas's biography of Delmore Schwartz, Eileen Simpson's memoir of her marriage to Berryman, *Poets in Their Youth,* Ian Hamilton's *Robert Lowell,* John Haffenden's life of Berryman, and sizable collections of Schwartz's and Jarrell's correspondence. Biographer and critic Jeffrey Meyers has just come out with *Manic Power: Robert Lowell and His Circle,* the first fullfledged group biography. Out of the welter of documentation we are witnessing the emergence of a historical entity known as the Lowell Generation.

I expect that the lives and reputations of these poets will be reckoned every bit as strenuously as those of Eliot, Pound, Frost, and Stevens have been. This is not to say that they are all of the same stature—only Lowell and Bishop sustained greatness in their work—but they have captured the eye of posterity with the lurid drama of their lives. Look at the biographical headlines. Lowell, Jarrell, Berryman, Schwartz, and Roethke all suffered the devastations of mental illness. Excepting Jarrell, they were all alcoholics. Berryman and Jarrell and, later, Lowell's protégées Sylvia Plath and Anne Sexton committed suicide. The affairs and wrecked marriages are beyond enumeration. They achieved their art at the expense of great destruction. And much of the art was *about* that expense. As Lowell put it—rather mildly—in "Dolphin":

I have sat and listened to too many
words of the collaborating muse,
and plotted perhaps too freely with my life,
not avoiding injury to others,
not avoiding injury to myself—

The Critic's Work

to ask compassion . . . this book, half fiction,
an eelnet made by man for the eel fighting—

my eyes have seen what my hand did.

It will be objected that these were extreme cases, that such intense disorders were not common among the stable, hardworking majority, that the relatively serene careers of other poets of that generation—Richard Wilbur, Richard Eberhart, Stanley Kunitz—give the lie to mania. True enough. But there is *something* in all this madness and tragedy, some extent to which it tells the story of a specific epoch in American cultural life.

These poets were the last outriders of a spent ideology—Romanticism. This is where their heroic aura comes from. It's no coincidence that the lines popularly regarded as their collective epitaph (Lowell adapted them for his poem "To Delmore Schwartz"; Eileen Simpson mined them for her title) belong to Wordsworth:

We Poets in our youth begin in gladness,
But thereof come in the end despondence and madness.

The auto-da-fé that they made of their lives illuminates a great deal about the place of poetry in American life, both in their time and ours.

What drove these individuals? Personal circumstances were, to be sure, at the root. "Each of these poets," writes Jeffrey Meyers (referring to Lowell, Berryman, Jarrell, and Roethke), "had an unhappy childhood. They suffered from unmanly or absent fathers and from strong, seductive mothers. . . ." And later: "The poets' serious problems with their parents led to tempestuous marriages, which were characterized by infidelity, alcoholism, violence and mental breakdowns." Their literary ambition was part of the drive for psychic compensation—they would redeem their flawed pasts through art. Not surprisingly, some of them were the first to break with the constraints of impersonality and to pioneer what we now call confessional poetry. But fame, which they all considered the secular equivalent of absolution, was never enough. Even when they had it, they made life hellish for themselves.

Robert Lowell I

Unhappy childhoods, though, can't explain the whole tortured phenomenon. Poets since the days of Homer have grown up in blighted families. Doubtless there are thousands writing today whose need for artistic redemption is every bit as great as that felt by Berryman, Jarrell, or Roethke. No generation is exempt from the miseries that are our human lot. How is it, then, that we have seen nothing that can rival the public and private catastrophes wrought by this group? *What happened?* To understand them, we obviously have to look past psychobiography.

Meyers's book, for all the promise of its title, is not very useful in this respect. Though he has laid out the well-known case histories of his players with some care, he does not examine the conditions that shaped the larger milieu. This is a shame, especially as his opening chapter, "The Dynamics of Destruction," introduces this tantalizing suggestion:

> The poets' careers began in the 1940's and coincided with the emergence of the United States as the most powerful country in the world. They believed they were the truthtellers, bearers of culture, sacrificial victims driven mad by a need to escape from an increasingly crass and ugly society. As their audience diminished and their significance decreased, the poets felt they must transcend this hostile society through a finer and more intense conception of reality.

I can see why Meyers is loath to press the connection further. Nothing could be more difficult to assess than the impact of global politics and the attendant social transformations upon the practice of a small group of poets. But this inchoate play of forces may well have been the prime catalyst for their mad excess.

If the Romanticism of the late eighteenth and early nineteenth centuries was in large part a response to the encroachment of industrialization and utilitarian ideologies (read Shelley's *A Defence of Poetry*), then couldn't this midcentury explosion of tormented lyricism have been a reaction of the same kind—against the postwar centralization and bureaucratization of power? Where the French and American revolutions sparked the hope of change, so, too, did the confident prosperity that followed our emergence from the war.

I referred to these poets earlier as the last outriders of Romanticism. What I meant was that there was a period in the late forties and early fifties—before the balance tilted decisively away from them—when it was possible for poets to sustain a Romantic faith. They could believe for a time that intellect and imagination had a shaping role to play in American life.

Maybe every poet—every artist—feels this kind of optimism at the outset of his career. What was different about this group was that it was able to nurture the dream for a prolonged period. Our society did not congeal into monolithic imperialism overnight. There was an interval—from the end of the war to Eisenhower's landslide defeat of Adlai Stevenson in 1952—during which the future seemed open. The poets gave vent to their great ambition. Only when that future failed them did their work wither into tormented confession (the last discharge of Romantic protest); only then did their lives start to slide into chaos.

Politics, of course, was only part of the story. There were other factors at work, too. We can't forget, for one thing, that these poets came of age under the tutelage of the New Critics. Their masters—John Crowe Ransom, Allen Tate, Cleanth Brooks, Robert Penn Warren—were not only poets themselves (Brooks excepted), but were the prominent teacher-critics who had put the rigorous study of poetry at the very center of the liberal arts curriculum in the American university. The energies first released by Eliot and the modernists had not yet dissipated. A poet could still believe that his endeavor placed him at the very hub of the culture. And indeed, for these young poets nothing—but *nothing*—mattered so much as their trade. As Lowell wrote in his obituary for Jarrell: "Woe to the acquaintance who liked the wrong writer, the wrong poem by the right writer, or the wrong lines in the right poem!" You will not find devotion like this among poets writing now.

Again, *what happened*? Meyers cites "an increasingly crass and ugly society," diminishing audience, and decreasing significance. Who is to say what congeries of forces brought all this about? Material prosperity combined with internationalist politics combined with reactionary anti-communism combined with industrial and bureaucratic standardization combined with the electoral debacle—"egghead" Stevenson was crushed by "Ike." Lowell caught the mood in "Inauguration Day: January 1953":

Ice, ice. Our wheels no longer move.
Look, the fixed stars, all just alike
as lack-land atoms, split apart,
and the Republic summons Ike,
the mausoleum in her heart.

That mausoleum was where the bright hopes of the Lowell circle were finally interred.

Saul Bellow conveys a vivid sense of these atmospheric changes in his novel *Humboldt's Gift*. When we first meet the eponymous Von Humboldt Fleisher (the character was modeled directly on Bellow's longtime friend Delmore Schwartz), he is flush with egomaniacal passion. America, he believes, is the poet's mission. Its vast material reality is there to be melted down in the crucible of the imagination, to be transformed into art such as the world has never seen. But Humboldt mistakes his early success—he reached a poet's equivalent of stardom in the thirties and forties—for a nod of confirmation from the larger world. He soon finds out the truth. When his later books are not so well received, when his bids for academic power are repeatedly frustrated, he suffers mental collapse. Though his failures did not directly cause his illness, it's clear that they created a favorable climate for it.

Humboldt dies of a heart attack in a seedy New York hotel. When he sees the obituary, Charlie Citrine, Bellow's narrator, responds with anguished indignation:

The *Times* was much stirred by Humboldt's death and gave him a double-column spread. The photograph was large. For after all Humboldt did what poets in crass America are supposed to do. He

---

The Critic's Work

chased ruin and death even harder than he had chased women. He blew his talent and his health and he reached home, the grave, in a dusty slide. He plowed himself under. Okay. So did Edgar Allan Poe, picked out of the Baltimore gutter. And Hart Crane over the side of a ship. And Jarrell falling in front of a car. And poor John Berryman jumping from a bridge. For some reason this awfulness is peculiarly appreciated by business and technological America. The country is proud of its dead poets. It takes terrific satisfaction in the poets' testimony that the USA is too tough, too big, too much, too rugged, that American reality is overpowering. . . . So poets are loved, but loved because they just can't make it here. They exist to light up the enormity of the awful tangle and justify the cynicism of those who say, "If *I* were not such a corrupt, unfeeling bastard, creep, thief, and vulture, I couldn't get through this either. Look at these good and tender and soft men, the *best* of us. They succumbed, poor loonies."

Bellow has hit upon something here. In a psychically obscure—but very real—way, Humboldt/Schwartz, Jarrell, Berryman, and the others were brought to the edge of their precipice—and over—by the proudly brutal apathy of their culture. They caught sight of a nobler fate for themselves, and then every chance of attaining it was taken away. The fact that they had glimpsed the alternative was what set them up for tragedy.

It is now a full decade since Lowell, the last surviving member of Meyer's core group, died. Things in the poetry world feel very different now. We don't see nearly so much torment and self-destruction—and for the sake of the potential victims and their families, we should be glad. More and more, poetry is becoming a safe, grant-and-university-sponsored kind of thing. I'd say that the change—the "calm"—has a great deal to do with societal changes and with the disappearance of certain hopes and expectations. Things have come to such a pass in Olliemanic–Silicon Valley–Star Wars–Wall Street–*cynical* America that no one even considers that poetry—or art of any kind—might make a difference. As history reveals, the Romantic vision comes alive only when some chance of transformation is felt to exist. The French Revolution lit up the poets once; our emergence from World War II sent up a much smaller spark. Still, there was a moment when the balance seemed to teeter—before it tipped for good.

The Critic's Work

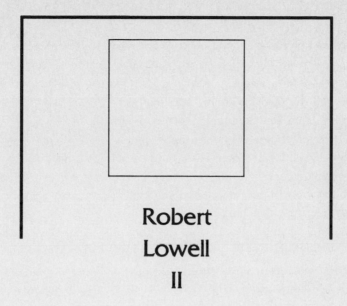

Robert
Lowell
II

I once had a friend—a scholar and a bookman—who believed that it was a sacrilege to annotate a printed text in any way. When he absolutely *had* to mark a passage, he would take out a special pencil and move it with a surgeon's care along the margin—his trace would be no darker than the shadow of an eyelash. I thought of him just now: I was thumbing my way back through Robert Lowell's *Collected Prose* and I realized with a guilty twinge how much I had disfigured the borders of the text. I had marked everything I thought worth returning to—and it turned out to be most of the book.

I had not expected such riches. Most posthumous collections turn out to be sad salvage operations, mercenary efforts to trade on the luster of a name. Although I had read a few of the pieces when they first appeared as prefaces or eulogies, I stubbornly held to the idea that Lowell had directed his genius into his poetry, with little left over for the more quotidian medium of prose. I was mistaken. Nearly everything between these covers—reminiscences, estimates of fellow poets, general essays, craft interviews, and autobiographical narratives— shows the hand of a master. The very best of the pieces shimmer like skywriting over a contemporary landscape gone drab with academic verbiage.

The first of the book's three sections is in many ways the best. Here, in eighteen essays, you find Lowell celebrating, measuring, dickering with, and thoroughly engaging the lives and careers of the poets of his day. After poetry itself, the essay/memoir was his ideal mode of expression. Indeed, the prose has been schooled at the feet of poetry—it is quick, allusive, sensitive down to its least syllable to the subtle phonetic surges of language. And like so much of Lowell's poetry, it conveys a sensory engagement with particulars. No dead space. Listen to the opening paragraph of his "Visiting the Tates":

> April 1937—I was wearing last summer's mothballish, already soiled white linens, and moccasins, knotted so that they never had to be tied or untied. What I missed along the road from Nashville to Clarksville was the Eastern seaboard's thin fields chopped by stone walls and useless wilderness of scrub. Instead, plains of treeless farmland, and an unnatural, unseasonable heat. Gushers of it seemed to sprout over the bumpy, sectioned concrete highway, and bombard the horizon. Midway, a set of Orientally shapely and conical hills. It was like watching a Western and waiting for a wayside steer's skull and the bleaching ribs of a covered wagon.

The poet's eye never stops moving. And that "set of Orientally shapely and conical hills" is pure joy: you feel the tires twisting along the sinuosities of the terrain. All this in anticipation of the human encounter.

Lowell knew that deadness is the enemy. "Dullness and the sad, universal air of the graduate schools have descended on close literary criticism," he wrote in an essay praising Stanley Kunitz. Things may have been bad then, but they're a damn sight worse now. The critic-poets of Lowell's day included Allen Tate, John Crowe Ransom, Delmore Schwartz, R. P. Blackmur, John Berryman, Yvor Winters, I. A. Richards, and Randall Jarrell—and most of them were his friends. Not least among the delights of this section is a view of an epoch from the front lines. Biographies (like Ian Hamilton's *Robert Lowell*) and memoirs (like Eileen Simpson's *Poets in Their Youth*) have already presented many of the anecdotes and legends, but none has cut as close to the living nerve as Lowell does. Here, for instance, is his report of an encounter between Berryman and Jarrell at Berryman's home in Princeton, New Jersey:

> Both poet-critics had just written definitive essay-reviews of my first book, *Lord Weary's Castle*. To a myopic eye, they seemed to harmonize. So much the worse. Truth is in minute particulars: here, in the minutiae, nothing meshed. Earlier in the night, Berryman made the tactical mistake of complimenting Jarrell on his essay. This was accepted with a hurt, glib croak, "Oh, thanks." The flattery was not returned, not a muscle smiled. . . . On the horrible New Jersey midnight local to Pennsylvania Station, Randall analyzed John's high, intense voice with surprise and coldness. "Why hasn't anyone told him?" Randall had the same high, keyed-up voice he criticized. Soon he developed chills and fevers, ever more violent, and I took my suit coat and covered him. He might have been a child. John, the host, the insulted one, recovered sooner. His admiration for Randall remained unsoured, but the dinner was never repeated.

Lowell, too, had the greatest admiration for Jarrell. Like every poet of his generation, he could not rest easy with the publication of new work until the verdict had been passed from on high. ("Randall was so often right that we sometimes said he was always right.") Lowell does not try to compete. When he writes about poets, he nearly always praises. This is not a sign of weakness, fear, or flaccid powers of judgment—Lowell is always exacting and never hesitates to quarrel with a line, a stanza—but more a kind of restraint exercised in the service of his true vocation. He refuses to set himself up as a critic. But if you want to see what the beast is like with his claws unsheathed, you should consult his review of A. E. Watts's translation of Ovid—the poor professor gets knocked around like a catnip mouse.

Mostly, though, Lowell is kind. He loves beauty and excellence and wants everyone else to love them, too. When pointing out the finer features of a poet or poem, he is especially contagious. This is because passion, not intellection, is generating the language. On the image of a pond in Kunitz's "Father and Son," he writes: "The pond must somehow touch the remembered father, and is a puff of blue smoke from everyone's childhood, when ponds, water lilies, and nature were closer and more demandingly mysterious." Break the branch anywhere and it oozes sap.

The short middle section is not nearly as distinguished as the first. Lowell's longtime friend and editor Robert Giroux is guilty of some padding. He includes, for example, "The *Iliad,*" written when Lowell was a senior at St. Mark's School in 1935; the piece has little to offer beyond archaeological interest. He also brings in a tedious and unfinished—it breaks off midsentence—lecture entitled "Art and Evil." Provocative as the title may sound, the words on the page have not yet been sculpted into shape. Since this is a paragraph of cavils, I might also add that the arrangement of contents throughout the collection is quite confusing. Giroux has opted for thematic consistency over chronology. But with a writer who changed as much as Lowell did—his career moved from the fervid and formalistic Catholicism of its beginnings through the liberations of a secular, confessional mode on into the hard-won notational freedom of its final phase—such a strategy is flawed. Time and again I found myself flipping to find the date appended to a certain essay, or pausing to calculate just where in the career trajectory a certain passage belonged. It would have been more rewarding, I think, to partake of the changes and expansions in Lowell's outlook directly.

The last section, which includes the two lengthy craft interviews and three autobiographical essays, more than compensates for the shortfall. The first of the interviews, by poet Frederick Seidel, has long been available in the *Paris Review* series; the second, with Ian Hamilton,

---

The Critic's Work

appeared in the London journal *The Review*. Poets as well as Lowell aficionados will be happy to have the two side by side. For these are exemplary dialogues, sustained and intelligent. Lowell details the stages of his poetic formation and brings the clarity of hindsight to the key transitional periods, supplying an invaluable counterpoint to the interpretations of critics, biographers, and scholars.

The Hamilton interview, done in 1971, ten years after the Seidel, captures Lowell in his period of exile to England. A veteran of divorces and hospitalizations for manic depression, the poet sometimes strikes a weary note. But his estimates of his own work, and the work of his colleagues, are direct and incisive. Asked about Sylvia Plath, for instance, he responds: "I glory in her powers. I don't know whether she writes like me. In an extreme life-and-death style, she is as good as Sir Walter Raleigh; no, she's not as good, but no poetry has a more acid sting." You feel the tensile power of the mind: He locates the unexpected comparison, weighs it, then modifies. There's a pause during which the essence of Plath and the essence of Raleigh are held together under the inspecting lens; you're both startled and instructed.

"Antebellum Boston" and "91 Revere Street," the first two memoirs, make another perfect diptych. The latter is well known (Lowell included it in his collection *Life Studies*); the former has never been published. Read together, they give a most intimate picture of Lowell's family background. The setting is Beacon Hill in the early decades of the century. Through the eyes of a preternaturally observant child, you see the heirloom-and-bric-a-brac-packed rooms of his boyhood house; you clamber along the branches of the family genealogy until you gaze at last at the unhappy parents. Although his father belonged by blood to the great patrician dynasty of New England Lowells, the family was forever at the margins, neither powerful nor prosperous. Lowell's father was a career navy man, a failure to himself and his wife. As his son writes: "He was a man who treated himself with the caution and uncertainty of one who has forgotten a name, in this case his own." By contrast: "Mother, her strong chin unprotected and chilled in the helpless autumn, seemed to me the young Alexander, all gleam and panache. . . ." Though these pieces cover just over fifty pages, Lowell's concentrated use of detail gives them the impressionistic depth of a novel.

Robert Lowell I

Finally, there is the remarkable, hitherto unpublished memoir "Near the Unbalanced Aquarium." Lowell begins: "One morning in July 1954 I sat in my bedroom on the third floor of the Payne-Whitney Clinic of New York Hospital, trying as usual to get my picture of myself straight." Alternating the description of daily routine with the recording of memories—of the deaths of his parents, mainly—Lowell reconstitutes the harrowing vicissitudes of mental illness. He gives you a sense of how composure can suddenly yield to the vertigo of mania. Here is how Lowell describes one such attack. He is sitting in the clinic lounge, watching a couple at the piano:

> Anna giggled with tremulous admiration as Roger insisted that the clinic's music instructor could easily teach her to read more skillfully. Suddenly I felt compelled to make a derisive joke, and I announced cryptically and untruly that Rubinstein had declared the eye was of course the source of all evil for a virtuoso. "If the eye offends thee, pluck it out." No one understood my humor. I grew red and confused. The air in the room began to tighten around me. I felt as if I were squatting on the bottom of a huge laboratory bottle and trying to push out the black rubber stopper before I stifled. Roger sat like a rubber stopper in his black suit. . . .

The scene continues, culminating in violence. The painful—tragic—thing was that Lowell could see and understand what he was doing, but was powerless to intervene against himself.

When Ian Hamilton's biography was published, many of the poet's friends protested that there was too much focus on the manic episodes, that the warm, witty, brilliant side of Lowell had been slighted. They should take some solace: Those qualities are preserved here in great abundance. I would urge you not to conclude with "Near the Unbalanced Aquarium," but to glance for a second time at the pieces in the front of the book—to cut the sadness with some of the fire of love.

*T*he *Collected Poems of Paul Blackburn*—close to seven hundred pages of text—weighs as much as a bag of groceries and has "definitive" written all over it. When the book was published last year there was almost nothing of Blackburn's to be found; now we have everything. Which is physically—visually— almost too much. I'm not suggesting that any lover of the language ought to be less than grateful for the editorial labors of Edith Jarolim, but it is somewhat disconcerting to see a poet of thin collections and fugitive appearances suddenly immured in the wrappings of respect- ability. What's more, I suspect that this compendium will not exert an immediate magnetic appeal upon readers hitherto unfamiliar with the poet. For Jarolim's decision to dismantle the unities of the original book appearances, and to proceed, instead, strictly in the order of ascertainable date of composition, presents the fidgety newcomer with a massive and unbroken edifice of poems. While the reader is, it's true, given a closer insight into the sequential evolution of a style, he is also deprived of any sense of how the poet wished to present himself during a particular phase. And Blackburn, we soon discover, was supremely alert to the movement of signal waves from one poem to another: Over and above the individual poems there was always the "poem" that they composed through their arrangement. While Jarolim has included a letter code in her index to tell us what book a given poem originally appeared in, we have no precise indication of positioning.

I wanted to get this cavil out of the way straight off, for there is much to celebrate in the carefully garnered abundance. And, to give Jarolim's editorial decision its due, the chronology is instructive. For Blackburn was striving above all else to capture the moment: Each poem marks the one-time intersection of a particular inner state with a particular setting and circumstance. The temporal ordering of these "moments" turns the volume into an odd sort of autobiography. I say "odd" because Blackburn never supplies any antecedent material for his notations, and he does not confess himself except through arrangement of detail and rhythmic shifts. The conventional contents of autobiography are the very thing that this poetry has excised. And yet, for all that—because of it!—we feel the sharp pulsations of a life that was fought for and enjoyed from one day to the next.

Blackburn's poetic "career"—if we can apply such a tainted word to an enterprise so open-ended and exploratory—spanned just over two decades, from the late 1940's when he was at the University of Wisconsin (but most likely getting his real education through his correspondence with Pound and Creeley) until 1971 when throat cancer finally claimed him. His production was ample by any poet's standards, and even a collection trimmed of garrulous excess—for Blackburn did indulge in a good bit of ephemeral word-sport—would have a commanding heft. The temptation for the critic, naturally, is to seek out the trajectory, the arc of development. And one kind of arc is clearly discernible in these pages: From first to last the poetry shows a pro-

The Critic's Work

gressive annexation of experience and locale—better: experience *in* locale—and a compositional control that becomes more instinctive, more uniquely a signature, by the year.

In early Blackburn, for example, we still feel the trace markings of his apprenticeship: Pound and Provençal (between 1954 and 1957, Blackburn lived in France and Spain, doing many of the translations that were later gathered in *Proensa: An Anthology of Troubadour Poetry*), the powerful dogma of Olson's projective verse theories, and the cat's paw choreography of Williams. Later, however, through the decade of the sixties, an idiosyncratic personal force increasingly sweeps away any sense of learned procedure. A defiant loosening of form and idiom convinces the reader that the words were rushed to the page along an avenue of timed traffic lights. The poems are sharp, aggressive, edgy with urban adrenaline. A turbulent emotionality is felt to abut almost every line, but it is never itself brought forward as a subject. Finally, as the seventies encroach, the shadow of the wing of mortality passes over the poems—even as, paradoxically, the poems themselves achieve a wry, stoical calm. Reading the pieces from the last year of Blackburn's life, we are hard pressed to realize that this quick-eyed, whimsical man is dying of cancer.

It would be too simple, nevertheless, to think of Blackburn's progress as an ever more direct confrontation with the real. For this would imply that the poet was getting more and more of his inner being onto the page—and this is manifestly untrue. Throughout his poetry, Blackburn silences the inner man in order to favor the present-tense creature of the senses. He rarely declares overt emotion and searches no psychological depths. Everything he wants to tell us is there in the patterned observation of the moment. As Gilbert Sorrentino once noted in an essay on Blackburn: "The exquisite ordering of the common materials of the poet's life is the architecture by means of which he not only deployed them in balanced design within the poem, but by means of which he changed them into instances of artifact. His poems are as artificial as those of his beloved troubadours." This is the central tension and the source of much of Blackburn's force: that in his pursuit of the immediate present he never relinquished his aesthetic purchase, never stopped controlling the strokes with which he regis-

Paul Blackburn

tered the chaotic profusion of the world. As jumbled and casual as his surfaces at times appear, they nearly always obey the dictates of a strict and subtle music.

Neither, in tracing Blackburn's development, can we neglect the profound influence of the times and the milieu. Where some poets evolve hermetically, following only the urges and imperatives of the voice, Blackburn did everything he could to enlarge his susceptibility to the here and now. He limned as honestly and accurately as possible the force lines of the moment, recognizing implicitly their extension into the past and future. To speak, therefore, of a formal relaxation, or of an intrusion of disruptive energies into his work in the sixties, as if these were merely private poetic tendencies, would be delusive. Blackburn was opening his pores to the strange electricity moving through the culture, especially the frontier that was the Lower East Side of Manhattan. If ever the spirit of a time and a place found its way into poetry, it was in the magnesium flashes of some of these lines.

"Suerte," written in 1956 during Blackburn's first European sojourn, is a concise example of the restrained lyricism of his early poetry. Here we find the imagist echo, as well as the thoughtful balancing of rhythmic requirements with breath intervals:

You shall not always sit in sunlight watching
                    weeds grow out of the drainpipes
                    or burros and shadows of burros
                    come up the street bringing sand
                    the first one of the line with a
bell
always.
          With a bell.
          Grace is set
               a term of less than a year.
Another bell sounds the hours of your sun
          limits
               sounding below human voices,

The Critic's Work

counts the hours of weeds, rain, darkness, all
        with a bell.

The first one with a bell always.

Simple, relaxed, and precise. The careful line breaks and spacing,
as well as the shy distancing of self (in spite of the fact that the poem
is self-addressed), recall Williams. This most unassuming of lyrics succeeds through a subtle aural engineering: First it breaks five lines of
sedate, if breathy, observation with a lurch and a wobble ("bell/al-
ways. / With a bell"); thereupon Blackburn instigates a lovely alternation between the long *a* sounds and the sibilants and punctuates this
with the repetition of the word "bell." The final "bell always" links the
separate effects and closes the poem with a delicate suggestion of ex-
piring echoes. When poets and critics speak of Blackburn's "ear"—and
they always do—it is this keen feel for the way that sounds separate
and coalesce, and this confident handling of rhythmic gradations, that
they have in mind.

Blackburn's poems of the sixties have a variety and vegetal profusion that make it impossible to cite a representative passage. The poet
moves from the most free-spirited and fanciful sort of wordplay:

stink, stank, stunk,
stinker.
the septic tank over
flows, *estanque,* to
save it, tanker, to hold it,
stack?

—from "The Word" (1965)

to an anecdotal urban reportage:

"C'mon, get out,
y'gotta get out," sez Milly,
"stop sleeping'n get out, I call the cop."
The old man
crumples up his check and drops it onto the sawdust floor.

—from "Sunflower Rock" (1966)

Paul Blackburn

to the most pruned lines of requia:

> Two years ago
> Jim died
> doing battle with a truck
> on Third Avenue
> from a motorbike seat
> shaking and
> cold sober
>
> Love is not enuf
> Friendship is not enuf
> Not even art
> is/Life is too much

—from "16 Sloppy Haiku" (1966)

What strikes us most as we read this middle section of the book is Blackburn's porosity, his willingness to sound out all registers of his experience. The lyric tenderness so evident in the early work has not disappeared, but pain and confusion have now been accepted as a necessary part of its setting. This maturing shift becomes increasingly apparent as we read in sequence. Indeed, I would argue that Blackburn is best read in batches of a dozen or more poems at a sitting. Only then can we begin to appreciate the contrapuntal variety, the way that a quip can become a defiant affirmation by virtue of its positioning, or how the somber context of one poem can throw its shadow over the bright effusion of another. This reasoning, pursued far enough, would end by having us consider Blackburn's whole output as a single long poem. Possibly this is what Jarolim had in mind when she decided to unravel the separate collections. Without a doubt, the poems acquire an enlarged referentiality when read in sequence. This is *not* to consider them as entries in an ongoing diary (though they are often highly diaristic)—the rhythmic variety, the precision of the modulations, and the attention to balance and closure preclude any such facile comparisons. But each separate shape can be said to secure its larger completion with reference to the other shapes, all of which are organically bound to the ongoing motion of a life.

The Critic's Work

An example might clarify this. Among the poems written in 1966, we find a series—which includes "16 Sloppy Haiku"—that takes as its subject the death of Blackburn's friend Bob Reardon. It is a bitter interlude. And at the end of his poem "The List," where he speaks through the persona of Reardon, Blackburn comes as close as he ever will to hitting the elegiac note:

"No rites
but some friends reading words I loved, mostly
other men's words, only a few of my own, other
friends hearing them. Regret
only what was not finished, regret only the loss
of afternoon sun thru the window at McSorley's, that
table's wood whitened as my bones are in the fire, the
cold rain of this later date, all that.
Say goodbye for me."

Without the sound of these lines in our minds, a later poem, "The Island"—set, presumably, in McSorley's—would be little more than a well-turned mood sketch. But once we have the larger picture, the closing lines carry a beautiful hint of redemption. I would even say that they touch lyric profundity:

Six men stand at the bar
Seven men sit at the tables
            now eight
                now nine
a sixteenth man in the urinals
Matty behind the bar
George in the back   .
Silence there is &   2   conversations
                sometimes   3   .
It's March 9th, 3:30 in the afternoon

The loudest sound in this public room
is the exhaust fan in the east window
            or the cat at my back
                asleep there in the sun

Paul Blackburn

bleached tabletop, golden
shimmer of ale

The poem, in a very important way, requires the earlier passage. Without it we partake of the languor of a quiet March afternoon, nothing more. With it in mind, however, we feel an immemorial recognition: This is just how the living resume the momentum of habits after a death. The numeration is ominous. But then comes the "golden / shimmer of ale": It is like a light winking at us from beyond.

In September of 1967, Blackburn was awarded a much awaited Guggenheim fellowship; he embarked promptly for Europe. The period that followed is often spoken of as one of inner renaissance for the poet. He met Joan, his third wife to be, and his work took on a directed and energized immediacy. In April of 1968 he wrote the first of the many journal poems that he would write in the few years remaining to him.

The designation "journal" is somewhat misleading, for these more personalized pieces are every bit as much *poems* as anything Blackburn was to write. The word indicates more of a shift in focus than in technique or mode of presentation. We find the same linear acrobatics, the same discursive wordplay, and no slackening in attention to spacing or line breaks. But from this point on there is a greater unity about Blackburn's production. It is as if the poet had finally decided that his own immediate experience—with his own persona as the acknowledged center—was material enough for all the poetry that he wished to write. With the transition comes a perceptible rise in temperature. The poems are more genial; they also tend to be looser, freer in their rambling. Conceiving of poems as journals seems to have allowed Blackburn to take a freer hand, to work in more personal reference. This latter trait becomes a liability as soon as we pry individual poems loose from their surroundings; much of the depiction then looks one-dimensional. But the fact is, as I indicated earlier, we have to take Blackburn on his own terms, to read him serially and to keep track of his autobiographical signposts. Thus, we cannot but follow along with the course of Joan's pregnancy, the visit with the Cortázars at Saignon,

The Critic's Work

the birth of their son Carlos, the stages of the family's trip through the
American West, and so on. Blackburn forces us to hew to the informal
and often chaotic progress of his life.

A few excerpts from "Journal: July 21/22, 1969" will give some
indication of Blackburn's way of modulating between the poetic and
notational poles:

Those boys comin' back fr/the moon
   Armstrong, Aldrin & company, & I
         make my own countdown   :   score
be
tween
dusk & midnight, I
missed one rabbit & got one, I think,
                rear wheels, one small bird,   &
also about dusk
     (the small ones do a dance in front of the
                    windshield in pairs)

a young hawk crossed
right to left &
cut back

     hit the upper right side
     the VW truck's window
         W H A P
           & bounced off.

and:

     Springfield (Mo.) to near to Boise City (Keyes)
         OKLA

         HOMA

         500 miles in a day
     then Raton, Cimarron, Eagle Nest
     Joan drove those mountains   , Raton to

Paul Blackburn

Taos on 65   .   111 north to Tres Piedres &
            285 straight up
            into those hills (2 rainstorms, in the
                        distance lightning) & at La Jara, 14
miles south of our mark, our Car-
los starts
            HOWLING   . we . stop .   feed,
                        walk him around a bit

These passages reveal a great deal both about the range and the limitations of Blackburn's journal approach. The first discovers a narrative momentum and sustains a nervous and complex energy as it oscillates between the ironic (and defensive) reckoning and careful descriptive miming. The hesitation between "I think" in line 7 and "rear wheels" in the following line, for example, catches the pace of the perception exactly; likewise, the staggering of line clusters, the movement from right to left and back as it plays off the depicted motion of the hawk resolves perfectly in the flat "W H A P." The second passage, on the other hand, seems to me full of gratuitous elements. The information is only of private interest, and the staging of the lines and breaks serves no purpose that I can detect. There is, of course, the punning line break of "Car- / los," but the bulk of the verbiage is the kind best consigned to the private travel log.

Blackburn's effort, as his career matured, was to bring more and more of the language of prosaic daily experience into the poetic matrix. To some extent his was a tactic of framing: The choreographed lines would signal to the reader that the words were to be assessed for their aural, visual, and semantic functions. Heightened attention would reveal the underlying poetic bedding of all utterance. The ultimate goal—and Blackburn must have thought about this—would be to keep the transformative lens in place at all times, to come to see all language as poetry. Conceptual artists from Duchamp on have had similar ambitions for the visual sphere. If they have not finally succeeded, it may be because they have not paid sufficient heed to the law of diminishing returns, and to the fact that the "poetic" or "aesthetic" achieves its status in relation to the ordinary, the uninteresting. This, at times, is Blackburn's failing as well—when, for instance, he attempts to turn a recipe or a set of highway directions into poetry. Exercises like this do not so much poeticize the subject as weaken the transformative potential of the framing device.

Fortunately, most of the journal poems—which come to dominate his *oeuvre* in the last two years of his life—work. They are alert and witty, uncluttered transcriptions of events, moods, and observations. And once we learn of Blackburn's illness, their lightness generates a reverse effect.

The first direct mention of Blackburn's cancer (there are very few in these pages) comes in the entry titled "17.IV.71," written some months after the diagnosis:

Cities & towns I have to give up this year
on account of my cancer: Amster-
dam, Paris, Apt, Saignon and Aix,
(Toulouse I'll never loose), Peripignan and Dax,

All at once we understand that his casual, playful, deprecatory humor has all along been a form of stoicism, that the humor and lightness have looked suffering and death in the eye and are thereby all the more humorous and light. For a poet with cancer to make verbal play with the homophonic "Amster" is evidence of an absolute vocational purity. Of itself, it may not stand as profound; but once we have engaged the life behind the poems, the unwavering dedication to the clarity and joy of language, it transmits a considerable moral and spiritual largesse. The remaining journals are affecting in much the same way. Though Blackburn does not deviate from his earlier manner—not once does he take his sufferings as a subject—his every observation is now backlit by our awareness. The daily life of the body and its senses becomes profound, as the poet always meant it to be, as it always has been.

Paul Blackburn

May
Swenson

Reverse chronology appears to be enjoying a vogue among publishers of collections of poetry. I can't see the logic of it myself. If the poet in question has improved over the years, shedding bad habits, widening the reach, then we are apt to get increasingly demoralized as we turn the pages. If, on the other hand, the poet has declined, then the arrangement scarcely serves his or her best interests—though, admittedly, when that's the case any policy other than self-censorship is a bad one. And if the poet has not so much progressed or declined, has simply changed? Well, then the result can be quaint, like watching the dog running backward over the lawn while the ball arcs back into the hand; or, provided our study is motion and change, instructive.

May Swenson's *New & Selected Things Taking Place* has been put together in just such a fashion. I read it, as I'd been trained, in the Christian manner—proceeding from left to right, top to bottom, front to back—and after a time I realized that I was participating in a most curious event: an eclipse of personality. Section by section, I felt voice and expressiveness yielding ground to formal precision. Subject matter was increasingly framed and distanced. I was disappointed, not because I couldn't enjoy the poems themselves, but because I'd missed the experience of the real process behind the career. Where I should have felt some of the exalting sensations of struggle and self-liberation, I traced only diminution. Any transposition I make now is intellectual and *a posteriori*.

Not every reader, I suspect, will agree that the changes in Swenson's poetry represent positive growth. Those with a bias toward strict form might argue that her poems have declined from purity. The early work has a structural self-containment largely absent from recent offerings; artifice is prized. Those who value poetry as a vehicle for personal expression, on the other hand, will want to praise the human event: Here is a poet who has, with patience and determination, made her way from a detached fascination with otherness to an increasingly subjective recognition of the self as an agent in the chaotic here and now. The inevitable question arises: What do we cherish more, technical excellence or voice? In Swenson's poetry the latter has been achieved to some extent at the price of the former.

The transformation I would chart is a gradual one, and there are exceptions to the pattern everywhere. I can locate free-spoken lines in *Another Animal*, the earliest included section, and formal austerities in *Things Taking Place*, the latest. But the overall steady displacement of aesthetic distance by personal involvement seems incontestable. A few sample poems might make my distinction clearer. Here, from *Another Animal*, is "Horse and Swan Feeding":

Half a swan a horse is
how he slants his muzzle to the clover

forehead dips in a leaf-lake
as she the sweet worm sips
spading the velvet mud-moss with her beak
His chin like another hoof he plants
to preen the feathered green
Up now is tossed her brow from the water-mask
With airy muscles black and sleek
his neck is raised curried with dew
He shudders to the tail delicately
sways his mane wind-hurried
Shall he sail or stay?
Her kingly neck on her male
imperturbable white steed-like body
rides stately away

Note the control. In almost every line the natural flow of the language is subverted, either syntactically, through subject-predicate reversal, or through the elided pronoun ("forehead dips in a leaf-lake"). Persistent artifice, grafted upon the mythic conceit, gives the poem an autonomous character; it is something fashioned *out of* language, not discovered *in* it. The horse has been seen with astonishing accuracy, and the diction expertly serves its ends ("His chin like another hoof he plants" or "Up now is tossed her brow from the water-mask"), but its animal life is passed to us through a mesh woven, at least in part, of the cadences and imaginings of Marianne Moore. Compare it with the first stanza of Moore's "No Swan So Fine":

"No water so still as the
dead fountains of Versailles." No swan,
with swart blind look askance
and gondoliering legs, so fine
as the chintz china one with fawn-
brown eyes and toothed gold
collar on to show whose bird it was.

Moore announces her aestheticism, struts it; Swenson is less flamboyant. But in both poems the attention is less focused upon the

---

May Swenson

intrinsic merits of subject, more upon the delays and revelations possible through careful clause manipulation.

Now, from the front of the book, from *Things Taking Place* (and we might remark the two respective titles, the one—*Another Animal*—signaling modest detachment, the other a more embracing sense of activity), here is a poem called "The Willets":

One stood still, looking stupid. The other
beak open, streaming a thin sound,
held wings out, took sideways steps,
stamping the salt marsh. It looked threatening.
The other still stood wooden, a decoy.

He stamp-danced closer, his wings arose,
their hinges straightened,
from the wedge-wide beak the thin sound
streaming agony-high—
in fear she wouldn't stand? She stood.

Her back to him pretended—
was it welcome, or only dazed
admission of their fate?
Lifting, he streamed a warning
from his beak, and lit

upon her, trod upon her
back, both careful feet.
The wings held off his weight.
His tail pressed down, slipped off. She
Animated. And both went back to fishing.

That Swenson's diction has loosened is obvious immediately. The lines, still tensed, are now open to the event, and the literary nimbus has been blown off. A word like "curried" would be as out of place in this poem as "stupid" would be in its predecessor. But the most fundamental change is of vision. Though both poems belong to the same genre—nature observed—they are as unlike as can be. In "Horse and

Swan Feeding," nature has been entirely appropriated by art. "The Willets," while it acknowledges the poet's projections ("in fear she wouldn't stand?"), does not varnish or transform the real event. What's more, it embodies a wisdom, a note of mature reconciliation, that the earlier poem does not. The limitations of language are implicit—we can reflect upon the world around us, but we cannot penetrate its strangeness. What a difference between "white steed-like body/rides stately away" and "She/Animated. And both went back to fishing." Diction is the least of it. The conceptual gulf is as wide as that between Tennyson and Auden.

Swenson's aesthetic has always been exclusionary. We sense, especially in the early poems, that every choice of subject also involves the deliberate avoidance of other subjects. And in this, I think, her debt to Marianne Moore and the early Elizabeth Bishop is most conspicuous. (One cannot but wonder in what ways aesthetic reticence is bound up with the privacies of sexual preference, whether the line between private and public is not differently drawn.) The complexities of animal life and natural form are eagerly seized upon, while the intricacies of the social order and the human emotions are not so much overlooked as proscribed. Perception sustained; feeling overruled. It is as if the greater part of Swenson's psychic endowment has been channeled into the sense organs, which then become capable of the most precise registrations. The early sections are filled with *tour de force* lines and images, and playful imaginings that are in no way held by the gravitational field of the emotions. In the poem "At East River," for instance, Swenson artfully turns floating gulls into "ballet slippers, dirty-white," points out how a plane "Turns on its elegant heel:/a spark, a click/of steel on blue," and concludes by describing Brooklyn as "a shelf of old shoes/needing repair."

These early poems, outward looking though they might be, are not all of a kind. Self-exempted from the hazards of voicing emotion, Swenson is free to try on different styles. (Or is this a polite way of saying that she has not yet forged her own distinctive idiom?) In the opening lines of "Two-Part Pear Able" (from *A Cage of Spines*), we see her making use of a lucent, Williams-like diction:

May Swenson

In a country where
every tree is a pear tree
it is a shock to see
one tree
(a pear tree undoubtedly
    for its leaves are the leaves
    of a pear)
that shows no pears

It is a fairly tall tree
sturdy
capable looking
its limbs strong its leaves glossy
its posture in fact exceptionally
pleasing

The play of long *ee* sounds against sharply articulated consonants leaves a vivid impression of etched branches. The very same section, however, also finds her using these clotted lines to characterize a squirrel:

Furry paunch, birchbark-snowy, pinecone-brown back,
    a jacket with sleeves to the digits.
Sat put, pert, neat, in his suit and his seat, for a minute,
    a frown between snub ears—bulb-eyed head
    toward me sideways, chewed.
                    —from "News from the Cabin"

Which would we say is the definitive Swenson? Or should we look instead to the shaped quickness of "Fountain Piece"?:

A bird
    is perched
        upon a wing

        The wing
    is stone
  The bird
is real

The Critic's Work

This is where the perspectives of hindsight turn out to be useful. If we read from the vantage of Swenson's later *Iconographs* phase, then "Fountain Piece" is the more prophetic. If, on the other hand, our ear is more attuned to the most recent work, then the cadences, as well as the relaxed presence of the first-person pronoun, of a poem like "Waiting for *It*" will seem to be the truest heralds:

> My cat jumps to the windowsill
> and sits there still as a jug.
> He's waiting for me, but I cannot be
> coming, for I am in the room.
>
> His snout, a gloomy V of patience,
> pokes out into the sun.
> The funnels of his ears expect
> to be poured full of my footsteps.

The lines are vigilant and precise, hovering at the edge of humor. The language is transparent, stripped of excess vowels and consonants; the living creature fills the space exactly. Swenson may have tossed human nature out with a pitchfork, but it has found a way in through the back window. The nonhuman order vibrates at a frequency very near that of the human. A charming domesticity results.

The natural world in Swenson's early poetry is delicately perceived, and its hierarchies are carefully set out. If the household cat reigns over the near end of the spectrum, its counterpart roars at the other:

> In the bend of your mouth soft murder
>   in the flints of your eyes
>   the sun-stained openings of caves
>
> —from "Lion"

In the intervals between we come upon pigeons, owls, butterflies, horses, and monkeys, to name a few. Here, though, is one way in which Swenson differs from Moore. Moore would pounce upon the peculiarities of nature, allowing her observations to coax her language to the idiosyncratic extreme. Swenson is more intent upon charting the distance between creature and human; peculiarity is merely a by-prod-

---

May Swenson

uct. Thus, the cat is in intimate alliance ("He's waiting for me"), while the squirrel occupies a middle ground—in nature, but wearing "a jacket with sleeves to the digits"—and the lion is emphatically other: "in the flints of your eyes / the sun-stained openings of caves."

The animal kingdom is just one part of Swenson's subject. Geographical and geological environments are of nearly equal importance. Her poetry moves freely among the different kinds of urban habitat, but it annexes just as avidly the less tenanted places—mountains, plains, shores, and waters. She finds poetic material wherever the eye can discover movement or form. And, I might add, the nuances that she fastens upon are predominantly visual; the delicate measuring tool of the ear works to underscore the masses and details of the seen world. One could put together quite an anthology of kinds of settings, moving from city:

> From an airplane, all
> that rigid splatter of the Bronx
> becomes organic, logical
> as web or beehive. Chunks
>
> of decayed cars in junkyards,
> garbage scows (nimble roaches
> on the Harlem), herds of stalled
> manure-yellow boxes on twisting reaches
>
> of rails, are punched clean and sharp
> as ingots in the ignition of the sun.
> —from "Distance and a Certain Light"

to garden:

> You've put out
> new nooses since
> yesterday.
>
> With a hook and
> a hook and a hook
> you took territory
>
> —from "A City
> Garden in April,"
> *The Vine*

The Critic's Work

to lakes:

> The hazel waves slip toward me,
>   the far arcade
> honed by the sunset; nothing tears
>   the transparent skin that water
> and sky and, between them,
>   the undulant horizon wears.

—from "A Lake Scene"

to the sea (and note here the remarkable interiorization of the imagery):

> Slowly a floor rises, almost becomes a wall.
> Gently a ceiling slips down, nearly becomes a floor.
> A floor with spots that stretch, as on a breathing
> animal's hide. It rises again with a soft lurch.

—from "A Hurricane at Sea"

Nor is Swenson content to observe the limits of the terrestrial. There are poems that survey landscape from the air, poems that observe clouds from the windows of a plane, and then, with increasing frequency, poems about the sun, the moon, the galaxies. In more recent work the landing of the Apollo astronauts becomes a topic of some fascination. Swenson delights in rendering the technological penetration of the unearthly in terms of the most archaic human images:

> A nipple, our parachute
> covers the capsule: an
> aureole, on a darker aureole
>
> like the convex spiral of
> a mollusc, on a great breast:

—from "'So Long' to the Moon
from the Men of Apollo"

May Swenson

The more adventurously Swenson ranges among the outer universe of images in these poems, the more conspicuous is her rejection of the human subject. So successful is she at keeping her gaze trained outward that one begins to wonder if she is not in some way using the whole natural world as a correlative for the psyche and its processes. Indeed, couldn't we argue that the psyche is bound to represent itself, its repressed contents, in whatever images it selects, whatever rhythms it convokes? Or is the dissociation of self a better explanation? Eliot, of course, maintained that the progress of the artist was a "continual extinction of personality." But then Eliot did not foresee that posterity would read his poetry with a watchful eye on the individual conspicuously positioned behind the arras of his words. I am not going to debate here whether dissociation or psychic determinism is the key to interpretation. But Swenson's work, as we shall see, makes the question a live one.

In her contribution to a volume entitled *The Contemporary Poet as Artist and Critic* (1964), in her discussion of fellow formalist Richard Wilbur, Swenson wrote: "The modern lyric is autonomous, a separate mobile, having its own private design and performance. It may be little on the page, yet project a long and versatile dance in the mind. Its total form and gesture is not a relative, it is an absolute, an enclosed construct." This would have been written at about the time that Swenson published *To Mix with Time: New and Selected Poems* (1963). Her description is striking, for it joins together the precise fixities of something constructed and the fluidity of dance—form and freedom. Certainly she had her own work in mind. As it happens—and as the phrase "a separate mobile" suggests—Swenson was beginning to develop an interest in the semantic possibilities of a poem's appearance. A number of poems in that collection explore the relationship between the look of a poem and its meaning. Some even put the visual and phonic elements on an equal footing, trusting that the disjunction between the seeing and hearing would set up an unexpected propulsion of parts:

> They said there was a   Thing
> that could not   Change

The Critic's Work

They could not	Find
it so they	Named
it	God
They had to	Search
so then it must be	There

—from "God"

To my mind, any attempt to subvert the aural foundation of poetry is doomed to failure. Not only is the natural integrity of the genre compromised—for no effective oral performance is possible—but our own allegiances are strained. A poem like this asks us to admire its concept even more than its verbal reality. It is, in a sense, the ultimate attempt to pry poetry loose from the spoken idiom. To make of words "an enclosed construct" is to follow the formalist impulse for its own sake; and pure form, as Hans Castorp discovered on the Magic Mountain, is death.

Swenson continued for a time to move in this direction. Some time after the 1963 collection came *Iconographs,* in which, as is obvious from the title, the visual aspects of the poems were dominant. Some of the artifacts, typographically too complex to be reproduced here, were clearly to be considered as artistic shapes in their own right. Poem and world, form and idiom, were set into opposition.

If we were to draw a figure (how apropos) representing Swenson's poetic development, *Iconographs* would mark—according to bias—either an apogee or a nadir. By insisting that the poem function visually, she drew the elastic to its limit. Since that time, obedient perhaps to the laws of elasticity (otherwise known as dialectics), she has been moving decisively in the opposite direction, toward a poetry of natural diction. The change in orientation could not be more complete. I will not presume to theorize about the deeper causes of this change, but a closer look at the shape of some of the *Iconographs* poems might give us some idea about the tensions involved.

Let us accept, for argument's sake, that poetry—indeed, any mode of expression—is entirely determined by the forces of the unconscious. We could agree, then, that both the linguistic and the visual choices in these poems were responses to specific psychic pressures—

in which case, the iconographic features would be most telling. Now, even a glance at the poems in this collection will reveal that a great number of them are in some way fissured or fractured, that their layout strains against the unity implicit in our conception of poetry. Here are just two examples:

Stop bleeding   said the knife.
I would if I   could said the cut.
Stop bleeding   you make me messy with this blood.
I'm sorry   said the cut.
Stop or   I will sink in farther said the knife.

Don't   said the cut.

—from "Bleeding"

What does love look like?   We know the shape of death
Death is a cloud, immense   and awesome. At first a
lid is lifted from the   eye of light. There is a
clap of sound. A white   blossom belches from the
jaw of fright.

—from "The Shape of Death"

Of course, not all of the poems are iconographically split—some essay other effects—but the tendency is pronounced enough to give pause. There is, as I see it, a fundamental contradiction at the heart of the matter. The dominant impulse sponsoring the visual construction is a formal one; it is a desire for aesthetic wholeness and self-containment. Swenson certainly described her lyric ideal unambiguously enough in the sentences I quoted. How is it then that the artifacts themselves are so often emblems of rupture? Does it seem too farfetched to say that the tension between form-making and form-destroying forces deter-mines this phase of Swenson's career? Or that the obvious movement away from "enclosed construct[s]" in the subsequent poetry marks a victory for the deeper—repressed—demands of the self? The poems in *Things Taking Place* are, with few exceptions, repudiations of the credo cited above. It is almost as if *Iconographs* allowed Swenson to discharge her own imperatives once and for all, as if the artifacts self-

The Critic's Work

destructed out of their own inner necessity, freeing her to move in a new direction.

Things Taking Place, comprising mainly work from the 1970's, is an uneven collection. In some ways it is like a first book, exhibiting that on-off quality that often accompanies a new poet's search for voice. But with this important difference: that the poems that do achieve that expressive synthesis of subject and tone are unquestionably the work of a mature and sophisticated artist. Though there is a paradox here, it shouldn't be too perplexing. For in one very important sense this is a debut. In a long lifetime of writing, Swenson has never before tried to bring her own self forward.

The change is conspicuous, but not dramatic. Readers familiar with Swenson will find many of her customary subjects—there are poems on landscape, animals, the moon landing, and even a few more formal exercises that hearken back to earlier work. But then, alongside this archive of the known, Swenson has included a dozen or so longer pieces that are different from anything she has done before. Not only does she take her own experience as a central subject, but she allows a stubborn and distinctive personal voice to emerge. Restraint has not vanished—hers is not a declamatory "I"—but the ideal of a pure and autonomous poetry has been left behind.

The austerities of observation, once central, are now placed in the service of the voice. Swenson uses the first-person pronoun without coyness or artifice; formerly this could not have happened. Here is a section from an earlier poem called "Riding the 'A'":

> I ride
> the 'A' train
> and feel
> like a ball-
> bearing in a roller skate.
> I have on a gray
> rain-
> coat. The hollow
> of the car
> is gray.

May Swenson

The "I" is a situating device, utterly opaque. Compare this with the opening lines of the recent "Staying at Ed's Place":

> I like being in your apartment, and not disturbing anything.
> As in the woods I wouldn't want to move a tree,
> or change the play of sun and shadow on the ground.
> The yellow kitchen stool belongs right there
> against white plaster. I haven't used your purple towel
> because I like the accidental cleft of shade you left in it.

Measured against the best work of a generation of autobiographical poets, this sort of expression does not command special attention. When compared to Swenson's previous work, however, the departure is quite startling.

Swenson begins *Things Taking Place* with a series of poems about travels in the American West. (As she was born in Utah, this could be interpreted as a gesture of homecoming.) Her description of spaces, mountains, and natural detail is calm and loving. Though their subjectivity is tentative, the poems diverge from previous efforts in that the perceptions are not rendered out of omniscient objectivity, but are controlled by the vantage of the speaker:

> Great dark bodies, the mountains.
> Between them wriggling the canyon road,
> little car, bug-eyed, beaming, goes
> past ticking and snicking of August insects,
> smell of sage and cedar, to a summit of stars.
> Sky glints like fluorescent rock.
> Cloth igloo erected, we huff up our bed,
> listen to the quaking of leaf-hearts
> that, myriad, shadow our sleep.

> —from "The North Rim"

The lines have a casual, intimate fall. I would even say that they stray over into cuteness—with the punning "bug-eyed, beaming," and the oddball pairing of "ticking and snicking." Nature is not so much the fierce and fabulous architect as a friendly—though still bewitching— presence. The poet herself, as part of the "we," has moved forward

---

The Critic's Work

into the middle distance. She is not exactly confessional, but she is *there*.

Throughout *Things Taking Place,* we feel Swenson looking for a comfortable way to lodge herself in her settings. Her most successful mode, and the one that she resorts to most often, is both personable and precise. She gives us the human element, but her incessant detailing keeps us at arm's length from intimacy, even when the situation is relatively "unbuttoned":

When, squint-eyed from the flashing river,
we climbed into farmyard shade, I spied
the squeaking door of a little privy
of new pine board, among trees beyond
where the blond horse crops. The bright
hook worked like silk. One seat, and no wasps,
it was all mine. An almanac, the pages Bible-thin,
hung by a string through a hole made with an awl.
Outside, steady silence, and in
the slit-moon-window, high up, a fragrant
tassel of pine. Alone, at peace, the journey done,
I sat. Feet planted on dependable planks, I sat.
Engrossed by the beauty of the knothole panel before me,
I sat a nice long time.

—from "The Beauty of the Head"

Earlier parts of the poem have set up the relentless swaying of the boat; the square solidity of the privy comes to seem like the very image of heaven—or haven. The delicacy of the description ("The bright / hook worked like silk" and "An almanac, the pages Bible-thin, / hung by a string through a hole made with an awl") yields beautifully to the flat, emphatic repetitions of "I sat." My delirious ear hears "satisfaction" and "satiety"; my Swiftian self bids I add "shat."

Emotion is still problematic for Swenson. While she has begun to address herself and her fellows as subjects, protocols of reserve are studiously observed. When she does allow her gaze to settle on another person, it is generally from a distance, either literal, as in this painterly composition:

May Swenson

I see Captain Holm
in yellow slicker,
right hand behind him
on the stick of the tiller,
feet in the well
of his orange Sailfish:
like a butterfly's
single wing, it slants
upright over the bay.

—from "Captain Holm"

or, as in this poem on the death of her mother, through the scrim of a
conceit:

Mother's work before she died was self-purification,
a regimen of near-starvation, to be worthy to go
to Our Father, Whom she confused (or, more aptly, fused)
with our father, in Heaven long since. She believed
in evacuation, an often and fierce purgation,
meant to teach the body to be hollow, that the soul
may wax plump. At the moment of her death, the wind
rushed out from all her pipes at once. Throat and rectum
sang together, a galvanic spasm, hiss of ecstacy.

—from "That the Soul May Wax Plump"

This conflation of the spiritual and profane senses of *pneuma* is not my
idea of an emotional farewell. It achieves a note of liberation, but
precisely because it bypasses the expected pieties. Swenson's extreme
detachment keeps her hovering between the exacerbated directness of
Villon and the nervous tittering of Monty Python.

In "Poet to Tiger," Swenson attempts a good-humored love poem.
But even here, she cannot free herself for apostrophe before she has
turned the object of her affections into a hyperbolic dream-creature:

Or else you wake me every hour with sudden
          growled I-love-yous
     trapping my face between those plushy
shoulders. All my float-dreams turn spins

The Critic's Work

and never finish. I'm thinner
now. My watch keeps running fast.
But best is when we're riding pillion
my hips within your lap. You let me steer.
    Your hand and arm go clear
    around my ribs your moist
    dream teeth fastened on my nape.

Still, this is a less restrained Swenson than we're used to seeing. The active pressure of the lines—not to mention their content—shows a woman's determination to assert herself more vigorously. The to-and-fro modulations between dream and wakefulness make it clear that the contest is, at least in some sense, between the unconscious and conscious parts of the self.

Much as I approve Swenson's effort to present more of herself in her poetry, I do not find that she has fully mastered her new voice. For one thing, there are a number of instances—like the mother poem—where she cannot align her address with her subject. She is skillful when the narration is centered upon material surfaces, but often irritating and unconvincing when she tries her techniques on popular or topical subjects:

Sent aloft by a leather toe,
a rugged leather baby
dropped from the sky and slammed

into the sling of your arms.
Oh, the feel of that leather bundle.
Oh, what a blooper and fumbler
you are, that you couldn't nest it

                       —from "Watching the Jets
                         Lose to Buffalo at Shea"

Like, everyone wants to look black
in New York these days.
Faces with black lenses, black
frames around the eyes,
faces framed in black

May Swenson

beards. Afros on all the blacks—
beautiful. But like,
everyone looks puff-headed.

—from "Fashion in the 70's"

This brings me to the heart of my complaint about Swenson. She is a poet of obvious gifts, among them a lively imagination and a most delicate sensory apparatus. But I rarely find her gifts working on behalf of her full sensibility. The material has always been thought through or imagined through; it has seldom been felt through. The eye does work that the heart should be doing. I cannot speak for everyone, naturally, but I find that poetry not fundamentally rooted in the tears of things is quickly forgotten and seldom, if ever, returned to. Entirely too many of these pieces are of this stamp.

To be fair, though, there are several praiseworthy exceptions; poems, indeed, that distinguish themselves by striking a balance between the inner claim and the external detail. And, as it happens, they tend to be the very poems that take aging and death as their subject. Swenson's reticence and her way with natural images stand her in good stead. In "October," for instance, one of the finest lyrics in the book, she allows the images to hew to the track of the unstated emotion. The yield is an unaffected and clear-sighted eloquence:

Now and then, a red leaf riding
the slow flow of gray water.
From the bridge, see far into
the woods, now that limbs are bare,
ground thick-littered. See,
along the scarcely gliding stream,
the blanched, diminished, ragged
swamp and woods the sun still
spills into. Stand still, stare
hard into bramble and tangle,
past leaning broken trunks,
sprawled roots exposed. Will
something move?—some vision
come to outline? Yes, there—

The Critic's Work

deep in—a dark bird hangs
in the thicket, stretches a wing.
Reversing his perch, he says one
"Chuck." His shoulder-patch
that should be red looks gray.
This old redwing has decided to
stay, this year, not join the
strenuous migration. Better here,
in the familiar, to fade.

The clean observation, always a feature of Swenson's poetry, is no longer serving strictly aesthetic ends. The images, carried by a steady voice, take their place naturally in a procession that is simultaneously outward and inward. We do not have to be told that the landscape is itself *and* the correlative for the past as it presents itself to memory. The hard-won calm that suffuses the lines could never have been manufactured; the daring of that single "Chuck" certifies that we are in the hands of a genuine poet. I have but one quarrel: that the poem itself belies the final adjuration. Its strength and its grasp of the surrounding world point less to fading than to that singing that comes with the tatters of the mortal dress. Passionate proclamation may yet be in the cards.

May Swenson

Adrienne Rich

A drienne Rich's career as a published poet is now thirty-five years old. This is a straightforward enough statement of fact, but everything about it feels wrong. First, I can't get comfortable with the word "career"—as serious and assertive as her endeavor has been all along, Rich has never appeared interested in tending her place as a poet in the way that many of her peers have. Her poems strike me, increasingly with the passing of years, as bulletins from a front: The real work is being done off the page. Second, the time-frame is somehow deceptive. Rich does not come across as one of the Old Guard, though by rights she should. The work feels fresh, suspicious of certainties and fixed opinions, very much subject to further growth. She has matched the velocity of cultural change with her own inner velocity—it's impossible to cashier her with the badge of distinguished service.

At the same time, however, there *is* something venerable about Rich, and it emerges, perhaps for the first time, in *Your Native Land, Your Life*. Her confident assumption of authority, combined with a significant enlargement of her moral domain, contributes to the impression: She is not just a representative figure, a spokeswoman; she is an exemplar, an active agent in the service of the good. Nor is she oblivious of this:

> Sometimes, gliding at night
> in a plane over New York City
> I have felt like some messenger
> called to enter, called to engage
> this field of light and darkness.

So she writes in her long poem "North American Time." She undercuts her claim in the very next line—"A grandiose idea, born of flying"—but that sense of an important calling is manifest throughout this collection. I find it admirable that Rich can acknowledge frankly her hard-won position as a model and a guide.

For the past few decades, of course, Rich has been revered as an oracle in certain quarters. She has won the passionate partisanship of thousands of feminists, many of whom have been less interested in her poetry as poetry than as a written validation for their own struggles. Her books have been mined for slogans as well as for clues about allegiances, stances, and positions, for Rich herself has traversed the long arc of feminist self-definition. The dutiful, precocious formalist of *A Change of World* became the disaffected questioner of *Snapshots of a Daughter-in-Law,* the radical feminist of *Diving into the Wreck,* and the lesbian separatist of subsequent books. Though always conscious of her emblematic political status, Rich has never lost sight of the claims of her craft. Her movement has been ever in the direction of a freer, more expressive idiom, toward a line that can transmit anger as well as compassion without lapsing into banality. The newest poems show no slackening of control.

The Critic's Work

Rich has always linked the cultural status of women with that of other oppressed groups, but the travails of the former have hitherto been dominant. *Your Native Land, Your Life* brings a shift of emphasis. While her feminist perspective remains unaltered, new subjects emerge to claim her attention. These latest poems look for ways to come to terms with age, physical pain, and the deep issue of racial heritage. For the first time in her poetry, Rich brings herself to face her Jewishness, and in the process she finds that she must come to terms with the ghosts of her father and her former husband. Out of this self-inquisition emerges a wider sense of responsibility. When Rich titled her earlier collection *The Dream of a Common Language,* she meant a language common to all women. In *Your Native Land, Your Life,* I sense an impulse toward a more inclusive human commonality.

The book is divided into three sections. The first, "Sources," is a long suite of twenty-three parts. The sequence looks to answer the question posed early on: *"With whom do you believe your lot is cast?"* The line, incidentally, was first used in "The Spirit of Place," from *A Wild Patience Has Taken Me This Far,* and that poem, in retrospect, appears to be a preliminary step toward the open questioning of her Jewish heritage conducted here. "North American Time," the middle portion of the book, preserves continuity with Rich's writing of the last decade; the nineteen poems, many of them composed in serial chunks, carry on, whether directly or through the mediating personae of other women (Ellen Glasgow, Emily Carr), her search for the roots of responsibility, both personal and social. The last grouping, "Contradictions: Tracking Poems," comprises twenty-nine quick-flash lyrics and adjurations. These, in their sum, give us a sharp glimpse of Rich as artist, lover, and spokeswoman; they also show us, for the first time, her private grappling with the debilitating pains of arthritis.

"Sources" is, to my mind, the weakest part of the book. For one thing, the constant voicing of italicized questions—*"From where does your strength come, you Southern Jew?"*—is distracting and feels self-conscious. The poet is pushing herself, badgering herself, toward a deeper grasp of identity, but from the material presented in the lines we are unable to account for the sudden urgency. Also, Rich's longing does not come across as convincingly spiritual. She writes:

Adrienne Rich

but there is something else: the faith
of those despised and endangered

that they are not merely the sum
of damages done to them:

But while this expresses a kind of religious reasoning, it does not reach
to the emotional core, the heart's yearning *toward* something. Nor does
Rich ever reveal what, beyond continuity, rootedness, the faith may
signify. Surely the racial bond cannot be cleanly extracted from the
surrounding body of belief.

My other reservation about the "Sources" sequence has to do with
the way in which Rich tries to come to terms with her father. Here is
the second paragraph (the addresses to father and husband are given in
prose) of her brief:

> After your death I met you again as the face of patriarchy, could
> name at last precisely the principle you embodied, there was an
> ideology at last which let me dispose of you, identify the suffering
> you caused, hate you righteously as part of a system, the kingdom
> of the fathers. I saw the power and arrogance of the male as your
> true watermark; I did not see beneath it the suffering of the Jew,
> the alien stamp you bore, because you had deliberately arranged
> that it should be invisible to me. It is only now, under a powerful,
> womanly lens, that I can decipher your suffering and deny no part
> of my own.

As valuable as this insight may have been to Rich, I see it more as
an undigested journal entry than as a passage worthy of inclusion in a
cycle of poems. I am not disturbed that it is in prose, but that it *is*
prose. Rich, who generally excels at making public lines out of private
conflicts—who understands at just what point the personal becomes
universal—here fails. She is not so much uncovering a new perception
as revealing the radical insufficiency of a former one. Worse still, she
prides herself ("a powerful, womanly lens") upon having seen the forest for the trees.

Most of the poems in "North American Time" try to discover just
how the self—private and artistic—fits into the larger social order.

The Critic's Work

Rich achieves a credible tension by cross-examining her own actions and motivations. "We move but our words stand," she writes in the title poem, pushing toward a recognition of the accountability of writers before the signs they put to the page. It cannot be otherwise, she finds, for there is no creation that is self-contained:

> Try sitting at a typewriter
> one calm summer evening
> at a table by a window
> in the country, try pretending
> your time does not exist
> that you are simply you

But in "Yom Kippur 1984," she complicates the situation by bringing to collision the imperatives of the artist with those of the Jewish faith:

> Find someone like yourself. Find others.
> Agree you will never desert each other.
> Understand that any rift among you
> means power to those who want to do you in.
> Close to the center, safety; toward the edges, danger.
> But I have a nightmare to tell: I am trying to say
> that to be with my people is my dearest wish
> but that I also love strangers
> that I crave separateness
> I hear myself stuttering these words
> to my worst friends and my best enemies
> who watch for my mistakes in grammar
> my mistakes in love.
> This is the day of atonement; but do my people forgive me?

The contradiction is as old as art. Though Rich gives it no striking new expression here, her appeal to a vision rooted in culture rather than gender makes the poem a milestone in her own search.

Rich's ongoing self-interrogation seems to have pulled her back into an inner battle zone. Indeed, it is almost as if her continued growth as a poet depends on her finding a way to challenge any posi-

---

Adrienne Rich

tion she arrives at. The separatism implicit in her lesbian advocacy is now opposed by a drive toward a more encompassing racial solidarity. The conflict forces her to reassess her responsibilities. The last section of the book ("Contradictions: Tracking Poems") does not come to any resolution, but it clearly suggests the intensity of her inner debate and sets out some of the opposing terms. The second poem, for example, invokes 1980's America:

> Heart of cold   Sex of cold   Intelligence of cold
> My country   wedged fast in history
> stuck in the ice

But when we lift our eyes from these concluding lines and look to the next poem, we find:

> My mouth hovers across your breasts
> in the short grey winter afternoon
> in this bed   we are delicate
> and tough   so hot with joy we amaze ourselves

Public versus private; abstract versus sensual. The larger realm of responsibility cannot be shuttered off by our natural gestures of love, nor will those gestures be curtailed by its presence. How can we irradiate that realm from our narrow privacy? Rich's poetry has always answered thus: by living bravely, by denouncing and combating oppression, no matter how small-scale and local, and by making, as she puts it so beautifully in "Homage to Winter," "the visible world your conscience." Even in these last lyrics, writing out of her acute physical pain, she keeps marking out the vital connection between the individual and the world. Here is Rich at her secular best:

> You who think I find words for everything
> this is enough for now
> cut it short   cut loose from my words
>
> You for whom I write this
> in the night hours when the wrecked cartilage
> sifts around the mystical jointure of the bones
> when the insect of detritus crawls

The Critic's Work

from shoulder to elbow to wristbone
remember: the body's pain and the pain on the streets
are not the same   but you can learn
from the edges that blur   O you who love clear edges
more than anything   watch the edges that blur

Adrienne Rich

Frank
Bidart

—The second part of my ballet
Le Sacre du Printemps
                    is called "THE SACRIFICE."

A young girl, a virgin, is chosen
to die
so that the Spring will return,—

so that her Tribe (free
from *"pity," "introspection," "remorse"*)

out of her blood
can renew itself.

———————

Frank Bidart

The fact that the earth's renewal
requires human blood

is unquestioned; a mystery.
. . . .
The dancer I chose for this role
detested it.

She would have preferred to do
a fandango, with a rose in her teeth . . .

The training she and I shared,—
training in the traditional
                    "academic" dance,—

emphasizes the illusion
                    of *Effortlessness,*
Ease, Smoothness, Equilibrium . . .

When I look into my life,
these are not the qualities
                    I find there.
                    —from "The War of Vaslav Nijinsky"
                    in *The Sacrifice*

Reading Frank Bidart's poems, I react at first a bit the way that dancer reacted to her role: I do not "like" them. They do not make use of the sonorous properties of the English language, they do not incorporate the poetic tradition in any obvious way, they avoid the concentrating power of metaphor, they offer none of the tensing satisfactions of meter, and, finally, they seize and explore only what is most frightening, wounded, and compromised in our souls. Madness, suicide, guilt, the devious choke holds that one will can put on another—these are not things one "likes" to read about. A fandango would be much nicer: effortlessness, ease, smoothness, equilibrium. But alas, like Vaslav Nijinsky, when we look into our lives, these are not the qualities we generally find. Frank Bidart's sharp, unlyrical, excruciatingly forthright work (I almost hesitate to call it

---

The Critic's Work

poetry) assays our defended places. And though I do not "like" it, though it does not give me pleasure, I *am* discomforted, challenged, and moved by it. I respect it as I respect anything that can rouse the inner man from his sleep of habit.

Bidart was born in Bakersfield, California, in 1939. He grew up in California, studied there, and, as he has said, dreamed of making great movies. Then came literary ambition, graduate school at Harvard, the East. ". . . I made myself an Easterner," he reports in the poem "California Plush," "finding it, after all, more like me/than I had let myself hope." In Cambridge, Bidart formed friendships with Robert Lowell and Elizabeth Bishop. (His role as reader/critic/editor of Lowell's later work has been documented in Ian Hamilton's biography *Robert Lowell*.) He has remained in Cambridge; currently he teaches at Wellesley College.

With the first poem in his first book, *Golden State*, Bidart signaled his independence from Bishop and Lowell (one could have done worse than be influenced by either) and embarked on a declarative enterprise that continues through his very latest poems. "Herbert White" begins:

> "When I hit her on the head, it was good,
>
> and then I did it to her a couple of times,—
> but it was funny,—afterwards,
> it was as if somebody else did it . . ."

Most of his distinctive traits are already present: the monologue spoken through the mask of an afflicted character, the explicitly violent subject matter (in other poems the violence is inward, but it is no less explicit), the strangely affectless voice. *Golden State* drew the contour line of Bidart's own state. He would speak, out of others, and out of himself, of the tragedy of unanchored being. This last phrase suggests that there is an existential/religious dimension in the work. Yet it is more than just a dimension, or layer; these concerns are the very pivot of Bidart's poetry. In the poems leading up to *The Sacrifice,* and in this new book especially, the question is repeatedly, implicitly posed: What meaning can we have without connection to something greater than the self?

Frank Bidart

Herbert White, the killer, is unconnected, as is the father Bidart describes in "California Plush," "The Book of Life," and "Golden State":

> You punished Ruth
> when she went to Los Angeles for a weekend, by
> beginning to drink; she would return home
> either to find you in the hospital,
> or in a coma on the floor . . .
>
> The exacerbation
> of this seeming *necessity*
> for connection—;

The father drinks to punish, to lacerate himself, to force guilt, but the "connection" he needs is of another sort. Bidart acknowledges this near the end of "Golden State." Stepping back, speaking with a detachment that his father could not possess, he writes:

> in the awareness, the
> history of our contradictions and violence,
> insofar as I am "moral" at all,
> is the beginning of my moral being.

The "insofar as I am 'moral' at all" is the crucial line, and "insofar" is the key word. Bidart's intent is to locate, through the insistent presentation of "contradictions and violence," this "moral being"—its order and its source. This is the connection that the father drank to find.

With *The Book of the Body,* Bidart moved away from the externalized, anecdotal narrative that he had used in *Golden State* and began to search for an idiom that would articulate both the static and the mobile aspects of inwardness. At the same time, he took on opposition and polarity as his subject matter: the body versus the spirit, assent to life versus refusal. The conception is dualistic, even Manichaean. Matter, the body, the appetites are evil; they affront the spirit and inevitably produce guilt. But Bidart also perceived the inverse dynamic that operates between body and spirit: that hatred of the body is at the same time obsession with it, that the most devout yearning can be expressed through the most extreme bodily fetishism.

The long poem "Ellen West" represents this ambivalence in extreme form. Bidart based the poem upon Ludwig Binswanger's "The Case of Ellen West" a study of a young woman with anorexia nervosa. In the poem, internal monologue is counterpointed with short, clinical progress reports (Ellen West is in the hospital). The terms of the struggle—the fundamental split in her psyche—are set out immediately:

I love sweets,—
          heaven
would be dying on a bed of vanilla ice cream . . .

But my true self
is thin, all profile

and effortless gestures, the sort of blond
elegant girl whose
               body is the image of her soul.

Bidart's interpretation of anorexia, like Binswanger's, is existential: It is a turning of the spirit away from the flesh (an interpretation not shared by all psychologists). Ellen rejects the body, its sexuality, its mortal obligation; she hurls herself toward weightlessness, spiritual freedom, the kind of angelic innocence that she imagines is beyond death. Her contradiction, the embattled other self, expresses its claim through food obsession. Each surge of appetite is also a flaring-up of her sexual being; each willful denial is a scourging of her sinfulness. The result is a parable of sainthood. When Ellen finally poisons herself, the struggle is over. Attached to the hospital report is this observation: "She looked as she had never looked in life—calm and happy and peaceful."

The title poem, "The Book of the Body," expresses a conflict of another sort. Through "YES" and "NO"—the poles of acceptance and denial—Bidart writes of his "terror" at accepting his homosexuality: "The NO which is YES, the YES which is NO." In sharp, telegraphic lines he outlines the stages he passes through before his "reconciliation

Frank Bidart

with the body." This "reconciliation," in Bidart's case, requires the vanquishing of a deeply rooted guilt—about the body, sexuality, unsanctioned sexuality. The poem has a violent, jagged movement: One does not break a taboo calmly.

"The Book of the Body" is painful to read, and I'm not sure that it succeeds. The references to the stages of passage are private, the psychic ground traversed is vast, and the dialectical form of the final acceptance (cited above) is difficult to absorb. The poem does, however, raise important questions. In what ways is Bidart's "terror" connected to the expressions of violence in "Herbert White" or the vicious self-lacerations of Ellen West? Does a rage against the body underlie the thrust of Bidart's metaphysics? Are guilt and violence inextricably linked in the soul's economy?

The Sacrifice, Bidart's newest collection, is very much the successor to *The Book of the Body.* And "Ellen West" and "The War of Vaslav Nijinsky" are the two parts of a hinge. "Nijinsky" transfers the struggle between spirit and flesh to a larger stage; it modulates the more private, existential guilt of Ellen West into the guilt of Western man. In *The Sacrifice,* Bidart finally pushes open the door to the religious. First he presents us with the tormented expiations of Nijinsky; then, in "Confessional" and "The Sacrifice," he conducts fevered meditations on guilt and salvation; finally, in "Genesis 1–2:4," he takes it upon himself to prune and resyncopate the opening passage of the Old Testament. The movement is toward an expanded sense of spirit, but it is nothing like Dante's journey from darkness to pure light. Indeed, though Bidart's frame of reference is explicitly religious, it is not necessarily that of a believer. "Genesis 1–2:4 is not meant as a trumpet call or an announcement of reconciliation. Rather, it is a harsh statement about necessity: For better or worse, the mystery and myth of our creation *ex nihilo* will always be at the core of our collective imagination. We can no more free ourselves from it than we can shake off our dependence on the moral imperatives set out by Christianity.

Like "Ellen West," "The War of Vaslav Nijinsky" is both a narrative and a dramatic monologue. Bidart employs emphatic capital letters—a distinctive feature of his style since *The Book of the Body*—to present the crescendo moments of the inner life of the "mad" dancer;

the alternating sections, given either in the voice of Nijinsky's wife, Romola, or as objective narrative, are unemphasized. These skillful typographical modulations put Nijinsky's bitter soul struggle into relief. The Western Front does not stop at the body's outer perimeters: It is a spiritual war that, for Nijinsky, calls up the ancient impulse to sacrifice. Here Bidart brings together both pagan and Christian conceptions. Nijinsky's *Le Sacre du Printemps* is pre-Christian; Nijinsky himself, conscious of guilt and sin, is a martyr of the Christian stamp:

> I said to myself:
>
> *I must join MY GUILT*
> > *to the WORLD'S GUILT.*

And:

> Then, I said to myself:
>
> > HISTORY *IS* HUMAN NATURE—;
>
> TO SAY *I AM GUILTY*
> > IS TO ACCEPT IMPLICATION
>
> IN THE HUMAN RACE . . ."

And:

> Tomorrow, I will go to Zurich—
> to live in an asylum.
>
> *MY SOUL IS SICK,—*
> > *NOT MY MIND*

Bidart has choreographed the poem masterfully. With every movement the screw is tightened: Nijinsky's self-interrogations grow shriller, his plaints more manic. At last he snaps—evil is more durable than the mind. The most celebrated dancer in the world ends up on all fours in an asylum in Zurich. "Let this be the Body/through which the War has passed." So he had asked in his extremity, and so it was granted.

Bidart does not argue, as lesser poet might, that Nijinsky's madness was, in fact, sanity. No, the dancer *was* mad. The point is that his

---

Frank Bidart

madness was consistently spiritual. Bidart, though, is questioning the spiritual impulse itself—might *it* not be a kind of madness? But then, supposing it were, would we not have to say that madness is ethically superior to sanity? This is the essence of Bidart's procedure: He peels away the layers of received response until all is contradiction. Nijinsky is both hero and madman; his martyrdom is both insanity and the purest, most valorous act of soul; his ruin was inevitable *and* it was freely chosen.

"Nijinsky" epitomizes the Bidart style. The lines are broken and staggered on the page, but not according to any "poetic" principle. They are arranged to transmit as precisely as possible the pauses and stresses of the declarative voice. This is where Bidart parts company with most poetic norms: The "speaking" is of paramount importance. Everything is sacrificed to its imperatives. There is no metric or stanzaic underpinning—the lines are arranged and controlled to serve the movement of the voice. Spacing, line breaks, punctuation, and typography are all-important. To dispense so completely with the poet's arsenal is to walk a tightrope. Where there is no structure, where all is voice, a single false note can undermine the reader's trust. Bidart's poems come to hold the beat and nuance of the inner voice.

"Confessional" is, as the title suggests, a poem of self-excoriation. The conceit itself—that these are words spoken to a priest—violates the sacrament: We read with voyeuristic absorption Bidart's dissection of his relationship with his mother. He has found a remarkable counter-narrative in Saint Augustine's *Confessions* (the poem's title thus has a double resonance), for Augustine's reconciliation with his mother is a paradigm of spirituality:

> As Augustine and Monica stood leaning at that
> window in Ostia, contemplating
>
> what the saints' possession of God is like,
>
> they moved past and reviewed
> (Augustine tells us)
>
>   each level of created things,—

Monica has won her once-wayward son back to the Church. Secure that his soul has been saved, she falls into a fever and dies. "My mother," writes Bidart, "JUST DIED."

"Confessional" is a harrowing poem. As in "Nijinsky," guilt is at the core; only Bidart's guilt is nothing so grand, or "mad," as a guilt for humanity—it is the most private, self-bound thing:

> and then he found
>
> that what had made his life
> possible, what he had found so deeply INSIDE HIM,
>
> had its hands around his neck,
>   strangling him—
>
> and that therefore, if he were
> to survive,
>
> he must in turn strangle, murder,
> *kill it* inside him . . .

TO SURVIVE, I HAD TO KILL HER INSIDE ME.

This is the universal separation process that Bidart is anatomizing. What makes the poem so remarkable is the poet's determination to track the guilt to its deepest rooting place, to find its connection to his moral being.

Nietzsche proposed the "superman" who would be free of the burden of guilt: To live without a conception of morality was the imperative that followed from the death of God. Bidart works in the opposite direction. He looks into his heart and discovers guilt. Guilt, in turn, implies a moral nature, and a moral nature presupposes some foundation. Of course, Bidart is not psychologically naïve. He knows that the guilt may be generated by the Freudian superego, that the religious dimension is not logically necessary. But at a certain pitch of affliction, logical truths are not sufficient; suffering must bring its appeal to a higher court. I am not saying that Bidart has turned to God. But he has found in the religious tradition a framework that will accommodate his urgent questioning. Whether that tradition is valid or archaic is beside

---

Frank Bidart

the point—it stands for the need that is at the psyche's core. I cannot read "Genesis 1–2:4" as ironic, artful, or blasphemous. I see it as a most serious homage, if not to God then to the lost and fearful beings that had to make Him:

In the beginning God made HEAVEN and EARTH.

The earth without form was waste.

DARKNESS was the face of the deep.
His spirit was the wind brooding over the waters.

John
Ashbery

John Ashbery's *Selected Poems:* that forlorn codex, garden of branching paths, termite tree of the late Millennium . . . The assignment was to *review* it, and I find I cannot. To review is to have read and to be looking back. I have read *at,* toward, near, but never with that cinching tug of understanding. I have moved my eyes and felt the slow dispersion of my sense of self. I have been flung back into the boredom and rage of childhood, when the whole world seemed to rear up against me, not to be had or understood. I find no sequence, no way of seriously discussing the poems as poems. I can only report on the defensive reflexes that their insistent refusal of meaning triggers in me.

John Ashbery

Ashbery cannot be approached as an isolated phenomenon, sui generis, though most critics do exactly this. For better or worse, the work is part of a broader cultural tendency; it belongs with that groundswell opposition against the hierarchies of reason and determinate meaning known as deconstruction. While Ashbery practices no critical jujitsu himself, he is one of the brethren by temperament. I will explain.

Deconstruction is but the latest development in a process that began early in our century with the linguistic theories of Ferdinand de Saussure, and which continued (mainly in France) in the movements of structuralism and semiotics. Deconstruction has taken Saussure's premises to a radical extreme. Its thrust, as I understand it, is to demolish the deeply rooted conceptions of the Enlightenment, presumably so that the culture can evolve in new directions. Deconstruction itself offers no signposts for this evolution, only a method for taking things apart. In this, deconstructionists are like members of a terrorist sect.

Saussure instigated a revolution in linguistics with his idea of "difference." Briefly, he asserted that words (signs) do not signify by virtue of any relation to a referent, that they do so solely because of their differentiation from other words. Any combination of sounds can mean anything, so long as it is distinct from other combinations. In essence, Saussure divided the closed order of signs from the world.

Deconstructionist thought goes even further. Where Saussure held that the sign is made up of two elements, the signifier (word) and the signified (its meaning), deconstructionists insist that there is no demonstrable connection between the two, that we can never get past the signifier to find the pure signified. Look up any word in the dictionary—you will not find meanings, only other words. What this leads to is the assertion that meanings are imprecise and unstable, fluid entities that dissolve and coagulate along the so-called chain of signifiers. The deconstructionist operation is to unmask any discourse that pretends to clarity and stability. The favored method is to turn logic against itself, to pulverize the ruling assumptions by showing that they rest upon uncertain foundations.

Ashbery is not, as I said, a deconstructionist. His poetry has nothing to do with this cross fire of logic. Rather, it moves in the wake of the demolition. Ashbery's lines are what we find after the clear crystal of meaning has been shattered. Many readers, I suspect, fail to understand this and misread him. They treat the poems as if they were playfully obscure, but nonetheless part of the project of meaning. No. Ashbery makes a practice of *seeming* to mean while *not meaning*. In the process, he is able to capture many of the sensations that are part of the register of contemporary sensibility. The collapse of meaning in his poetry resonates beautifully with our intuition of larger social collapse. This is obviously an enormous subject and I cannot explore it here. Suffice it to say that sensation, not meaning, is what the poetry is all about.

Ashbery partisans are forever telling me that I lean too hard on that old business of cut-and-dried meaning, that I need to accept that there are innumerable other ways in which language signifies and intimates. That I should, in other words, loosen up and let the poem work its way with me. I do have a problem with this. For me, verbal reference and linguistic structure are fundamental elements in the rule system of a game called meaning. It is a game—I see that—but by my lights it's the only game in town. I can respond to Dada and surrealism, but only so long as they are an excitement at the edge of a larger system of coherence. The fact that I link Ashbery with the deconstructionists, that I see him as temperamentally favoring their pernicious undertaking, forces me to take his procedure seriously. If this makes me a wet blanket, so be it.

Ashbery's poetry is at war with grammatical logic and referential meaning. It sets out to mime—indeed, intensify—that condition of confused unknowing which language evolved to remove us from. Maybe this is why so much of it simulates in me the all-but-forgotten feelings of early childhood—then, too, the world overran whatever feeble structures I had devised for myself. The poetry is, according to this formulation, tautological to the core: It uses language, by definition an ordering system, to shake the reader loose from order. Ashbery can evoke profound sensation, but the profundity is that of confused emotion and drifting boundaries characteristic of the prelinguistic psyche.

John Ashbery

Ashbery joins the deconstructionists in believing that linguistic propositions give a false and consoling impression of order, that they organize and whitewash what is essentially flux and foster the illusion of understandability. We string words into sentences and imagine that we have thereby ordered our lives. The poetry tilts at every moment against that illusionistic impulse. It makes use of our grammatical and semantic expectations—much as the deconstructionists make use of logic—in order to overturn them, to disclose what Ashbery holds to be a larger truth: that we are unanchored, psychically dispersed among a welter of stray sensation and unattainable signification. By staying short of meaning, the poetry becomes, implicitly, a poetry of yearning. Of melancholy.

> There is that sound like the wind
> Forgetting in the branches that means something
> Nobody can translate.

These opening lines of "Summer" are a good example of the procedure. They read as though they ought to mean; they activate the salivary glands of logical expectancy. We believe that if we work at them long enough, the sense will spring loose. But it never does. Break it down: The *sound* (like that of wind forgetting in the branches) means something (that) nobody can translate. The opacity has been very carefully engineered. First, that the sound means something that nobody can translate implies, logically, that meanings can be translated, carried over. They cannot. Meanings are the entities that translation serves; words are translated so that meaning can pass between languages.

Second, the sound is said to be *like* that of wind *forgetting* in the branches. The transitive verb "forget" has been used as an intransitive. Wind, the fundamentally insubstantial movement of air, has been personified as a consciousness that can forget, that has something *to* forget. This is, undeniably, poetic: Forgetting *is* a losing, a leaving behind. An essential perception about wind has been registered. But the promise of revelation that it carries keeps us moving back and forth among the lines—combining them—longer than is warranted. Shuttling back and forth, avid to *get,* we find ourselves driven like squirrels on a wheel—for the nonsensical premise, neither proposition nor metaphor, ensures that we will never come to rest at sense.

Try another:

The concept is interesting: to see, as though reflected
In streaming windowpanes, the look of others through
Their own eyes.

—from "Wet Casements"

Here we have not only the logical disjunction—"to see" is not a "concept"—but also the slippery setup of a comparison that asks us to imagine a *look* reflected in streaming windowpanes. This is somewhat easier to parse, for we know that a look is registered on a face and that a face can be reflected. But even with this clarification, a logical problem arises. Intended, of course. A look is something that A may give or—if we think of it as appearance itself: "his new look"—manifest, but that only B can see. These lines are finally asking us to imagine A seeing with his own eyes the expression that those eyes are giving out—the effect is Möbius-like.

If the unattainable ideal of linguistic communication is a one-to-one ratio between grammatical structure and semantic content, then Ashbery's approach is to tinker with that ratio until it reaches the point at which communication looks possible but is not. The kind of slippage that I have shown as working within the sentence can also be made to work *between* sentences or lines. That is, each individual unit can be said to make, or approximate, sense, but the discourse (poem) itself, governed by semantic, not grammatical, logic, is elusive. Consider the complete poem "We Hesitate":

The days to come are a watershed.
You have to improve your portrait of God
To make it plain. It is on the list,
You and your bodies are on the line.

The new past now unfurls like a great somber hope
Above the treeline, like a giant's hand
Placed tentatively on the hurrying clouds.
The basins come to be full and complex

John Ashbery

But it is not enough. Concern and embarrassment
Grow rank. Once they have come home there is no cursing.
Fires disturb the evening. No one can hear the story.
Or sometimes people just forget

Like a child. It took me months
To get that discipline banned, and what is the use,
To ban that. You remain a sane, yet sophisticated, person:
Rooted in twilight, dreaming, a piece of traffic.

I could go over this a hundred times and it would mean nothing more than it does on a first reading. The suggestion of sequence, of a narrative, quickens the semantic desire; the lines resolutely refuse to deliver. We find out neither how the days to come are a watershed, nor what the portrait of God has to do with anything. The two uses of "it" in the third line divide, rather than consolidate, possibility. What "line" the bodies are on is never specified, or even suggested. The whole is a slap—and to my mind a not too friendly slap—at the reader. Nor is there any point in invoking the surrealist example. This has nothing to do with surrealism. The latter is based upon the transcription of spontaneously recovered, alogical unconscious materials; this is a calibrated verbal contraption.

Ashbery has a fat magician's bag of devices and tricks, all of which he uses to mock and undermine determinate meaning. It would be no trouble at all to work up an Ashbery "kit," a how-to manual for would-be epigones. Let me list a few of the components and methods:

1. Use the definite article with nouns, "the," not "a." This conveys the impression that there is a clear context behind the poem, even if no one but the poet knows what that context is. The reader believes that if the other side exists, it can be reached; he keeps trying.
2. Use vague and inclusive pronouns—"we," "you," "it"—mixing or "shifting" them frequently. This technique effectively breaks down identity lines, creates the sense that we're all just parts of some large, unbounded consciousness.
3. Construct an indeterminate time-frame. Make something un-

specified just have happened or be about to happen. Useful words: "later," "before," "soon," "always," "then" . . .

4. Import the unexpected, jarring word every so often—a word from another language or discourse. This keeps the reader from ever settling in, reminds him that language worlds are constantly impinging upon each other. Also: unexpected spurts of playful colloquialism—"O gosh!"—and obvious clichés.

5. Refer knowingly to some place or event, but make sure never to mention it again. The reader needs to realize that the world is always out there, material and inexplicable, and that things just happen. This works well with No. 1.

6. Confer concrete properties upon abstract or nonexistent entities: "a picture of treason" or "your portrait of God."

7. Finish poems with elusive, important-sounding statements. They should feel like closure. ("In his book there was a picture of treason only/And in the garden, cries and colors.")

8. Repeat procedures from book to book.

As talk-show hosts are wont to say after doing their best to humiliate an audience member: "But hey, folks, this is all just good fun, right?" Well, only in part. I find that the bulk of Ashbery's poetry is formulaic, and that the dross/beauty ratio is weighted dramatically on the side of the dross. Poems like "We Hesitate" far outnumber the gems upon which the reputation has been founded.

But what about those gems? I have said nothing about the instances—lines, passages, whole poems—where Ashbery makes beauty. They certainly exist. The three lines about the wind that I cited earlier, for instance. Though they finally escape the reader, are they not tonally marvelous, themselves the wind? They weave a spell, enlarge our sense of mystery. And the same kind of thing happens again and again in the poems (though often as an isolated passage in an otherwise incomprehensible setting). We feel a blurring of bounds, a subjective liberation from the constraints of order. Nor, to be sure, can we help but project our own intimations and desires onto certain lines.

Listen to the closing section of "As One Put Drunk into the Packet Boat" and you'll see what I mean:

John Ashbery

The night sheen takes over. A moon of cistercian pallor
Has climbed to the center of heaven, installed,
Finally involved with the business of darkness.
A sigh heaves from all the small things on earth,
The books, the papers, the old garters and union-suit buttons
Kept in a white cardboard box somewhere, and all the lower
Versions of cities flattened under the equalizing night.
The summer demands and takes away too much,
But night, the reserved, the reticent, gives more than it takes.

This, I think, is as good as Ashbery gets. While the lines cannot be corralled into meaning, they do nudge the sensibility toward contemplation. They make a music that feels like significance. We can enjoy the word-sounds, and the tranquil, almost weary rhythm. The "moon of cistercian pallor" delights, as does Ashbery's use of words like "installed" and "business"—the recontextualizing works to freshen the language. Alas, this passage is more the exception than the rule. More often than not, the reader gets the non sequitur, the portentous and obviously contrived proclamation; he experiences over and over the frustrations of narrative interruptus.

The cliché among Ashbery exegetes is that the poems reproduce the "logic"—or flow—of dreams, that they bathe us in an effluvium of primary sensation. And truly, when a poem does work, we are sent paddling into a Heraclitean flux, a dark Heideggerian "Being" wherein we can never lodge, but only recognize ourselves as en route *toward*. However playful the work may at times appear, it is implicitly frightening, for—as in Heideggerian philosophy—that *toward* is always *toward death*. The gathering surge of confusion breaks only there, if it breaks at all.

I won't deny that Ashbery's poetry at times has this effect, or that when it does it affects me deeply. Nor will I pretend that there are no uses or pleasures in a poetry that mimics the dispersal of meaning that I feel all too often as an inescapable part of the contemporary condition. But I cannot on this account turn from another, more philosophic concern. Simply: that this is an enterprise that repudiates sense and mocks our faith in the sufficiency of our language structures. It turns against the word in its attempt to uncover the undistilled feelings and sensations that are behind it. In a sense, Ashbery's poetry works backward along the evolutionary spiral, undoing. Granted, this might be necessary. Maybe it's true that, as creatures of meaning, we are at a historical dead end, unable to see past the regress of our rational constructions. Ashbery is staking himself on a wager. If another way exists, then demolition might be in order, and his work will be seen as a pioneering move in that direction. But if there is not another way, if we have made for ourselves the best, the only, tool, then the poetry will prove to have been a dead end—interesting, at times beguiling, ultimately nihilistic.

John Ashbery

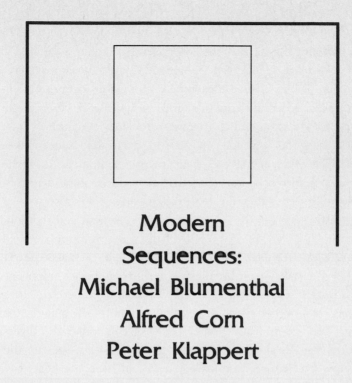

Modern
Sequences:
Michael Blumenthal
Alfred Corn
Peter Klappert

M. L. Rosenthal and Sally M. Gall have expended considerable effort to advance a claim that the long sequence is the central poetic form of our time. One need not be a haruspex to know that their text will be slow moving and redundant; a quick parse of the title—*The Modern Poetic Sequence: The Genius of Modern Poetry*—will suffice.

The sequence, as the authors tell us at the outset, is different from both the long poem and the linked series ("a group of poems related to one another by their tonal range, or by a shared context, or by the repeated use of the same verse forms"); it organizes disparate lyrical energies around a single affective center. But as Rosenthal and Gall declare without debate that the long narrative is not a suitable vehicle for the sensibility of our times—indeed, they cite approvingly Poe's dictum that a long poem is "merely a succession of brief ones"—and as the linked series and the sequence are not *that* categorically different, there is nothing much to contend about. The authors have only to work their way through a clutch of exemplary sequences—from Whitman to Adrienne Rich—and prove that their strategies and effects are ultimately unitary and that they do in some way reflect an expansive urge. This they do. Alas, much patient demonstration is leavened by little surprise; the reader nods in agreement and then nods off.

To establish that the key works of the modern canon are sequences is, in my view, to subtract something from their particular power. It is to impose the dullest and broadest generic resemblance upon poems as anarchically various as *Song of Myself, The Cantos, The Bridge, Life Studies,* and *Crow.* Is not the work in every case more sui generis than *like* anything else? Poets from Homer on have celebrated the diversity of the world over its similitudes—new taxonomies are the last thing we need. How much more stimulating it would have been for Rosenthal and Gall to question seriously why the long poem can no longer serve the needs of modern sensibility or to assess the impact of changed collective experience upon poetic form. Their study tells us nothing at all about modern sensibility, yet they assume it throughout. "These sequences," they write, "have been written in the spirit of our changed world. . . ." Since the 1920's "the outstanding poets writing in English have used the sequence to accommodate the complexities and passions of contemporary experience." What *is* the "spirit of our changed world"? As for "the complexities and passions of contemporary experience," I am at a loss. Yes, I agree that the world is different than it was, but I want to know why Rosenthal and Gall think so. I especially want to understand how the myriad shifts have impinged upon the sphere of poetry.

A living criticism (or scholarship) must locate poetry in the world and must dare to draw connections. The preeminence of the sequence cannot be argued without some rigorous discussion of the larger determining forces of culture. These are, of course, inchoate and diffuse. But no one ever said that the interpreter's job was easy. Rosenthal and

The Critic's Work

Gall have attempted to evade difficulty. Reading their book, one falls under the sway of the old illusion and begins to believe that poetry is a province unto itself, an order closed to the order of human circumstance. The authors, to take just one example, repeatedly commend the loose, relativistic arrangements of the sequence; they refer to its dynamic equilibrium. Not once, however, do they mention the ideas of relativism current in the sciences or historiography of our times. Nor, for that matter, is there any reference to the shattering of the picture plane in the visual arts, or the subversion of the melodic line carried out by Schoenberg and others. We get no sense at all of poetry as an event among events, a developing art bound to a changing culture. The deeper implications of sequential composition have not been taken up. Our guides find it too easy to go on about "progression[s] of specific qualities" and "intensities of emotionally and sensuously charged awareness." *The Modern Poetic Sequence* is an expensively appointed dreadnought.

Poets write at length, in sequence and otherwise, for any number of reasons: to do justice to the scale of a subject (Pound's vision of history), to achieve expressive effects denied to the shorter lyric (Eliot's explorations of musical recurrence in *Four Quartets*), for larger cognitive reach (Olson's archeologies in *The Maximus Poems*), or to encompass material that is in itself sequential (Lowell's and Berryman's graphing of successive states of the psyche in time; Merrill's tracing of his Ouija board experiences). Doubtless they have other motivations, too, that derive from the particular demands of expression. But as I survey the pile of recently published book-length works before me—most of them by younger poets—I have to wonder whether there might not be other factors involved as well. In almost no case did the artistic ends warrant the length. Either the talent would not stretch to support the conception, or else the conception was a cobbled-together pretext for something else. So my reasoning went. And that something else? I confess that I thought first of the A word and the E word. If anything disfigures the natural life of poetry in our times it's Ambition and Egotism.

I don't believe that most of these young poets are writing large sequences because they have great themes, important cognitive designs, or zeal for new expression. No, more likely they are trying to declare their importance to the world in terms that the world understands. Marginal to the life of our culture, isolated from spheres of power, these poets cynically declare—*contra* Mies Van Der Rohe—that more is more. This is both understandable and excusable—psychologically. Unfortunately, even as permissive a mode as the sequence must argue its necessity. The reader will tolerate more slackness and discursiveness than he would in a shorter lyric, but he expects to be rewarded in some commensurately large way for his tolerance. I would like to examine in this light three sequences by highly touted younger poets— Michael Blumenthal's *Laps,* Alfred Corn's *Notes from a Child of Paradise* (which is, strictly speaking, a narrative), and Peter Klappert's *The Idiot Princess of the Last Dynasty.* The hazards of foliation are evident in each; only *The Idiot Princess* could be said to surmount them.

In his first two collections, *Sympathetic Magic* and *Days We Would Rather Know,* Michael Blumenthal established himself as an imaginative, if inconsistent, lyricist. From the start there was evidence of a divisive tendency, toward a demotic humoresque on the one hand:

> The reward for good work is more work,
> she says when it's over, placing
> your head like a pat of butter between
>
> her breasts, the reward for good work is
> a kind of fatigue and desolation like arriving
> at the end of a long hike to find
>
> blood in your shoes, amnesia clotting
> your memory for names   oh darling
> it was good and I am full of you
> > —from "Fatigue Is Its Own Reward"

and an insufficiently tempered mawkishness on the other:

> Holding your eyes
> in your fingertips,

The Critic's Work

touching
to see me,
insisting
that the mind's eye lay in the heart,
that the world's one dimension was darkness,
that touch was the light,
sense the window.

And now still
your lesson:

Only those who will touch can see me,
Only those who can't see will listen. . . .

Only the blind reach out to find me.

—from "Johanna"

Blumenthal's talents clearly favored wryness and detachment; they could not support much naked emotion. But the poet seemed very much to want it both ways, to be idiosyncratic *and* romantically serious, conventional and surreal—we sensed the determination to span a wide subjective range.

This determination—which at times resembles indecisiveness—is very much evident in *Laps,* Blumenthal's sequence about a half-mile swim. If short lyrics are like affairs, then sequences are like marriages—shortcomings and faults cannot be concealed for long. Contrary impulses are as conspicuous in *Laps* as they were in the earlier books. But where Blumenthal could make a mosaic of his divergent tendencies in the latter, the sequence lays its constraints of unity down. Warring energies must either find synthesis or else determine a structure that will accommodate them. Nothing of the kind happens in *Laps*—it is a well-intentioned failure.

I say "well-intentioned" because it is very clear what Blumenthal is after. He would like his poem to attain a fluidity that would represent consciousness itself, where the most oblique or witty observations could dilate naturally into larger pronouncements—something like what Joyce achieved in *Ulysses.* He would compose a music that could demolish contradictions by revealing them to be different aspects of a single substance—the psyche. And what better way to express and celebrate these modulations than in a long fluid poem? The ambition is admirable. Blumenthal, however, cannot get the desired music onto the page; his various inner voices refuse to organize themselves around an affective center. I agree with Rosenthal and Gall that the sequence cannot find coherence otherwise.

Blumenthal begins with a prologue in which he invokes the Greek philosopher Aristippus, "whose chief tenet," the footnote explains, "was the primacy of pleasure as a source of moral good." The lead-in beguiles us with a witty sort of doggerel:

> Oh sacred father of desire,
> who found duty good, but pleasure higher,
> might I, a moral Jew, be blessed
> to find the key of life here, half undressed?

We heed the promise of the witty, throwaway deprecations—it's not Alexander Pope, but it might be fun.

Turning to the first section, however—and here we glimpse the design: Each of the thirty-two sections represents a length of the pool*—we are jarred by the following:

> Tired of everything I know,
> I turn to what I do not know,
> hoping to find where I am, hoping
> to find where I must go.

I hear Eliot and Gertrude Stein harmonizing. Is *Laps* going to be a parody-pastiche? The confusion is not speedily resolved. A few lines down we find:

> *What does it mean to be in pain?*
> No more than that the rain is rain,
> and flood flood. Deep we are, and deep
> is where we have to go. As seed goes deep.
> As rain goes deep to bring forth the flower.

---

*Two corrections. First, a half mile equals thirty-six, not thirty-two, *lengths* of the pool. Second, a lap equals two lengths—Blumenthal repeatedly uses "lap" to mean length.

The Critic's Work

The sense is knotty. Is Blumenthal actually saying that pain can be nothing more than an event in the natural order, a kind of weather? Is he jettisoning the possibilities of moral transcendence? The tonal shift—swerve—is troubling as well. The archness of the prologue is still quick in the ear. The poet's several strains are already pulling us in different directions.

The remaining thirty-one lengths/sections do not provide a satisfactory resolution. Increasingly we are persuaded that Blumenthal views the swimming pool as a vast receptacle, a volume somehow equivalent to the world—the world as it is present in consciousness, that is—and that the speaker's progress back and forth is actually meant to suggest a pilgrimage from station to station. Further, we sense that the liquid element and the automatic repetitions are supposed to spring that speaker from the responsibilities of consecutive thought or orchestrated performance. What we have, finally, is a psychic impressionism that does not resolve into clarity, no matter how many backward steps the mind takes.

The best way to illustrate this bewildering heterogeneity is by taking a few sample "dips":

And what a strange thing too
the body: an envelope
of flesh and necessity,
a loose coincidence
of orifice and appendage,
the soul's wet suit,
the mind's a capella
accompaniment, the one note
so often out of tune
in the Vienna Boys' Choir
of the soul.

—from 3

How Prussian of me,
I now realize,
to make of this act

of pure movement
and loss of thought
an act of thinking. Jung
would call me
a *thinking type,* which
implies that feeling
is my *inferior function.*

But Oh hell
what a feeling
of pleasure
these wet and baptismal
thoughts bring

—from 14

A misanthropic ardor
rises as I flip to find
a truant in my lane:
a *jeune* nymphotic *fille* in red
who uddles forward
toward my outstretched arms
and makes me think,
at first, of: *bed.*

—from 16

Ecco: "the soul's wet suit," Jung, the "uddling" of a "*jeune* nymphotic *fille*" . . . The phrase from the first citation—"a loose coincidence"— prophesies the rest of the poem's tone. What aesthetic permits phrases like "an act of thinking. Jung" or "implies that feeling" to stand as lines? Where is necessity? I find a most serious misalliance here between ends and means, contents and form. It is possible, I'm sure, to write a long sequence that would capture something of the psyche's diversity—but not by following this procedure. Turns in a pool cannot serve as a structural base for a meditation on consciousness and identity. There is nothing inherently significant about the progress—it begins, it has a terminus, and that's all. The swimmer may find that emblematic—how like life, and so on—but only a Beckett would

---

The Critic's Work

know how to turn the obvious back on itself so as to release both the absurdity of the action and the profundity of absurdity. In Blumenthal's treatment we cannot get around the feeling that the poet finds this an ingenious subject. Worse still, we suspect that the thirty-two sections were filled up like so many sausage skins. It can be argued, of course, that Dante, too, wrote to fill out a numerical scheme. But in his work the numerology was close-fitted to spiritual design, and what turns he made were along a vertical axis.

Poor Dante. If he were to repeat his anguished descent again and pass through these parts on the way, he would have to add a circle to his great design to house his imitators. For what greater sin could there be against the noble art he so prized than its travesty? Where Blumenthal's ambitions can at least be seen as having an artistic goal—he wants to sing of variousness—Alfred Corn, in *Notes from a Child of Paradise,* is up to nothing larger than self-celebration. However, not only is his persona bereft of the least charm or interest, but his larger plan—to assimilate his tale to Dante's—is so presumptuous that it tests the reader's credulity. If ours is the culture of narcissism, Corn is one of its many prophets. The only way through this book is by forced march.

If the word "paradise" in the title did not tip one off, or the apportionment of the narrative into ninety-nine sections, the second stanza of the first—canto?—would clinch the matter:

> At the desk again, a curling snapshot
> Of you, leaning against the spine of my
> Old Grandgent *Commedia* makes me want
> To dub under it the laughter-silvered
> Tones that just now firmed up plans to visit . . .

Notes from a Child of Paradise undertakes to tell the story of a love—the shy inception, the binding of souls in matrimony, the dissolution—against a backdrop of *Zeitgeist.* The callow Alfred meets Anne:

> a young woman—tawny
> Silk-straight, Beatnik-style hair free-flowing far

Modern Sequences

Down the back; wrapped in a Bogart trenchcoat;
A Camel in the left hand, Gore Vidal's
Julian in the fine right; brown eyes well up
To Provençal standard (say Peire Vidal's)—

in Europe in 1964 during a year of study abroad. He lets us know by the third canto that his previous *amour* had been a tease—and a *he;* the seed of our doubts about the new romance is planted—but to Anne he says: "Somehow you didn't see *me* in that light."

Gradually, clumsily, the relationship begins. Corn rehearses the remembered ambience of those times in glib, jaunty lines. Of their studies, for example, he writes:

Doctrinal variants on Western Civ:
Marxism-Leninism, "l'art pour l'art";
A faith in Jung or Christian Science, naive
Materialism—Pope was right, to err
Et cetera. If some would charge, say, Scève
With lifting Dante's old New Style, a mere
Pointed mention of Guinizelli, of,
Well, Virgil, Plato, Homer (overkill)
Should clear him.

Is it too soon to call attention to the Merrill pastiche—the flip, in-the-know and of-the-happy-few tonality? (Merrill tells us on the back of the book that "a pot of gold lies in store for each reader.") The giddy self-absorption cloys instantly. Just imagine a real human being—someone, say, who works for a living—coming upon these lines:

I did detect, though, some reluctance on
Your part to join your . . . friend. His name was Norm?
No, Bert. Malicious rhymes were roiling in
My brain. "You'll write? American Express
In Florence." "Oh, Al, sure I will. What fun!
You're off to Florence, aren't you lucky!" *(Kiss)*
Then, told your four-week jaunt in—*Germany?*—
Was courtesy his Yamaha, I guess
I blanched or something.

The Critic's Work

Well . . .

I don't know how much point there is in following through in any detail the joys and sorrows of Alfred and Anne. Perhaps it's enough to say that they end up living together in New York, furnishing a palatial apartment; studying, writing; they separate, come together again, get married. . . . For half of the second book, (*Purgatorio?*) they are in Paris, lingering at the fringes of demonstrations. But no matter where they are, we are subjected to quips and bulletins about their friends in Berkeley or the Village, or the latest developments in the counter-culture (for this is the late sixties, and Corn takes it upon himself to make sense of the experience of a generation):

Changes: they argued of and for themselves, as
Hemlines soared to write another chapter
In the red book of hotline revelations,
Airwaves spinning with the London latest
That fans in pea-jackets shook their mare's nest
Curls to, then dropped, to play a California
Riff on new guitars from some oldtime
Blues or country tune.

The times are nowhere assessed for their significance; every observation is served up in caption-ese, as though Corn had gone back to old issues of *Time* magazine to jog his memory.

And Alfred? Anne? They are not even a generic couple of the times. The psychic and emotional complexities of a relationship are undetectable. I would wager that more of interest transpires between two deep-sea sponges. "Telling our story is . . . painful as anything/I've ever done . . ." writes Corn. But *why*? Search as I may, I can find nothing more in these pages than an itinerary of moods and movements. The lens may be finely polished, but there is nothing on the other side to look at. A list of pretensions does not add up to a personality.

The third book opens as Alfred and Anne return from Europe. Tireless travelers that they are, they are soon off on a cross-country trek to the Northwest. Desperate to confer unity and scope upon their passage, Corn hits upon a disastrous device. He interleaves their wanderings with bits of narrative about the Lewis and Clark expedition, carrying the parallel along to the parting of Clark and the resourceful Sacajawea. As Alfred and Anne realize that they can no longer remain together (we have no more idea about why they're separating than we did about why they got together in the first place), so, in the same neck of the woods, the white explorer takes leave of his guide:

> She sees them turn and go, preceded by their long
> Sunset shadows; pause at the top of a hill
> And then turn to wave, turn, and then sink out of sight. . . .

> (The ties of myth and memory connect them still,
> Strong as cable, invisible as *caritas,*
> This three-figured emblem outside history.)

The linkup is made in the very next canto:

> Then, having struggled to say the right farewells,
> And not long after seen you snapped up by someone else
> (Your new Victor, whom I judged suitable, as you did

> My new Walter)

How interesting this all might have been had Corn taken the complexities of sexual identity as his subject. Alas, no. The return to former proclivities is treated episodically; mysteries of sexuality remain unplumbed.

We are almost through. There remains just the final cadenza, the unfurling of the celestial rose. For this is, after all, rigged to *The Divine Comedy;* apotheosis is a sine qua non:

> Now an antiphon with instruments of silence
> Notes all things that are made in heaven, petal

> And star, perpetual salutation inscribed
> In the soaring of the eagle, radiance of this temple
> Of fire crowning the young watergold domain,

> Inception here at journey's end, the former sunset
> Land restored to light, where all build in common
> Ecstasy a city raised up in trees and flowers.

The Critic's Work

This storm of fire, these rainbow tears that make
You stammer, this sweetness intricate through every limb
Witness now what will not be written nor ever said:

. . . .
. . . .
. . . .

Appended to so many pages of banal reportage, this Dantean cadenza falls flat. We cannot accept this modulation as a part of Corn's natural register; nor, indeed, has the ground been prepared in any way for a vision of sweetness and reconciliation. The effect is ultimately the reverse of what was intended. We are not so much moved as reminded of all the posturing that went before. We understand that we have been staring at an elaborate cartouche: much scrollwork, nothing at the center.

Peter Klappert's *The Idiot Princess of the Last Dynasty* is the eccentric guest at this table. Indeed, it is so unlikely a work that it requires some preliminary explanation. In Klappert's own words:

> These are the imaginary monologues of "'Doc' Dan Mahoney," speaking in Paris in 1939 and 1940. Daniel Mahoney has had at least three previous incarnations: as the vulgar and queeny title character in Robert McAlmon's story "Miss Knight," as "Dr. Matthew O'Connor (Family Physician to the Ryders)" in Djuna Barnes' first novel, *Ryder,* and as the more arch, flamboyant, and declaratory "Dr. Matthew-Mighty-grain-of-salt-Dante O'Connor" in Miss Barnes' celebrated *Nightwood.*

There are conflicting stories about the flesh-and-blood Mahoney, but from a composite of recollections emerges the image of a brilliant, dissolute homosexual savant, a habitué of low-life Parisian dives during the period between World War I and the German occupation. The link between Klappert's Mahoney and Djuna Barnes's Dr. O'Connor will be obvious to anyone who has read *Nightwood.* Because of this—so the story goes—*The Idiot Princess* could not be published so long as

Miss Barnes was alive; the fine points of the case are unknown to me. At any rate, Djuna Barnes has died, and Dan Mahoney's monologues are now out. They constitute the strangest poetic sequence in recent years.

The Idiot Princess is, at first—and second, and third—sight, a maniacal assemblage. The sections are linked insofar as they are all monologues spoken by Mahoney (in varying stages of intoxication), but there are few filaments of narrative; auditors and settings shift according to the principle of the kaleidoscope. What's more, the contents of Mahoney's mutterings and jeremiads are often personal, local, or have direct, unexplained reference to historical and political situations that few readers will know. (I prepared by reading *Nightwood* and Herbert Lottman's *The Left Bank,* a fascinating documentary history of the period in question, but a majority of these references escaped me nonetheless.) The monologues, writes Klappert in his preface, "assume an audience in a café which is familiar with French history and with political events between 1919 and 1940. . . . But even that audience would miss some of Mahoney's references. Such is his manner, such the angularity of his mind, the pace of his conversation."

Here is something taken quite at random from one of the early monologues:

The King of the Belgians

journeyed all the way to Paris
to hear a man with an aspirating anus
toot out airs. And Le Pétomane could snuff a dip
at half a meter—not the last Pierrot
to "pay no author's royalties."

Indeed, why *not*

a few lies of Paradise?
Because these are the only lies that are never believed.
Saint Artemius.

Saint Febronia! In Byzantium

the battles are not fought in the arena,
they are fought among the lookers-on.

This?

The Critic's Work

I call this number
   Caught on the Teeth of Time, or *Life*
Torn Full Circle.
                   Ammonia.

Spikenard, ginger, siphium—and pepper. And goodnight.

Many people will not know who, or what, Le Pétomane is, what "snuffing a dip" is—is it done differently at a meter's distance?—or identify Saints Artemius and Febronia. And why would the latter merit an exclamation?

Still, there is something thrilling about the very opacity of the passage—we heed the rhythmic glide, the witty way in which the sibilance of line 3 is cut (so to speak) by "toot," the sudden shift from near absurdity to the frank declaration of the italicized line. Rabelais and Villon stand in the wings. I would argue, further, that the absence of clear sense unsheathes the sound values—and that this is Klappert's intent. For the early sections are far more obscure in this way than the later ones. It's as if the poet wanted us to limber the tympana, to listen to the work first as a modern chamber piece and only later to grasp it as a lament.

We begin, then, by accepting certain terms: that the speaker is a drunk with an overfurnished mind and that not everything that he says will be clear to us, that what intelligibility there is will be more serial than sequential in its expressions, that words will be used as much for their sounds as for their designatory value. In exchange, we soon realize, we will be treated to a Stravinskian whirl of rhythm and tone. We are the more delighted when we start coming upon passages knit by sense:

                The rest?
We'll keep going, thinking no more than a drone
or a worker with some place to go
and get back from.
                Until one day comes
a snag in the back or a tight
rim around the chest when you inhale, or your eyes

Modern Sequences

cloud up and you say, "Sinuses."
But truly it's the lacuna in your life, the pock
at the center of that gaze
you construct night after night in a glass.
And while you water yourself with drops
and butter your cheeks with creams, the hole
in your face grows larger and you feel
perhaps you've missed it, whatever it was,
and it's gone clear on through.

Mahoney's monologues draw us in increasingly as we read. We get accustomed to his drunkard's transitions, the sudden jumps from trivial observation to impassioned apostrophe, as well as to his posturings; he is, by turns, sorrowful, catty, perverse, outraged, penitent . . . We catch on, too, to the premise of the book—that this anomalous individual, drunk or not, feels in his soul the tremors from the future. He is very close at points to being the Old Testament Daniel that Klappert evokes in the later sections: He sees the outlines of catastrophe, not just in Hitler, but in the smug anti-Semitism of the French, in the faces of young fascist thugs roaming the streets of the city. He senses all about him the eroding of the will to resist; he can anticipate the double-dealer and the collaborationist. The squalor and wretchedness of the alleys and *boîtes* are for Mahoney the outward emblems of a morally bankrupt civilization. Once we grasp this, the sequential sense of the monologues comes to matter much less than the emotional import of his words. His outpourings come from every part of the soul's register:

My little lisper, cher ami,
had you thought our days were tallied
in rational ciphers? Or that you alone
were guyed up to horses and stretched
to the four extremities? The aspic
of congealed death-do-us-part, the flat
aluminum horizon of memorization,
L'Afrique off to the south full of hot mirages,
and that jawbone of a cow called Land's End

The Critic's Work

where a deaf-mute combs the shingle.
                    —from "Does Daniel Believe in Order?"

            Be discreet
and circumspect with him, when his eyes
grow wide on opera, when he elliptically
enjoys a retinal spasm or in abstraction
doodles severed heads,
when he eats bonbons, pralines, dragées, Torte, Toffee,
Zuckerwerk und Kuchen,
but fails to purge his gloom.

Poverty clasped him to her breast,
Dame Sorrow was his foster mother.
Ayez-en soin. Seien Sie vorsichtig.
Faites attention. See how he cleans his mouth
at the quarter hour, how he lives
in fear of horses, microbes, moonlight, his own
flatulence and body odor.
                    Il faut être très prudent:
that man will never humble himself to drink on his knee.

His oratory wilts his collar.
His being stiffens in a stream of speech.
His jugular grows turgid like a hose.
                        He goes mute
in panic, sucks his little finger, whistles "The Big Bad Wolf."
                    —from "Adolphe, or the Sad Young Man"

        When the mistral sends all awnings flapping
and an impatient sea rolls over—jade, cobalt suddenly
gone obsidian under the chop—just there,
just then you'll hear the pre-dawn milk-train
counting cobbles up le boulevard Saint-Michel,
see all of the hours of the world unwinding
round the *New York Herald*'s clocks, and sense
grey bats, the risen ghosts of church mice,

skimming among the unsounding, violet towers.

    "——Is there yet small verdure
      on the market tables?"

        "——Immortelles
        in Pere-Lachaise?"

                "——Are there bayonets,
black pins, parading on the bridges, a black gear
        grinding above the Senate?"

              "Offizieren at the Closerie?"

In the aurora borealis of exhaustion

    "——Is there a dome of fever under the famished skull?"
"Is there life, up there, on Earth, in Paris?"
              —from "Daniel's Other Love Song"

No quilt of snipped bits can give an accurate sense of the modulations of Mahoney's despair. The effects are cumulative and orchestral. Consonantal vituperations are set against vowel-heavy lamentations; vulgar argot bleeds together with unaffected tenderness. Mahoney is a French-speaking American Irishman, and Klappert has taken full advantage of the linguistic possibilities. James Joyce (*Finnegans Wake* was published in 1939) is never out of earshot.

The book is, finally, a drunkard's fever dream. Mahoney's ruined synapses fire as they will. He brings the glass to his lips to steady himself. Everything in the world connects; everything, therefore, is doomed. This drinker drinks because he cannot bear the world. He cannot bear the world because it is unbearable. *In vino veritas.* Klappert insists that Mahoney is as much a visionary as he is a toper. To his last section he appends an epigraph from the Old Testament book of Daniel: "And he said, Go thy way, Daniel." Clearly it is in his prophetic capacity that he sees the coming of apocalypse.

For all of its strangeness—because of it!—*The Idiot Princess* succeeds. Klappert has taken on a most daring and difficult conceit in order to hurl new tonal possibilities our way. English-language poetry has been so dispirited in recent years, dividing its estate between the ever more aerated constructions of the formalists and the solipsistic exhalations of the free-verse opposition. Klappert has vaulted right over the controversy—his eccentricity renders the terms of the debate irrelevant to his book. I expect that *The Idiot Princess* will have a liberating effect on younger poets. It points the way back to an adventurous use of sound and proves that there *are* new possibilities of arrangement. The opacities may be troublesome, but they may also, as I suggested, open the way to a purer hearing. Not the least of Klappert's accomplishments is to have stripped some of the soil away from the rich Gallic seam of our language. If the poet's job is to invigorate the speech of the tribe, then here is a poet who is earning his keep.

Modern Sequences

Derek Walcott

O n October 17, 1983, in one of the more unlikely cere-
monial moments in the world of poetry, Derek Wal-
cott mounted the high pulpit in New York's Cathedral Church of St.
John the Divine to read his "Eulogy for W. H. Auden." The event was
part of a week-long commemoration of the tenth anniversary of Auden's death. What could have been a greater study in contrasts—a
powerfully knit black poet from the Caribbean declaiming lines to
honor the whey-faced and rumpled don of English-language letters?
And what could have been more appropriate? If poets are, by definition, suitors of the Muse, then these two have been, in our age, among

her special favorites. They have perceived more than others that she is a woman with a past.

Walcott has been writing poetry for some four decades now. He apprenticed himself to the English tradition and has never strayed far from the declamatory lyrical line. His mentors, the voices that one hears running as a weft through his lines, include the Elizabethans and Jacobeans, Wordsworth, Tennyson, Yeats, Hardy, and Robert Lowell (who himself sought to incorporate that tradition into his work). Reverberating against this diction one hears the local influences, the dialect phrases and constructions of the Caribbean. The whole heritage is there, but it is quickened and jazzed—and entirely unique.

In the crisis-ridden decades of the 1950's and 1960's, when poets took up various cudgels—for free verse, projectivism, Beat prosody, confessionalism, a return to American roots, and so on—Walcott's work was little heeded. He was always to one side of the current excitement. But power and craft like his could not be kept off the stage forever, any more than poetry could keep going without its central sustenance: metric structure. In the last ten years, as the productions of our tenured poets have proved increasingly feeble and enervated, Walcott has moved forward to claim his rightful place. *The Star-Apple Kingdom* and *The Fortunate Traveller* were both major collections. The poet had found a way to fuse the diction of his masters with his own energetic and sensuous idiom. Now in *Midsummer,* with all the grace and gall of a writer at his prime, he has essayed the most hazardous of ventures.

Midsummer is a fifty-four-poem sequence that was written over the course of two summers in Trinidad. We don't need a calculator to figure out that's about a poem every other day—and these are solid seventeen- to thirty-line compositions. Poets have been known to compose at such a rate—think of Byron, Neruda, Berryman, or Lowell in his *Notebooks* period—but it is hardly common practice. The risks are so obvious: repetition, slackness, the stretching of material. But Walcott has taken them on for a shot at the rewards—velocity, immediacy, and freshness. And he has upped the ante by avoiding dramatic progression or continuity of subject. These are the meditations of a middle-aged prodigal son, nothing more. The intent is evident. By taking away drama, subject, and any sort of finishing varnish, Walcott is forcing the full weight of scrutiny onto the lines. The poetry has nothing to hide behind—no tricks, no feints. It's an all-or-nothing gamble, and it succeeds.

Poetry in recent years has become more and more bound up with the magazine industry. A poet puts out twenty or thirty separate "pieces" and then collects them into a book. The ancient tribal song has been groomed and pomaded until it looks like a whisper. *Midsummer,* ragged-edged and robust, is anything but a magazine book. Its lines are like the links of a chain saw moving through the broad trunk of a life. We are to look at the cloven bole, its rings, whorls, and irregularities. Connections and links have not been engineered—they are implicit and organic. If there are chips and splinters, so be it. Walcott would have it no other way. Here is his own metaphor:

> My palms have been sliced by the twine
> of the craft I have pulled at for more than forty years.
> My Ionia is the smell of burnt grass, the scorched handle
> of a cistern in August squeaking to rusty islands;
> the lines I love have all their knots left in.
>
> —from XXV

Midsummer: boredom, stasis, the harsh afternoon glare of self-assessment. Midsummer equals midcareer, middle age, Dante's *"mezzo del cammin di nostra vita. . . ."* The only real narrative prop that we have for any of these numbered poems is given in the first. The poet, comfortably identified with the "I" of the speaking voice, is returning by air to his old island home. The plane descends over "pages of earth . . . canefields set in stanzas," and as the wheels touch the tarmac he exclaims:

> It comes too fast, this shelving sense of home—
> canes rushing the wing, a fence; a world that still stands as
> the trundling tires keep shaking and shaking the heart.

Walcott has the Ovidian gift; his compressions, associations, and transformations appear effortless. So, in this poem, the jet is likened to a silverfish that "bores . . . through volumes of cloud," clouds are

---

Derek Walcott

linked to the coral shapes below, and both become "pages in a damp culture that come apart." As the clouds part to reveal the island, while the jet's shadow ripples over the jungle "as steadily as a minnow," Walcott suddenly wrenches open the frame to apostrophize a fellow poet:

> Our sunlight is shared by Rome
> and your white paper, Joseph. Here, as everywhere else,
> it is the same age. In cities, in settlements of mud,
> light has never had epochs.

But two lines later he is back, noting "steeples so tiny you couldn't hear their bells." Space and time are like baker's dough to this man; he kneads, stretches, and punches them as he sees fit. Nor is he afraid to hook a thought to its prompting detail, however unlikely the connection. His faith in the elasticity of the metered line is complete.

The poems that follow are no less various in their internal composition. Though mainly grounded in the Caribbean, and attentive to local detail, they are as diverse as Walcott's own nature. There are passages of intense expressionistic observation:

> Monotonous lurid bushes
> brush the damp clouds with ideograms of buzzards
> over the Chinese groceries.
>
> —from VI

side by side with solemn brooding:

> I can sense it coming from far, too, Maman, the tide
> since day has passed its turn
>
> —from XV

and sudden celebratory surges:

> Midsummer bursts
> out of its body, and its poems come unwarranted,
> as when, hearing what sounds like rain, we startle a place
> where a waterfall crashes down rocks. Abounding grace!
>
> —from VIII

The Critic's Work

The range is restricted only by the circumstances of compressed composition and the psyche's inevitable recurrences.

The visual is one strong component in Walcott's work. He has a painter's eye for shape and color value and a strong sense of proportion. Descriptive elements in the poem are arranged as if words and their sounds were equivalent to pigments:

> Gnats drill little holes around a saw-toothed cactus,
> a furnace has curled the knives of the oleander,
> and a branch of the logwood blurs with wild characters.
> A stone house waits on the steps. Its white porch blazes.

—from XXV

This structure and detail-oriented instinct can be said to represent Walcott's objective pole. But the subjective counterpart is there in equal portion. Sharply etched descriptions give way to dark surges, upright consonants lean over like palms in a storm. At times Walcott will flash back and forth between the two poles; at other times he will force them into fusion. These are his supreme moments—when he modulates into passionate declaration:

> O Christ, my craft and the long time it is taking!
> Sometimes the flash is seen, and a sudden exultation
> of lightning fixing earth in its place; the asphalt's skin
> smells freshly of childhood in the drying rain.
> Then I believe that it is still possible, the happiness
> of truth . . .

—from XIII

If nothing is rarer in poetry than this note, it is because nothing is riskier. Full-throated ease is something our culture has unlearned.

It is impossible, of course, to give a fair account of a cycle like this. Walcott is trying to fix, in sharp, living lines, the particular texture of his inner life during the course of two summers. The ambition carries certain hazards in its train. A certain monotony, for one thing. Reading the undifferentiated stanzas from start to finish can be like wandering around in a rain forest. There is something almost vegetal in the pro-

Derek Walcott

liferation of Walcott's lines. How can anyone produce so many naturally flexed hexameters so quickly?

Walcott is not, of course, blind to the repetitious nature of his project—he wants it to be that way. He tests the constraints of subject that seem to inhere in metric verse, but he does so from within. Like Cézanne, who painted hill after hill because hills were not what he was interested in, Walcott writes poem after poem with little differentiation of subject. His settings and descriptions are, in a sense, pretexts. He would like to throw out as much as possible in order to clear a path to his real subject: language becoming poetry.

Poetry, like speech, is a complex connivance of sound and sense. The lyrical ideal is a condition in which the two are seamlessly joined. Or, better yet, a condition in which it becomes clear that sound is a kind of sense, and vice versa. For as sense is proper to the mind, so sound is to the heart. And the heart, as great lyric poets have always known, is the tribunal before which reason lays its spoils. "To betray philosophy," writes Walcott, "is the gentle treason / of poets. . . ." He is reducing, or eliminating as much as possible, the ostensible subject of the poem, so that the plaiting movement of sound and sense can show itself. This is not an evasion of subject so much as a deeper perception of the poet's function.

Walcott is reestablishing the sound, the music, as a connection to felt and perceived experience. When he writes:

> The oak inns creak in their joints as light declines
> from the ale-colored skies of Warwickshire.
> Autumn has blown the froth from the foaming orchards,
> so white-haired regulars draw chairs nearer the grate
> to spit on logs that crackle into leaves of fire.
>
> —from XXXVI

he is promoting the status of sound as meaning and is arguing against the notion that meaning is some kind of detachable content. The treason of poets is to believe that sonorousness and rhythmic emphasis establish a body circuit through experience that reason alone cannot achieve.

The Critic's Work

Walcott writes a strongly accented, densely packed line that seldom slackens and yet never loses conversational intimacy. He works in form, but he is not formal. His agitated phonetic surfaces can at times recall Lowell's, but the two are quite different. In Lowell, one feels the torque of mind; in Walcott, the senses predominate. And Walcott's lines ring with a spontaneity that Lowell's often lack:

> White sanderlings race the withdrawing surf to pick,
> with wink-quick stabs, shellfish between the pebbles.
>
> —from XLVIII

There is not a single forced emphasis. The lines are at once mimetic—the "withdrawing surf" is perfectly offset by the "wink-quick" beaks—and perfectly natural.

Though Walcott is very much aware of the assaults that modernism has waged upon the metric line, he has elected to work with its possibilities. In part this is a matter of temperament. But there is also the matter of the poet's unique relation to the English language. He acquired in the Caribbean an English very different from that spoken by his counterparts in England and America. Not only is the region a linguistic seedbed, with every kind of pidgin and dialect, but successive waves of colonization (and oppression) have left phenocrysts of all descriptions. As Walcott said in a recent interview in *The Threepenny Review:*

> . . . it's very hard for people to understand my love of the Jacobean—it's not from a distance. If you hear a guy from Barbados, or Jamaica, speaking English, and you listen to that speech, you hear seventeenth-century constructions. I once heard in *Henry V* a soldier speaking in a Yorkshire dialect and it sounded like pure Barbadian speech.

Walcott's traditional metric is more than a simple act of homage to the past—it is the most expeditious way for him to organize his complex linguistic heritage. Controlled by a firm structure, each element of that heritage can declare itself. And the various distinctions, as anyone in the third world can testify, are not just historical; they are political as well:

Derek Walcott

for so much here is the Empire envied and hated
that whether one chooses to say *"venthes"* or *"ven-ces"*
involves the class struggle as well.

—from XLIII

There is no one writing in English at present who can join power
with delicacy the way Walcott can. He is the outsider, the poet from
the periphery, but it may be time to center the compass at his position
and draw the circle again.

Melissa Green/ Patricia Storace

Several years ago, when their debut books were still manuscripts looking to grow, Melissa Green and Patricia Storace read together at a celebration for *The Agni Review*. I was in the audience, prepared to like, nod, applaud, smile at, congratulate—not at all prepared to feel the envious, uncomfortable, exultant sensations that come when work does what it's supposed to: when it hurts and connects and makes you want to hear more. Both young women got to me in just that way. And yet what a difference between them! Green unrolling her bolts of melody, the burled textile of her long eclogue, calling up our New England landscape in its every fit particular. Storace, by contrast, pivoting dextrously from mode to mode, from pointed, wry musings to sharpened (maybe even dangerous) invective. Pastoral meditations on memory and loss in one voice, acetylene scriptures on faithless love in another. There was no choosing between them, nor should there be. And now that the books are here, one can set them side by side on the shelf as if to say, "Both."

The Squanicook Eclogues by Melissa Green is a rara avis, a first book that bears none of the customary feather markings of that species. There is nothing erratic, imitative, or lopsided about the work. Whatever influence her teacher Derek Walcott may have exerted upon her style or her way of staging material has dissolved past immediate recognition. Green is entirely her own poet; she is not to be mistaken for anyone else.

The power of her art is rendered all the more conspicuous by her refusal of pyrotechnics—her idiom is unapologetically traditional—and by the static, in many ways unfashionable nature of her subject matter. The title poem, for instance, is a long descriptive pastoral composed in twenty linked sections. "Last Year's Snow" and "The Attic Bird," the two long poems that follow it, present stages in the life of a man and a woman, respectively, through carefully conceived tableaux. Green's imagination is deeply, almost completely preoccupied by the flora of her native Massachusetts and by the details of a vanished mode of twentieth-century life. With a firm grip on seen particulars, she builds up her vision of the hazards—and the inevitability—of human isolation. In this one respect she resembles Robert Frost.

Green achieves her effects through painstaking art and a vigorous verbal imagination. As we learn from her fourth, and final, poem, "The Housewright's Mercy," the poet has a very nearly mystical feeling about *making* ("The hipped roof. Elegant. The downspout, turned/where fascia boards and soffits met. The weight/of stories borne by joists and summer beams"). Her own edifices are exquisitely carpentered. The lines are rhythmically disciplined tetra-, penta-, and hexameters. Her end rhymes are precise and ingenious. One 19-line section—I choose almost at random—plays off the following pairs: seize/size, color/collar, fret/fruit, guard/gourd's/God's. Green's artful finish extends to lovely consonances and assonances, as well as to the ceaseless tightening of expression through internal rhyme.

This love of the challenges of technique is matched by her faith in the beauty and rightness of our naming words. Confucius, who believed that all the ills of the body politic could be traced back to careless usage, would have appointed Green to an important civic post. Listen to a short section from "Thanksgiving 1908," part of the "Attic Bird" sequence:

> A kitten's caterwaul
> astonished her under the nail kegs. Each
> implement in its gloomy niche
> was forged for use—a goose-wing broadax
>
> and lathing hatchet, barrel staves
> hooped on a peg, an Ashley stove's
> six-lidded top and damper starved
>
> for polish near a pomace rake,
> upended in a broken hayrack.
> A mud wasp's nest in firebrick
>
> festooned with harnesses that coiled
> like snakes. Old snaths and sickles, scaled
> by spiders, crowned a toothless scroll
>
> saw, and where a fallen cleaving froe
> had ploughed a mound of grain, a farrow
> of spotted piglets scratched the furrow.

At this level of precision, naming almost reaches back to the origins of *poiesis*. (As Emerson wrote in "The Poet": "Every word was once a poem.") This passage is an etymological feast. The "caterwaul" reactivates the Middle English *cater,* for "tomcat"; "pomace" harks back to the Latin *pomum,* for "fruit"; and the "froe" turns out to be an early Americanism, a special use of the now archaic "froward." We get not just a catalogue of implements but an implicit inventory of uses. Lines like these tell us more about farm life in the early twentieth century than could pages of historical description.

Melissa Green/Patricia Storace

But even with all these strengths, the poetry would not come alive, would not manifest such absolute distinctiveness, did Green not also command that most uncommon amalgamating power: insight. Behind its beautifully wrought surface, Green's work is a perpetual discerning of the movement of spirit within an arena of matter. Her mission, from first to last, is to track this fugitive element and measure the momentum of its surges.

Nowhere is this more evident than in the long title sequence. "The Squanicook Eclogues" unfolds in four groupings of five sections each. These are titled by month—April, August, October, and January—and each includes two poems superscribed "from the sketchbook," two "from the notebook," and a closing celebration of one of the four fundamental elements: water, fire, earth, and air.

Dramatically speaking, little happens. The speaker/poet and her father—to whom the poem is dedicated—choose on Sundays "the iconography of trees/Instead of church." Their seasonal walks, during which father teaches daughter piety before the beauties of nature—the notebooks and sketchbooks reflect her efforts at close observation—culminate in his illness and presumed death in the final January passages.

> *He paused, then reached into his pocket for a pen.*
> *Don't ever make things up. Write only what you see.*
> *Name the woods and you'll have named the world,* he said.
> He tore some pages off and handed me his pad.
> I heard the current crimp, mimetic, on the pond,
> And larch or beech or birds murmuring over me. The task
> Was how to write *birch* when I saw the crumbling, pale tusk
> Of a fallen mastodon bridging the path, or *ash,* when the air
> Was frenzied with the head of a neighbor's rain-black mare.
> Sycamore waved at me like drowned Ophelia's hair.

Compressed in this passage is the whole logic of Green's sequence. The child takes from the father a faith in creation. Though his injunction wars with her natural tendency to see all things in an exuberantly associative manner, she curbs her impulses and learns to look at things as they are. Having imparted a faith and a technique (a kind of "reality

---

The Critic's Work

principle"), the father leaves the child. She takes what she has learned and fashions a memorial for him. This memorial is all the more powerful for restricting itself to the hard work of *'Nam[ing] the woods."*

Green's organization of the sequence is straightforward and unobtrusive. The independent sections, almost bare of narrative exposition, become panels in a seasonal book of hours. The life of the poem is found in line after line of exaltingly accurate perception.

Green assembles a wide range of observational perspectives, which vary from the open and panoramic evocation of the opening lines:

> After a blustery, fretful March, the fields have yawned,
> Tossing off their goosedown coverlets to thaw.
> In airing upstairs farmhouse rooms, the sunlight paints
> A sudden gold-leaf on the dresser drawers and wall.

to the kind of close-focus scrutiny found in this later notebook passage:

> The shadblow shivers like a shaved corsage, bronze
> And apricot powder dusting every palsied leaf.
> A spinster of chicory fearfully clasps a lilac stalk
> With virginal fringe, guarding her single-day's bloom.

Both citations show a seeing eye that is at every instant engaged, rendering the surroundings with the utmost precision and at the same time enacting the metaphoric transformations whereby we bind ourselves to what is Other. If the linguistic resources are those of a mature poet, the perceptions themselves retain all of the freshness and intensity of the child's first stirred sightings.

Green reaches her apotheosis in this poem in the closing "element" sections. These allow her to lift her absorbed gaze from the flora around her and to conjure a larger connectedness. Here, complete, is "Water":

> Father, I'm drowsy in April's humming sun and think
> A girl the color of autumn kneels at the Squanicook's bank,
> Who is the river's daughter, dressed in driven skins,
> Who knows a cedar wind at Nissequassick brings
> The schools of alewife, herring, yellow perch ashore.

Melissa Green/Patricia Storace

The Place of Salmon roars with light. She steps, sure-
Footed onto stone; lithe as poplar, bends over
The water. Wren feathers, shells, seven quills quiver
In her sable hair. Her eyes, a spring-fed stream,
Like silica, seek bottom. Deep in her mossy brain,
The white-tailed mouse is born. She carries in her supple
Body all of spring—a tree frog in the apple,
A kit fox dozing in the brush, a brash otter
Diving her river-veins—the new, young, utterly
Green morning beads her skin. How simply she leans
Into understanding, baptized by light and the delicate lines
Of shadow from cedar. A goldfinch has flown its ribbed nest,
Dusting her cheek with its wing, a hummingbird throbs in her
    wrist,
She's drenched in waking. Wonder, a long-legged doe,
Drinks in deeply, as all instinctive creatures do,
And laughs, leaping the current, printing the fields with dew.

The lyricism is generous and unstrained, but Green never once
hands herself over to rhetoric. The passage is, of course, an homage to
Keats, to the spirit he apostrophizes in "To Autumn." But while Green
appropriates the conception, she works the imagery into a distinctively
North American evocation. The girl—the imagined deity of the
place—has been fashioned, at least in the opening, as an Indian princess. Described in her skins and ornaments, she emerges with vibrant
immediacy from the natural setting. Mention of Squanicook and Nisse-
quassick affirms the immemorial potency of place names; the innocence
of perception is implicitly linked to the mythos of the uncorrupted
native cultures.

But then, quite boldly, Green alters the outline of her imagining.
Drawing directly upon Keats's "And sometime like a gleaner thou dost
keep/Steady thy laden head across a brook," she uses the mediating
element of water to turn the Indian maiden into an all-pervading and
all-encompassing spirit. The girl bends over, sees herself, and in that
moment of transparency, the change is effected. From this follow images of containment. The mouse, the tree frog, the kit fox, and the

---

The Critic's Work

otter are presented as being *inside* this "river's daughter." But Green is not done—still further transformations ensue. The goldfinch is described as "Dusting her cheek with its wing"—restoring a sense of the deity's finite, and human, outlines. Finally, Wonder, given the animate form of a doe, drinks in deeply and bounds away. Drinks *her* in deeply? It's hard to say. Logic breaks down here. But as we have accepted an Ovidian porosity of boundaries by this point, we are not disturbed. To the contrary, the image of the doe leaping the current and printing the fields with dew is one of pure liberation.

The Squanicook Eclogues contains, in addition, three other lengthy poems in sections. "Last Year's Snow," which manages in three panels to unfold the childhood, marriage, and death of a man, showcases Green's ability to compress significant action in maximally suggestive ways. I cannot possibly do justice to the braided complexity of the entire sequence, but let me try to sketch its motion along the track of its dominant image, that of snow.

The first section, "Child's Play," begins with the imaginings of a young boy at play. One of his treasured toys, we learn, is

> a hefty paperweight,
> a globed duck's egg, which seemed to hold
> the essence of winter; snow, a sleigh,
> the steady changeless motion of its perfect sphere.

Green then moves us inside the soul of the dreamy child, describing through his eyes the life within that miniature world, following his fantasy as it becomes a scenario of adventurous escape. He clutches the flowing mane of the horse and tries to ride beyond the demarcated boundaries of home. But he cannot get away, even in dreams. The inhibiting reins of home, as well as a sudden sense of the inevitability of death, pull him back:

> But his mother would be crying in the lyre-back
> chair beside the banjo clock, her bracelets
> wrangling on the tambour sewing table,
> his father roaring into his decanter.
> Something flew in his eye, a grain, a seed.

Melissa Green/Patricia Storace

He knew he could never ride ahead of the snow.
It would track him down.

A deft depiction of a child's first intimations of mortality. The domestic image draws upon Robert Lowell's family portraits, a recognition that Green acknowledges with a deliberately Lowellesque diction and phraseology ("her bracelets/wrangling" and "his father roaring into his decanter").

Section II, "The Bridegroom," begins with a grown man awakening on his wedding day. The imagery of the opening lines looks forward to his eventual ruin by drink:

His wedding morning woke him.
Fog hung over the shoulder of the coast,
a crony's sleeve, its headland nursing the tide
like a stevedore his stout.

There follows, much as in the first section, a kind of blurring out into fantasy. Anticipating the day, the man pictures the wedding cake and, more specifically, the miniature figures planted on the icing. Among them is a small Christmas sleigh. His reverie then moves into a long cadenza. He is whisking his bride away over the snow:

This time, they'll follow the fluted road,
and cross the chaste horizon,
a stream of wrought hexagons
under their bright-runnered sleigh.
Beyond the curve of seneschal firs,
a frosted cottage waits in winter air,
a granite step soon to be swept of powder
and the petals of his boutonniere.

But now the snow and winter take on a more ominous undertone. Ensconced in his dream cottage, alone with his bride, he recognizes his own insufficiency—the cold invulnerability of his (and maybe his bride's) heart:

His skin surrendered where she kissed him,
his breath came out in plumes, frost etching
its intricate signature on his glass heart.

The Critic's Work

"Armistice," the final section, brings us to the bedside of the dying man. He is delirious, confused. He descries the nun at the foot of his bed as one of the Pleiades "who stepped down to earth/to bathe his face in snow." In fact, he is being asperged:

He wanted to sit up, to explain how the labors
of love had burdened him, and bad luck
dogged his every move, but light
was blizzarding about her face,
she was lifting away years of failure,
an adamant shroud.

Green now makes a last encompassing move. She identifies the man with his historical epoch. He is "the child whose cradle rocked/when Argonne's candelabrum flared," and his death falls (literally?) upon the anniversary of the Armistice. In the closing lines of the poem, his child steps forward to pronounce an *in memoriam*:

Requiescat, father. Day is done.
The Squanicook unlocks its jaws at last—
a peeling rowboat buoyed on the failing current
turns to commemorate the Armistice.
A sprinkling of bleached petals flakes
from the widow's hand at the oarlocks,
they ride the shallows under a stone bridge
where the shadows of seven soldiers site
November's opaque sky, and fire,
snow and shards of ice falling
for days across the shaken globe.

Innocence and experience collide, as do the smallest and largest scales of perception, in this play with literal and figurative meanings in the image of "the shaken globe."

"The Attic Bird," a long sequence picking up stages in a woman's life, is less successful. Again, Green aims for a larger resonance, this time by choosing important public days for her points of reference. Thus, the poem begins with a section entitled "New Year's Day 1986," and continues on with "Easter 1900," "Labor Day 1905," and so on.

From materials found in the attic of the old woman, the narrator reconstructs her story—her girlhood, young love, the early death of her husband in World War I, and the subsequent withering of her heart. Though the local beauties are many and various, the sequence is not as compelling as its predecessors. There is something too pat, perhaps, about Green's decision to write a poem that is at once the story of a life *and* the story of an age. The "Labor Day 1905" section, for instance, modulates from a tranquil evocation of setting:

> Edwardian simplicity,
> that summer's wickerwork settee,
> a gazebo under willow trees
>
> where hours droned in leisurely flux,
> the century's mill wheel winnowing flecks
> of mica from gold—a time transfixed
>
> by its reflection in a pool.

to a concluding reminder of contrasting historical context:

> It is a temporary peace,
> this picnic gotten for a price
> by Knights of Labor and police,
>
> from fireworks and men that boast
> their stones' and nightsticks' volley burst
> above the scabs' and strikers' breasts.

Green's determination to be all-inclusive draws her away from the real psychological material that should be at the core of such a poem. The reader wants less enumerative description and more penetration, especially since in the closing section of the poem we are to grasp the woman's devastated soul.

The final section of "The Attic Bird" is marred by obscurity. The closing stanzas reveal that the woman has borne a son, and that that son will in time engender "a grandchild who could rhyme/and fist her fury's fiercely hoarded blade." The poet is, in effect, closing the circle, bringing back the narrator, who, as in "Last Year's Snow," will put a

---

The Critic's Work

shape on the foregoing material and shape it into a legacy for herself. But Green's last stanza mystifies me completely.

To begin with, she describes herself, without giving sufficient background, as somehow imprisoned by this old, embittered woman: "I thrash exhausted at the bars and lose/my voice, the world dissolving in this cell." Then follows her conclusion:

> I've done with legacies, all striped by welts
> of war, and dare myself to die, infirm
> and greedy as my kin, when in my eyes
> there rises up a slender, laughing form,
> and suddenly my resolution wilts—
> my lover, Wilfred Owen, threads the maze,
> death's honor guard, lieutenant to the Muse,
> who'll bend me down in our consonantal waltz,
> and take me down to dinner on his arm.

I'm confused not by the *sense* of the passage, but by its placement and intent; that after ten long sections devoted to the life of this woman, the poet should put herself so conspicuously forward. The entwined desires for death and creation, emblemized in the figure of Wilfred Owen, do not seem to have their origin in the preceding narrative. The poet has not established for herself a persona capable of such pronouncement. A private dream, or perhaps another poem, has intruded itself.

But this weakness scarcely undermines the performance as a whole. *The Squanicook Eclogues* is stamped in every line with decisive singularity. Green has obviously found her idiom not by looking outward but by mining herself. She has already attained the authority of necessity. These are lasting poems, honorable additions to the small hoard of timelessly contemporary poetry.

Midway through "Spring Afternoon," the first poem in Patricia Storace's *Heredity,* we meet with these arresting and disturbing lines:

> I pass shops offering whips, spiked collars, devices
> I don't need; to rack my neck requires

Melissa Green/Patricia Storace

implements no sharper than a pair of lips,
and for bondage, simple genitalia suffice.

So much of what is distinctive about Storace's vision of human relationships is openly exposed here. Her charged, violent metaphors sing
the call note of the Catullian *odi et amo,* a note sustained throughout
this provocative volume.

It is risky, of course, to read a group of poems as if they were
leaves from the poet's autobiography. But some poets—and Storace is
one of them—project an emotional volatility that forces the reader to
reckon with its source. Though we may not be sure about the circumstances of the poet herself, we cannot help pondering the identity and
psychic makeup of the speaker. Indeed, certain connections and hypotheses are hard to avoid.

To put it simply: At the core of this book is a consistently iterated
legend of failed love. Men and women are locked into patterns of
treachery and betrayal; they are fiercely carnal, appetitive. But they
cannot, virtually without exception, give of themselves in selfless or
trusting ways. There is bondage, but no bonding. And this deep, irre-
solvable failure manifests itself in descriptions of suggested or explicit
violence.

In "La Valse," for instance, Storace depicts the "helpless" dance
partners who "hurtle on

while the spectators applaud
the risk that makes the sport so good,
the chance that love with a ballistic force
might throw the missile-couple off its course
while the fuselage of music melts
and the two careen past tenderness
beyond the gravity of hate
flash past the blur of other lives
and neither one survives
neither one survives.

More dramatically, "The Archeology of Divorce" examines "not
sacked cities, but sacked lives." The investigating team comes up with
a horrifying hypothesis:

The Critic's Work

Here is the table; note these fine archaic knives.
The flesh we scraped from one might indicate
a practice occurring even at this date:
perhaps the two ate each other alive.

At any rate, a struggle: the outcome isn't known.
Look, the chairs overturned in terrible haste,
the bowl of fruit left to rot and waste,
and this carcass of love, gnawed to the bone.

And finally, every bit as visceral and shocking, these lines from "Simple Sums":

A mouse inches forward, circles a cheese shard—
like an errant ace cut into its deck,
his body's dealt forever to a flat steel card.

The arithmetic of love or pain is so exact.
Think of a woman's womb; its nine-month estimate,
rounding off a percentage of desire.
One animal tonight miscalculates
and writhes out a correction of its error.
Exemplary scholar, its neck snaps—
describing precisely the structure of its trap.

I'm struck, not just by the honed accuracy of the imagery and the detached coolness of the presentation—in each case an extended analogy—but also by the curious recurrence in each excerpt of the word "love." We have "love with a ballistic force," a "carcass of love," and, in the last, an "arithmetic of love," which is likened to the functioning of a trap. I have to wonder about Storace's conception. For *agape, caritas,* and their myriad cognate powers have no apparent bearing. Storace has focused herself entirely upon sexual passion—eros. That other love, which in usage at least is set off against hate, is missing from these scenarios. Love, as she ponders it here, can barely be distinguished from its opposite. What underlies and animates the play of tropes is rage.

Now, with this frightening array of tortures and lacerations in

---

Melissa Green/Patricia Storace

mind, we can turn to one of Storace's cornerstone poems, "Il-legitimacy." It is one of the most powerful pieces in the book and worth quoting in full:

I

An hour or two in bed—my family history.
I'm caught in your act—like those cameras
planted in hotel rooms to catch
politicians at illicit sex,
I am the evidence of your kisses,
the proof of acts best unrecorded,
the reel of film replaying
the one domestic moment we three shared—
you begetting and begetting me.

Hence, the stigma of the illegitimate
in whom father and mother
are left coupling forever
so the child appears,
as it were, impaired,
conclusive proof of the social fear
that love outlasts lovers, and *is* eternal.
We bastards know it.
Trapped here in the love
that used a man and woman
as its instruments, it seems clear
that when the weather at last
turns radioactive,
and the temperature vaults
past boiling point
when the earth slips from the universe
like a hand from a black glove,
love will rush into the vacuum—
and caress it.

II

Caught as I was in the spokes of your kissing,
I know the world as a web of unions

The Critic's Work

that words are the matings of syllables
that piano keys breed
as they lie beside each other,
that scissors are men and women;
two blades, they cut through anything
that obstructs their joining.

III

Mother and Father,
lavish and careless
you left kisses everywhere
on the sheets on the glasses
on the walls on the night—
before you knew kisses were permanent.
One settled on my face,
and trembles there—
my mouth its imprint.

Storace commands her image sequences beautifully, moving from the tabloid atmospherics of the opening lines to the ironic wordplay of line 14 ("impaired"), from the apocalyptic fantasy that follows that to the proliferating conceits of the second section. The final lines startle us with their contained precision. The echoes from some of Storace's other poems work to strengthen the effect. The love that, in the first stanza, is said to use a man and woman as its instruments recalls the melting fuselage of "La Valse"; the sense of causal inevitability is the same we find in "Simple Sums."

But I cannot hover over these adjacent expressions with New Critical neutrality, any more than I could when faced with work by Berryman or Plath. I feel compelled to postulate the psychic dynamic that might weld the separate poems into some kind of unity. Briefly and crudely: the primary fact of illegitimacy and abandonment (in "Spring Afternoon," Storace writes: "half-resigned to my legacy of absent Spaniard,/vanished Jew, true scion *ex nihilo* . . ."; she titles her book *Heredity*) is vitally bound up with the vision of love that is expressed throughout. The speaker bears the brand of a narcissistic injury, an injury that has left in its wake a lasting rage, a deep suspicion

---

Melissa Green/Patricia Storace

of all love contracts, and a consuming desire to redress the balance. How else are we to make sense of such a thorough skepticism about the workings of the human heart?

This bitter view, prevailing in poem after poem, confers tremendous unitary power upon the book. It is also responsible for some of its central flaws. These are, mainly, Storace's occasional lapses into gratuitous cynicism, even sadism, and an accompanying metaphoric excessiveness. Let me get these objections out of the way before I revert to the many excellences of the work.

The poem "Barbie Doll" will illustrate my first reservation. Here is the opening section:

I

Her body, which is perfect,
is impenetrable.
It is her capsule,
orbiting
through childhoods which follow
childhoods which follow
childhoods,
the nest of decades
that emerge from one another.
Children are her oxygen.
The life oils in their hands
have made her plastic
tougher than muscle or bone.
The one way to destroy her
is dismemberment.
Her perfection is a violence.
Fling her to the soil;
she stands upright and
quivers, a thrown knife.
Grasp her carelessly,
her feet and hands
can damage, the flesh
laddered suddenly with blood.

The Critic's Work

One of the small things
that cause consequences;
a slap, a razor,
a pinch of cyanide.
One of the small things
whose smallness is a honing;
a piranha,
the switchblade of the ocean.

At issue here, I think, is proportion. The cool fury of the description, the inventory of imagined violences, is not commensurate with
the object of focus. What is being addressed, of course, is not the doll
itself but the sexist ideology that markets it to a susceptible population.
But somehow this cannot excuse the brutality that fantasy wreaks
upon an iconic human form. We lose the message, finally, and keep the
rage.

As for metaphoric excess, it's a fine line that I would draw. Storace
has a way, throughout, of achieving forward momentum through an
incessant manufacturing of tropes. Her inventiveness generally stands
her in good stead. Indeed, her lines are imbued with all of the tension
and vitality of incipient transformation. But there are times when she
overreaches, when too many different kinds of analogies are packed
together too closely. A few lines from "Still Life" might suggest what I
mean:

Somehow, the two of us sit in a café
bordering the park. Its grass succumbs
again to chronic green, and I see,
obedient, what I don't want to see—
lacerating tulips, leaf-racked trees,
hear steps as gunshots on the street,
heel and pavement sniping at each other.
The corner of your mouth bleeds geography
in the form of Côtes du Rhône.
And the sunset is cossack,
reddening the West with its pogrom.

Melissa Green/Patricia Storace

Admittedly, Storace is being somewhat campy here, but the tendency is evident in more serious poems as well:

> Tonight, lovers leaping to each other's arms
> across the precipice of past,
> as limbs merge in erotic galaxies
> now, as the Olympic blood wheels fast
> runs with red gospels through the arteries,
> can parent-current and tide of child converge,
> and God make us ardent, and merciful,
> for what we are about to conceive?

—from "Bedtime Prayers"

Over such a short interval we meet with past as precipice, limbs as parts of galaxies, blood cells as Olympic runners carrying gospels, parents and children as current and tide . . . The reader succumbs to what I call flea-market psychosis—coming away with nothing.

But as a poem like "Illegitimacy" shows, Storace can combine keen imaginings into passages of considerable expressive force. What's more, she has a broad array of modes and voices that she can press into service. When she turns from her more cynical vision of the physics of passion (which does produce, let me emphasize, some unforgettable passages), Storace can bring across subtler and more useful messages. "Pamina's Wedding Speech," to cite one example, is a most delicately wrought caution. Here are two excerpts:

> I hope I won't darken our celebrations
> if I affirm my marital consent
> with an honest, but agnostic epithalamion,
> in praise of that dubiety, sustained connection,
> and love, that questionable reality,
> unlikely, but possible, like resurrection.
> I say this as I place a husband's hand
> beneath the breast so intimate
> in act two with a knife,
> exchanging steely certainty of blade
> for malleable gold of wedding band.
> . . . .

The Critic's Work

Love is, in supreme form, concentration.
Enough of this. Raise the veil, beloved,
now I've made it dark enough to kiss
and teach those guests we've rendered skeptical
love passionate as doubt, as radical.
By these hands' imperfect light
receive a resonance of knowledge,
through flickering palms, lucid embrace,
read by this uncertain flame,
achieve description of a face.
Pray that we withstand the shock of blessing,
assembled friends, with lowered heads,
pray urgently that we may make
for good the crucial and ecstatic risk
we take, following brilliant torches to this bed.

The voice that addresses us here is wise, self-possessed, open-eyed before the frightful deceits of love, but at the same time tender, willing to risk. Difficulty and doom are acknowledged; they are also mastered. The tense equipoise brings Rilke to mind.

Storace can also reach to the other end of the spectrum. Her brightly vicious "Forties Movie, Starring Joan Crawford" vibrates not to the idiom of the master of Muzot but to the brashness of Villon:

I don't dream of my husband: I sleep with him,
when he's not shacked up with his girl, that toilet,
with her double-bed ass, and her three fat brats
she keeps in sneakers and denim, that sloven,
she didn't have the brains to saddle cash,
        that factory discount courtesan.
I'm sure that's the word, if that's how you pronounce it.

Her couplets blasting the clichés of Southern Gothic show that she is at home with frank, and fecund, earthiness:

And the one grand house is empty; its peeling columns stand
like discarded muskets, emptied of ammunition.

Melissa Green/Patricia Storace

Everything's costumed; hoopskirted rustling oak trees
furred with Spanish moss, whisper at factitious pedigrees.

The scattered lakes glint hot and jagged as trash tin,
And slaughtered Indians sun there, reborn as water moccasins.

The squatter woods are full of decomposing cars,
and menopausal, yellowed, hag refrigerators.

The screen-door cooks unhinged in the sun;
a tubercular mattress dies at length, coughing cotton.

—from "Deep South Carol"

Finally, Storace shows herself capable of elegant wit and considerable formal resourcefulness. The concluding poem in *Heredity,* from a sequence called "Personal Pronouns," is the intricately fanciful "It (Lullaby)":

Little it, little eunuch, little culprit,
struck match dropped that burns the house
of the five-year-old who didn't mean to do it.

Little understudy, hid behind curtains, tacit:
all that the tongue-tied point to when
they've lost the name of whatchyamacallit.

Misplaced earring, ticket, stolen loot,
the cache of emeralds the detective found
after the bandit confessed to it.

Half-wit, victim, little scapegoat;
alone and cornered by a crowd of bullies—
"Oh beat it, oh kick it, oh pummel it!"

Focus of tenderness and regret;
peace and quiet and time will heal it,
but it's a pity, oh it's a pity, isn't it?

Little grain, olive pit, conduit
through which the world poured when God saw

The Critic's Work

that it was good; creation's seed, atom—
and infinite.

Woven through these six short stanzas are, by my count, thirty-one *it* sounds (I include close homophones like "regret," "ticket," and "hid"). Storace has great fun modulating from literal to idiomatic usages, playing off from many angles to build a sense of the pitiable insignificance of the pronoun, and then rounding on us—for all of these tiny "its" comprise, in agglomeration, everything. With the strategic placement of "infinite," she imparts to her casual play an unexpected hint of the metaphysical.

I chose that last word with some deliberation. For I cannot end without remarking Storace's affinity—in vision somewhat more than poetics—with the Metaphysical tradition. The point is most easily made by setting her work alongside Green's. The latter, ever faithful to the word over the concept, the particular over the abstract, is a Keatsian Romantic. Her melodies arise directly and naturally from the agitations of language. Storace, while she delights in words and sounds, clearly discovers her momentum through the unfolding of the conceit. She is thinking her way across the page. What makes the work so compelling is that she is thinking about subjects that compress great emotional residues; her motion is guided by more than just the imperatives of logic.

Storace's great concern is, as I've said, with the treachery, if not impossibility, of human love. Insofar as this powers some of her most energetic and incisive work, one would not wish her cured. But then the poems that lean out from decided despair and venture more ambivalent, embattled stances gain her greater dimension and credibility. And when she sparks off in other directions, into more playful or formal idioms (or both), then she is simply delightful. If this first book is uneven, it is also exciting. A great many passions are tested and exercised. The best of the poems show a sophisticated intelligence in the service of a staunch fighter's heart.

Melissa Green/Patricia Storace

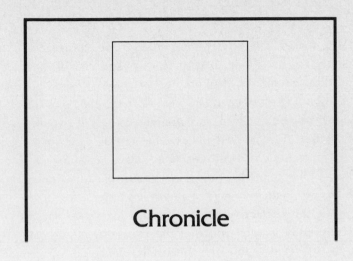

Chronicle

Brad Leithauser

In a recently published appreciation of poet Richard Wilbur, Brad Leithauser offers the following observation:

> Free verse and its various half-disciplined siblings have of course been around a great many years, but it's only now, for better or worse, that we are witnessing the ascendency of the first generation in the history of English-language verse never to have worked seriously in form.

Our immediate response is to assert that there are good reasons for this, that formal verse can no longer respond adequately to the discords of modern experience. In fact, there seems to be a consensus in all the arts that it is hopelessly retrograde to ply formalism in an age nervously biting its cuticles over decline and fall.

With this in mind, what are we to make of Brad Leithauser's debut? *Hundreds of Fireflies,* the work of a man not yet thirty, is an overtly formal book. Given the present context I would even say brashly formal. It is marked by extreme control, personal reticence, and a calm, confident virtuosity that makes us think of Elizabeth Bishop or Wilbur himself. And more remarkable than the style is the subject matter. Leithauser writes almost exclusively about the natural world—not the implacable nature of Jeffers or Frost, but the benign, pastoral, optically infinite nature of the Dutch landscape painters. His poems are so detailed and unemphatically lucid that we cannot help but wonder where and how the poet weathered the experiences of the past decade.

> Ahead, brown and white shorebirds,
> Probably sandpipers, fled from us
> Calling with small chipped voices;
> So quick, their matchstick legs
> Blurred, like hummingbird wings
>
> —from "Along Lake Michigan"

Or:

> Inches and yet far below, thin
> as compass needles, almost, min-
> nows flicker through the sun's
> tattered netting, circling past
>   each other as if lost.
>
> —from "Angel"

We have been schooled to approach poetry in a certain way, taught to extract content, a message, and then to summarize and report. Leithauser's poems resist these tactics. His lines embody the perceptual experience, *are* that experience; they hug their content and will not give it up. The poems are not about anything. Their meaning consists of the progress of the eye across the texture of the page, the movement through beautifully patterned clauses. The formal underpinning is clearly not gratuitous. It is there because attentiveness of such high degree discloses order. Yielding to the exigencies of form we become tensed and alert. The eye slows down, starts to move on tiptoe. And when we come to the end of the poem there is closure, the obscure, half-unconscious appeasement of our appetite for balance and clarity. The qualities of the poem become—briefly—our qualities.

It is impossible to argue the relative merits of formal versus informal poetry in a short review. I would say, though, that Leithauser's work is proof that the heritage of formal verse is more arsenal than obstacle, that the problem, where there is a problem, lies not in the rigidity of the forms but in the rigidity of their user. Here is a clear case of a supple and subtle intellect deriving maximum benefit from its interaction with formal strictures. The maturity of these poems is to some extent derived from the maturity of poetic form itself. And as for the criterion of relevance—any doubts we may have vanish as we begin to read. We discover what it means to pay attention:

> Theirs seems a gimpy flight, crude
>   Aerial gallop, yet they live
> By hunting on the wing—swoop to strain
>   The quick night air for food—
>
> As an outflung vision, surer
>   Far than sight, sounds the treetops
> At clearing's edge, the outcrops
>   Of stone, the ferns, the dense, standing
>
> Water in the overhung ditch,
>   And returns as rumpled echoes to
> Ears that map the field according to
>   Its shifting, imperfect pitch.
>
> —from "Additional Bats"

Hundreds of Fireflies is not without its weaknesses. At times the reader will long for greater variety of subject matter or a less imperturbable tone. Also, it might be argued that the poet falls victim to his own skill in places—his knack for pure resolutions sometimes limits his access to less-predictable side roads. In the same way, there could be more burr, more rasp, more protrusion of recalcitrant fiber: in other words, less smooth precision. But this is quibbling before a stunning maiden voyage. We would do better to break a champagne bottle belatedly against the hull, to praise the courage and obstinacy required to stand so far apart from gangs and trends. Here is a man with a love of the world and its words and the exceedingly rare capacity to express the first by means of the second.

Jorie Graham I

In the sixth book of Virgil's *Aeneid,* Aeneas descends into the underworld to speak with the shade of his father, Anchises. As they stand together by the banks of Lethe, Anchises points to a crowd "to whom fate owes a second body," and the hero cries out in protest:

> But, Father, can it be that any souls
> would ever leave their dwelling here to go
> beneath the sky of earth, and once again
> take on their sluggish bodies? Are they madmen?
> Why this wild longing for the light of earth?
> —trans. Allen Mandelbaum

Two millennia later, in a poem entitled "At Luca Signorelli's Resurrection of the Body," Jorie Graham writes:

> See how they hurry
>   to enter
> their bodies,
>   these spirits.
> Is it better, flesh,
>   that they
> should hurry so?

When Virgil wrote his lines, the commerce between bodies and spirits was popularly assumed. In our time we are apt to regard it as a poetic conceit. But Jorie Graham, pondering Signorelli's fresco, choosing to

---

The Critic's Work

ponder it, is every bit as serious as her predecessor, and every bit as
literal. *Erosion,* her second book, gives passionate voice to that all-but-
unmentionable entity, the human soul.

Graham brings the poem to a close by recounting and reimagining
a story about the painter:

When his one son
        died violently,
he had the body brought to him
        and laid it

on the drawing table,
        and stood
at a certain distance
        awaiting the best
possible light, the best depth
        of day,

then with beauty and care
        and technique
and judgement, cut into
        shadow, cut
into bone and sinew and every
        pocket

in which the cold light
        pooled.
It took him days
        that deep
caress, cutting,
        unfastening,

until his mind
        could climb into
the open flesh and
        mend itself.

The stitch-pattern lines and incremental accelerations are characteristic
of Graham's prosody. Pauses and line breaks are carefully manipulated.

The momentum is heady, but expert tacking keeps it under control. She is a difficult poet to quote in snippets; one hesitates to cut short such urgent, delicate breathing.

In the Signorelli poem, as elsewhere throughout the book, Graham reveals her preoccupation with the split between body and mind, flesh and spirit. Like Blake, she indicts excessive rationality, the impulse to break everything down into components and particles. Poem after poem restates the problem and then summons formidable energies of imagination to close the rift. Images of mending, healing, and stitching abound. What reason has sundered, imagination will make whole. And Graham, with her unusual metaphysics, her belief in higher spiritual orders, has a range of imaginative association that is rare in contemporary poetry. In "My Garden, My Daylight," for instance, a neighbor brings her fresh-caught bottom fish. Graham quickly turns a commonplace into a dynamic cosmogony:

> Once a week he brings me fresh-catch,
>   boned and skinned
> and rolled up like a tongue. I freeze
>   them, speechless, angelic
> instruments. I have a choir of them.
>   Alive, they feed
>
> driving their bodies through the mud,
>   mud through their flesh.
> See how white they become. High
>   above, the water thins
> to blue, then air, then less . . .
>   These aren't as sweet
>
> as those that shine up there,

Fish that resemble tongues become a choir of angels. All at once we sense a synchronized activity—below, in mud, and above, in ether. With superb economy Graham has touched to life a hierarchy of spirit.

In "I Watched a Snake," the sinuous movements of a small reptile in the grass yield an imagining worthy of Donne:

This must be perfect progress where
    movement appears
to be a vanishing, a mending
    of the visible

by the invisible—just as we
    stitch the earth,
it seems to me, each time
    we die, going
back under, coming back up . . .

This would be a clever conceit and nothing more were it not for the fact that Graham believes her imagery. Her diction is sincere. There is no sense of barrier between poet and poem. And as we entrust ourselves to the language, we experience the interpenetration of matter and spirit on the grandest and also the most microscopic of levels. In the poem "Erosion," running pebbles through her fingers, Graham remarks: "Each time/some molecules rub off/evolving into/the invisible."

But for all of this concern with spirit and matter, Graham is not an overtly religious poet. The poems are religious only *en passant*. She will address Santa Chiara or Saint Francis, but even on these occasions it is more the intensity of their faith that she celebrates and less its Christian meaning. Graham, like Rilke, invokes a spiritual force that defies clear-cut definition:

Who is
    the nervous spirit
of this world
    that must go over and over
what it already knows,
    what is it
so hot and dry
    that's looking through us,
by us,
    for its answer

Chronicle

Graham is not quite as ethereal as I have perhaps made her sound. There is a fibrous resilience in these poems as well. She is very much aware of the world enduring outside the self, and she knows that the mind can never penetrate it deeply enough. Because "there is / no deep enough."

> Isn't the
> honesty
> of things where they
> resist,
> where only the wind
> can bend them
>
> back, the real weather
> not our
> desire hissing Tell me
> your parts
> that I may understand
> your body,
>
> —from "The Age of Reason"

Readers seeking the staple goods of late-twentieth-century poetry—flat narration, wry autobiography, exhumed solitudes—will find little satisfaction here. This is an enterprise of a higher order. "Why this wild longing for the light of earth?" asked the grave Aeneas. Even as Jorie Graham takes up the hero's question, the longing he spoke of thrills through her lines.

Jorie Graham II

You can't open a poetry journal these days without catching a whiff of musket smoke. The battle that started modernism has been rejoined, this time by the vanquished party. Born-again prosodic conservatives contend that free verse has exhausted its original strengths—novelty and surprise—and that in the absence of metrical constraints it can offer little to make up for the deficit. Free-versifiers, in their turn, tilt at formalist pomposity and say that there is no returning to the golden age. They bear aloft their standards of innovation and naturalness, but embattled as they are, they make little mention of intellectual or spiritual imperatives. The recent work of Jorie Graham, if heeded, might strengthen their hand; it brings the reminder that artless utterance is not the alpha and omega of nonformal verse.

The End of Beauty is Graham's third collection. In the four years since her last book, Erosion, she has made a decisive turn—away from accessibility and resolution and into a realm of difficult ambiguity. My guess is that she has fallen under the spell of Rilke, for her voice has taken on something of his tone of prophetic intimacy. What's more, Graham has adopted a Rilkean approach to subject. Focusing on a biblical or mythological episode—Adam and Eve, Apollo and Daphne, Demeter and Persephone—she breaks the familiar narrative line into freeze-frame sections to highlight the confusion of contending forces. She is confident enough about her approach to dare to retell Rilke's own retelling of the Orpheus and Euridice legend.

Graham's tactic of slowing and interrupting narrative sequences affords her an enormous freedom of expression. In less gifted hands, chaos would quickly result. But she has ways of preserving control. In a poem like "Self-portrait as the Gesture Between Them," which culminates with the plucking of the apple in the Garden of Eden, she relies upon the shaping suspense of the foreseeable—inevitable—moment. Other poems, like "Pollock and Canvas," sustain cohesion through a careful braiding of discrete narrative strains. In that poem, Graham arrests the painter's gesture before his brush ever touches canvas. Into this dimension of pure possibility, she intercuts a parallel image-sequence of a fishhook aloft in the suspended moment of the cast and another of God resting after the creation:

> And then He rested, is that where the real
> making
>   begins—the now—Then He rested letting in chance letting in
> any wind any shadow quick with minutes, and whimsy,
>   through the light, letting the snake the turning
> in.

Chronicle

The poem is nine pages long and, as this excerpt suggests, some-what abstract in its argumentation. Graham ultimately works it around so that the two ideas of freedom are paradoxically inverted: The Cre-ator's stepping back and "letting in chance" reverses the termination of freedom represented by the painter's first stroke. "Pollock and Canvas" is not without its passages of turgid opacity—Graham sometimes over-reaches and loses her reader—but its ambitiousness, the thrust and parry of images and ideas, is liberating. If it's true that free verse has been languishing, then this work brings the possibility of rejuvenation.

Graham's vision embraces flux and transformation. She discovers in her narrative the critical or pivotal moment; she then slows the action to expose its perilous eventual consequences. "Freedom" and "neces-sity" are, in Graham's world, crude coordinates; her scenarios are thick with ambiguity. Indeed, the first of all stories, the taking of the fruit, is a paradigm of the blurring between free action and necessary order—here is a case of necessity including a provision for freedom. "Self-portrait as the Gesture Between Them," written in short, numbered sections, asserts this paradoxical awareness:

23

the balance that cannot be broken owned by the air until he
    touches,

24

the balance like an apple held up into the sunlight

25

then taken down, the air changing by its passage, the feeling of
    being capable,

26

of being not quite right for the place, not quite the thing that's
    needed,

27

the feeling of being a digression not the link in the argument
a new direction, an offshoot, the limb going on elsewhere,

The Critic's Work

28

and liking that error, a feeling of being capable *because* an error,
29

of being wrong perhaps altogether wrong a piece from another set
30

stripped of position stripped of true function
31

and loving that error, loving that filial form, that break from
    perfection

Graham demands patience and application from her readers. And when
she rewards them, it is not with neatly finished artifacts, but with a
sense of the hazards and unknowns of poetic thinking. *The End of Beauty*
is open and provisional. Its vector reaches right off the page.

Amy Clampitt
Christopher Jane Corkery

There is no point in introducing Amy Clampitt here. Her rapid ascendancy and success, after years of neglect, have passed into literary folklore, and her first book, *The Kingfisher,* has the status of a modern masterpiece. It is axiomatic, of course, that the follow-up work will be received less enthusiastically—sudden acclaim invariably puts the writer in the damned-if-you-do, damned-if-you-don't situation. To continue in the original vein is to be resting on laurels; to depart is to betray the gift. Clampitt, in *What the Light Was Like,* plays shrewdly down the middle, neither quite repeating nor betraying. If the result is not as striking as *The Kingfisher,* it's less because her performance has fallen off, more because her idiom has revealed its intrinsic limitations.

With *The Kingfisher,* Clampitt injected a much-needed serum of the baroque into the bloodstream of English-language poetry. Indeed, so starved were readers for her kind of verbal richness and stylization—who can explain what the public craves at any given time?—that sins of excess were either overlooked or forgiven. And there were excesses, grand cadenzas of ornamental description that almost completely bur-

---

ied the object or event in question. Aware of her tendency, Clampitt cleverly looked for subjects that would let profusion appear appropriate. In "Botanical Nomenclature," for instance, she wrote of:

> foliage
> blued to a driftwood patina
> growing outward, sometimes to the
> size of a cathedral window,
> stemrib grissaile edge-tasseled
> with opening goblets, with bugles
> in miniature, mauve through cerulean,
> toggled into a seawall scree,

and so on. Her enterprise was only in part concerned with perception or even sense. It was also determinedly intent upon overturning the dictatorship of unemphatic plainness. Heeding the law of compensation, she threw herself in the opposite direction—at times, it seemed, choosing words for their strangeness more than their utility. Still, her civilized bombardiering was widely applauded.

What the Light Was Like is divided into five sections, all of which can be seen in relation. "The Shore," "The Hinterland," and "The Metropolis" are geographical panels; "Voyages: A Homage to John Keats" and "Written in Water" bear an obvious titular connection. But the sense of wholeness comes retrospectively: Every section in some way meditates on death, art, and the mysterious relation between the human spirit and the natural elements that house it and compose its habitat. "The thinnest of osmotic boundaries contain what once/was called the soul," writes Clampitt in "A Curfew." This awareness pervades the poetry and underwrites the astonishing precision of many of her lines.

As in The Kingfisher, Clampitt is at her best—and also at her most inflated—when describing the natural world. What the Light Was Like is an archive of magical detailings. Eiders trail "a knit-and-purl of irresistibly downy young behind them"; a warbler is "dapper in a yellow domino/a noose of dark about his throat"; a gooseberry is flavored with "the acerbity of all things green/and adolescent" . . . But then, right alongside these perfect registrations, are passages where the verbiage is so disproportionate to its subject that baroque degenerates into

---

rococo: "Mulleins hunker to a hirsute/rosette about the taproot."
Though Clampitt can render the slightest quiver within the natural
order, she can also cause us to lose sight of that order completely.

"Voyages: A Homage to John Keats" consists of eight long biographical poems. Helen Vendler (to whom the section is dedicated)
once praised the "Keatsian luxury of detail" in Clampitt's writing. The
affinity between poets is worthy of remark. It also explains, I think,
why this sequence—the most ambitious in the collection—is so disquieting. The poetry itself is as exquisitely nuanced as anything by
Clampitt. The problem is that the sensibility of Keats, the ostensible
subject of the section, never acquires an independent resonance. Dozens of ingenious echoes and appropriations stand in the way:

> how beautiful
> the season was—ay, better than
> the chilly green of spring, the warmed hue
> of grainfields' harsh stubs turned pictorial
> with equinoctal bloom, the tincture of
> the actual, the mellow aftermath of fever:
> purgatorial winnowings, the harvest over.

The representative passage, from "Winchester: The Autumn Equinox,"
is a skillful tatting of the relevant description from Keats's letter to J.
H. Reynolds and key signals from Keat's autumn poem itself; "ay,"
"mellow," "winnowings" . . . But Clampitt has neither carried us further into the Keatsian sensibility nor improved upon the poetry.

Cavils aside, there is much to celebrate in Clampitt's book. The
landscape sections give an evocative thrill, and the long poems on the
death of her brother and, in the title poem, of an old lobsterman, are
heartfelt and strong. Strong, too, is "Black Buttercups," Clampitt's
farewell to a childhood house and to childhood itself:

> I remember waking,
> a February morning leprous with frost
> above the dregs of a halfhearted snowfall,
> to find the gray world of adulthood
> everywhere, as though there never

had been any other, in that same house
I could not bear to leave, where even now
the child who wept to leave still sits
weeping at the thought of exile.

All adornment has been sloughed off; mood and setting have come together like the two images in a viewfinder. The lines suggest that Clampitt could move away from the baroque without surrendering her special power.

I have not the space to offer anything but the most general praise for Christopher Jane Corkery's first collection, *Blessing*. Unlike Clampitt, Corkery eschews decoration and curbs every impulse to pure style. What these poems offer is an obdurate vision of grace, a careful sounding of human circumstance that omits nothing of its dreads and despairs, but which nonetheless manages to find under just what conditions beauty and redemption are granted. This is one of the most honestly made and least assuming first books I have encountered. Corkery is difficult to excerpt, for her poems are carefully woven wholes. Here, nevertheless, is the opening passage from "Letter from Marcellus, Maker of Fountains, to Cominia His Mother":

. . . Yes, I understand quite well. Within
two days the Senate's edict will be out,
my fountains tightly gagged. The central cistern
will be rimmed by crowds who wait in lines for what
they thought was theirs. They'll think they only mind
the wait. They will not know it is the absence
of the leap enfeebles them and queers their dreams
at night. The surge the spirit needs to live
is gone without the fountains.

With little adjustment these words can be said to describe the place of poetry in our or any culture.

The Critic's Work

Alice Fulton

Alice Fulton's first book, *Dance Script with Electric Ballerina,* careered around the poetry corner like a cartoon fire engine, with two wheels in the air and an extension ladder cantilevering perilously over the street. Well, that might be an exaggeration; it was certainly a distinctive—and much remarked—debut. Fulton's quick, jaggy lines caught the music of growing up tough ("This boy liked me once:/two cries and a clutch") and her gift for transforming commonplace objects and actions into lit-up signals was singular. As she wrote in "From Our Mary to Me," an early poem in that book, her mother left her "neither her optimism nor charm,/only imagination, kicking like a worm in a jumping bean." She was wrong about only the charm.

All first books are, in a sense, written to the world; second books tend to have a smaller target—mainly, the readers of the first. Improvement or departure is obligatory. As Fulton had achieved a kind of perfection within her chosen mode in *Dance Script,* the latter choice was natural. In *Palladium,* therefore, we see the artist installed in front of a larger canvas, equipped with more brushes and paints. The poems are longer, the subjects and stances have greater variety—the results are mixed.

Fulton's ambition is evident straight off in the organization of the book. There are six sections, each prefaced by a different definition, or legend, of the word "palladium": a platinumlike element, a safeguard, a music hall, a photographic printing process, a legless effigy or cult object, and a magic-working totem that dropped from the heavens into the city of Troy, only to be stolen by the besieging Greeks. Though Fulton does work out certain thematic connections between the section headings and the poems—the music hall section, for instance, presents lively character studies of relatives—the unifying strategy is finally unconvincing. Why palladium? The reader feels either that some larger significance eludes him, or else that arbitrariness has donned the mask of order.

In her irrepressible inventiveness, as well as in her aesthetic of profusion, Fulton recalls Amy Clampitt. Both poets are capable of stunning virtuoso turns, but both are also capable of switching on the image-making machine while they rest from their exertions. When her heart is in it, Fulton can come across with a Gould-playing-*Goldberg* effervescence:

> Collars and cuffs are dipped in the hot
> icing of starch: crisp wings, crackable
> as willowware. She tacks the scrapping
> armfuls on five lines: shirts, bloomers,
> livelier than when worn,
> doubledare the wind. They'll freeze soon enough—
> her fingers are stiff as clothespins.
> She sings. The sound forms quick clouds
> that mark the time: "Take me out to the ball-
> game, take me out to the . . ." After dark she'll drag in
> the tough sheets. They'll score the snow toward home.
>
> —from "Days Through Starch and Bluing"

The skillful syncopation of consonantal sounds turns the humdrum event of laundry into domestic choreography.

At other times, though, an equally persuasive rhythm can get undermined by the surface clutter of similes and metaphors:

> up North where windows ignite early,
> hanging the dark
> with inner lives like tiny drive-in screens
> showing underrated grade B stars,
> and bingo-playing ladies
> hover, intent as air controllers
> above their cards in social halls.
> At tables long as football fields, they acquire
> a taste for the metallic:
> coins, flat Coke; and Bic lighters
> puff like the souls of exclamation
> points as winners collect
> their macrame plant cradles.
>
> —from "Aviation"

The Critic's Work

In thirteen lines we have inner lives likened to grade B drive-in scenarios, bingo ladies to air traffic controllers, tables to football fields, and Bic lighters to exclamation points. Passages like this convince me that Fulton's pen holds a bottomless reservoir of images, that she has only to move the point across the page for a poem to start shaping up.

This is my central complaint about this prodigiously gifted poet: I cannot always feel the pressure of inevitability, the sense that here is a poem that *had* to be written. This disturbs me most often with her longer, more discursive meditations—on faith healing, on peripheral vision—and in set pieces like "The Ice Storm":

> militant
>   yet democratic, ice built this
> superstructure of light, flinging
> beaded shawls around the meanest shrubs,
> tinting shadows a catatonic mauve,
> making weeds brittle as invalids'
> glass straws.

Even in these lines, of course, Fulton struts verbal skills that lesser poets would envy. Her ear for sound valences—watch how the *i* and *t* sounds play against the repeated *sh*'s—and startling juxtapositions ("catatonic mauve") ensures that whatever she produces will have some way of delighting us. But even her most skillful compositional exercises pale beside her heartfelt expressions. When Fulton puts her precision and daring in the service of true feeling, the result is a durable, living poetry:

> Papa, who said of any gambler,
> roughneck, drunkard, just "I don't think much
> of him," and in his stiff denims
> toted his lunchpail's spuds
> down a plumbline of twelve-hour shifts:
>
> farmed, lumbered, and cow-kicked,
> let the bones knit their own
> rivet, oiled big wheels that bullied

Chronicle

water uphill, drank stout, touch animals only
unawkwardly, drove four-in-hand, and sired six.

—from "Plumbline"

My complaints notwithstanding, *Palladium* is a collection to own and explore; like its namesake metal, it will not tarnish at ordinary temperatures.

Baron Wormser

Baron Wormser lives and works in Mercer, Maine. We learn this from the author's note on his first collection of poems, *White Words,* and again on his second, *Good Trembling.* Determinedly laconic, Wormser wants us to know that he is a man of place, and, more importantly, that he is not one of that proliferating species: the urban-dwelling, workshop-affiliated "poet." The work certainly bears this out. It is steady, unaffected, subject oriented, and honorably loyal to a kind of American life that has slipped out of the literary viewfinder—not because it doesn't exist, but because American poets either ignore that experience or else pat themselves on the back for taking it up.

I do not want to give the impression that Wormser is a chronicler of rural or small-town U.S.A. He is not. He is an intelligent and sophisticated man who happens to live and enjoy that life. He takes his subjects from the world around him; they prompt his observations and set him to thinking. What's more, their solid, unvarnished reality curtails any temptation he might have to rhetorical or lyrical inflation. His exposition may, at times, be complex, but it is never false. Wormser refuses to throw a brocade of language over anything.

The best of Wormser's poems arise directly out of occasion. We are never forced in the direction of poetry; rather, poetry discloses itself naturally, even demurely. In "Stitches," the poet describes some embroidered handkerchiefs he has found on a roadside "odds 'n' ends" table:

They are not beautiful but they are pretty
And better than anything they are someone's

Precious time—be it by a window or in
A little attic room or on a veranda—they
Are someone's time which you can see
In each small stitch that is too small to see
But is there the way the funny yellow ducks
Are there or the purplish five-petal flowers.

Note the perfect poise of "They are not beautiful but they are pretty." Wormser avoids pity and condescension, and manages it not through adroitness but native humility. We sense implicitly the connection between the artifact and the private industry that produced it, and that privacy is respected. The concluding stanza sustains the balance while calmly widening the focus:

Each moment in them is straight and steady and
You can see that a hand is a body
And a body is a life and a life is
The habit of time and seems, to someone who
Happens by later like this, the remainder of design.

Wormser's appeal is immediate. The source of his power, however, is a more subtle matter. It has to do with the poetry inherent in the thinking process itself. For these lines bring us repeatedly to the inner threshold at which the observation of the particular is abstracted from and enlarged upon until it becomes thought. The poem "In Baseball," for example, looks searchingly at the great American pastime:

Neither forces nor bodies equivocate:
Each action holds a telltale trait
Each moment convokes an actual fate.

Reality, being precious, becomes a game
In which, nature-like, no two things are the same—
Whatever is remarkable is nicknamed.

Abstract, yes. But it is not abstraction for its own sake. These are clearly the meditations of a watcher who has been pricked deeply by the magic of the game—their accuracy is confirmation. And the poem moves on surefootedly: "It's the keenness of conflict that appeals / To the citizen so sick of the abstract 'they.'" The ghost of Auden smiles behind the lines.

But America is more to Wormser than baseball and roadside stands. There is a dogged, idiosyncratic spiritual energy that he would record. His "Poem to the Memory of H. L. Mencken" is exemplary. I quote the second stanza:

> I see you at your typewriter, bemused and irascible,
> Unappalled by yesterday's perishable headlines,
> Appalled by the unbridled asininity of some current
> Maker of the so-called news. Journalism was the brine
> Of celebrity. There were more fools than there was time.

So, too, there are more riches in *Good Trembling* than I can show. Wormser can find the current of poetry just about anywhere—at a stock car race, in a girl's dreams of Elvis, in a postcard taped to a refrigerator door. This dowser's intuition, coupled with an accuracy of phrasing that is, to me, the surest sign of respect—for oneself and for the world—make Wormser a poet to watch, and read.

Christopher Middleton
Samuel Menashe

Christopher Middleton is a poet of pure and private resource. He fishes by obstinate isles, far from the often academic agitations that ruffle the waters of the American poetry scene. British by birth, a professor and translator of German literature by vocation, Middleton has lived for the last few decades in Austin, Texas. These statistics from his *vita* only partially map his singularity. His poetic temperament determines the rest. Middleton is a European modernist; his expression transects a Germanic (Rilkean) lyricism with the synaptic disjunctions of Dada. Needless to say, his name lights up few of our poetry marquees— modernism has never really found a place in our literature. Thus, while the publication of *Two Horse Wagon Going By* (timed to coincide with Middleton's sixtieth birthday) should be an occasion for redressing the balance, winning for him the readers and critics he deserves, things will probably not change. Idiosyncrasy and difficulty remain a guarantee of marginality.

Two Horse Wagon Going By is divided into two sections, "Silent Rooms in Several Places" and "Apocrypha Texana." The poems in the latter section tend to be based in the geography—and, in some cases, built around the speech patterns—of Middleton's adopted locale. Insofar as they implement a recognizable narrative structure, they offer an easy entry point to the work of an otherwise demanding artist. Stanzas like the following, about the killing of a coral snake, are almost entirely transparent:

> When I looked again
> The small black head with its yellow nape band
> Was pointing up and the mouth, opening, closing,
> Snapped at air to repel the blind force
> Which held him down.
>
> I could not do it, not to him, looking so
> True to himself, making his wisdom tell,
> It shot through me quicker than his poison would:
> The glory of his form, delicate organism,
> Not small any more, but raw now, and cleaving,
> Right there, to the bare bone of creation.
>
> —from "Coral Snake"

But this is hardly the conventional Middleton mode. We are more likely to find an accelerated, compacted idiom, as in this section from the long poem "Rilke's Feet":

> Or Rilke had no feet at all
> What he had was fins
> Up he twiddles into the air
>
> Sycamore seed going the wrong way
> Lands in my tree
> Owl's eyes large liquid

Blink at me　　　Contrariwise
He has no body just a head
Thought a little girl

No body in his clean but threadbare
Clothes crossed the room
And took a cake with Mama later

Off again
Somehow bowing
Where can he have put that cake

Middleton is playing, but as anyone who has been a child can tell you,
there is nothing more serious than play. In these fleet fifteen lines he
finds both the truth and the absurdity within the popular image of the
incorporeal poet. The vertical liberation, moving through rapid con-
versions from aqueous fins, to airborne propulsion, to the copter rota-
tions of the sycamore seed, to the gathered stillness of the owl's
blinking eyes, is decisively joined to the droll imagining of the little
girl—Rilke has gone from having no feet to having no body at all. The
clever aptness of "Somehow bowing" puts the final spin on the passage.

In truth, there is no "conventional Middleton mode." Poems, as he
wrote in his essay volume *Bolshevism in Art,* are "active structures of
eccentric feeling." Middleton's poems are flowerings, zones of sensibility that have erupted into rhythm. He writes of "the birth of a
phrase" as the origin of poetic composition. The poem, then, moves
within the orbit of a given rhythmic trace, exploring and fulfilling its
imperatives. This would account for the absolute distinctiveness of
each separate poem—no set metric or agenda has been allowed to
interfere with the life of the emerging organism.

In his prose poem "Bivouac," Middleton recalls the belief of the
Polish Hasidim that a "pneuma" (or spirit breath) dwelt within the
pages of the sacred texts. I like to think of Middleton's own poems as
small gusts of pneuma, captured and shaped, waiting to be released by
the eye and ear of the reader. Readers tired of the water diet of
contemporary American poetry should break their involuntary fast
here.

The Critic's Work

*   *   *

Middleton once characterized the prose style of Robert Walser as one of "snailhorn delicacy." The phrase, as I hope I have suggested, applies no less to his own work. But it can also be used with reference to the calibrated minims of Samuel Menashe. Like Middleton, Menashe is a poet of subtle breath stops and fine detail. He differs in that he is also a poet of overtly formal tendencies. Whether his occasion is light and celebratory:

> Sky thrust from town
> Vaults high towers
> But comes down
> To flowers

—"May"

or elegiac:

> Darkness stored
> Becomes a star
> At whose core
> You, dead, are

—"untitled

or epigrammatic:

> Sharpen your wit—
> Each half of it—
> Before you shut
> Scissors to cut
>
> Shear skin deep
> Underneath wool
> Expose the sheep
> Whose leg you pull

—"Scissors"

Menashe finds a way to let rhythmic expectation and rhyme work on his behalf. Spatial constriction appears to spark his inventiveness. Indeed, the reviewer very quickly begins to feel verbose and imprecise. I

would as lief be brief: The garden is small, but the flowers grow tall.
Portion the joy lest the rhyme start to cloy. This is good stuff; that
said, enough.

Gary Snyder

Reading Gary Snyder's *Left Out in the Rain: New Poems 1947–1985* is a
bit like going to a four-star restaurant on the chef's day off. We get
many of the courses that a collected poems would put before us, as
well as some of the panoramic pleasures, but we don't leave the table
with the glow of a fully gratified palate. I question the publishing
strategy. Right at that point in the poet's career when we might look
for a fat retrospective volume, we are presented with four decades'
worth of outtakes. Poems that Snyder for one reason or another decided not to include in other collections are now amassed under the
rubric "new poems."

The danger, of course, is that trigger-happy critics might use this
as a basis for measuring the whole *oeuvre*. *Left Out in the Rain* would not
stand up well under such scrutiny. Too many of the inclusions represent near misses, poems saved for an image, an idea, or because they
had some associational meaning for their author. Don't get me wrong,
though. The book is not a disaster. Its spirit is of such confident, genial
permissiveness that we end up enjoying it for what it really is: a glance
into the poet's laboratory.

Left Out in the Rain is portioned off into epochs, beginning with two
poems from the late 1940's. While that work still shows the haphazard
wingbeats of the fledgling, it does allow us to see what Snyder had to
outgrow in order to reach poetic maturity. The familiar subject matter
is there, but the perception is still alloyed with rhetoric. Snyder has
not yet learned the sharp adze strokes that will eventually become his
trademark. The lines, like these from "Elk Trails," have yet to be pared
into distinction:

I have walked you, ancient trails,
Along the narrow rocky ridges

The Critic's Work

High above the mountains that
Make up your world:

It won't be long, though, before "I" becomes *eye*.

What's interesting about Snyder, to my mind, is the fact that he schooled a deeply Western sensibility in Eastern ways, without ever becoming ersatz-Eastern. His minimalism retains a hard American bite. Here, complete, is "Seeing the Ox" from the central 1959–1969 section:

Brown ox
Nose snubbed up
Locking his big head high
    against telephone pole
    right by Daitoku   temple—
Slobbering, watching kids play
    with rolling eye,

Fresh dung pile under his
    own hind hooves.

I like the intimated clash of perspectives: ancient, heraldic creature and telephone pole, temple and dung; the ox's indolent immobility is foregrounded against the play activity. Snyder is not straining to get any recoil effect from the juxtapositions. Only the slight double take in the spacing between "Daitoku" and "temple" alerts us to the bemused perplexity of the outsider. It's not vintage Snyder, but it's nice to have.

Snyder's enduring contribution is to have trained a disciplined, facet-cutting eye upon the primeval terrain of the Pacific Northwest. His pure, staggered lines have become the signature of a kind of perception, a respectful registry of a durable and deeply structured *out there*. In this, they are not unlike Cézanne's delicately layered planes. But *Left Out in the Rain* shows little of this side of Snyder. What we get instead is episodic snapshots from the many locales of his life—the Indian Ocean, Kyoto, Lookout Mountain, Turtle Island. Still, underneath the changing surface of subjects and occasions, it is possible to sense the willed life gradually becoming the real life. Style tells the whole story.

Chronicle

Early Snyder is very much the poet trying to fit himself into an admired mode. We can almost feel the muscular expenditure behind the reductions in these lines:

Flickering eye
Peers from a birdcage
    shivering lips of bone
    scratch, and a taste of shell

Feathers cram the mouth.

        —from "A Change of Straw" (1949–1952)

Whereas a poem like "The Net" from the 1974–1984 grouping allows us to see how natural such moves have become:

A man in a canoe
Catching fish by dancing—

  "hey, fish by casting with a net!"

Women in the evening circle
casting, round a fire

A man in a canoe
Dances with a net.

The first quotation belongs to a poet who is trying to tell us everything he knows; the second just hints at a bountiful lore, understands that worthy subjects can never be fully encompassed.

    The least successful part of this collection is the section placed last: "Satires, Inventions, & Diversions 1951–1980." If the thrust of Snyder's effort over the years has been to refine a cleansed and natural idiom, then these are exercises in self-opposition:

You joyous Gods, who gave mankind his culture,
And you, brave nymphs, who taught him love of Nature,
        —from "Sestina of the End of the Kalpa"

Or:

Here's the last drunk song I'll sing
Of all the balls we had this Spring.
        —from "Ballad of Rolling Heads"

The Critic's Work

Every poet, to be sure, sends out tracers in different directions. But not every poet puts them in a book. The unintentional effect of these sorties is to remind us of what we most treasure about Snyder. He has spent forty years now doing "the real work"—it's time we had a volume honoring *that*.

Paul Muldoon
Tony Harrison
Christopher Logue

"Where there is amenability to paraphrase," wrote Osip Mandelstam, "there the sheets have not been rumpled—there poetry has not spent the night." The poet was championing a particular kind of language-oriented lyricism. The ear, believed Mandelstam, would infallibly lead the pen away from abstraction, from ideas. He would have delighted in following the evolution of the young Northern Irish poet Paul Muldoon: His every developmental stage is marked by poems more accurately and more adventurously *listened* onto the page.

The earliest work gathered in Muldoon's *Selected Poems, 1968–1986* is the most conventional. Deft anecdotal sketches follow the off-kilter ripple and roll of a situation or build upon the telling irregularity of some vernacular utterance. Already, though, the special gift is evident. There is an eccentric precision to the narrative strokes, a willful obliquity that transforms the commonplace, and a clear fondness for the sounds of words:

> Old photographs would have her bookish, sitting
> Under a willow. I take that to be a croquet-
> Lawn. She reads aloud, no doubt from Rupert Brooke.
> The month is always May or June.
>
> Or with any stranger on the motor-bike.
> Not my father, no. This one's all crew-cut
> And polished brass buttons.
> An American soldier, perhaps.

Chronicle

> And the full moon
> Swaying over Keenaghan, the orchards and the cannery,
> Thins to a last yellow-hammer, and goes.
> The neighbors gather, all Keenaghan and Collegelands,
> There is story-telling. Old miners at Coalisland
> Going into the ground. Swinging, for fear of the gas,
> The soft flame of a canary.

—"Ma"

But these are just the first evolutionary stirrings. In the poems that follow, from the books *Why Brownlee Left* and *Quoof,* the trademark Muldoon style starts to emerge. The poet is more willing to let language have its head and to be led along to singular discoveries. Wordplay is taken seriously, allowing for an idiosyncratic lyric edge. A poem like "Truce," for example, obviously came to life more from a fidgeting with half rhymes than from some embracing thematic conception:

> It begins with one or two soldiers
> And one or two following
> With hampers over their shoulders.
> They might be off wildfowling.

This is not to say, however, that Muldoon ignores the deeper claims of subject. The obdurate real world can nearly always be found, startlingly there, at the far side of his words.

Nearly always. Muldoon does have a penchant for a kind of lengthy humoresque in which surrealistic situations are strung out (rather in the manner of middle-period Bob Dylan) until little but verbal sport remains. Lines like the following, good for a nod and a wink, don't really stand up under much rereading:

> The billiard-player had been big, and black,
> Dressed to kill, or inflict a wound,
> And had hung around the pin-table
> As long as it took to smoke a panatella.
> I was clinging to an ice-pack
> On which the Titanic might have foundered
> When I was suddenly bedazzled

The Critic's Work

By a little silver knick-knack
That must have fallen from his hat-band.
I am telling this exactly as it happened.

—from "Immramm"

But Muldoon's most recent poems, from the collection *Meeting the British,* easily redeem these stretches of gratuitous cleverness. The *tour de force* of this group, representing the poet at his most daring and auditorially complex, is the long sequence "7, Middagh Street," which sets forth in their different voices the notorious *and* unconventional lodgers—Carson McCullers, Gypsy Rose Lee, Benjamin Britten, Salvador Dali, among others—of the Brooklyn Heights rooming house that W. H. Auden presided over for a time. The work suffers under the excerpting knife, but a small cutting (in the voice of Carson McCullers) might serve to suggest the charm and sophistication of Muldoon's latest idiom:

The magnolia tree at my window's a bonsai
in the glass globe
I jiggle like a cocktail-
waiter from the Keynote Club,
so that Chester's Kwaikiutl
false face and glib,
Jane and Paul Bowles, the chimpanzee

and its trainer, Gypsy
and hers, are briefly caught up in an eddy
of snow; pennies
from heaven, Wynstan's [sic] *odi*
atque amo of Seconal and bennies:
then my cloudy
globe unclouds to reveal the tipsy

MacNeice a monarch
lying in state on a Steinway baby grand
between the rotting
carcasses of two pack-mules from *Un Chien Andalou*

---

picks out a rondo
in some elusive minor key.

The Englishman Tony Harrison, born and raised in working-class
Leeds, educated at the University of Leeds, is in many ways Muldoon's
opposite number. Where Muldoon goes in search of the singular shape,
the unrepeatable lyric signature, Harrison is a man for the syllable
count and the rhyme. To the extent that such a practice defines the
formalist, he is a formalist. But he is no maker of filigrees. There is
nothing decorous or formally ingenious about his lines or structures
(most commonly sixteen-line sonnets). His antecedents are the piston-
stroke lines and straight rhymes of Kipling, of Auden's ballads, of stage
and music hall.

Like his contemporary the Scots poet Douglas Dunn, Harrison
alternately celebrates and scorns the status of the "barbarian" working-
class outsider. His very best poems play off what are perceived as the
awkward and gnarled speech idioms of that class against the linguistic
expectations of the ruling culture. We see this clearly in a series of
coming-of-age poems, included from his aptly titled collection *The
School of Eloquence:*

Outside the whistled gang-call, *Twelfth Street Rag,*
then a Tarzan yodel for the kid who's bored,
whose hand's on his liana . . . no, back
to Labienus and his flaming sword.

Off laiken', then to t'fish oil all the boys
off tartin', off to t'flicks but on, on, on,
the foldaway card table, the green baize,
De Bello Gallico and lexicon.

It's only his jaw muscles that he's tensed
into an enraged *shit* that he can't go;
down with polysyllables, he's against
all pale-face Caesars, *for* Geronimo.

He shoves the frosted attic skylight, shouts:

Ah bloody can't ah've gorra Latin prose.

The Critic's Work

His bodiless head that's poking out's
like patriarchal Cissy-bleeding——ro's.

—"Me Tarzan"

In the deeply affecting sequence that follows this chronicle of an ill-sorted youth, Harrison narrates the deaths of both his parents. First, the mother dies, leaving father and son together in an empty house and bringing on long-deferred kinds of reckoning. Then the father is gone, too, and the son is forced to search out what belongs to him, both in his vanishing heritage of class and in his only partially conquered "higher" world of school and literature. Here, too, Harrison thrusts the spoken idiom up against the standardized, eliciting humor as well as pathos, holding both in check with rhyme and meter:

Last meal together, Leeds, the Queen's Hotel,
That grandish pile of swank in City Square.
Too posh for me! he said (though he dressed well)
If you weren't wi' me now ah'd nivver dare!

I knew that he'd decided that he'd die
not by the way he lingered in the bar,
nor by the look he'd give with one good eye,
nor the firmer handshake and the gruff *ta-ra,*

but when we browsed the station bookstall sales
he picked up *Poems from the Yorkshire Dales*—

'ere tek this un wi' yer to New York
to remind yer 'ow us gaffers used to talk.

The broken lines go through me speeding South—

As t'Doctor stopped to oppen woodland yat . . .
and
wi' skill they putten wuds reet i' his mouth.

—"The Queen's English"

Reading a number of Harrison's poems in sequence, however, one starts to feel the ear go a bit slack at the monotony of the rhythms. And occasionally the suspicion arises that the poet finds it rather easy

---

to "do" a certain kind of poem. Or that rhyme is the principal mode of transport from one notion to the next. This is especially evident in some of the longer poems he includes—"The White Queen" and "A Kumquat for John Keats"; the ceremony of marrying two word-sounds seems more important than the love that purportedly brought them together. The bulk of the book, though, remains original, thoroughly convincing in its projection of embattled identity.

Most readers of poetry by now know the story behind Christopher Logue's *War Music: An Account of Books 16 to 19 of Homer's Iliad:* how Donald Carne-Ross, then at the BBC, invited (or incited) the poet to try his hand at rendering parts of the *Iliad;* how Logue had the temerity, being without Greek, to stitch together—cutting, taking cues from other versions, *inventing*—what has proved to be an astonishingly beautiful, sui generis artifact. Is it an *Iliad?* I think even Logue would say no. For one thing, he has eliminated precisely those elements, the stock words and phrases, upon which its status as an oral epic was based (according to Milman Parry and Albert Lord). But it *is* a living, breathing entity, a poem that builds itself up not from the manipulation of translated idioms but from freshly imagined—newly seen, tasted, felt—details and sensations.

Logue has isolated the episodes that make up from Book 16, or *Patrocleia*—which, he notes in his preface, "might be described as a miniature version of the *Iliad,*" and which culminates in the death of Patroclus—through Book 19, or *Pax,* which has "disaffected allies settling their differences in order to avoid defeat at the hands of a mutual enemy."

But plot is not so important here. What will mesmerize the reader is the sharp, swift, sensuous presentation of a wholly gripping narrative. Logue has learned much of his compositional method from Pound—his use of the vibrant image, his way of quick-cutting to expose the dominant shape of an event—but his eye and his sinewy rhythms are entirely his own. Here is a section from one of the battle scenes of *Patrocleia:*

Patroclus aimed his spear where they were thickest.
That is to say, around

The Critic's Work

The chariot commander, Akafact.
But as Patroclus threw
The ship's mast flamed from stem to peak, and fell
Lengthwise across the incident.
   Its fat waist clubbed the hull's top deck
And the ship flopped sideways.
Those underneath got crunched.
And howling Greeks ran up
To pike the others as they slithered off.
   This fate was not for Akafact:
Because the mast's peak hit the sand no more than six
Feet from Patroclus' car, the horses shied,
Spoiling his cast. Nothing was lost.
   As he fell back, back arched,
God blew the javelin straight; and thus
Mid-air, the cold bronze apex sank
Between his teeth and tongue, parted his brain,
Pressed on, and stapled him against the upturned hull.
His dead jaw gaped. His soul
Crawled off his tongue and vanished into sunlight.

There is so much to remark and to praise: the rich yet accurate phrasing—"Its fat waist clubbed the hull's top deck"—the forceful originality of the verbs—"flopped," "slithered," "stapled"—and, not least, the rhythmic control. Observe how the thronging stresses of the penultimate line—"His dead jaw gaped. His soul"—set up the startling lightness of the last: "Crawled off his tongue and vanished into sunlight." What lovely things can result when the crusts are broken off the classics.

Irish Poets

Poetry anthologies are big business these days, much bigger than the publication of volumes of poetry. Commodious and costly, they are seldom targeted on the lay reader. Their real function is canon making.

Chronicle

Generations of students absorb the categories and valuations promulgated and fix them in the mind as "knowledge." When the content is the poetry of a beleaguered culture like the Irish, however, the consequences are as much political as aesthetic.

Thomas Kinsella hints at some of this in his preface to *The New Oxford Book of Irish Verse.* "New," as it turns out, is a very civil way of putting it. The fact is that the previous *Oxford Book of Irish Verse* pretty much ignored all poetry not written in English. It presented, in other words, the leaves and outermost branches, while suggesting that the tree (like that posited by the Irish philosopher George Berkeley) did not exist. Kinsella's volume, which moves with tact and taste through the whole legacy of Gaelic, Latin, and English (he translates everything himself), entirely supplants that collection. The unmaking of an exclusionist canon can now begin.

The wonderful thing about Kinsella's anthology is that in addition to reflecting the historical development of Irish poetry—and it fulfills its pedagogic aims unobtrusively—major portions of it can be read for the pleasures of imagery and verbal music. Indeed, the particular charm of the latter can be traced in part to the historical collisions that shaped the Irish soul. The formative event was clearly the imposition of Christianity, with all of its missionary asperities, upon the native Celtic paganism. What we see, from the earliest recorded verses on, is an artistically fruitful tension between monkish asceticism on the one hand and unquenchable delight in the natural world on the other. Thus, in a selection of anonymous ninth-century monastic poems, we find an injunction like this:

> A salt and meagre diet
> with mind bent on a book;
> no disputation, visitation;
> conscience serene and calm.

coexisting with a purely sensory effusion:

> The little bird
> let out a whistle
> from his beak tip
>   bright yellow.

The Critic's Work

He sends a note
across Loch Laíg
—a blackbird, a branch
   a mass of yellow.

The advantage of having all translations by one hand—the deft
hand of an acclaimed poet at that—is that we have unity and quality
throughout. But we are, at the same time, subjected to a single poetic
intelligence; other options of cadence and phrasing are lost. Kinsella
might have made some use, I think, of Seamus Heaney's vigorous and
fresh rendering of the twelfth-century *Buile Suibhne* (Sweeney Astray),
which seems in all parts livelier than his own. Or, in the case of the
blackbird poem, Frank O'Connor's version would have added some
welcome dash:

What little throat
Has framed that note?
What gold beak shot
   It far away?
A blackbird on
His leafy throne
Tossed it alone
   Across the bay.

Still, we should be grateful for what has been given. The panorama
is vast and inspiriting. From the vigorous devotions and laments of the
Middle Ages, through the lovely infusions of courtier verse, which
reaches Ireland in the wake of the Norman Conquest, harshness and
sweetness—briar and rose—continue plaiting. If there is a lull, a falling off, it comes in the sixteenth and seventeenth centuries. Kinsella
himself, in his informative notes, finds little to extol.

With the eighteenth century, however, we see a major change of
idiom. English replaces Irish as the dominant poetic language. Jonathan
Swift and Oliver Goldsmith hold the stage. But their witty and urbane
verses, measured against the Irish demotic tradition of centuries, do
not feel central. Far more compelling—and, for subsequent poets, in-
spirational—is Brian Merriman's earthy and argumentative long poem

"The Midnight Court." Written in Irish in the 1780's, this battle of voices puts the Irish bachelor on trial, and scornful women give their verdict in no uncertain terms:

> We enact hereby as a law for women:
> a man, twenty-one and not yoked to a mate,
> to be forcibly dragged by the head, without pity,
> and tied to this tree beside the tomb.

But the earthiness of Merriman's blast dissolves in the current of sentimental Romanticism that comes with the nineteenth century. Thomas Moore, James Clarence Mangan, Samuel Ferguson, and Thomas Davis (the last three claimed as influences by Yeats) infect a whole age with rousing and rhyming patriotism. Of all centuries, including the early Christian period, the nineteenth feels, for the American reader, the most remote from our own. It took the genius of Yeats to curb and temper that music, and to forge a poetry that joins the ancient tension between nature-love and spiritual desire to the complex disaffections of modernity.

After Yeats—and no one goes to anthologies for his work—Kinsella attends to the other poets of our century, covering all bases and offering, finally, few surprises. This part of the anthology is disappointing. Ireland is, after all, in the midst of an astonishing poetic renaissance right now. With only these samplings to go by, we would never guess it. What good fortune, then, that Faber has released Paul Muldoon's compendium, *The Faber Book of Contemporary Irish Poetry*. Modestly cutting his own contribution out (and, alas, those of Seamus Deane and Richard Murphy), Muldoon proposes very ample selections from Patrick Kavanagh, Louis MacNeice, Kinsella, John Montague, Michael Longley, Heaney, Derek Mahon, Paul Durcan, Tom Paulin, and Medbh McGuckian. There's not a weak poet in the lot.

The urge to enumerate delights exceeds available space. I was struck by Paulin's tough and tussocky evocations of place, Mahon's shrewd way of intercutting irony and compassion, and Durcan's winnowed obliquities, which seem to infuse the least bit of whimsy with ominous possibility.

The strong spine of the book, however, the language cable con-

---

The Critic's Work

necting Irish poetry in our times with its origins, runs most conspicuously through Kavanagh, Montague, and Heaney. Here is the love of
the land, the embattled awareness of self, the lyrical impulse flying in
the face of historical exigency. Muldoon has done well to include entire Kavangh's durable epic of life on the land, "The Great Hunger," as
well as a strong selection of his shorter poems. Reading through these,
it's hard to dispute the contention by Heaney and others that Kavanagh was, no less than Yeats, the authentic fount for Irish verse in
our century. Even the slightest fragment, like this from "The Long
Garden," reveals a man capable of finding bounty and affirmation
wherever he turns:

> It was the garden of the golden apples,
> A long garden between a railway and a road,
> In the sow's rooting where the hen scratches
> We dipped our fingers in the pockets of God.

I urge every lover of poetry to dip into a less exalted pocket and get
this book.

PART IV:

Poets in Translation

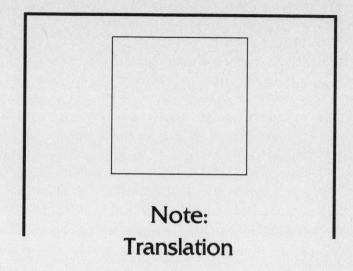

Note:
Translation

The case against translation is irrefutable, but only if we are presented, in Ibsen's phrase, with "the claims of the ideal." In actual performance these claims cannot be met or allowed.

—GEORGE STEINER

T ranslation is, invariably, falsification. Traducement. And if we high-mindedly leave matters at that, we will never read poetry except in the original. As soon as we forfeit "the claims of the ideal," however, the gates of discussion are open again.

We live in the midst of a vast and various literary culture, most of which—if we are strict with ourselves—is beyond our reach. Should we live with our backs to it?

Or should we strike a different kind of bargain? For it could be that the subtle (but often all-important) losses incurred through translation may be offset—in part—by other gains. I may not be able to read Czeslaw Milosz or Zbigniew Herbert in the original Polish, and may not, therefore, truly *know* their work. But I would argue that having read them in translation has not been without benefits. In the process, I have strained my Amero-centric prejudices against a whole other set of cultural assumptions. I have become, if not in a deep way then surficially, cosmopolitan—at least for the duration of my reading.

For though much is lost, *some*thing does come through. And that something is what burns against my rootedness, against my preconceptions. Because I recognize that the language is not solidly under my feet—the way it is when I read Keats or Auden or Roethke—I walk differently. I develop other muscles and new sets of reflexes. The ultimate effect may be to make me a better reader of poetry in English.

In spite of my views, expressed in earlier sections, about poetry's embeddedness in its originating language, I believe that we must do all we can to get at works from other cultures. I don't see this as a contradiction so much as an effort to have it both ways. I know that I cannot get at poetry except in the original, but I cannot stop trying.

This said, there remain a number of distinctions, or considerations, to be set out. To begin with, we find among different kinds of poetry different degrees of translatability. Some poetry grows directly out of the secret life of the language; it derives its main power, interest, and importance from its stirring up of the linguistic depths of words. We can think of Mallarmé, Mandelstam, Hölderlin.

On the opposite extreme are poets whose central force arises from image creation or the juxtaposition of ideas and perspectives. Tomas Tranströmer could be said to exemplify the former, Zbigniew Herbert the latter. This does not mean that these poets are any less careful in their use of language. It does mean, though, that less is lost through translation. The poetry uses words, but it does not originate phonically *in* the word.

Another distinction must be made between different kinds of translations. Some, like Baudelaire's Poe or Logue's Homer, use the original as a pretext for injecting new or refurbished aesthetic values into literature. Their effort is less to translate than to make new art.

Others, in attempting to serve the original, manage through a happy convergence of talent and temperamental affinity versions that may be accounted as exceptional poetry even in their second language. Many of Richard Wilbur's translations are of this order.

Wilbur is, of course, an artisan of rare distinction. Most translations fall far short of their originals and are not to be thought of as poetry. But even these may perform a service for the life of the imagination—if not the reader's, then that of the writer. Who would deny that our contemporary poetic idiom has been significantly influenced by ultimately inaccurate renderings of Neruda, Rilke, and a dozen others?

The last of the distinctions would be among the different ways in which we read translations. And here I can make use of my own experience with poets and texts.

The Polish poets (Milosz, Herbert, and Zagajewski) were, linguistically speaking, the most distant. As I could not sound out the originals, I was forced to take the translations on faith. Though I was not happy with having to read at such a remove from the source, I did feel that their way of writing—with distinct images and idea sequences—made these poets at least partially accessible.

Pasternak was a different story. If ever a poet worked from the sound materials of a language, it was Pasternak. Fortunately, I had studied enough Russian in college to be able to make out the sound structure of the one poem that I chose to focus upon. And as I explain in my essay, Joseph Brodsky was good enough to read the poem into my tape recorder and to give me a word-by-word crib. I had, therefore, some sense of how a Russian would hear the rhythm. A dictionary helped me fill in some of the remaining gaps. *Some.* I don't flatter myself that I "got" the poem completely. I could never—even if I had completed my study of the language—have caught its manifold lateral associations and resonances. But in the hours that I spent going back and forth, repeating and listening, I felt myself beginning to penetrate the language surface. I felt my hands close momentarily around the quicksilver life of the poem.

The Rilke project was instructive in a different way. In that case I was looking at as many versions as possible within the full span of the *oeuvre*. I tried to piece together what I could from the German (which I

Note: Translation

can play with but which I don't *know*) and the various English renderings. A peculiar kind of linguistic triangulation ensued. For the multiple
possibilities of expression would sometimes correct and refine my understanding until, looking at the original, I imagined that I was able to
read it.

Finally, with the Octavio Paz poems, I was closer to home ground.
I had studied Spanish for years in high school. Though I had forgotten
all but the rudiments, I found that I was quickly familiar with constructions, syntactic possibilities, and sound values. By working back
and forth between languages, I could occasionally feel that I was inside
the skin of a particular poem.

Obviously, then, these are not the essays of a skilled comparativist.
Readers searching for a trustworthy guide to the inner workings of
these poets should hasten in the opposite direction. I cannot vouch for
my findings and assertions. By the same token, though, I would not
rule out that unfamiliarity and its accompanying unease might have
pushed me at times to a more concentrated kind of listening.

I include these seven essays as tokens of the spirit in which they
were undertaken. They are explorations, forays, inconclusive ventures
toward a larger view of literature. They make possible certain discus-
sions of politics and mysticism that a straight diet of English-language
poetry would not easily permit. Let's accept, too, that the Muse is
multilingual, even if we are not. Are we not drawn on, always, by the
sense that there are untold treasures just on the other side—behind
that undulant curtain of sounds?

Rainer Maria Rilke

Boris Pasternak chose to begin his memoir, *Safe Conduct,* with a curious description of an incident:

One hot summer's morning in the year 1900 an express left Moscow's Kursk Station. Just before it started, someone in a black Tyrolean cape appeared outside the window. A tall woman was with him. Probably she was his mother or an elder sister. They talked with my father about something familiar to all three of them and which evoked the same warm response. But the woman exchanged occasional phrases in Russian with my mother, while the stranger spoke only German. And although I knew the language perfectly well, I had never heard it spoken like that. For that reason, between the two rings of the departure bell, that foreigner on the crowded platform seemed like a silhouette among solids, a fiction in the thick of reality.

The obliquity, sustained for several pages, is pure Pasternak. When we have all but forgotten the episode, he names the shadowy stranger: Rainer Maria Rilke. The older woman, whom Pasternak does not identify, had to have been Rilke's friend and former mistress Lou Andreas-Salomé. The precocious onlooker was ten years old at the time of the encounter.

When Pasternak does finally name the poet, he reveals the true nature of his enterprise: to write an autobiography that would recover not what happened, but what *mattered*. He begins with his first—and only—glimpse of Rilke because Rilke had come to embody his ideal of poetic perfection. Pasternak was not alone in his veneration. When he died in 1926, Rilke was recognized as the undisputed giant of European poetry. Marina Tsvetaeva called him "poetry itself."

Sixty years later, Rilke's stature remains undiminished. Indeed, his *oeuvre* has engendered so much activity among translators of late that it almost seems he is still out there, producing. Poems hitherto unknown in English turn up in almost every new collection, and collections appear quicker than one can read them. More remarkable, however, is the fact that this surge in publication and popularity (the books do sell!) flies in the face of prevailing literary trends. In literature as elsewhere, this is the era of quotidian caution, while Rilke is the prophet of the terrors and ecstacies of soul making.

Are we, then, in the throes of another highbrow fad? Or are readers finding a genuine spiritual guidance that is unavailable elsewhere? Or is it simply a matter of poetic excellence reaping its due recognition? Yes to all three questions. But that explains little. For no single Rilke exists in all that welter of books. The trajectory of the poet's career passed through a number of sharply defined, at times even antithetical, phases. From the extreme Romanticism of the early work (*The Book of Hours, Stories of God*) to the long-fought-for "objective" vision in the *New Poems* of 1907; from the call for inward transformation in the

Duino Elegies to the elegant lightness of the last poems written in French—Rilke made a unique art at every turn of his life. One does not just *read* the man—one joins up with him at one point or another on his pilgrimage. Before we can assess the boom, we must assess the career.

In 1900, when Pasternak saw him, Rilke was twenty-five years old, poised at the brink of poetic maturity. Though he may have looked like a "silhouette among solids," he was of this world enough to be a canny self-promoter. He had been sending his youthful poems, stories, and plays to editors and publishers all over Germany and central Europe. (The popular image of Rilke as a creature of pure spirit, aloof from the hustle of the marketplace, derives more from his later years. Then, thanks to the devotion of his publisher, Anton Kippenberg, and the generosity of a number of wealthy friends, he was free to cultivate his Muse as he saw fit.) Recent biographies by Wolfgang Leppmann and Donald Prater show just how much of his energy Rilke consecrated to flattering, wheedling, and beseeching the influential.

Rilke's traveling companion, Lou Andreas-Salomé, was, by 1900, looking for ways to put distance between herself and her young admirer. Though she had a reputation as an outspoken freethinker, she was also a married woman old enough to be Rilke's mother (she had broken Nietzsche's heart some fifteen years before). By the time of this trip to Russia, their second, the poet had been demoted from lover to friend; Lou would soon resort to geographical distance.

Rilke didn't seem to mind this first change of status. What mattered most to him, judging from the lifelong pattern of his relationships, was the proximity of a sympathetic female presence. He would almost never be without some gifted, emotional woman within earshot. He had his Odilies, Sidonies, Loulous, and Magdas. . . . A certain kind of woman found the poet irresistible. It was only when the beloved showed signs of wanting something more permanent that he invoked his amatory credo: Love me, love my solitude. Or, as he put it in his First Duino Elegy: "Isn't it time that we lovingly/freed ourselves from the beloved and, quivering, endured . . . (?)" How much of this ambivalence had to do with his mother—a hysterical,

---

Rainer Maria Rilke

doting woman, who liked to outfit her young son in dresses—is for the psychologists to decide.

When the Russian journey ended, Lou imposed a separation. Rilke traveled by himself to the artists' colony at Worpswede near Bremen and fell in love with a young sculptress named Clara Westhoff. Their precipitous marriage was a mistake. The bald chronology tells it all: 1901, Rilke and Clara are married; that same year, the birth of a daughter, Ruth; 1902, Rilke moves to Paris, alone. The charade was carried on for years—Rilke would establish quarters; he would send for his family. It never happened. But as late as 1906, he was still writing to Clara that the touching of their solitudes was the highest possible affirmation of their love. As John Berryman put it in his third *Dream Song:* "Rilke was a *jerk.*"

But jerk or no, Rilke did become a sublime poet. And it was in Paris, Walter Benjamin's "Capital of the Nineteenth Century," that the sublimity first manifested itself. Perhaps "manifested itself" misleads in emphasis—the lyrics and prose writings of Rilke's Paris period resulted from the strictest discipline. The young poet finally abandoned his rhetorical spiritualism for an art rooted in sensory vividness. The two bright stars by which he steered his course were Rodin and, some time later, Cézanne. Rilke learned as much from their punishing ethic of daily work as he did from their aesthetic example.

Clara was useful in at least one respect—she gave Rilke an introduction to Rodin. Upon his arrival in Paris, Rilke went immediately to the master's studio in Meudon. Before long, he was visiting regularly. He followed Rodin, watched him work, and began to assemble notes for a study. Rodin's work habits—the sculptor never stopped—astonished Rilke. If only the poet could work like that! Then, with great speed and resolve, Rilke found a way. He would direct his gaze outward; he would forge his objective impressions into a more sculpted kind of lyric. Scarcely three months after his arrival in Paris, Rilke had written "The Panther," the signature poem of his new style.

To grasp what a *volte-face* was involved, we need only glance at Rilke's earlier style. The prose of his *Stories of God* (1900) and the poems of the first part of *The Book of Hours,* written immediately after his return from Russia, show the poet struggling with spiritual ultimates. Strongly influenced by Nietzsche, as well as glimpses of the Russian peasant culture, Rilke was evolving his idea of God as an entity yet to be created. As he wrote in *The Prayers,* a lengthy cyclic poem of the period:

> We are building Thee, with tremulous hands,
> And we pile atom upon atom.
> But who can complete Thee
> Cathedral Thou?

Compare this with the rigorously framed perception of animal otherness in the justly celebrated panther poem:

> His gaze has from the passing back and forth of bars
> become so tired, that it holds nothing more.
> It seems to him there are a thousand bars
> and behind a thousand bars no world.
>
> The supple pace of powerful soft strides,
> turning in the very smallest circle,
> is like a dance of strength around a center
> in which a mighty will stands numbed.
>
> From time to time the curtain of the pupils
> silently parts——. Then an image enters,
> goes through the taut stillness of the limbs,
> and is extinguished in the heart.

—trans. Edward Snow

Soon would follow masterpieces like "Orpheus. Euridice. Hermes." and "Tombs of the Heterae."

Rilke searched during this crucially formative period not so much for a poetry of objective description as for a way of displacing focus from the observer to the thing observed. The poem was to be a bridge thrown from an *in here* to an independently existing *out there;* the poet strove to purge his perception of subjectivity. This is, of course, an impossible project; language cannot attain anything like the neutrality of color or clay. But in the effort, Rilke learned an aesthetic rigor that would henceforth temper his tendency toward Romantic effusiveness.

Rainer Maria Rilke

(The tendency was indulged freely in his correspondence, however, which he used as a proving ground for images, impressions, and turns of phrase.) The *New Poems* have often been cited as a pioneering of the principle that T. S. Eliot would later dub the "objective correlative."

Rodin was, as Rilke found out, a temperamental master. The poet served for a time as his secretary and factotum. He was fired during one of Rodin's rages. But Rilke's admiration for the artist remained unswerving: He published two separate essays on the man and his art. The first, dating from 1903, is an intoxicated proclamation of Rodin's creative force. The 1907 essay, far more subdued, acknowledges the enormous difficulties inherent in all artistic endeavor. The poet had clearly learned a few hard lessons in the intervening years.

Rilke's encounter with the genius of Cézanne came at the exhibition of the Salon d'Automne in 1907. If exposure to Rodin changed his work, the paintings of Cézanne confirmed his decision and spurred him further along his chosen path. In a remarkable sequence of letters to Clara—now published as *Letters on Cézanne*—Rilke set down the day-by-day impact of his visits to the salon. His letter of October 13, 1907, shows more clearly than any manifesto how much his sense of artistic mission had changed:

> If I were to come and visit you, I would surely also see the splendor of moor and heath, the hovering bright greens of meadows, the birches, with new and different eyes; and though this transformation is something I've completely experienced and shared before, in part of the Book of Hours, nature was still then a general occasion for me, an evocation, an instrument in whose strings my hands found themselves again; I was not yet sitting before her; I allowed myself to be swept away by the soul that was emanating from her; she came over me with her vastness, her huge exaggerated presence, the way the gift of prophecy came over Saul; exactly like that. I walked about and saw, not nature but the visions she gave me. How little I would have been able to learn from Cézanne, from Van Gogh, then.

Later, in the same letter, he adds: "[Cézanne] knew how to swallow back his love for every apple and put it to rest in the painted apple forever"—his aesthetic ideal of the Paris years could not have been put more eloquently or concisely.

Those years—from 1902 until the outbreak of war in 1914—were by no means stationary. Almost every few months, Rilke would interrupt the ordeals of composition in order to travel. There were reading tours, guilty—and brief—visits to Clara and Ruth in Germany; then there were the more pleasurable trips to Capri, Venice, Egypt, Spain, and elsewhere, most of them subsidized by his patrons and friends. (Rilke's social successes were such that he never soiled his hands with anything worse than ink so long as he lived—quite an accomplishment for the son of a retired railroad official.) Every departure from Paris marked Rilke's desire to shake off oppressive solitude and the recurrent threat of artistic stagnation. Similarly, with every return he announced his resolve to recover the productive power of his first happy Paris season. He had a new project now: Shortly after his poetic breakthrough, Rilke had begun working on the prose experiment that would eventually be published as *The Notebooks of Malte Laurids Brigge.*

Malte was, for Rilke, an enormous effort of spirit. The book was nearly plotless, a sequence of meditations moving back and forth through the memory of its eponymous narrator. If the *New Poems* represented a distancing from the subjective claim, *Malte* was the poet's effort to impose sculptural shape upon his deepest preoccupations. It is the closest thing we have to a portrait of the artist as a young man. Rilke drew many of the feverish, gritty descriptions of street life in the poorer quarters of Paris directly from his own journals. Where Malte diverges from his creator is in his memories of growing up in a haunted Danish manor—the solidly bourgeois poet (born in Prague) had to draw these chiaroscuro passages out of his own imagination.

In *Malte,* Rilke first extensively developed the theme that would be central to his *Duino Elegies* and *Sonnets to Orpheus:* that death is the hidden "other half" of life; that we carry it within ourselves like a seed that we must tend as it germinates and grows. Already Rilke was building his philosophy around a welcoming, rather than refusing, of the inevitable. His late lyrics are utterly singular in fusing death obsession with a spirit verging on the celebratory.

No less important is Malte's powerful retelling of the parable of the Prodigal Son, with which Rilke chose to end the book. In his version, the son leaves home in order to escape the stunting force of his family's love. He returns only after he has come to understand how earthly, mortal love perverts the intransitive love that is God's. The prodigal does his best to endure everyone's "vain" and misdirected affections. The book ends with these most enigmatic sentences: "He was now terribly difficult to love, and he felt that only One would be capable of it. But He was not yet willing." The words obviously embody Rilke's own conviction. For one who had single-mindedly turned his back on the flawed love of his fellow mortals, the phrase "not yet" must have conjured a terrifying hollowness.

Rilke nearly collapsed from exhaustion after finishing *Malte,* and for the next two years all production stopped. The poet began to wonder if he might not have depleted his powers once and for all. A period of restless traveling followed: Germany, Italy, Prague, Algiers, Cairo . . . Then, in October of 1911, he accepted the hospitality of Princess Marie von Thurn und Taxis-Hohenlohe, going to stay at her magnificent castle at Duino on the Adriatic Sea. The story of his first great inspiration is well known: how in January of 1912 he interrupted the writing of a business letter to walk on the castle ramparts, how he heard a voice call out of the wind the beginning of what became the First Elegy: "Wer, wenn ich schriee, hörte mich denn aus der Engel Ordnungen?" By the evening of the same day Rilke had written the whole of that elegy, and in the days immediately following he completed the Second; the Third and Sixth were written a year later. But the follow-through, the creative burst that would bring the cycle of ten to completion, would not come for a full decade.

Erich Heller has written, in an essay entitled "Rilke in Paris," that "for the time being, for the ten years between Duino and Muzot [where the sequence was finished], Rilke did not quite understand what the voice that was in the storm demanded of him, the voice that then at last did speak to *him.* . . ." Heller's point is a good one. Rilke could not have been ready for the whole dictation. The *Duino Elegies,* along with the quickly written *Sonnets to Orpheus,* are the very apotheosis of inwardness. Their ultimate claim is that it is the destined human task to transform the materiality of the world into spirit ("We are the bees of the Invisible," wrote Rilke to his Polish translator). But in 1912, the poet was still very much occupied with the obdurate reality of the *out there*. He had not yet relinquished one vision of poetic salvation for its opposite. Indeed, it may be that Rilke's inability to write any poetry during the long war years had less to do with his sorrow at the geopolitical struggle than with the fact of a psychic contest between two very different ways of understanding experience.

On June 20, 1914, before the outbreak of the war, Rilke wrote as follows to his old friend Lou: "Lou, dear, here is a strange poem, written this morning, which I am sending you right away because I involuntarily called it 'Turning-point,' because it describes *the* turning point which no doubt must come if I am to stay alive." The poem, too long to quote here in entirety, ends with these lines:

> For there is a boundary to looking.
> And the world that is looked at so deeply
> wants to flourish in love.
>
> Work of the eyes is done, now
> go and do heart-work
> on all the images imprisoned within you; for you
> overpowered them: but even now you don't know them.
> Learn, inner man, to look on your inner woman,
> the one attained from a thousand
> natures, the merely attained but
> not yet beloved form.

—trans. Stephen Mitchell

On the surface, this looks like a complete reversal of Rilke's program. In truth, it is a most radical extension. "Work of the eyes is done," he writes. Only now, after the objective seeing of the world has been undertaken, can the next phase begin: transformation. Implied in the phrasing is a larger vision of interdependence. For the poet is not merely bringing the *out there* back into the crucible of his subjectivity. No, the world "wants" to flourish in love. As Rilke would later ask in the Ninth Elegy: "Earth, isn't this what you want: to arise within us, *invisible*?" Poet and world are no longer seen as separate; a single breath of spirit seems to move through all things.

Rainer Maria Rilke

As Rilke once held that mankind had to make God, so he affirms in "Turning-point" that all of creation needs man in order to realize its ultimate destiny as pure spirit. What Hegel began as philosophy—the idea of the self-realization of a World Spirit through history—Rilke sought to bring to completion in his poetry. And what is this vision, finally, but a secular eschatology? If the redemption of the world cannot be had through God, or Son, then the task falls to us. The similarities between Rilke's aims and Nietzsche's have often been remarked. There is, however, one crucial difference. Where Nietzsche adjured his superman to *will,* Rilke—as the cited passage suggests—called for pliancy and receptivity above all. His "inner woman," who here sounds very much like the Jungian *anima,* is a figure of maternal gestation, not conquest. The last lines of the Tenth Elegy, similarly, imply that final happiness is something *granted:*

And we, who have always thought
of happiness as *rising,* would feel
the emotion that almost overwhelms us
whenever a happy thing *falls.*

Eight years would elapse between "Turning-point" and the completion of the *Elegies.* It was to be a creatively barren time for Rilke. Though he greeted the outbreak of war with jubilation—he actually began a series of hymns to the god of battles—he quickly perceived his own foolishness; he thereupon succumbed to an inertia that lasted until long after the war ended.

Reading about this period reminds us of the difficulty—even futility—of the biographer's job, especially when his subject's activity was almost entirely internal, as Rilke's was. And when there are not even writings, nothing but the artful posturings of the letters, all purchase disappears. It is as if the poet, in the prime of maturity, had simply stopped living for a decade. Prater and Leppmann have both scratched the ground for revealing details, but neither has turned up much besides the expected string of amours. We get the clear impression that Rilke remained almost immune to the surrounding catastrophe. Apart from a brief interval in uniform—influential friends quickly got him released from duty—the poet spent most of the war years living in stylish security in Munich. In both of these biographies, he recedes from view; and he never fully reappears in either.

We can blame the confusion of war, the paucity of information, any number of things—but isn't it possible that the outer man *did* more or less disappear? After all, the creative explosion of 1922— when Rilke wrote five elegies and the complete cycle of fifty-five *Sonnets to Orpheus* in a two-week period—did not come from nowhere. The preceding years would have seen a great hoarding of inner resources. If you compute the sums, not much remains for living.

Except as it is revealed in his art, Rilke's inwardness stayed hidden. Before the mystery of the creative artist, said Freud, psychoanalysis must lay down its arms. The same applies to biography. For all that they have uncovered about the circumstances, places, and people in Rilke's life (Prater is painstaking to a fault; Leppmann moves swiftly, but tends to glibness), neither biographer has begun to answer the central question. How did the selfish, snobbish, and decidedly unsympathetic man portrayed in their pages come to produce such an utterly singular body of work? Even a modicum of theorizing would be welcome.

In 1919, after years of doubt and depression, Rilke left Germany for Switzerland. There he eventually secured for himself the isolated château at Muzot—it would be his last, his only, real home. Those were the walls that he stroked "like a big animal" on February 9, 1922, when the second immense inspiration came to him. On February 11, he could write to Marie Taxis:

> Only just now, Saturday the *eleventh* at six in the evening, did I finish! —Everything in only a few days, it was an indescribable storm, a hurricane in my spirit (like *before* at *Duino*), everything that is fiber and tissue within me was strained to the breaking point. There could be no thought of eating, God knows who nourished me.
>
> But now it's done. Done. Done.
> Amen.

In the next nine days, Rilke wrote twenty-nine more sonnets—only then was he really done.

Rainer Maria Rilke

One convulsive shudder had produced two very different kinds of masterpieces. Where the *Duino Elegies* are declarative, their long lines bearing a freight of images, expostulations and ideas, the *Sonnets to Orpheus* hover with wingbeat delicacy at the very edge of the expressible. The *Elegies* argue the transformation of the world; the *Sonnets,* through the mediating persona of Orpheus, come closer to enacting it. With the very first lines—"A tree ascended there. Oh pure transcendence! / Oh Orpheus sings! Oh tall tree in the ear!"—Rilke announces the highest possible claim for poetry and song: the conversion of all that exists into sound.

It is impossible, of course, to do any more than hint at the visionary force of either work. But neither am I convinced that their central mysteries can even *be* elucidated or paraphrased. For Rilke's insistence was upon language and song as experience, as events in the ear. There are no shortcuts. Readers, even practiced readers, are likely to be rebuffed again and again. Those who have no German face an additional obstacle. No translation, however skillful, can reproduce the sound values of the original. And the sound values, especially in the purely lyrical *Sonnets,* are fully half the experience. Compare the texture of the German of the first two lines from the well-known Sonnet 13 (second cycle):

> Sei allen Abschied voran, als wäre er hinter
> dir, wie der Winter, der eben geht.

with Stephen Mitchell's semantically faithful rendering:

> Be ahead of all parting, as though it already were
> behind you, like the winter that has just gone by.

The meaning has been carried with some elegance, but the dense weave of vowels, consonants, and rhymes—"als wäre er hinter/dir, wie der Winter"—has been sacrificed. The problems every translator faces are here exacerbated, for sound itself is an intrinsic part of Rilke's theme.

When the *Elegies* and *Sonnets* were at last finished, Rilke enjoyed an enduring sense of accomplishment: He spoke of having fulfilled his poetic mission. He did continue to write poetry, but no longer in

German. He felt that he had taken his mother tongue to the limit and could do no more with it. In his last years, then, Rilke wrote over four hundred lyrics in French, most of them in thematic sequences. In their near-transparent lightness, they are cousins of the *Sonnets.* But every so often, as in this section from *The Roses,* one can also hear echoes of the Rilke of the *New Poems.* This evocation of the rose has quite a lot in common with the description of the pacing panther:

> All that spinning on your stem
> to end yourself, round rose,
> doesn't that make you dizzy?
> But drenched by your impetus,
>
> in your bud you just ignore
> yourself. It's a world that whirls
> around so its calm center dares
> the round repose of the round rose.
>
> —trans. A. Poulin, Jr.

Rilke died on December 29, 1926, not from the prick of a rose-bush thorn, as the legend would have it, but from a rare and painful form of leukemia. He did prick his finger while gathering roses for a visitor, and the resulting infection may have hastened the eruption of his final illness, but the myth only simplifies and trivializes a long struggle and denies the poet what he most insisted upon: that he be allowed to die his own death. He was buried at the cemetery in Raron, Switzerland; chiseled on his stone is this most beautiful epitaph:

> Rose, pure Contradiction, Delight
> to be No-one's Sleep under so many
> Lids.
>
> —trans. Rika Lesser

By the time he died, Rilke had achieved world renown. The cele-bration of his birthday in December of 1925 brought greetings and *Festschrift* honors from every side. Among the salutations was one from the painter Leonid Pasternak, whom Rilke had met in 1899 during his first visit to Russia. Replying to Pasternak's letter, Rilke added a few

---

Rainer Maria Rilke

words of praise for the poetry of his son, Boris. The compliment was passed along, not without effect. "It's as if my shirt were split down the front by the expansion of my heart," an ecstatic Boris wrote to his sister. He promptly wrote a reply to his idol:

> The magical coincidence that I should come to your notice was a staggering event to me. . . . I was alone in a room; none of my family were here when I read the lines about this. . . . I rushed to the window. It was snowing, people were walking outside. I could take nothing in, I was crying.

In the same letter, Pasternak urged upon Rilke the kindred genius of his friend Marina Tsvetaeva—would Rilke permit her to write to him? Soon letters were passing from poet to poet; only Rilke's final illness brought the three-way volley to an end.

I don't know that a more passionate document exists than the recently published *Letters, Summer 1926.* Personal confessions and poetic celebrations are charged with eroticism; emotions run high. Rilke: "Yes and yes and yes, Marina, all yeses to what you want and are, together as large as YES to life itself. . . : but contained in the latter there are, after all, all those ten thousand noes, the unforeseeable ones. . . ." Tsvetaeva: "Rainer, just always say yes to all that I want—it won't turn out so badly, after all. Rainer, if I say to you that I am your Russia, I'm only saying (one more time) that I care for you."

Letters are, of course, letters. And since we shouldn't even really be reading them, we make certain allowances. But even with allowances, the whole business cloys. Is this the soil of temperament required for the nourishing of a vital lyricism? Or is this more like the hypertrophy—rhetorical emotion consuming itself—that must prove fatal to any romanticism? Who *was* this Rilke (this Tsvetaeva, this Pasternak)?

Our removal in time makes this question very hard to answer, and reference to the historical epoch does not clarify matters any. After all, by 1926, Eliot had published *The Waste Land,* Hemingway had written the tough prose of *In Our Time,* and Auden was already putting together the impudently discordant poems that would make his reputation. The Rilke-Pasternak-Tsvetaeva letters represent, if anything, the last phosphorescence of the nineteenth century. The large-scale abrasions of modernity make these outcries of feeling and sensibility sound hysterical and outmoded—more remote from us than anything in the Roman elegists, or even Sappho.

The idiom of Rilke's work is, fortunately, a good deal more austere and demanding than the idiom of his correspondence. And if we can't say precisely who he was as a man, we can at least try to make some sense of his legacy. Who is Rilke for us today? What cultural forces—or needs—underlie the flourishing Rilke industry?

Rilke is not, let us note, one of those suddenly discovered "greats." Editions of his work have been available in English since the late 1930's. And he has always had a following. Not just among poets and literati, either. Romantics of every stripe found the singing-master of their soul in the difficult, breathless cadences set out by M. D. Herter Norton and J. B. Leishman, his two most prolific early translators. Generations of English and American readers came to know the *Duino Elegies* through the peculiar Germanized English of the Leishman/Stephen Spender version:

> Every Angel is terrible. Still, though, alas!
> I invoke you, almost deadly birds of the soul,
> knowing what you are. Oh, where are the days of Tobias,
> when one of the shining-most stood on the simple threshold,
> a little disguised for the journey, no longer appalling,
> (a youth to the youth as he curiously peered outside).
> Let the archangel perilous now, from behind the stars,
> step but a step down hitherwards: high up-beating,
> our heart would out-beat us. Who are you?
>
> —from the Second Elegy

The sense is no more problematic than in any translation of the *Elegies,* but there is no suggestion that the work belongs to the genus of the modern.

The Rilke boom that we are presently witnessing is very much bound up with the retranslating of the *oeuvre.* A. Poulin, Jr., Stephen Mitchell, and Edward Snow—to name the three most energetic workers—have among them brought a good part of the output over into a

---

Rainer Maria Rilke

swifter, simpler, more Americanized idiom. They have sought to release Rilke from the trappings of the awkward and archaic and to give him a place in the modernist pantheon. Rilke's current popularity has everything to do with his new readability.

The 1977 publication of A. Poulin, Jr.'s versions of the *Duino Elegies* and *Sonnets to Orpheus* may have been the first herald of change. Look at Poulin's rendering of the very same lines:

> Every angel's terrifying. Almost deadly birds
> of my soul, I know what you are, but, oh,
> I still sing to you! What happened to the days of Tobias
> when one of you stood in the simple doorway, partly
> disguised for the trip, radiant, no longer appalling;
> (a young man to the young man as he looked out amazed).
> If the archangel, the dangerous one behind the stars,
> took just one step down toward us today: the quicker
> pounding of our heart would kill us. Who are you?

A "journey" has become a "trip," "hitherwards" is now "today"— indeed, the gravity of the older version has been eliminated. In its place, a hopped-up ("Every angel's terrifying") phraseology, a freer narrative line. As Robert Lowell wrote: "It's hard to imagine the *Elegies* first written in English. Rilke has sealed them in German, which is part of their essential mystery and foreignness. . . . Now, because of Mr. Poulin's translation, I experience the *Elegies* almost as English." Lowell, of course, was anything but a purist when it came to issues of translation. His own *Imitations* (he takes on several of Rilke's lyrics) were blasted by scholars and translators alike for their brazen deletions and alterations.

Poulin, too, was drubbed by a number of critics. But the taboo had been breached. His translations made it much easier for those who would follow. Of these, Mitchell has been the most prolific and consistently skillful. He has singlehandedly reprocessed the *Letters to a Young Poet, The Notebooks of Malte Laurids Brigge,* both the *Sonnets* and the *Elegies,* as well as a number of the lyrics. Mitchell's idiom strikes a compromise between the kind of stripped and speeded voice that Poulin found, and the more ceremonious and awkward diction of some

of the earlier translators. His rendition of the stanza in question runs as
follows:

> Every angel is terrifying. And yet, alas,
> I invoke you, almost deadly birds of the soul,
> knowing about you. Where are the days of Tobias,
> when one of you, veiling his radiance, stood at the front door,
> slightly disguised for the journey, no longer appalling;
> (a young man like the one who curiously peeked through the
>   window).
> But if the archangel now, perilous, from behind the stars
> took even one step down toward us: our own heart, beating
> higher and higher, would beat us to death. Who *are* you?

Mitchell keeps the stateliness of the Leishman/Spender translation, but
he combs out its worst knots. "Still, though, alas!," "shining-most,"
and "hitherwards" have all been eliminated. But "I invoke you" has
won out over Poulin's colloquial "I know what you are." Mitchell is
generally canny in his choices. He tries to position himself midway
between poet and reader, effecting at every turn a solution that both
gratifies the poet's expressiveness and the reader's desire to understand. Erich Heller, one of the better explicators of Rilke, has written
of Mitchell's renderings: ". . . the *Duino Elegies* succeed almost always
in converting the energies of thought into telling images. . . . A list of
these happy transformations of the abstract into concrete pictures
would fill pages. In accompanying this most impressive 'imaging' in
English, Stephen Mitchell proves his mastery of the art of translation."

Whatever cavils native German speakers might have about word
choice or idiom (I have heard it said that *any* translation of Rilke's
German into English is doomed to be a travesty), the fact is that the
poet is now available in a reasonably plain English. But availability is
one thing, popularity another. It would seem that more and more
readers are looking to Rilke because they think—or already know—
that he has something they want, or need. Why Rilke?

I can think of several possible reasons. The most obvious: that in
our ironic, materialistic period, Rilke's poetry represents a distillation
of the most endangered values. Rilke stands for inwardness, spiritual

quest, the primacy of feeling over intellection (the same things that Hesse represented for young idealists in the sixties). To read Rilke—whether you understand him or not—is to cast a vote against the status quo.

In one sense, obviously, this is true of nearly all poetry and reading of poetry. But Rilke is something of a special case, because his work offers a complete secular cosmology. It is a system (a most elusive and vague one, true), a way, an answer. The poet announces a grand, and ultimately beneficent, spiritual order behind this world of appearances. What's more, his system is being set before us precisely at a time when other systems, other ways, seem to be losing their appeal.

In an essay about the Emerson "revival," Richard Poirier made an observation that pertains most closely to the reception of Rilke as well. One factor adduced by Poirier "has been the exhaustion of T.S. Eliot's version of modernism, and of the Christianizing New Criticism that went with it." Simply, if you take God out of the picture, you leave a habit and a hunger that is not easily appeased. Rilke's poetry provides all of the drama of intense spiritual struggle and offers some promise of solution. Moreover, this solution does not seem to depend upon a transcendent or immanent deity; it requires, instead, an assent to death, a liberation of yearning. How enticing, how secular, and how inchoate are these lines from the Ninth Elegy:

> But because *truly* being here is so much; because everything here
> apparently needs us, this fleeting world, which in some strange
>   way
> keeps calling to us. Us, the most fleeting of all.
> *Once* for each thing. Just once; no more. And we too,
> just once. And never again. But to have been
> this once, completely, even if only once:
> to have been at one with the earth, seems beyond undoing.
> —trans. Mitchell

Condense this and you get, essentially: Life, in spite of death, matters; that things perish makes them all the more precious. Ancient wisdom, but we never tire of it. As Paul De Man has written (in *Allegories of Reading*): ". . . Rilke's work dares to affirm and to promise, as few others do, a form of existential salvation that would take place in and by means of poetry." But De Man makes a point of greater suggestive power when he writes of the reader using Rilke "as a reflector for his own inner image." This allows us to explain, perhaps, how Rilke can be at once so vague and difficult and so popular. Lines like the ones I just quoted are, in effect, like the burnished surface of a mirror. One can read into them at any depth one chooses. Like the verses of the *I Ching* or the *Tao Te Ching,* they offer no impediment to interpretation. Like the Eastern texts, too, Rilke's *Elegies* and *Sonnets* have behind them the authority of a world comprehended. One reads harder, projects more vividly, because one has invested the text with a scriptural potency—it seems to know the reader better than it will ever *be known.*

I don't want to make it sound as though the work has no determinate value of its own. It does. But that value may have more to do with giving shape and expression to perpetually obscure psychic processes, and less with supplying answers to our deepest questions. Rilke was one of the great explorers and colonizers of the inner realm. No poet in our age—and possibly no poet ever—has gone so far in representing both the violent rushes and subtle tropisms of the interior life. Rilke invented an idiom of his own for emotional and spiritual events. Moreover, this idiom, unlike the language of psychoanalysis, is neither taxonomic nor explanatory. It incorporates movement and desire—it *expresses.* And through its particular imagistic richness and intensity— those "concrete pictures" Heller identified—it directs the reader steadily toward a recognition of his spiritual needs. Again, De Man: "Many have read him as if he addressed the most secluded parts of their selves, revealing depths they hardly suspected or allowing them to share in ordeals he helped them to understand and to overcome." Like Dostoevsky, Rilke splays the curtain of the everyday to disclose the primary truth of our condition: that we have all been, as the existentialist philosophers would say, "thrown into being." Like Dostoevsky, too, he continually reminds us that our vaunted material progress has not brought us one step closer to explaining that fact. Whether we think of Rilke as a prophet or a spiritual rhetorician, we can't deny that he is a barometer for the atmospheres of essential desire.

Rainer Maria Rilke

Gunnar Ekelöf/ Tomas Tranströmer

In 1745 Emanuel Swedenborg heard the clamoring of God at his ear and took it as a mandate. He devoted the last three decades of his life to setting down his elaborate vision of "correspondence," where each particular of the natural world was a cipher for some other entity in the celestial. An ultimate poetics, we might call it, or a poetics of the ultimate. A part of his scheme took on a second life in the following century. Through Baudelaire's famous poem "Correspondences" (*"La Nature est un temple où des vivants piliers/Laissant parfois sortir de confuses paroles"*) the idea of the poet as a broker between orders of being became a part of the symbolist credo, and it has been a tributary thread in the history of poetry ever since.

Swedenborg was an anomaly in his day, to say the least. He retained his high standing with the Swedish court not on account of his traffic with angels, but because he was, to the last, a canny and useful scientific intelligence. His views were no less controversial in his day than were the occult pronouncements of August Strindberg 150 years later. Orthodoxy has never gone unchallenged in Sweden. Today it is the orthodoxy of "the middle way": Swedish society is conscientious about its social programs, progressive in its ideology and mores, and careful with its managed economy. But in the larger economy a balance is still maintained. The more enlightened public life becomes, it seems, the more avidly artists and writers will peer into dark private corners.

The two foremost Swedish poets of our century, Gunnar Ekelöf and Tomas Tranströmer, illustrate this logic of compensation perfectly. Though poetically very different, they share an appetite for the unknown and a vision of life as a difficult mystery. Both deny the primacy of the ego and turn against the faith in reason that is inseparable from that primacy. This disposition is, of course, common to poets everywhere. And yet, there is something recognizably Swedish about the work of these two men, an introverted intensity that has no tonal counterpart in German, Russian, English, or even Norwegian writing. Doubtless the matrix of the mother tongue is responsible for one part of this, and the singular saturations of place for another. But it also would not be too farfetched to find in both, however refracted, the vigorous otherworldliness of Swedenborg and some remnant of the *épater le bourgeois* spirit that drove Strindberg. In smaller countries the influences of the local giants are less easily escaped.

"Poetry is something which is only done by the whole man."
—Gunnar Ekelöf

Gunnar Ekelöf came to poetry by a circuitous route. He first studied music in Paris, and when he abandoned that it was to move to London to pursue Oriental studies. It was not until illness forced him to drop his plan of traveling to Asia that he finally turned to poetry. He did not relinquish either interest—and the poetry of his later years has often been characterized as a kind of Eastern music—but many years had to pass before such a synthesis could be effected. First there came a surrealist phase, and then, for decades, lyrical and metaphysical impulses merged to shape a unique and constantly changing idiom. This "middle phase" forms the bulk of Ekelöf's production and is crucial to any tracing of his full trajectory. Leonard Nathan and James Larson have made a judicious selection and a careful translation of poems from these decades (1938–1959). In *Songs of Something Else* we have for the first time a full sense of Ekelöf's poetic dynamic. After reading this volume—sequentially—we are better prepared to follow his ultimate mystical undertaking, the Byzantine triptych comprising the *Dīwān over the Prince of Emigon, The Tale of Fatumeh,* and *Guide to the Underworld.* No previous selection has managed to impose perspective upon the spiritual growing pains of this most volatile poet.*

Ekelöf's first collection, *Late Arrival on Earth,* which he referred to as his "suicide book," was published in Sweden in 1932. That mordant epithet may allude to some felt impulse; it may on the other hand signal a belief that one has to die to all competing aspirations in order to be reborn as a poet. Ekelöf never treated his calling as anything but sacred.

Late Arrival on Earth reflected the strong influence of the French surrealists, even though Ekelöf repudiated the undisciplined working methods of Breton and his followers. But a more profound influence was Rimbaud, whom he translated, and in whom he found the appealing vision of poet as scientist:

> The poet makes himself a *seer* by a long, gigantic and rational *derangement of all the senses.* All forms of love, suffering, and madness. He searches himself. He exhausts all poisons in himself and keeps only their quintessences . . . he becomes among all men the great patient, the great criminal, the one accursed—and the supreme Scholar!
>
> —Rimbaud, letter to Paul Demeny, 1871,
> trans. Wallace Fowlie

*Most of the previous translations of Ekelöf have drawn from this middle period, but none has paid close attention to the sequence—Ekelöf's evolution from phase to phase is both interesting and important for the poetry. The fine Muriel Rukeyser/Leif Sjöberg versions *(Selected Poems of Gunnar Ekelöf)* are out of print. Robert Bly's seventy-five-page overview in *Friends, You Drank Some Darkness* is sketchy but does include some of the early surrealist poems. The late triptych is in disarray. Penguin released, under the misleading title *Selected Poems,* the Auden/Sjöberg translation of the first two panels. But now that Rika Lesser has completed the third *(Guide to the Underworld),* the Penguin edition is out of print.

Gunnar Ekelöf/Tomas Tranströmer

And, truly, Ekelöf's early poetry was a strenuous Rimbaldian assault upon poetic respectability, its tendencies both gnomic:

> Hair and fingernails grow slowly into the silence
> The door's lips are closed to reversed values
> > —from "At Night," trans. Robert Bly

and frenzied:

> crush the alphabet between your teeth yawn vowels
> the fire is burning in hell vomit and spit now or
> never I and dizziness you or dizziness now or never.
> > —from "Sonata for Methylated Prose," trans. Bly

Late Arrival on Earth may have been shocking in its day, and it did bring the stream of surrealism northward, but one could not really say that Ekelöf had found his voice. These lines have little in common with the unique, haunted sonorities of the later lyrics. I would speculate that the transition from early to middle phase was prompted by Ekelöf's discovery of his own unique vocal instrument. Most likely there were transitional poems—for few poets step unerringly into mature style—but these are not represented in *Songs of Something Else*. Here, right from the start, we hear the clear, unconcealed speech of a man.

In their introduction, Nathan and Leonard discuss the phenomenon of Ekelöf's voice:

> As our familiarity with and affinity for the poet grew, Ekelöf's poetic voice came to seem to us the most important formal element in these poems. This voice is impossible to describe in general terms—inward, remote, reflective, formal, severe, yet somehow colloquial—but we became convinced that if we could convey something of the quality of this voice in English, our problems would be solved.

It is a measure of their success that, for all the diversity and tonal variation of these lyrics, a clear print of identity is struck on the page. To speak of a "voice" in this way is not just to speak of sound or characteristic diction, either. Voice, in this higher sense, is realized

---

inner speech; it is the all but intangible quality that marks off greatness from high competence in a writer. For there is no voice without the daring of self-exposure. In Ekelöf this self-exposure is critically linked to a vision of self-transformation: He was, by his own avowal, a mystic in pursuit of enlightenment. Poetry was for him the agency of soul making.

The spiritual aspiration was present from the start—the early study of Oriental religions was already purposeful. And the subsequent transformations comprise a continual movement toward the "something else" that he apostrophizes in his poems. The mystic, by definition, cannot believe in the sufficiency of the material world. He believes in the soul and the possibility of its communion with a universal force. For some mystics that force manifests itself as a pervasive moral order, a *logos* deriving directly from a deity. For others—and Ekelöf was of this stamp—it is sheer being, a potency pervading all, a *tao* (though he never names it as such) bearing no moral imperative, requiring only submission. Ekelöf's poetry, from the middle period on, is a path toward submission. The convolutions of that path indicate just how much of a struggle with contrary tendencies was involved.

In "Elegy," the very first poem in this collection—from the section dated 1938—Ekelöf writes:

And fall will return again
however much of spring there was!
What does it matter to life
that someone calls himself "I"
and pleads for his wishes!
What does it matter to earth
which slowly turns itself around
from season to season
that someone struggles against its turning!

We humans lack patience,
we have no time to wait,
but darkness is all around us
and darkness has ample time:
Suns and stars are wheels

Gunnar Ekelöf/Tomas Tranströmer

that move the eternal clock
—slowly, infinitely slowly
everything is altered
to eternally the same.

Both Eastern and Western mysticism call for the overthrow of the "I"—it is illusion, obstacle, sin, *maya*. Here, though Ekelöf is declaring the frailness and inconsequentiality of the "I," he opposes nothing to it but infinite magnitude and endless time. No sense of higher animate being is given. Implacable, mechanistic law is implicit, but the "I" has no connection to it. It "pleads" and "struggles," while the earth, active but indifferent, "slowly turns itself around." What tension there is in the poem derives from the simple contrast between the finite and the infinite orders. We find simplicity, plainness of utterance, and, in spite of the exclamation points, calm—the calm of the stoic's sidereal perspective. But a familiarity with Ekelöf's later torments suggests that it is an unearned, mentally grounded calm. The Ekelöf who speaks here, or in the lovely short poem "Coda," also from this period, has not yet passed through the purging fire. The grip of intellect has not yet been shattered.

Everything has its time, even this darkness
and these catacombs—finally
life needs those who want a meaning.

What would the weave of events be without
the red thread, the thread of Ariadne,
vanished now and then but always woven in!

And even now in these deadly times,
something still holds fast: that he alone
who serves life shall survive.

—"Coda"

There is a striking difference between these two poems. Life, in "Elegy," is rendered as utterly neutral ("What does it matter to life/that someone calls himself 'I'"). In "Coda" Ekelöf establishes some ground of interdependence ("finally/life needs those who want a meaning"). A slight red thread makes all the difference; the scale is completely different. The closing lines discover a wisdom entirely free of moral suggestion.

The well-known Zen parable relates that before initiation mountains are mountains, that during initiation mountains are no longer mountains, that initiation is past when mountains are once again mountains. Ekelöf's development embodies something of this movement. From the relative serenity of these early poems, he moves into a phase of disruptive intensity: the straight way has been lost. And the change in style is immediately obvious. We find a dialectical velocity, the goal of which, it seems, is to uproot the dialectical process, to destroy all categories of thought, to get rid of the *ratio*.

> You say "I" and "it concerns me"
> but it concerns a what:
> in reality you are no one.
> Reality is so without I, naked and shapeless!
>> —from "Write It Down"

Lines like these, though they recall those of "Elegy," already carry an acceleration of breath, a greater urgency. And this soon intensifies:

> What is it I want? What is it I mean?
> I know what it is—and I don't know what it is!
> It has no name, no place, no kind
> I can't call it, I can't explain it
> It is what gets a name when I call
> It is what gets a meaning when I explain
> It is this—but before I have yet called
> It is this—but before I have yet explained
> It is this which still has no name
> What has got a name is not something else—
>> —from "The Gymnosophist"

Or:

> O deep down in me
> from the surface of the eye of black pearl

Gunnar Ekelöf/Tomas Tranströmer

is reflected in happy half-awareness
a picture of a cloud!
It is not this that is
It is something else
It exists in what is
but is not this that is
It is something else
O far far away
in what is distant
there is something close!

—from "Absentia animi"

In these poems Ekelöf is hunting the paradox; he negates his negations, tries to point by way of a stream of cancellations at that "something else" that cannot be named, but that exists, essential, in spite of every mental operation. From a philosophical perspective it appears that he is trying to break through from the phenomenal to the noumenal reality—which, according to Kant, is impossible. The problem is, of course, the "I," that net of deceptions. Ekelöf tries to repudiate the "I" in "Write It Down," but he cannot. At best he can frame its indeterminate status. As we see in "The Gymnosophist," he requires an "I" as a provisional pivot. Without it, he cannot hurl himself at the surrounding flux. These epistemological assaults are not, perhaps, the most successful poems in the Ekelöf canon—their single-mindedness limits them—but they demonstrate an energy and commitment that are not to be denied. Ekelöf, so obviously not interested in being innovative or "different," is forcing his poetry to accommodate and act upon a crisis of the soul.

This period of struggle—roughly the decade between 1941 and 1951—also brings forth a sequence of sarcastic, mocking poems that logically accompany the involuted interrogations, and they signal that Ekelöf is by no means unaware of the larger social panorama. He certainly knows what an absurd figure the tormented poet cuts in the public eye. The poem "Interview" makes clever play with this and is a good example of his cutting style. Ekelöf makes a strong case for the immediate expulsion of the poet from the Republic:

What do you think your task is in life?
I am an utterly useless person.
What is your political creed?
The old order is O.K. Opposition
to the old order is O.K. You could also
imagine a third—but what?
Your view of religion, if you have one?
The same as my view of music: That only
the truly unmusical can be musical.
What do you look for in people? My relations
sorry to say have little or no steadiness.
What do you look for in books? Philosophical depth?
Breadth or height? Epic? Lyric?
I'm seeking the perfect sphere.
What's the most beautiful thing you know?
Birds in cemeteries, butterflies on a battlefield,
somewhere in between. I don't know.
Your favorite hobby? I have no hobbies.
Your favorite little vice? Masturbating.
And finally (as briefly as possible):
Why do you write?
For want of anything better to do. *Vade retro.*
Being witty, eh?
Yes!—I'm being witty.

—"Interview"

If the tensions of the poet's struggle are manifest in the poems of this period, the process of inner reconciliation remains opaque. We feel a change as we read through the last poems of the 1941–1951 section. Sarcasm, negation, and argumentation, the armature of the earlier poems, are gradually replaced by lyricism. The tone becomes less and less strident. Acceptance ousts opposition. We can only guess at the sources of this reconciliation: Did Ekelöf succeed in destroying his dialectical bent, was he granted some transfiguring insight? Whatever the explanation, Ekelöf is no longer at war with the premises of his being. The "something else" is not some impossible antagonist or unattainable *fata morgana,* but a fount of inner replenishment. As Ekelöf writes in the closing lines of "I Heard Wild Geese," closely recalling Hopkins:

Deep in me abides a freshness
that no one can take from me
   not even I myself—

The poem "Raga Malkos," which also dates from this time, gives us one kind of clue about Ekelöf's turnaround. Not only does it show his imagination repossessing the East, but it also suggests that Ekelöf is looking in that direction for spiritual resources. His invocation of the Hindu god Krishna combines languorous rhythms with a vision of immersion in experience that is far removed from the dialectical to and fro of the earlier poems:

Beautiful-eyed one, you walk
with the sway of your loins
to bathe yourself in us
the dark reeds and obscure waters
which hide the struggle
the struggle through beauty to joy
childhood through fortune
flailing fortune
wisdom and eternal life—

Night and good cheer!

—from "Raga Malkos"

The final section—1955–1959—marks a completion of the cycle. The lyrical note returns but now it is very different from that in the earlier poems. There the lyricism depended upon a vision of transience. What Ekelöf stated directly in "Elegy" also emerged in more crepuscular fashion in "To Remember":

Voices near
and voices in the distance—
the sadness of spring twilight . . .
We used to stand on the bridge.

We stood there a long time
in the deepening blue nights
when the pike leaped
—saw the rings spread,
saw the moon path become
a winding serpent
in last year's reeds . . .

But in the poems from the late 1950's it is clear that Ekelöf has changed the whole basis of his perception. The "I" has been vanquished, and what was formerly suffered as transience is now celebrated as the truth of eternal movement. Eastern spirituality is everywhere evident. Poem after poem is now imbued with the idea of the Void—the Nothing that is the plenum through which all creation passes:

This music is like ankle-rings
if nothing is the ankle and nothing the rhythm
in which the foot stirs itself and slowly stamps
round round a rounded carpet.

—from "Like Ankle-rings"

And:

That's why you sing for me bird, that's why the raw
          chill feels fresh
Seductive tones, seductive tones, o hunger that can
          be satisfied only
when you have caught in your beak the insect of nothing
that every moment vanishes in the empty air.

—from "Why do you sing my bird"

The "insect of nothing" is quite compatible with the lyric mode. If we read "Why do you sing my bird" right after "Elegy," we can see that a complete transformation of vision has been effected, with no sacrifice of delicacy or poetic power.

Ekelöf is, I have stressed, a poet for whom creation and self-discovery are a single process. He is not being rhetorical when he writes: "Poetry is something which is only done by the whole man." This identification cannot but raise the stakes: Each finished poem is there for itself *and* as a moment, or step, in a sustained search. We do not know the eventual issue of that search any more than the poet does. The *oeuvre* reminds us, more than any single poem, that identity is not a gift passively received, but a determined creative action in the midst of a vast unknown. Ekelöf's evolution from Western skepticism to Eastern mysticism is a fascinating *pas de deux* of mind and spirit, all the more fascinating in the way that it bypasses Christianity entirely. His path is eccentric—but no more so than that of Yeats or Merrill. Complex souls have complex expedients. For our part, we must hope that *Songs of Something Else* will prompt the publication of all three parts of Ekelöf's triptych. Then we will be able to start assessing the full meaning of these expedients.

Here I come, the invisible man. . . .

—Tomas Tranströmer

Tomas Tranströmer has been publishing his sharp, disquieting poems in Sweden since 1954. English-language translators—Robert Bly, May Swenson, Sam Charters, and Leif Sjöberg—only began to catch up with him in the late 1960's. And we have had to wait until 1981 for a compendium. The publication by Ardis of Robin Fulton's translations gives us our first full overview of this singular poet. Here we have generous selections from the first six books, and complete texts of *Baltics* and *The Truth Barrier,* Tranströmer's two most recent books. (An interview by Gunnar Harding is included as an appendix.) The translations themselves, compared with other versions, appear to be somewhat flat. But if the delicacy of Tranströmer's pacing has been slighted, the odd curvature of his vision is more or less intact on the page.

Tranströmer, like Ekelöf, is a poet preoccupied with the unknown, with all that is excluded by the bright efficiency of an aggressively modern country. Time, identity, the bottomless psyche, and death—these are the boundary stones of his terrain. Where Ekelöf has the mystic's drive to get past the phenomenal, however, Tranströmer does not. He roots himself in it. In his work, the perceived world—stones, trees, cars, electric razors—reverberates with phenomenality. Instead of stripping away the perception of the here and now, Tranströmer uses it. His images tirelessly animate the object world: Fluttering laundry is a butterfly; bicycles are beasts with horns; rubber stamps are the hooves of horses. . . . Nothing escapes his Ovidian eye. The result of this thorough reprocessing of the world is, for the reader, a sharp sense of displacement. For there is no point of rest, no place at which things hug their usual forms or conform to our expectations. This obsessive animation is the expression of a dissolving ego. In Tranströmer's poems the "I" is not a coherent entity; it is almost entirely porous to the surrounding world. Each poem is a vibrant, uncentered perceptual field, a mystery. But Tranströmer is not a mystic. The mystery is there for itself. The poet will not put a higher interpretation upon it. The suggestion is now and again made that there are hidden windows and doors and that they will lead somewhere. Nothing, however, comes of it. And where all is provisional, including the self of the narrator, the ethical dimension is necessarily absent.

In Tranströmer's poems the image is dominant, prevailing over the line, and the individual poem progresses by way of stacked perceptual units. This is where Tranströmer reveals his mastery: He is an engineer of uncanny effects. Synesthesia, telescoped metaphor, unpredicated transitions and leaps, sudden shifts in scale all combine to form tight linguistic circuits working at maximum load capacity:

The albino sun stood over tossing dark seas . . .
—from "The Four Temperaments"

An old house has shot itself in the forehead.
—from "The Journey's Formulae"

. . . the jet plane curtsying in its skirts of noise . . .
—from "Noon Thaw"

Underlying this image world is a great metaphysical unease, the absence of a higher claim. The surface of the work is varied and rich, but beneath it we find a man in deadlock. The images conjure great mystery and strike the complacent senses with all kinds of startling connections. The reader is plucked from the network of the familiar and hooked into something self-contained and ominous. But while intimations gather and build pressure, they ultimately lead nowhere because there is, in the vision of the self dissolved, no place to get to:

> The squat pine in the swamp holds up its crown: a dark rag.
> But what you see is nothing
> compared to the roots, the widespread, secretly
>   creeping, immortal or half-mortal
> root-system.
>
> I you she he also branch out.
> Outside what one wills.
> Outside the Metropolis.
>
> A shower falls out of the milk-white summer sky.
> It feels as if my five senses were linked to another
>   creature
> which moves stubbornly
> as the brightly-clad runners in a stadium where
>   the darkness streams down.
>
>   —"A Few Minutes"

Tranströmer is intent upon the provisionality of all structures, whether internal (structures generated by the psyche), conceptual (social orders and world views), or even literal (objects and the edifices of material civilization). He is suspicious of the very *idea* of order. And thus, his eye is always looking for the anomaly, the slip, the contradiction, whatever will buttress his case: that we live blindly in the midst of the unknown, that we have evolved our personalities and social orders to defend us from this, that they are never quite adequate. As Tranströmer remarks in the interview:

> . . . you could at least say that I respond to reality in such a way that I look on existence as a great mystery and that at times, at certain moments, this mystery carries a strong charge, so that it does have a religious character, and it is often in such a context that I write. So these poems are all the time pointing toward a greater context, one that is incomprehensible to our normal everyday reason.

Poets in Translation

The poems set out to subvert this "normal everyday reason" and to open the reader to that "greater context." But what this greater context involves is never made clear. The reference to the "religious character" of the mystery is not very helpful, for there is no sense in which the work bears this out. At best we might say that there are moments of discontinuity in the psyche—when we go into sleep, or wake from sleep, or suffer sudden shock—that are avenues to higher apprehension. But "higher" only in that they are truer. These brief displacements are the only time that we come face to face with unstructured reality. They are glimpses of the noumenal through unexpected chinks in the phenomenal. We perceive that our "normal" order is a phantom architecture. Tranströmer re-creates in his poems the "feel" of a psyche suddenly jarred from its track.

If we look closely at the dynamic of these displacements, we see that they are, in fact, instances of collapsing ego. The "normal everyday reason," Plato's "charioteer," is nothing more or less than the conscious "I." As Ekelöf wrote:

> In reality you are no one.
> Reality is so without I, naked and shapeless!

But what for Ekelöf were superior forces permeating the universe are, in Tranströmer's poetry, the forces of the unconscious. (Tranströmer, it should be noted, is a trained psychologist.) In both poets there is a sense of the porous "I," an "I" that may at any time lose its contours. The difference is that for Ekelöf this effacement is a spiritual process, a surrender to a higher law; for Tranströmer there are overtones of psychosis: It is never clear whether the unconscious is a hoard of higher meaning or merely an undifferentiated mass of material, some of it useful, most of it anarchic and dangerous.

Tranströmer repeatedly searches out the line where the "I" stops and the unconscious begins. Once he has found the frontier, he will work from both sides:

> The roar of engines in the blue sky is deafening.
> We're living here on a shuddering work-site
> where the ocean depths can suddenly open up—
>   shells and telephones hiss.

Gunnar Ekelöf/Tomas Tranströmer

Beauty you can only see hastily from the side.
The dense grain on the field, the many colors in a yellow stream.
The restless shadows in my head are drawn there.
They want to creep into the grain and turn to gold.

Darkness falls. At midnight I go to bed.
The smaller boat puts out from the larger boat.
You are alone on the water.
Society's dark hull drifts further and further away.

—"Under Pressure"

The syntactic simplicity of the lines is deceptive. In the last stanza
there are two neatly managed reversals. First, by switching from the
"I" to the "you," Tranströmer effectively suggests the push that sun-
ders the two boats. The abruptness of the transition designates both
the indeterminacy of the "I" and the vastness of the id-like "you." The
shock of separation is delayed slightly by the fact that a plural "you"
has already been used in the second stanza; the manipulation of pronouns has set us up for this last maneuver. We accept that there is a
place in the psyche where all pronoun distinctions vanish. The second
reversal is subtler, but no less decisive. The smaller boat "puts out"
from the larger; two lines later it is "Society's dark hull" that "drifts
further and further away." The exchange of perspectives clinches the
pronoun switch. It closes the poem and at the same time aggravates
our sense that everything is liminal.

An interesting counterpoint to this movement into sleep is found
in "The Man Who Awoke With Singing Over the Roofs," where
Tranströmer sets up a vertical axis so that we can register the instant
at which the threshold between sleep and consciousness is crossed. The
airplane suggests both distance and instrumental control. Where the
imagery of boat and sea underscored the dark profundity of the unconscious, light, space, and transparency here give the impression of sur-
ficiality and insubstantiality:

Morning. May-rain. The city is still quiet
as a mountain hamlet. The streets quiet. And in
the sky a bluish-green aero-engine rumbles.—
     The window is open.

The dream where the sleeper is lying prostrate
turns transparent. He stirs, begins
groping for attention's instruments—
    almost in space.

To call Tranströmer's poetry a series of onslaughts upon the ego
would be too reductive. For one thing, Tranströmer does not confine
himself to the psychologist's standard map of the psyche. As a maker
of images he requires greater latitude. And if some of his premises have
empirical sanction, the effects he achieves from them place him well
outside the academy. Psychologists do affirm, for instance, that the
unconscious does not differentiate time, that it is, in effect, atemporal.
Tranströmer gets much poetic use out of this absence of tenses. When
he writes:

the stains pushing through the wallpaper
It was the living dead
who wanted their portraits painted.

      —from "From the Winter of 1947"

he is being neither metaphoric nor surreal. These unnervingly straightforward lines express the conviction that in the realm of the
unconscious the dead are very much alive. What's more, the unconscious, throughout Tranströmer's work, is shown to have as great as if
not a greater claim upon the real than does the ego. Thus, we keep
encountering these unclassifiable presences. They are not exactly
ghosts, or hallucinations, or memories—they are not even metaphors.
It is as if we are looking at time through the undiscriminating eye of
the id. Past, present, and future want to merge into a state of pure
duration. Only the structural limitation of the "I" prevents it:

Coming events, they're there already!
I know it. They're outside:

a murmuring crowd outside the gate.
They can pass only one by one.
They want in. Why? They're coming
one by one—I am the turnstile.

      —from "The Outpost"

Gunnar Ekelöf/Tomas Tranströmer

That inner frontier line between conscious and unconscious has a
spatial counterpart in Tranströmer's poetry in the ever-shifting boundary between the natural world and the structures of civilization. In a
sense they are the same line, for nature and the unconscious are vitally
linked, and technology is very much a conscious manifestation. This is,
of course, a simplistic mapping—as simplistic as correlating individual
and collective unconscious—but it may give us some access to Tranströmer's conceptions.

Tranströmer has been, from the earliest poetry on, attentive to
landscape and geography. As he notes in the interview: ". . . my
poems always have a definite geographical starting point." But he is
less interested in description or detailing per se than in finding the
various points of contact between the man-made and the natural order.
Just as he is fascinated by situations in which the balance of the psyche
teeters, so he wants to uncover terrestrial tension points. We find in
the poems a natural world penetrated by telephone cables and dotted
with industrial debris, suburbs where man and nature are in pitched
battle, and cityscapes that are subtly imprinted with other signs:

> Unidentified paws set their marks
> on the highest products dreamt up here.
> The seeds try to live in asphalt.
> . . .
> There's a secret door here. Open!
> and look into the inverted periscope
>
> downwards, to the mouths, to the deep tubes
> where the algae grows like the beards of the dead
> and the Cleaner drifts in his dress of slime
>
> —from "Traffic"

Nature, like the unconscious, is seen as an ultimately mysterious
entity, a code that will never be cracked. The tools of reason cannot
hope to penetrate their own original source—that would be a taut-
ology. Still, indifferent and dangerous, dangerous in its indifference,
nature may yet be where the saving powers are concealed. And though
there seems to be an undeclared war between nature and civilization,

reconciliation is not impossible. Perhaps it will be effected by some unknown principle within nature:

> And no one knows how it shall be, only that the chain
> perpetually breaks and is joined together again.
>
> —from "Traffic"

or else by some access of vision in man:

> Far away I happen to stop before one of the new facades
> Many windows merging together into one single window
> The light of the night sky is caught in there and
> the gliding of the tree tops.
>
> —from "In the Open"

The six books leading up to the long poem *Baltics* bring us repeatedly to these inner and outer border zones, startle us with uncanny imagery, force us to a recognition of peril, instability, and indeterminacy. The landscapes are depopulated and ominous, the voice always solitary. This consistency of effects would be a liability—or more of a liability—if Tranströmer were not so inventive with his surfaces: The poems are like mobiles, where the pendants and disposition of weights change, but where the principle remains the same.

But with the publication of *Baltics,* Tranströmer finally strikes out from his norm. His longest and most ambitious work (and a long poem is no small accomplishment for a poet accustomed to working with compacted image units), *Baltics* plaits history and locale, personal and communal memory, and generates an affecting texture of tenuously interconnected lives. The commerce between interior and exterior worlds is a great deal freer than what we have seen in the previous work. And, no less importantly, Tranströmer takes the liberty of a looser and freer line. There are fewer signs of compaction and construction, more bursts of lyricism. The imagery is now in the service of evocation, less calculated to startle:

> The wind is in the pine forest. Sighing heavily and lightly.
> The Baltic is sighing in the middle of the island also,
> far within the forest you are out on the open sea.
>
> . . .

Gunnar Ekelöf/Tomas Tranströmer

There's sighing, yes and no, understanding and misunderstanding.
There's sighing, three sound children, one in a sanitorium and two
    dead.
The great current blows life into some flames and blows others
    out. The conditions.
Sighing: Save me, O God; for the waters are come in unto my soul.
You go on, listening, and then reach a point where the frontiers
open
or rather
where everything becomes a frontier. An open place
          sunk in darkness. People stream out from the faintly
          lit buildings round about. Murmuring.

We sense that a new conception has thrown up its challenge. The poem moves with energy and assurance. Tranströmer has not changed his fundamental perception. He is still hovering among border zones, between day vision and night vision, always directing us to the mystery of things. But now the setting, an archipelago of islands in the Baltic, supplies structural freedom. The sea, all surrounding, is his mediating element. He has less need to set up transitions: The steady movement of water is itself perpetual transition. The narrative voice is free to shift among tenses, pronouns, and places. Not surprisingly, *Baltics* contains some of Tranströmer's freshest writing:

Maria's childhood ends too early, she's an unpaid servant lass
in perpetual coldness. Year after year. Perpetual seasickness
under the long oars, solemn terror
at table, the looks, the pike-skin scrunching
in her mouth: be grateful, be grateful.

Formerly Tranströmer avoided the human presence. One sensed a considered epistemological position: Other lives could not be known. His willingness, in *Baltics,* to evoke other lives indicates a major transition.

The Truth Barrier, the most recent collection, is a paradox in this light. It is, on the one hand, a consolidation of many of the gains made in *Baltics.* The poems are looser, with longer lines. Indeed, six of the fifteen are prose poems—further evidence that tight patterns have become stifling. The early Tranströmer would never have written lines like these:

> We squeeze together at the piano and play with four
> hands in F minor, two coachmen on the same coach,
> it looks a little ridiculous.
> The hands seem to be moving resonant weights to and fro,
> as if we were tampering with the counter-weights
> in an effort to disturb the great scale arm's terrible
> balance: joy and suffering weighing exactly the same.
> Anne said, "This music is so heroic," and she's right.
>
> —from "Schubertiana"

The problem is that the promise of transformation given in *Baltics* has not been realized. The humane discursiveness of "Schubertiana" is an exception. Too many of the other poems simply reenact the familiar Tranströmer procedures. A poem like "Homewards" is little more than self-pastiche:

> A telephone call ran out in the night and glittered
> over the countryside and in the suburbs.
> Afterwards I slept uneasily in the hotel bed.
> I was like the needle in a compass carried through
> the forest by an orienteer with a thumping heart.

More than half the poems are similar repetitions. A big step forward has been followed by a little step back.

I remarked earlier that there is an impasse at the core of Tranströmer's poetry, that for all of their brilliance his images are nondirectional. Stylistic shifts and the annexation of new material suggest that Tranströmer is aware of this and is looking for ways to change. But it is a deeply rooted problem. For twenty years now Tranströmer has been atomizing the ego. He has made its insubstantiality his central preoccupation. And out of this has come a distinctive poetic voice, a voice that does not depend upon authority so much as upon the undermining of authority. In the process, however, he has painted himself into a corner. For once the ego has been dismantled and the unconscious brought forward, there are few options left. The poet can either

---

Gunnar Ekelöf/Tomas Tranströmer

advance into surrealism and exploit the material, or else he can remain in his corner and try to vary his effects as much as possible—and for a time it looked as if this was Tranströmer's plan.

But there may be a third option: that of reclaiming and reconstructing the "I." The process would require a reversal, the repudiation of a unique project. In other ways, though, it would be a forward motion, a return from the underworld. Tranströmer's problem right now is that of the nihilist: The vaporized self cannot establish connection to any sort of moral order. And great poetry still depends upon this order. What Tranströmer will do remains to be seen. When Yeats felt in himself the severance of heart from mind, he made this solemn injunction:

> I must lie down where all the ladders start,
> In the foul rag-and-bone shop of the heart.

This may be where the deadlock breaks.

Boris Pasternak is that radium-rare, and possibly even oxymoronic, phenomenon, a subtle and demanding poet whose work is beloved by the masses of his native land. Any Russian speaker on the street, they say, will rattle off pentameter after pentameter, happy to unpack this treasure from the excelsior of sanctioned speech. We Americans have no way to really understand this, except possibly through the tangential example of Robert Frost. He, too, was a craftsman of uncompromising distinction who succeeded in winning the love of the fickle lay readership. But then, Frost was a maker of deceptively accessible surfaces; his poems beguile the reader with narrative simplicity and stable presentations of setting and detail.

Boris Pasternak

Pasternak's lines are something else again. They are as phosphorescent and centrifugal as catherine wheels. Pasternak made it his practice to jumble and telescope narrative, to conceal his referent situations, and to work together sound combinations of stunning intricacy. He pressed into service every imaginable synesthetic short circuit in order to catch hold of the moment. His lyrics are, to say the very least, difficult of access. The matter of his extraordinary popularity deserves some brief comment.

To begin with, Pasternak the poet is a very special emblem for the average Soviet citizen. As Max Hayward, who translated *Doctor Zhivago,* once explained it: "A man who seemed childishly innocent and ineffectual in his practical dealings not only withstood, almost alone, the intolerable pressures of the times, but also came to be seen by many as the last surviving focus of moral resistance to the infinitely cruel and merciless master of the country's destiny." The story has often been told—how Stalin called Pasternak on the telephone to ask for his impressions of Mandelstam. When their conversation was coming to a close, Pasternak told his interlocutor that he would like to meet him for a talk. "What about?" Stalin asked. "About life and death," replied the poet. The interchange, cited in Nadezhda Mandelstam's *Hope Against Hope,* may convey something about the man, but it suggests a good deal more about the potent mystery associated with his public image: poet as keeper of the secrets of power and survival. Small wonder that the poems were scrutinized like leaves from the Sibyl.

But I think that there is another factor of equal importance. It was Frost, interestingly enough, who said that sentence sounds often transmitted meanings as decisively as did the designatory contents of the words themselves. The implication, if I read him rightly, is that a kind of linguistic aquifer underlies the strata of our various locutions and expressions, a primary "genius of the language" that is intimately bound up with the emotional power of sounds and rhythms. The sense I get from Pasternak's Russian-speaking exegetes (Jakobson and Tynyanov, to name two) is that Pasternak's lyrics have in some unique way concentrated the tonal values and rhythmic tendencies, as well as the etymological relations, latent within the language. This might partly explain how a poet could bewitch a reader who could not fully explain his meanings.

Pasternak's name is certainly familiar to readers of poetry in this country. In fact, there is a whole generation that needs only to hear that triplet of syllables in order to resurrect the balalaika strains of "Lara's Theme" and the Technicolor ferocity of Omar Sharif's night of sublime inspiration. Knowledge of the poetry itself is another matter, however. Pasternak has been, so far as the translation of his work into English goes, one of the most ill served of twentieth-century masters. For decades his work was available only in a few dreadful renderings of uncertain provenance, or else in Valentine's gift samplers, which were packaged, as I recall, as "Love Poems of Yuri Zhivago." The one notable exception was Henry Kamen's slim collection *In the Interlude—Poems 1945–1960*.

The decade of the seventies saw Mandelstam and Akhmatova—the two great witness figures of the Stalin era—become a literary fashion. Translations from entrepreneurs as well as professionals appeared on every side. And zealous young poets began to affix their lines as epigraphs to their own productions—a clear sign of the burgeoning "International Style" in letters. Nothing of the kind happened with poor Pasternak, though. Was it that he did not appear to have *suffered* as much as the others—how *did* he secure safe harbor for all those years?—or had the gigantic popular success of *Doctor Zhivago* gobbled up his "serious" cachet? Whatever happened then, a substantial redress of balances is under way in the tranquilized eighties. Three new volumes in as many years. Is this the long-deferred recognition of his poetic virtues? Or are translators simply running out of important poets to "do"? I burrowed into the small stack of books with as much curiosity as trepidation. I saw a chance for breaking through my own long-standing reservations about the work.

I had tried before. Years ago, fired by the recorded praises of poets like Rilke, Tsvetaeva, and Mandelstam—for his ear, his ingenuity, the flash of language—I went looking for the Pasternak magic. I failed to find it. I was then—and am now—severely hobbled by my lack of Russian. The English versions I had, by George Reavey and P. C.

Boris Pasternak

Flayderman, were probably not the best avenues of entry: The poems were either woodenly inert or else swathed in rhetorical flourishes. They could not coax my ear out of hibernation. But now, with three fresh renditions, all of them by poets (Mark Rudman and Bohdan Boychuck, *Boris Pasternak: "My Sister—Life" and "A Sublime Malady"*; Lydia Pasternak Slater, *Poems of Boris Pasternak;* Jon Stallworthy and Peter France, *Pasternak: Selected Poems*), I would try again. This time, I had faith, sustained application would yield the living sap.

It was not to be, quite. For though I found much that was admirable—moments of real lyrical beauty in Rudman/Boychuck and marvelous recastings of form and rhythm in Pasternak Slater—I was still unable to catch hold of a voice or sensibility that was reliably Pasternak's. The question might be raised: Could I, without Russian, even hope to locate such an elusive thing? I can't swear to it, no. But I do feel that I have—erroneously or not—made contact with a single Rilke, Montale, Herbert, or Cavafy beyond and apart from the various filtering voices. With each, I have felt the pressure of a very specific vision; it exists for me even behind a screen of faulty English. I have yet to get this with Pasternak—or any Russian poet of that pleiad. At times I wonder if it would not be better to leave these poets robed in the unattainable syllables of their mother tongue. Does the difficulty arise from the kind of poetry that Pasternak (or Mandelstam, or Akhmatova, or Tsvetaeva) wrote, or does it have to do with a primary incompatibility between language values in Russian and English?

Henry Gifford has written as follows in his excellent critical study *Pasternak:*

Like Khlebnikov, Pasternak developed an extreme and almost morbid sensitivity to the formal relations between words as shown in their derivation from a common root, or in the chance entanglements of alliteration and assonance. Khlebnikov actually sought to determine the laws of primal utterance which he supposed to be hidden in families of words with similar sound and cognate meaning (this being at times conjectural). Pasternak can often in his earlier poetry be said to advance through assonance and rhyme;

the logic of this device becomes irresistible, and a whole stanza can fill up with tendrils growing out of a few words.

It stands to reason that a poetry thus propelled by phonic cell division and semantic whisperings—a poetry not situated on the track of linear idea or image development—would present extraordinary difficulties to the translator. After all, what remains if the subtle efflorescence of sound cannot be re-created? What can we be sure of? In Pasternak's case, especially with the early poetry, which reached its culmination in the epochal collection *My Sister—Life* (written between the February and October revolutions in 1917, first published in 1922), the answer depends to some extent on whether a poem is grounded aurally:

> She's here with me. Play on,
> flood, rip the dusk with laughter!
> Drown, float, at a tangent
> to love, like you, alone!
>
> > —from "Rain," trans.
> > Rudman/Boychuck

or visually:

> Summer waved goodbye to the wayside
> station. Then thunder
> took off its cap and snapped
> a hundred blinding photographs.
>
> > —from "Storm, an Endless Instant,"
> > trans. Rudman/Boychuck

In the first instance, we simply cannot gauge our distance from the original, particularly when a rival version reads:

> She's here with me. Come, strum, pour, laugh,
> Tear the twilight through and through!
> Drown, flow down, an epigraph
> To a love like you!
>
> > —trans. Stallworthy/France

Boris Pasternak

The image-centered lines, on the other hand, allow slightly less (but still considerable) leeway:

> Then summer took leave of the platform
> And waiting room. Raising his cap,
> The storm at night for souvenir
> Took snap after dazzling snap.

> —trans. Stallworthy/France

Accurate transposition, in other words, is not something that we can depend on.

Then there is the matter of the two languages. Russian is inflected and seems to permit greater line concision, as well as providing more possibilities for the strategic massing of sound values. At the same time, those sound values are duskier, emerge from the back of the throat and the glottis; English is frontal, chopped by the tip of the tongue and the lips. What range of solutions can the English translator have? His predicament is not enviable.

The more I read through these collections, the more disturbed I felt by the kinds of divergences I was finding. These were not three different soundings of one poet but three distinct creations. And who was I to say which came closest to reflecting or embodying the original? Each makes some kind of claim. The Stallworthy/France volume comes with the imprimatur of Pasternak's son, Yevgeny Borisovich Pasternak, and a commendation from no less a scholar than Clarence Brown. Lydia Pasternak Slater is, by the same token, the poet's own sister. She writes: "To translate my brother's poems without trying to preserve his melodies and rhythms is for me equivalent to not translating him at all." Then, as removed as can be from Slater's immaculate transcriptions, we have the prize-winning renderings by Rudman/Boychuck, which aim above all else to achieve lyricism in English.

The relativity of all things translated became increasingly obvious to me. I finally decided that I would be contributing very little were I to content myself with remarking similarities and differences and judging the work solely according to my ideas about what makes a successful poem in English. Instead, I resolved to get as close as I possibly could to the original rhythms, sounds, and meanings of at least one poem—as much to gratify my curiosity, in the end, as to complete my undertaking.

The Rudman/Boychuck translations give us *My Sister—Life* in its entirety (also included is Pasternak's long poem "A Sublime Malady," written between 1923 and 1928). The Slater and Stallworthy/France selections draw from the whole *oeuvre*. The area of overlap, therefore, is not that large. From it I picked, quite at random, a twelve-line poem entitled—with telling variety—"With Oars Crossed," "Oars Crossed," and "With Oars at Rest." Joseph Brodsky was kind enough to read the Russian into a tape recorder and to give me his word-by-word English crib. He could not understand, he said, why I had picked such a minor poem for my sample. "Brevity," I replied. But I was also thinking that a minor poem was probably as accurate a test of a translator as any *tour de force*.

What follows, then, is an exercise in cross-sectioning. While it may reveal certain aspects of the different translators' approaches, and may be in other ways representative, I'm aware that the quality of the part does not always reflect the quality of the whole. Taking the larger perspective, I would say that though the translations seem to be a fair index of Slater's art and that of Messrs. Stallworthy/France, Rudman/Boychuck's project is not fairly represented—their versions attain at times a richness not captured here. I should add that the phonetic transliteration is my own, taken in part from Brodsky's voicing of the poem, in part from my fumblings with the Russian orthography.

Lód ka	*ko ló tit sya*	*v'*	*són noy*	*gru dí,*
boat	knocking	in	sleepy	breast

Í've	*na vís li,*	*che lú yot*	*v'*	*klu chít se,*
willows	hang over	kiss	into	collarbones

Ve	*lók ti,*	*ve*	*u klyu chi ny—o,*	*po go dí,*
into	elbows	into	oarlocks oh	wait

É to	*vedj*	*mó shet*	*so*	*v' syá kim*	*slu chít sya!*
this	indeed	maybe	to	anybody	can happen

Boris Pasternak

É tim vedj v' pés ne te shát sya v'sé
it is indeed in song entertained everybody

É to vedj zná chit—pé pel sir é nye vey,
this indeed means ashes lilac

Rós kosh krosh é noy ro másh ky v' ra sé,
luxury crushed chamomile on dew

Góo by i góo by na zvéz dyi vi mé nyi ve!
lips and lips for stars to exchange

É to vedj zńa chit—ab yátj ne bos vód,
this indeed means to embrace heavens

Róo ki splés ti v'krug Ger á kla gro mád no go,
arms interlaced Hercules colossal

É to vedj zńa chit—ve ká na pral yót
this indeed means ages throughout

Nó chi na shél kan yi slá vok pro má tyi vot!
nights on trilling nightingales to squander

Pasternak's twelve lines are strictly patterned, with a consistent *a b a b* rhyme scheme, which invariably chimes the final syllables in the *a* lines and the penultimates, or antepenultimates, in the *b* lines. The poem moves very quickly, sped by its dactylic meter and the sportive use of assonances and consonances, as well as by the repeated words and constructions. Each stanza is dominated in its end rhymes by a different vowel: the long *i* in the first (*grudi/kluchitse/pogodi/sluchitsya*), the *e* in the second (*v'se/sirenyevey/v'rase /vimenyive*), and the alternation of *a* and *o* in the last (*nebosvod/napralyot—gromadnogo/promatyivot*). In addition, each stanza is knit together by its own intricate system of tonal relations.

The first stanza has, underscoring its lake imagery, a rich layering of *l* sounds. A heavy lapping is introduced in the first four syllables (*Lodka kolotitsya*) and is sustained through the next lines, tapering away after the caesura in line 3, only to be recovered at the very end of the next line (*sluchitsya*). In these lines, we also see how Pasternak builds semantic suggestion from the phonetic base. The sounds of *cheluyot* (kiss) and *kluchitse* (collarbones) in line 2 are merged in *uklyuchiny* (oarlocks), and then are rounded out in the final rhyme of *sluchitsya*. My guess would be that Pasternak first found the governing word, *kluchitse* (collarbones), by noting the physiognomic resemblance to a pair of splayed oars; that word might then have called up its rhyme—*sluchitsya*—and the oarlocks (*uklyuchiny*), at the same time producing the skein of a narrative. The jump from collarbones to elbows (*lokti*) may seem unlikely, but if we accept that Pasternak was a poet who generated his semantic connections out of sound relations, then the resemblance of *lokti* to the opening *Lodka* (boat) is basis enough. And it is at this point that we can begin to see the deeper implications of such a procedure.

First, the boat is said to be knocking, or beating, in a sleepy breast. Though the word for lake is not given, the logic of the conceit summons it up. Whereupon the rest of the stanza orchestrates two important phonetic blurrings, between the inanimate boat (*Lodka*) and the animate human elbows (*lokti*), and, similarly, between the collarbones (*kluchitse*) and the oarlocks (*uklyuchiny*). The result, facilitated by the steady lapping of *l* sounds, is a dreamy erasure of the boundaries between the breast and the lake (nature) and between the boat and the people in it—presumably lovers.

One could go on and on with a sound fabric like this, finding cross-stitchings and resonances. I will content myself with just a few observations about the second stanza. One of its conspicuous elements is the near parallelism of the first two lines—*Etím vedj/Eto vedj*—and its clever skewing by the chiasmic reversal of *pesne teshatsya* and *znachit—pepel*. Another is the sudden verticality achieved by the placement of repeated *sh* and *o* sounds in line 3 (*Roskosh kroshenoy romashky*) and their abrupt yielding to the clean echoing of *Gooby i gooby*. The liberation of the *oo* sounds fit perfectly with the introduction of stars (*zvezdyi*), creating for the reader a breakaway momentum that leads to the vast yearning invoked in the final stanza.

It should be obvious that a poem like this succeeds not because of the profundity or fascination of its ideas but by virtue of the phonetic

---

Boris Pasternak

inventiveness that the poet can sustain within the limits of his chosen form. Effective transposition to English would, in this case, depend upon the translator's ability to combine speed and intricacy with the threshold suggestions of the self melting away into its surroundings.

To begin with, here is the Stallworthy/France version:

Sleepy the lake's breast, the boat beats in it,
Willows stoop down, lips kissing collarbone,
Elbow and rowlock—o, wait a minute,
This sort of thing can happen to anyone!

This is just . . . this is all trivial . . .
This just means—with hesitant fingertips
Ruffling the petals of the white camomile,
Touching the lilac's pale flesh with your lips.

This just means—embracing the firmament,
Hugging great Hercules, this just means
For centuries, centuries on end
Squandering your substance on nightingales!

I find this to be an utterly undistinguished rendition. A desire to keep a rhyme scheme appears to have dictated syntactic choices and to have occasioned a number of misleading departures from the sense of the original. The whole second stanza might as well have been written by another poet. The literal version of its first line is: "Everyone is entertained with this in song." The translators' motive was clearly to pick up a catchy rhyme for "camomile." But "trivial" introduces an inappropriate note, turning what is meant to be registered in the light of human commonality into a mannered and ironic pose.

The rest of that stanza just compounds the sin. The "hesitant fingertips" are conjured from nowhere, the startling "ashes" is dropped, as are "luxury" (*Roskosh*) and "crushed" (*kroshenoy*), violating completely the fabric of the third line; trading "lips and lips for stars" becomes the insipidly effete "Touching the lilac's pale flesh with your lips." Not only is there no mention of lilac in line 4, but the close-up description (something from Huysmans) destroys the outward thrust that Pasternak so carefully implanted in these lines. The last stanza likewise offends, both because of its wasteful loading ("centuries, centuries") and its avoidance of the evocative *shelkanyi* (trilling). These kinds of liberties could be countenanced—and then just barely—only if the poets were fashioning an imitation *à la* Lowell, but these lines have none of the rhythmic or phonetic tension that that would require.

Rudman/Boychuck render the poem like this:

The rowboat rocks in a drowsy creek.
Dangling willows kiss our wrists,
our elbows, collarbones, oarlocks—but wait,
this could happen to anyone!

This is the drift of song.
This is the lilac's ashes.
This is the beauty of dew crumbled on daisies.
This is to barter lips and lips for stars.

This is to embrace the horizon,
encircle Hercules with your arms.
This is to swirl through time,
squander sleep for nightingales' songs.

These cadences are a welcome relief after the clotted hesitancies of Stallworthy/France. They have a pace that matches, even outstrips, that of the original, and a transparent clarity that poses no obstacle to the reader. But the simplifications have been attained at a high price. For one thing, all traces of Pasternak's controlling structure have been jettisoned. We miss the end rhymes as well as the ever ingenious play between the metric necessity and the syllabic variety. Indeed, this is the poem stripped of most of the elements that make it interesting in the original.

Rudman/Boychuck begin with the alliterative "rowboat rocks," picking up something of the rhythm set up by *Lodka kolotitsya,* but the lines do not go on from there to fulfill expectation. The word "wrists," absent from the Russian, is imported to mate with "kiss"—to parallel *cheluyot* and *kluchitse*—but this expedient forces the stacking of "elbows, collarbones, oarlocks," which becomes distracting through the jostling of so many *l*'s and *o*'s. In another circumstance this could be

---

Boris Pasternak

provocative, but the phonetic burden of this stanza is to create a sense of dissolving boundaries, and the mouthful of syllables here has the opposite effect: We feel the knocking and lose the dreaminess.

The second stanza adopts an aggressive tactic of repetition, pushing Pasternak's tendency to the extreme. Rudman/Boychuck begin seven of the poem's twelve lines with the word "this"—a decision that, to my mind, imposes more hortatory directness on the whole than is necessary. The middle section, in particular, loses much of its texture. Pasternak, as I observed earlier, builds that stanza toward the luxuriant and highly tactile third line (*Roskosh kroshenoy romashky*) and then tops that effect with the vaulting *Gooby i gooby*. "This is the beauty of dew crumbled on daisies" captures little of that sensation. The line contains, also, several misleading emphases. The "dew crumbled on daisies," while poetic, changes the original image of crushed flowers. Secondly, daisies cannot be substituted for camomile without a loss, for surely Pasternak intended a visual counterpoint between the white abundance of that flower and the stars in the night sky.

The Russian of Pasternak's third stanza once again invites speculation as to how the phonetic elements may have originated the semantic sequence. The rhyming of *gromadnogo* (colossal) and *promatyivot* (squander), which depends upon the stressed antepenultimate, seems to form the linguistic axis of the stanza. I suspect that *promatyivot* was the source word, pulling in its wake *gromadnogo,* then *Gerakla* (Hercules), and then the conceit upon which the first two lines rest. Whatever the instigation, the stanza is imbued with the spacious grandeur of the night sky, a sensation bodied forth by the alternation of resonant *o*'s and *a*'s in the rhymes. Pasternak uses, respectively, ten- and twelve-syllable lines to carry the tones. Rudman/Boychuck's lines count out at a skimpy 9-9-6-8. This accounts for their velocity. But the problem has more to do with a loss of gravity, which can finally be traced to an evasion of both vowel patterns and syllable strictures. The English version holds no dark notes, no suggestion of immensity, and this disappoints.

Still, in comparing Rudman/Boychuck's offering with Stallworthy/France's, I prefer the former. While Stallworthy/France struggle to keep a shape by upholding the rhyme pattern, they cannot get around mixed diction and troubling inaccuracies. Rudman/Boychuck, though unwilling to engage the disciplines of form, and though tending toward simplification of the music, nonetheless convey a control and decisiveness. They sacrifice the subtleties of linguistic interplay, but they get something of the headlong rush of Pasternak's lines.

Finally, here is Lydia Pasternak Slater's translation:

A boat is beating in the breast of the lake.
Willows hang over, tickling and kissing
Neckline and knuckles and rowlocks—O wait
This could have happened to anyone, listen!

This could be used in a song, to beguile.
This then would mean—the ashes of lilac,
Richness of dew-drenched and crushed camomile,
Bartering lips for a star after twilight.

This is—embracing the firmament; strong
Hercules holding it, clasping still fonder.
This then would mean—whole centuries long
Fortunes for nightingales' singing to squander.

Slater has done a masterful job of honoring the formal properties of the original. Indeed, the more closely we look, the more we are apt to be struck by the ingeniousness of some of her solutions. Looking at the whole, we might remark not only upon the solidity of the rhymes but upon her close reconstruction of Pasternak's rhythm. She recreates, with little sacrifice, the original alternation of ultimate (lake/wait) and substitutes penultimate (kissing/listen) rhymes for the antepenults; at the same time she hews to the sense more faithfully than either Stallworthy/France or Rudman/Boychuck. Though she cannot follow the changing vowel patterns in the rhymes perfectly, she does work out her own approximation. The second stanza pivots easily around the *i* sound, while the crucial *o* and *a* pattern of the third is upheld gracefully with strong/long and fonder/squander. Finally, Slater has made every effort to preserve the caesuras, a sign, perhaps, that she believes that the breathing of the Russian can be carried into English.

The first stanza begins with the distinct pulsing of *b* sounds (boat/beating/breast), and while this cannot create the effect of lapping

that Pasternak gets with his repeated *lo*'s, it does activate the suggestion of a heartbeat. But where Pasternak is able to braid his *l* sounds
throughout the stanza, thereby keeping the water aurally present,
Slater does not follow through. Her answer, meanwhile, to the *cheluyot*
(kiss)/*kluchitse* (collarbones) pairing in line 2 is quite inventive: "tickling
and kissing" is more active and playful than Rudman/Boychuck's "kiss
our wrists" or Stallworthy/France's inaccurate "lips kissing collarbone." Her response to the carryover of sound that Pasternak gets
with *uklyuchiny* in line 3 is to introduce a new pairing instead. Thus,
"tickling and kissing" spills over into "Neckline and knuckles." What
disappears, however, is the strong visual signal of the collarbones.
"Neckline" is vague, unsuggestive. Had Slater used "elbows and collarbones" she could have echoed the *b*'s of line 1 and had precision into
the bargain.

The next stanza works nicely. The strong caesura in line 2 is retained, and the weave of *r*'s and *d*'s in "Richness of dew-drenched"
keeps the tonal density of *Roskosh kroshenoy romashky,* especially when
the "crushed camomile" is appended. "Bartering lips for a star after
twilight," though, cannot capture the piercing quality of *Gooby i gooby*.
Slater's *bar*tering/star replaces deep transparency with a flat opacity.
And here, as accurate as the sense may be, we see just how much
Pasternak's lyricism depends on the subtle transactions of sound.

Slater's determination to keep the rhymes and rhythms of the original is responsible for certain weaknesses in the final stanza. She clearly
wanted the verb "squander" at the end, but this forced her toward the
weak phrase "clasping still fonder." What's more, she has tampered
with the literal meaning of the Russian, which has Hercules not holding but being held. Insofar as Pasternak is not putting great weight on
the conceit, but attempting more to convey magnitude, this is excusable. I am more troubled by the archaic sound of "clasping still
fonder"—the diction does not match the effortless clarity that the rest
of the translation has.

But this is a minor cavil. Slater has pulled off a mimetic triumph.
Quite possibly, this poem could not be brought into English any more
faithfully. Almost every detail has somehow been accounted for. The
semantic nuance, the beat, the firm clutch of the rhymes—all of the

elements have been assembled. I feel ungrateful, therefore, in saying that I do not find very much poetry in it. Poetry? I mean that when I read the words slowly and attentively, as if they composed a poem in English, I am unmoved. I feel no quickening in the ear. The sound interactions do not kiss the lines to life. And this is obviously not the case with the original. Even though I don't speak Russian, I can hear the movement of vowels and consonants; I pick up a sense of dynamic conversion, of materials being stretched and kneaded like dough. No amount of scrupulosity can generate that, only the poetic instinct itself.

I end up activating the old translation debate. Do we want absolute fidelity or lyricism? The letter or the spirit? Both, of course. But can we get both in a translation of a poet as structurally constrained as Pasternak? It may be possible, but I don't think it has happened yet. The would-be reader of Pasternak in English has a choice before him. If he is looking for the best *map,* the best representation of Pasternak's poetic procedure, I send him without hesitation to Lydia Pasternak Slater. Though the volume is thin, selecting sparingly from all phases of a long career, its integrity is absolute. Everything but the living ichor is there. If the reader desires, on the other hand, a poetic experience that is, while not pure Pasternak, at least under the master's aegis, then the Rudman/Boychuck volume is the one to get. There, in isolated spots, he will encounter authentic gusts of song:

> In this rich hypnotic country
>   you can't blow out my eyes.
> And after rain the slugs plug up
>   the eyes of garden statues.
>
> Water murmurs in the ears, the pine siskin
>   *shree* and tiptoe daintily.
> Go, smear their lips with blueberries,
>   they're blind to your mischief.

> —from "The Mirror"

As for Stallworthy/France, I can say only that it's unfortunate that their versions are the most widely distributed. Readers who look for Pasternak in those pages will not only be misled, they may very well wonder what all the fuss is about.

Boris Pasternak

Czeslaw
Milosz

H istory long ago put its mark on Czeslaw Milosz's brow and turned him against his natural grain. "My temperament was contemplative, little suited for active life," he tells us in his memoir, *Native Realm*. But if he wished that the cup be passed from him, the wish was not heeded. That same memoir documents the invasion of his homeland by German and Russian armies and the annihilation of an age-old way of life. It tells a tale of resistance, subterfuge, escape, and exile. Great success and honor have come to Milosz in recent years, but they are laurels edged with the dark of suffering: It has been the work of Milosz's later career to question on every level, in poetry and prose, the explosions of barbarousness in the modern age.

Czeslaw Milosz

Exile to the United States has given him freedom and geographical distance, but the ongoing history of his "corner of Europe" has never ceased to be his central preoccupation. And the suffering has gone on. Even as Milosz was presenting the Norton Lectures at Harvard in the winter of 1981–1982, jackbooted militiamen were swarming the streets in Poland, screwing the lid down on the hopes raised by Solidarity. Roundups, internments, bloody violence—the daily news gave a shadow lecture. Fittingly, Milosz's topic was the relation of poetry to history. He entitled his series *The Witness of Poetry,* not, as he explained, "because we witness it, but because it witnesses us."

These lectures have now been collected under the same title by Harvard University Press. Reading them on the page is quite different from hearing them delivered in the charged atmosphere of the auditorium. The crossover between the text and the newspaper headlines, which Milosz could establish with a pause or a lifted eyebrow, is necessarily missing. In print they seem more ruminative, more private. Exposition is compressed, and the shifts in scale and perspective are sometimes sudden. Alfred Kazin remarked on this in an article in *The New York Times Book Review.* He found in Milosz's "orphic rambling style a divide between one sentence and another." But Kazin's adjective "rambling" suggests a casualness that is never present in Milosz's writing. After several readings, I am convinced that the style is a fair reflection of the vastness and refractoriness of the subject matter. Milosz is taking on all of the big questions. The essays *are* ruminative, but if one is questioning the meaning and end of all human enterprise, polemical posturing is unseemly. As for the compression of argument and the quick shifts, these are a direct result of Milosz's determination to bring together as many perspectives as possible.

Some prior exposure to Milosz's work is most helpful. The reader who has absorbed the poetry in *Selected Poems* and *Bells in Winter,* the speculative essays in *Emperor of Earth,* and the autobiographical detail in *Native Realm* will be more equipped to take the measure of this book. The latter two works supply historical and philosophical context, while the poetry reflects something of the soul of the man. Both are essential. For if on an obvious level *The Witness of Poetry* is a response to the history of our time, it is, on a less obvious but no less important level, the testament of a man with a "God ache" (the phrase is Unamuno's). Milosz's views on history, poetry, and the fate of the race are actively shaped by the struggle between skepticism and the will to believe. Only when the tensions of this struggle are understood do the various perspectives fit together to declare a dynamic whole.

Milosz has added as an epigraph to these lectures a passage from his long poem "From the Rising of the Sun":

> My generation was lost. Cities too. And nations.
> But all of this a little later. Meanwhile, in the window, a swallow
> Performs its rite of the second. That boy, does he already suspect
> That beauty is always elsewhere and always delusive?
> Now he sees his homeland. At the time of the second mowing.
> Roads winding uphill and down. Pine groves. Lakes.
> An overcast sky with one slanting ray.
> And everywhere men with scythes, in shirts of unbleached linen
> And the dark-blue trousers that were common in the province.
> He sees what I see even now. Oh but he was clever,
> Attentive, as if things were instantly changed by memory.
> Riding in a cart, he looked back to retain as much as possible.
> Which means he knew what was needed for some ultimate
>   moment
> When he would compose from fragments a world perfect at last.

The passage is characteristic of Milosz in several ways. First, for the extreme sobriety of tone, especially in the opening line. It is understood that speech is indecent if it is inadequate to events. "My corner of Europe," Milosz states in *Starting from My Europe,* the first lecture, "owing to the extraordinary and lethal events that have been occurring there . . . affords a peculiar perspective." Milosz witnessed a violation of person and place that was historically unprecedented, in magnitude, if nothing else. And his vision of history, its tragedies, is fully documented by those few hard nouns and verbs. Indeed, in the poetics of Milosz and his East European contemporaries, brevity is a kind of

---

Czeslaw Milosz

shorthand for the enormity of the unspeakable. Adjectives and adverbs are very often eschewed in favor of nouns and verbs—the more rudimentary linguistic tools. But even these can do no more than set out the contours of event and draw the line that language cannot cross without great risk of false or inadequate sentiment. "My generation was lost. Cities too. And nations." The hierarchy is clearly marked: first the human loss, then the destruction of locale, and finally, almost as an afterthought, the loss of the more abstract entities—nations.

This would be all, the first and last word, were it not for the miraculous, absurd persistence of the heart. As Milosz wrote in the "Elegy for N.N.":

> We learned so much, this you know well:
> how, gradually, what could not be taken away
> is taken. People, countrysides.
> And the heart does not die when one thinks it should,
> we smile, there is bread and tea on the table.

It is the most deep-seated contradiction, that the heart does not die "when one thinks it should." The irrational smile sustains the race— grief and horror would otherwise have finished it off long ago. At the same time it is the measure of insufficiency, the revolt of the biological against the moral. We are made to withstand horror, and that in itself is a horror. Milosz knows both sides. And that may be why he is so fond of citing Simone Weil's maxim: "Contradiction is the lever of transcendence." Milosz's own experience has presented him with the moral contradiction of survival. We see the self-laceration in his post-war poetry. He cannot accept that he is sitting in a café, free in the realm of Becoming, while so many others are sealed in the room of What Has Been. With acid irony he pronounces: "We are better than those who perished." But more to the point is this invocation of the dead:

> and they look at me with a burst of laughter
> for I still don't know what it is to die at the hand of man,
> they know—they know it well.

> —from "Cafe"

Simone Weil's formula is not prescriptive; contradiction does not automatically produce transcendence. Great contradictions have thrust many into madness. Milosz's contradictions seem to have caused a significant split. One part of his nature—and I will take this up later—has been driven to seek religious transcendence. Another part continues to endure the tension imposed by the absurd—that is, irrational—privilege of survival. At times this appears to be a conscious, willed decision, as if moral and intellectual honesty demand it, as if achieving some liberation of spirit out of what was, finally, the most lamentable desecration would be falsifying the past. Milosz will not permit himself to bear false witness. To some extent, therefore, existence must be viewed as meaningless.

But these are not the only possible reactions; the complex soul has other needs and other expedients as well. In the epigraph passage, for instance, Milosz invokes the alternative order of memory. At its most potent, as an agency of recovery and redemption, memory overcomes contradiction—not by rising above it, but by effectively restoring the prior state, the former world. What is Proust's magnum opus but such a restoration? In the atemporal order of memory, sequence is liquidated; time past comes alive in the medium of the present, canceling the present. Thus, if eternity is not endless time, but the absence of time, then memory is the intersection of time and eternity in the soul. It can endure so long as the one who remembers endures. And that it not vanish entirely at death, man has art. *Ars longa, vita brevis.* Or Shakespeare's "That in black ink my love may still shine bright." There is a strong suggestion in the last line of the passage that Milosz has just this in mind, that the "world perfect at last" is the world carried by memory into the shaping current of language.

The religious component of Milosz's nature is most problematic; not that it should exist, but, rather, that it should exist side by side with a vision of meaninglessness. The two are, of course, incommensurable, mutually exclusive. There has to be some cycle of alternation: belief struggling with despair, despair fueling belief, reason wearing it away again. The cycle is bitter. Reading Milosz, especially the poetry, we can almost feel the pendulum swing. We realize that the man is fighting a battle in his soul, and that there is no still point, no securely

Czeslaw Milosz

held platform on which he can stand. This accounts for the tense movement of his thought and, at times, our difficulty in grasping it in its fullness.

Another section from "From the Rising of the Sun" may clarify the problem. We can consider it alongside the epigraph: for what recovery through memory is for the individual, the prophesied biblical End of Days is, in a sense, to human history. I think that Milosz intends the following literally:

> Yet I belong to those who believe in *apokatastasis,*
> That word promises reverse movement,
> Not the one that was set in *katastasis*
> And appears in the Acts, 3, 21.

> It means: restoration. So believed: St. Gregory of Nyssa,
> Johannes Scotus Erigena, Ruysbroeck and William Blake.

> For me, therefore, everything has a double existence.
> Both in time and when time shall be no more.

The passage is disturbing. The obvious sense is that the speaker has overcome all contradiction through a belief in ultimate restoration. Where memory works in time and resurrects the past inwardly, this restoration is outside of time and literal. Reason, naturally, balks. Indeed, Milosz's own skepticism balks. The jagged movement of the poem's many sections indicates that the struggle goes on and that contradiction has not been vanquished. The above assertion is to be weighed against the concluding lines of the poem:

> And the form of every single grain will be restored in glory.
> I was judged for my despair because I was unable to understand
>   this.

We cannot, obviously, draw any firm conclusion about Milosz's position. He remains embattled, plagued by intermittency and double vision. He cannot overcome the natural reflex to consider everything *sub specie aeternitatis* and to hold whatever is finite against a cold, sidereal backdrop. When he claims affinity with Pascal, as he does from time to time, it makes perfect sense: Pascal, too, had trouble keeping his faith steadily present—he went so far as to sew a reminder into the lining of his coat.

In the last paragraph of the second lecture, *Poets and the Human Family*, Milosz raises a key question:

> Is non-eschatological poetry possible? That would be a poetry indifferent to the existence of the Past-Future axis and to the "last things"—Salvation and Damnation, Judgment, the Kingdom of God, the goal of history—in other words, to everything that connects the time assigned to one human life with the time of all humanity.

He admits that it is a difficult question. And when he answers, he does not give a clear-cut yes or no—though his bias is already present in the phrasing. In a sense, everything in the lectures can be said to refer to this problem: What is the relation between the "time assigned to one human life" and the "time of all humanity"?

The question is best approached indirectly. As Milosz slowly circles his topic, so we should circle Milosz, addressing the first question with another, namely: What does Milosz believe about poetry? And to answer this, it is not inappropriate to introduce some of the ideas of Milosz's distant relative Oscar Milosz, to whom he devotes the long essay *Poets and the Human Family*. This is not the detour that it may seem. In discussing Oscar Milosz's views, Milosz comes the closest to presenting his own position. If he chooses to be circumspect, it may be because this position is so strikingly divergent from the rationalist temper of our times.

Czeslaw Milosz and Oscar Milosz do not espouse an identical poetics. Oscar Milosz, the mentor, was by far the more apocalyptic thinker. He was a visionary, which is something that the younger Milosz never claims to be. He was also the predecessor. He foretold the eruptions of history that the younger Milosz lived through; this is their bond and their difference. Milosz claims a certain spiritual kinship through his intense interest in the visionary tradition (he is a serious student of Blake and Swedenborg), and to some extent he validates Oscar Milosz's predictions by interpreting them to fit the data of his own experience.

Czeslaw Milosz   ·

Also, though Milosz is a poet of his time in a way that his senior never was, he has derived great benefit from the latter's arcane researches. It is possible that without the example of his relative, Milosz would not have delved into Swedenborg as deeply as he has, and without Swedenborg's influence, Milosz's later poetry would be very different. Milosz himself states that, through his writings and through personal contact, Oscar Milosz "to a large extent determined my own ways as a poet."

Oscar Milosz believed that from the time of the Enlightenment on, poetry had become increasingly estranged from its original sacral function, that the poet was no longer the go-between carrying the messages of the gods to men. This estrangement went hand in hand with the consolidation of the Cartesian tendencies of modern science, a process that was hurrying the race toward disaster; in his words, *conflagration universelle.*" But he was also a millenarian, a believer in restoration. "His model of time is dynamic," writes Milosz, "as is William Blake's, and historical movement takes the form of a triad: the time of innocence, the time of the fall, and the time of innocence recovered." After universal cataclysm there would be rebirth. And in the reborn world a new—more Einsteinian—conception of science would prevail. At such a time, too, poetry would regain its long-lost powers. The new poetry would be "spacious," biblically mighty, affirming in the fullness of language the ancient covenant between the poet and the "grand soul of the people."

Milosz does not tell us in so many words whether or not he believes Oscar Milosz's prognostications. But he does treat them with great respect.* As for the assertions about the fallen state of poetry, these are of central importance to Milosz. Time and again in the course of the lectures he questions why poetry should be so pessimistic, so impoverished, and so irrelevant to the great mass of humanity. Like Oscar Milosz, he believes that it has lost its sacred function. But he

---

*Milosz's Norton Lectures coincided, as I have said, with the military crackdown in Poland. In 1968, in a section of *Native Realm* devoted to Oscar Milosz, we find: "From observing the 'temps de laideur ricanante' and from his decoding of hidden prophecies, this heir of Rosicrucians learned that the cycle was closing and that we were entering the Apocalypse of St. John. He foretold the outbreak of war for the near future. It would be the war of the Red Horse and it would begin in Poland, or, to be exact, in the corridor where the Poles had built the port of Gdynia (Gdansk)" (p. 172).

Poets in Translation

does not lay the full blame at the feet of science or the Cartesian world-view. Poets themselves have been partly responsible. They responded to the encroachments of science by retreating. When the ancient link between poetry and the sacred was finally severed, the poets tried to turn their art into a religion unto itself. They sought the sphere of the pure word (Mallarmé), and by so doing cut themselves off from their lay brethren. Now, Milosz would say, poetry is paying the price for its refusal to address the real. He quotes Simone Weil with approval:

> I believe that the writers of this period which just ended are responsible for the miseries of our time. . . . Science in itself no longer possessed a criterion of value after science in the classical sense came to an end. But writers were by nature of their profession guardians of a treasure now lost. . . .

The contract between the writer and the human values, or, to put it another way, between poetry and history, is set out very clearly in a work by Oscar Milosz, *A Few Words on Poetry*. Milosz quotes from this at some length in the second lecture:

> That sacred art of the word, just because it springs forth from the sacred depths of Universal Being, appears to us as bound, more rigorously than any other mode of expression, to the spiritual and physical Movement of which it is a generator and a guide. . . . Sacerdotal in prehistoric times, epic at the moment of Greek colonial expansion, psychological and tragic at the decline of the dionysia, Christian, theological and sentimental in the middle ages, neoclassical since the beginning of the first spiritual and political revolution—namely the Renaissance—finally Romantic . . . poetry has always followed, fully aware of its terrible responsibilities, the mysterious movements of the great soul of the people.

Milosz has in mind this interdependence of poetry and history when he asks: "Is non-eschatological poetry possible?" And at the end of the second lecture he makes one sort of answer:

> It is possible that the gloom of twentieth century poetry can be explained by the pattern that resulted from the "schism and mis-

---

Czeslaw Milosz

understanding between the poet and the human family." This goes against the grain of our civilization, shaped as it is by the Bible and, for that reason, eschatological to the core.

In other words, poetry in the modern age has turned against its very nature—it has become noneschatological. The bond between the "word" and the "spiritual and physical Movement" (history) has been negated. When Milosz asks if a noneschatological poetry is possible, he is really asking if the present condition of divorce can last. For Oscar Milosz only *"la conflagration universelle"* could close the breach between the poet and the human family. Milosz is not so pessimistic—he does not require Apocalypse for things to be put right. He places a greater faith, as we shall see, in "the great soul of the people" and in the poet himself.

The Lesson of Biology, Milosz's third lecture, concerns itself, in part, with this severance of word from reality. Milosz maintains that the truth criteria of the once self-contained empirical disciplines have infiltrated all areas of thought, and that there has been a "rapid erosion of belief in any world other than one submitted to a mathematical determinism." And this, in turn, has led to a nihilism in the sphere of values. Milosz asks a very Nietzschean question:

Could we without perishing withstand a situation in which the things surrounding us lose their being, where there is no true world? Twentieth-century poetry answers that question in the negative. Its heroism is forced and offers no indication that we are on the verge of becoming supermen. When poets discover that their words refer only to words and not to a reality which must be described as faithfully as possible, they despair.

The discussion could almost stop here, for it would seem that there is no exit, no possibility for a turnaround. But Milosz knows other things about truth and human need. He finds in history's darkest hours an alternative to despair.

Milosz saw and experienced what happens to a people—and to oneself—when disaster overturns every certainty. Under extreme duress, he writes, "a hierarchy of needs . . . built into the very fabric of reality . . . is revealed." Urgency simplifies. And, as the hierarchy of needs is revealed, the attitude toward language changes: "It recovers its simplest function and is again an instrument serving a purpose; no one doubts that language must name reality, which exists objectively, massive, tangible, and terrifying in its concreteness." Disaster thus renews the bond between word and thing, and the poet, as servant of the word, is in a position to bring poetry out of its terrible isolation.

Ruins and Poetry, the fifth lecture, investigates the effects of the war experience upon Polish poetry. Although violence and destruction on such a scale can be said to constitute a special case, they may, for the very reason that they are unprecedented, supply a deeper insight into the ever-changing relation between poetry and history. Eastern European poetry, in the same way, and for the same reasons, is a special case, but no one will doubt that it illuminates more about the experience of our century than do the anxious ruminations that pour from our writing workshops. Looking at the postwar poetry of Tadeusz Rózewicz, Anna Swirszczinska, Miron Bialoszewski, Zbigniew Herbert, and Aleksander Wat, Milosz finds a range of linguistic responses to an experience that in its enormity all but shortcircuited language.

The work of these very different poets shares at least one common tendency, a poetics of restraint and indirection. They are one in their determination to avoid rhetoric, to speak only what can be spoken honestly. To call this a retreat of the word before experience would be too facile. Indeed, given the circumstances, it is astonishing that poets kept on writing. What we see is a victory, not a retreat. The work of these poets answers George Steiner's question—whether there can be a response to Holocaust other than silence. Language pushes on—differently, more hesitantly, it's true—but it does push on. The word is threshed and winnowed, but it remains the tenuous link between man and his historical self-consciousness. This is what interests Milosz and what gives him some measure of hope: that these poets did not fall silent, that they evolved their own austere response. Their restraint is an honest acknowledgment of the limits of language, but their activity is the highest affirmation of its durability. Thus, Swirszczinska composes detailed, nonmetaphoric word pictures, Bialoszewski strips the complexities of human activity to their most rudimentary components

Czeslaw Milosz

("First I went down to the store/by means of the stairs,/just imagine it,/by means of the stairs"), and Herbert, in what is perhaps the most effective response of all, finds a way to let everything that is absent from the poem stand front and center. He concentrates with the greatest possible restraint upon the description of a pebble: Beyond the curtailed horizon of the poem, almost palpable, are the menacing muzzles of the tanks.

The soul does not fall silent in the face of horror. Milosz reports that "probably in no language other than Polish are there so many terrifying poems, documents of the Holocaust. . . ." As documents they are terrifying, but as works of art—he admits that they are for the most part failures. This raises an important issue for Milosz. In *A Quarrel with Classicism,* the fourth lecture, he discusses the distinction between classicism and realism. The latter is committed to the impossible project of mirroring the multifariousness of reality. Classicism, accepting the impossibility of such an effort, is content to play literature as a game with rules, to perpetuate *topoi,* conventions that stand in the place of original or immediate response. The game, unfortunately, quickly becomes one of refinements and subtleties, and Milosz finds, as far back as Horace, the impulse to keep poetry out of the hands of *hoi polloi.*

At first sight, this discussion, interesting as it is, does not seem to fit with the material of the surrounding lectures. Why is Milosz bringing up the ancient form/content dispute? How does it connect? He does not gratify us by soldering this lecture to the others. We realize only gradually, after we have absorbed the material of all six lectures, in what ways the distinction has bearing. They are for the most part indirect. Milosz is roundaboutly buttressing his argument about the effects of disaster upon poetry.

If poetry is, as Milosz believes, vitally interfused with the movement of history, then disaster must transform poetry—and it most obviously has. But Milosz wants to determine the precise nature of the transformation. In order to do so, he first remarks upon the conventionality of most of the poetry that issued from the Holocaust. In most cases, he finds, the horror did not change the mode of response. The imagination siezed upon the *topoi* at hand, the established expressions and meters, and tried with these to convey unprecedented experiences and sensations. Milosz writes: "Because they use rhyme and stanzas, documentary poems belong to literature and one may ask, out of respect for those who perished, whether a more perfect poetry would not be a more appropriate monument than a poetry on the level of facts."

Milosz recognizes that history has forced a change upon poetry, that language has been subjected to an enormous shock, and that conventional (in this case "classical") approaches are no longer valid. The alternative, represented by the poets that Milosz does discuss, is sharply anticlassical. Explosions of the real have made impossible a poetry of "cherry blossoms, chrysanthemums and . . . full moon" like that Milosz satirizes in his poem "No More." For these poets, the world has come to exist as an indisputable, if frightening, fact. Their realism, stringent as it is, represents a rescue of the thing from the idea. The "passionate pursuit of the real," which Milosz claims as his own poetic program, is a response to the near destruction of "the real." Classical and realistic modes have been, at different times in history, bound up with different values. In our century, Milosz would argue, where the very continuation of "the real" is at stake, any manipulation of stylistic convention only aggravates the danger. To save the world we must first know it for what it is, and for this we still need language.

Concluding *Ruins and Poetry,* Milosz sadly reflects on the price that must be paid to bring poetry out of its alienated state:

> What can poetry be in the twentieth century? It seems to me that there is a search for the line beyond which only a zone of silence exists, and on that borderline we encounter Polish poetry. In it a peculiar fusion of the individual and historical took place, which means that events burdening a whole community are perceived by a poet as touching him in a most personal manner. Then poetry is no longer alienated. . . . If we choose the poetry of such an unfortunate country as Poland to learn that the great schism in poetry is curable, then that knowledge brings no comfort.

Czeslaw Milosz

We have seen that Milosz has a double vision of history:

For me, therefore, everything has a double existence.
Both in time and when time shall be no more.

We might expect, then, that his assessment of the present-day world, and his effort to locate some basis of hope, would be penetrated by the idea of redemption. After all, if history moves to an end, it must throughout be shaped to its destination. Interestingly enough, the concluding lecture, *On Hope,* has little or nothing to say about the restoration at the end of time. Milosz appears to be looking for a secular justification of the word "hope." But does this mean that the religious and secular visions are separable? That the event outside of time has no bearing on history? These matters have been disputed by churchmen throughout the ages and will not be settled here. But I do think that the separation of religious and secular is, at least on one level, a reflection of Milosz's struggle. His faith is not unwavering. It is always one element in a pitched struggle; it sharpens itself to match and surpass an active despair. If it appears to prevail in a poem like "From the Rising of the Sun," there is still no guarantee of final victory. Milosz is in many ways like the man in the Bible who called out: "I believe; help thou mine unbelief." The views of history presented here, therefore, are those of a man for whom the Kingdom is not a certainty. He is looking for a way to ground hope in man himself. He would like to make sense of history without God—just in case.

Hope. Whence hope? If we remove God and the prospect of eternity from the discussion, we are left with little more than the alarming visage of the world as it is today. And Milosz is under no illusion about the state of things: "It is possible that we are witnessing a kind of race between the lifegiving and destructive activity of civilization's bacteria, and that an unknown result awaits in the future." As for the unknown result, Milosz concludes that it depends upon so many different variables that not even a computer could calculate the right combination. For that reason, he says, "a poet with his intuition remains one strong, albeit uncertain, source of knowledge." It is as a poet—not as a sociologist, historian, philosopher, or scientist—that he looks to the future. He leaves us not with an argument or a program, but with a sequence of enigmatic intuitions.

Milosz takes his cue, as he does so often, from the writings of Simone Weil: "From where will a renewal come to us, to us who have devastated the whole earthly globe? Only from the past, if we love it." A puzzling assertion, Milosz admits. To clarify its import, he will refer to further pronouncements from Weil, and to an oracular phrase from Dostoevsky. But before we turn to these, it is necessary to establish a key point: that, for Milosz, the scientific, technological, and social transformations that have brought the world to its present imperiled state have also worked their effects on the mass of mankind:

> We can do justice to our time only by comparing it to that of our grandfathers and great-grandfathers. Something happened, whose importance still eludes us, and it seems very ordinary, though its effects will both last and increase. The exceptional quality of the twentieth century is not determined by jets as a means of transportation or a decrease in infant mortality or the birth-control pill. It is determined by humanity's emergence as a new elemental force. . . . Humanity as an elemental force, the result of technology and mass education, means that man is opening up to science and art on unprecedented scale.

And to what end? Milosz believes that this awakening humanity will, in time, turn away from the "Weltanschauung marked principally by biology," and that it will "increasingly be turning back to itself, increasingly contemplating its entire past, searching for a key to its own enigma." The revolution in communications, by breaking down the last vestiges of isolation, will open the masses to a sense of collective identity. And this, in turn, will initiate a collective existential questioning that will look past the scientific world view. Milosz's prediction (or hope) is quite different than Oscar Milosz's. The latter foretold that man would finally embrace the Einsteinian orientation, that relativistic vision would supersede the evils of the Newtonian conception.

It is, then, in the historical dimension that Milosz finds his grounds for hope. His formulation is a good deal more complex and mysterious

---

Czeslaw Milosz

than I have indicated; its dynamic requires close attention. First, we need to consider these two separate sentences. From Dostoevsky: "Beauty will save the world." And from Simone Weil: "Distance is the soul of beauty." Milosz cites both in his lecture, and the implication is that they fit together like two pieces of a jigsaw puzzle.

"Distance is the soul of beauty." There seem to be two layers of sense in the statement. One, that beauty is irreducible. (And this is corroborated by another sentence of Weil's: "Two things cannot be reduced to any rationalism, Time and Beauty.") The other sense is of objectivity, that what presents itself as beauty is purged of self, ego. In this, Weil is very close to Walter Benjamin's definition of "aura"— that it is "the unique phenomenon of a distance." If we consider distance in temporal as well as spatial terms, then we can surmise how the past, purified of the subjective element, can show itself objectively, as beauty. Beauty here is to be conceived in a larger sense—not simply as the fruit of aesthetic perception, but as the very revelation of meaning. As Saint Augustine wrote in the *Confessions:*

> And I said to all the things that throng about the gateways of the senses: "Tell me of my God, since you are not He. Tell me something of him." And they cried out in a great voice: "He made us." My question was my gazing upon them and their answer was their beauty.

In Augustine, of course, meaning is anchored in God, and thus transcendent. Milosz stresses that the attainment of self-consciousness is, in essence, a transcendence of the causal order of nature.

"Beauty will save the world," for Milosz, means that humanity's saving self-perception will come about through the revelation of beauty as meaning. Beauty will manifest itself as the passing of time and the change in mass consciousness will reveal the struggles of history under the aspect of objectivity. As an individual is said to come of age when he sees how the turmoils of his earlier years have shaped him, when he understands them objectively and from a distance, so, presumably, collective man will one day come of age. Implicit is Milosz's belief that such a perception will extirpate the warring instincts of the tribe.

Now, perhaps, the connecting line can be drawn between Milosz's epigraph and his closing remarks on hope:

> He sees what I see even now. Oh, but he was clever,
> Attentive, as if things were instantly changed by memory.
> Riding in a cart, he looked back to retain as much as possible.
> Which means he knew what was needed for some ultimate
>   moment
> When he would compose from fragments a world perfect at last.

And:

> This is not the place to say what will happen tomorrow, as the fortune tellers and futurologists do. The hope of the poet, a hope that I defend, that I advance, is not enclosed by any date. If disintegration is a function of development, and development a function of disintegration, the race between them may very well end in the victory of disintegration. For a long time, but not forever—and here is where hope enters. It is neither chimerical nor foolish. On the contrary, every day one can see signs indicating that now, at the present moment, something new, and on a scale never witnessed before, is being born: humanity as an elemental force conscious of transcending Nature, for it lives by memory of itself, that is, in History.

What humanity, by transcending nature, may accomplish for itself is not so different from what the poet, through his art, would compose from the ruins of the past. Or what the man who believes that "everything has a double existence" awaits from that date outside time. Hopes of this order, whether we share them or not, honor us all.

Czeslaw Milosz

Zbigniew Herbert

W. H. Auden once devoted some pages to the question of the translatability of the Greek poet C. P. Cavafy, concluding finally that because his poetry "speaks" rather than sings, and because his vision of the world was so unique that it transcended the confines of his immediate cultural background, some success was possible. I suspect that the same is true, for like reasons, of our Polish contemporary Zbigniew Herbert. And, indeed, his translators, Czeslaw Milosz among them, have testified to the *relative* amenability of his poetry to that "carrying across the threshold." They acknowledge that his tonal shifts are subtle, and that the structural mapping between English and Polish is problematic, but it appears that these liabilities

---

are compensated by the linearity of Herbert's thought and by what is sometimes called the "classicism" of his style—there are no gusts of moodiness or emotionalism in his work.

I would like to keep Cavafy's name up front for a moment, for a further instancing of similarities may be instructive. Here are two separate excerpts:

> I'm practically broke and homeless.
> This fatal city, Antioch
> has devoured all my money:
> this fatal city with its extravagant life.

> But I'm young and extremely healthy.
> Prodigious master of Greek,
> I know Aristotle and Plato through and through,
> poets, orators, or anyone else you could mention.
> I have some idea about military matters
> and friends among the senior mercenaries.

And:

> I received a many-sided education
> Livy the rhetoricians philosophers
> I spoke Greek like an Athenian
> although Plato I recalled
> only in the lying position

> I completed my studies
> in dockside taverns and brothels
> those unwritten dictionaries of vulgar Latin
> bottomless treasuries of crime and lust

The first citation is from Cavafy's "To Have Taken the Trouble" (translated by Edmund Keeley and Philip Sherrard), and the second is from Herbert's "The Divine Claudius," from the recently published collection *Report from the Besieged City* (translated by John and Bogdana Carpenter). I find more in common between the passages than the pronominal mask or the classical references. The two are on a stylistic continuum, presenting historical material in an unadorned manner that is at once intimate and detached. Translation has, of course, skimmed away the rich particularities of each mother tongue—the distance between Greek and Polish sounds is surely great—but it has disclosed all the more clearly a correspondence of vision.

I don't wish to press the Cavafy comparison too far. But as Cavafy's stance and tone and procedure of historical distancing are well known to readers of modern poetry, he can serve as a useful point of reference. The appearance of similar elements in Herbert's poetry cannot but raise some interesting questions. After all, Cavafy was writing about memory and about the slow decay of civilization—elegiac subjects. Herbert has situated himself in the heart of the "besieged city" that is Poland—refusing exile—and in his eyes slow decay might almost look like a utopian ideal. We have to ask: What kind of response does his poetic mode offer to a morally intolerable reality?

Report from the Besieged City offers three kinds of poems: those written about, or from behind the mask of, historical personages (Beethoven, Isadora Duncan, the emperor Claudius, the mythical Procrustes) or about historical events; topical or philosophical meditations; and poems spoken through the persona of his creation "Mr. Cogito," who comes across as a line-sketch caricature of an alienated intellectual of our times. The separation between kinds of poems is not clear-cut. For Mr. Cogito—and fully a fourth of the poems are in his voice—does a good bit of philosophical speculating, and history turns out to be one of his favorite subjects. The real continuity element, however, is tonal. The poems are, almost without exception, refracted through the complex crystal of irony:

> for a long time
> the conviction persisted
> man carries in himself
> a sizable reservoir of blood
>
> a squat barrel
> twenty-odd liters
> —a trifle
>
> —from "Mr. Cogito Thinks About Blood"

Zbigniew Herbert

I live now
in the best hotel

the dead porter
remains on duty in his room

from a hill of rubble
I enter directly
onto the second floor
to the suite
of the former mistress
of the former chief of police

—from "The Abandoned"

Irony of this sort is not so much a stylistic maneuver as a mode of consciousness. It is not part of the register of American poetry (only Weldon Kees comes to mind as an exception)—perhaps we have not suffered enough, collectively—and deserves some discussion. To begin with, we should get rid of the idea that its thrust is cynical or destructive. While it does represent the far—experienced—side of idealism, the ironic mode yet retains a connection to that idealism. It is resistance, not capitulation. The ironist protects against the erosion of all faith by inoculating himself with the serum of disillusionment. He never speaks of important things directly; he knows that the public disclosure of emotions or convictions destroys their fragile integrity— and in the modern age all truths are fragile.

If we look to the etymology of the word "irony," we come upon a telling paradox, at least with respect to Herbert's poetry. For the original Greek sense of the word was "dissembling"; to be ironic was to hold back, to refrain from speaking real thoughts, to be untrustworthy. But Herbert's consistently ironic poetry has been widely regarded as an instrument of sanity, a refusal of compromise, a bearing of witness. It would seem that a great deal has changed, either in the word or in the world, since the early period of usage. I would argue that Herbert's irony achieves its exemplary status because of a momentous historical inversion—because, in his part of the world, "polis" has become "police." The political order out of which—and of which—Herbert writes represents a willful deception so thorough that any flat assertion would be neutralized. You do not say of a barbaric deed: "That is barbaric"; to be more effective, to reach past the defenses of your auditors, you whisper: "That was lovely, most refined." Tone, then, becomes content; and tone is much more difficult to legislate. Irony represents, in a society like Herbert's, a language apart. Oblique, encoded, quarantined against rhetoric, it is the signature of a secret brotherhood, a covert emblem of truth. What is so frightening about reading Herbert's poetry is the realization that things have come to such a pass.

Herbert achieves a great many different kinds of ironic effects, and I have space to note only a few. In the poem "Mr. Cogito on the Need for Precision," for example, he manipulates the discrepancy between subject and tone masterfully. Here, in the middle of the second section, he uses a conventional tactic of understatement to set up his point:

> A few simple examples
> from the accounting of victims
>
> in an airplane disaster
> it is easy to establish
> the exact number of the dead
>
> important for heirs
> and those plunged in grief
> for insurance companies

But then, in the third section, he suddenly complicates things by taking up the issue of "those who perished / in the struggle with inhuman power":

> accidental observers
> give doubtful figures
> accompanied by the shameful
> word "about"
>
> and yet in these matters
> accuracy is essential

Zbigniew Herbert

we must not be wrong
even by a single one

we are despite everything
the guardians of our brothers

ignorance about those who have disappeared
undermines the reality of the world

The shift is clearly discernible. The second passage is frontal and eschews the primerlike tone of the "airplane disaster" lines. And yet the
undercurrent of irony cannot be shaken. Serious as this later passage
sounds, the cool sobriety is still at odds with the essential reality invoked. The fact that it is the two-dimensional Mr. Cogito who speaks
further heightens the dissonance. We end up heeding—and surely this
is Herbert's design—the detachment of Mr. Cogito's thought as much
as the substance of it. The tension between the *how* of presentation and
the *what* of real lives maps in miniature the enormous struggle between
totalitarian (or, for that matter, *any*) bureaucracy and the heart's desire
that every hair be numbered.

Historical subject matter supplies Herbert with other tonal options. Like Cavafy, he turns to his own poetic advantage the obliterat-
ing effects of time. The events and personages that he seizes upon have
already been cleansed of subjective particularity; little more than the
bare lines of narrative remain. This is a calculated operation on Herbert's part. For by choosing thus to address the past, he effects a
powerful reversal. The bleached bones of history show us more than
the past—they reveal implicitly the future's rudimentary image of the
present. Oppressor and oppressed will suffer equal oblivion—not a
consoling vision, even though it represents a relative gain for the latter.
For me this accounts for much of the bitter taste of a poem like
"Anabasis." Its irony—produced by the flat, retrospective generalizations—sends a shudder through the historian's time line:

The condottieri of Cyrus a foreign legion
cunning pitiless and yes they killed
two hundred and fifteen daily marches

—kill us we can't go any further—
thirty-four thousand two hundred and fifty-five stadia

festering with sleeplessness they went through savage countries
uncertain fords mountain passes in snow and salty plateaus
cutting their road in the living body of peoples
luckily they didn't lie they were defending civilization

the famous shout on Mount Teches
is mistakenly interpreted by sentimental poets
they simply found the sea that is the exit from the dungeon

they made the journey without the Bible without prophets burning
    bushes
without signs on the earth without signs in the sky
with the cruel consciousness that life is immense

Herbert's principal devices—tonal displacement and detached historical vision—are brought together in the powerful title poem, which is placed at the end of the book. The unnamed reporter/witness is situated in the "besieged city"; the time of the events is not specified. This last turns out to be an important strategic element. For at the beginning we locate ourselves in a near-mythic long-ago (much as we do in Cavafy's "Waiting for the Barbarians"):

Too old to carry arms and fight like the others—

they graciously gave me the inferior role of chronicler
I record—I don't know for whom—the history of the siege

But we are not allowed to hold that comforting scrim in place for long. By the halfway mark a more disturbing resonance has been created:

and so in the evening released from facts I can think
about distant ancient matters for example our
friends beyond the sea I know they sincerely sympathize
they send us flour lard sacks of comfort and good advice
they don't even know their fathers betrayed us
our former allies at the time of the second Apocalypse

Zbigniew Herbert

their sons are blameless they deserve our gratitude therefore we
    are grateful
they have not experienced a siege as long as eternity
those struck by misfortune are always alone
the defenders of the Dalai Lama the Kurds the Afghan
    mountaineers

And then comes the devastating conclusion:

cemeteries grow larger the number of defenders is smaller
yet the defense continues it will continue to the end
and if the City falls but a single man escapes
he will carry the City within himself on the roads of exile
he will be the City
we look in the face of hunger the face of fire face of death
worst of all—the face of betrayal

and only our dreams have not been humiliated

We have not the slightest doubt that Herbert is speaking to us out of the present, but the deliberately nonspecific opening section calls together the various historical tableaux that have preceded it in the book. The rays from vanished civilizations converge upon the point of the *now*. In that now, the City still lives; its invisible life is sustained in the hearts of loyal countrymen. But what will the next generation have to hold up against the "face of betrayal"?

"Too long a sacrifice," wrote Yeats, "can make a stone of the heart." The master ironist would appear to undermine this process by taking into his soul something of the hardness of the stone. But that armor must not be construed as callous resignation—behind Herbert's tonal facade is a man cupping his hands around a flickering match.

A recent review of Adam Zagajewski's *Tremor* (Renata Gorczynski, translator) by his fellow Polish émigré, the poet Stanislaw Baranczak, points up to me just how much historical context conditions the interpretive act. Baranczak, as a member of Zagajewski's poetic generation—the so-called generation of 1968—and who surely knows the poems in their original cadences, writes as follows:

> . . . the multidimensional meaning of Zagajewski's poetry can by no means be reduced to that of "a poetry of protest" or a generational manifesto. The book can (and should) be read also outside

the framework of Poland's recent history, and it will not lose much this way. After all, it has something important to say about life, death, love, loneliness, and other rather universal matters. And yet the keen sense of history that pervades and distorts contemporary existence seems to be something that cannot really be subtracted from Zagajewski's poems. While his work contains a wealth of sensuous imagination and philosophical perspicacity, the reader here is not able to forget that he is dealing with a poet born and raised in our age and in a certain corner of Eastern Europe.

While I will not set myself up to dispute Baranczak—my position on the far side of the linguistic barricade precludes even the possibility of that—I will say that I registered a very different response in my reading of the poet. What I found was a metaphysics born from a deep sense of contradiction, a will that had as its impossible goal the destruction of the space/time axis. The question is one of emphasis. Where Baranczak states that *Tremor* "can (and should) be read also outside the framework of Poland's recent history," it seems to me that "Poland's recent history" has driven Zagajewski to a larger vision of history itself, and that the work is only in part concerned with the generational experience of the Poles. In other words, the effects, which are metaphysical, take precedence over the causes, which are historical.

I will be the first to admit that mine is a privileged, and American, reading. But the simple fact is that these poems, even in translation, captured with unnerving clarity my own feelings about life in our terrifying epoch—they reach past the surface lesions in order to search out the wounding source. Which is something more than ideology and state power. This poetry is quickened—now and then made feverish—by the tension between two orders of time, the meaningful and the meaningless: between time as it was lived, felt, *inhabited* before everything changed, and time as we know it now, an abstract series of dissociated moments, a conceptual grid. The application is universal; the digital instruments of the free, capitalist West mark the same empty intervals as the clocks of the state. What happened? Did historical developments accelerate and then destroy our collective sense of meaningful time, or did Chronos himself undergo some mutation, carrying history in his wake? The second possibility is more frightening, for it denies us the idea of freedom. And Zagajewski will, on occasion, incline this way. In "Late Beethoven," for example, one of several meditations on the expiration of the nineteenth century, he writes: "Unending adagios. That's how tired freedom/breathes," as if to suggest the imminent collapse of human prerogative. So, too, in "Schopenhauer's Crying" we read:

> His vest. His starched collar.
> All these dispensables tremble,
> as if the bombs had already fallen
> on Frankfurt.

The implication, of course, is that there is a destiny inscribed on the fabric of history, and that the free acts of man are illusory. However—and this will become clear later—Zagajewski does not hold to any one position unequivocally.

Tremor begins with a breathless and image-haunted long poem entitled "To Go to Lvov." His trademark style is immediately obvious: the exploded syntax of his sentences, the prismatic juxtaposition of verb tenses, the massing of vivid threads of detail:

> To go to Lvov. Which station
> for Lvov, if not in a dream, at dawn, when dew
> gleams on a suitcase, when express
> trains and bullet trains are being born. To leave
> in haste for Lvov, night or day, in September
> or in March. But only if Lvov exists,
> if it is to be found within the frontiers and not just
> in my new passport, if lances of trees
> —of poplar and ash—still breathe aloud
> like Indians, and if streams mumble
> their dark Esperanto, and grass snakes like soft signs
> in the Russian language disappear
> into thickets.

Adam Zagajewski

The poem goes on for another seventy-odd lines, turning first into a catalogue of a vanished way of life, a dream picture of the European nineteenth century:

> . . . and joy hovered
> everywhere, in hallways and in coffee mills
> revolving by themselves, in blue
> teapots, in starch, which was the first
> formalist, in drops of rain and in the thorns
> of roses. Frozen forsythia yellowed by the window.
> The bells pealed and the air vibrated, the cornets
> of nuns sailed like schooners near
> the theater, there was so much of the world that
> it had to do encores over and over.

and then breaking its own reverie with this ominous metaphor:

> But scissors cut it, along the line and through
> the fiber, tailors, gardeners, censors
> cut the body and the wreaths, pruning shears worked
> diligently, as in a child's cutout
> along the dotted line of a roe deer or a swan.
> Scissors, penknives, and razor blades scratched,
> cut, and shortened the voluptuous dresses
> of prelates, of squares and houses, and trees
> fell soundlessly, as in a jungle,
> and the cathedral trembled, people bade goodbye.

Emotional narration finally gives way to a complex finale that mitigates its desperate cry with an unexpectedly consoling vision:

> . . . why must every city
> become Jerusalem and every man a Jew,
> and now in a hurry just
> pack, always, each day,
> and go breathless, go to Lvov, after all
> it exists, quiet and pure as
> a peach. It is everywhere.

Poets in Translation

I cite at length, both to show something of Zagajewski's manner, his idiosyncratic dovetailing of clauses, and to suggest the velocity—the gulped-air quality—that his longer poems often achieve. This, more than anything, establishes his stylistic distance from senior masters like Czeslaw Milosz and Zbigniew Herbert, both of whom sustain a certain intellectual/ironic fixity in their work; in Milosz particularly, the disruptive insanity of recent history is held up against a stable backdrop of natural order, childhood memories, and spiritual absolutes. Perhaps because Zagajewski is relatively young (he was born in 1945) and has had no direct experience of the prewar order, the past that he evokes is like a child's dream. But it is intention, not naïveté. In "To Go to Lvov," this romanticized perception of the past is what allows the poem to attain its shuddering and all but self-negating climax. The image of a child's scissors cutting away the beautiful past paves the way for the chilling interrogative: "why must every city/become Jerusalem and every man a Jew." Two vastly different orders of experience are pushed together: Jerusalem is at once the mythic setting of the child's Bible story and the ultimate site of loss and redemption.

The problem of redemption is posed by the last three lines, which are baffling both logically and in terms of their suggestion. If Lvov is indeed "everywhere"—that is, if it exists unscarred in the collective memory of a people, or in some state of duration that cannot be assailed by sequent events—then there is, literally speaking, no reason to be packing and rushing to get there. Similarly, if the poem is intended to be an elegy for a lost world, why would Zagajewski alter its impact with a sudden swerve, an intimation of perfect restoration? The best answer I can devise is that the reversal results from an utterly irrational act of faith. It is a lightning stroke of pure paradox: So much life could not be destroyed so quickly; it must exist—like Jerusalem for the Jew—as a final destination; because it is nowhere, it must be everywhere. This is the soul's logic, not the mind's—it generates an affecting and unforgettable poetry.

There is often a kind of impossibility—or unattainability—in Zagajewski's work. As he writes in his "Ode to Plurality": "a poem grows/on contradiction but it can't cover it." Historical truth and human desire move in opposite directions, the one telling us what *is,* the

Adam Zagajewski

other telling us what we are and, therefore, what *could be*. Destiny
versus freedom, reality versus art—the poet is the broker, the eternal
victim and beneficiary of the double vision. The tension of this is
sustained throughout the entire collection. If one poem declares a diminishing hope:

> He acts, in splendor and in darkness,
> in the roar of waterfalls and in the silence of sleep,
> but not as your well-protected shepherds
> would have it. He looks for the longest line,
> the road so circuitous
> it is barely visible, and fades away
> in suffering. Only blind men, only
> owls feel sometimes its dwindling trace
> under the eyelids.
>
> —"He Acts"

another, like "Kierkegaard on Hegel," will seem to countermand it:
"God/is the smallest poppy seed in the world,/bursting with greatness."

The reference of these quotations is deceptive, for Zagajewski is
not a religious poet. God is, for him, more like an emblem of a vanishing spiritual heritage, a manifestation of the desire that flies in the face
of the circumstantial fact. His own metaphysics is ultimately a good
deal more impersonal. In "Fire, Fire," for instance, he speaks of the
force that "ravages and burns cities/made of wood, of stone" but also
"compels Descartes/to overthrow philosophy." This Heraclitean sense
of flux and opposition is everywhere in Zagajewski; a self-
conflicted energy swirls at the core of creation:

> The force that grows
> in Napoleon's dreams
> and tells him to conquer Russia and snow
> is also in poems
> but it is very still.
>
> —from "That Force"

Poets in Translation

That stillness—which may represent the highest attainment of art, a surmounting of contradiction—is beautifully rendered in "A View of Delft":

Houses, waves, clouds, and shadows
(deep-blue roofs, brownish bricks),
all of you finally became a glance.

The quiet pupil of things, unreined,
glittering with blackness.

You'll outlive our admiration, our tears,
and our noisy, despicable wars.

But I cannot read this as a celebration of the final triumph of art.

Zagajewski writes comfortably in both compressed and extended forms. If the shorter lyrics at times resemble those of Milosz—direct, simplified statement enfolding a paradox or an irresoluble contradiction—the longer poems, *tours de force* many of them, announce his tonal distinctiveness. In these we feel most directly the impact of history upon sensibility, as much in the contents as in the syntactic cut and thrust. Indeed, the tremor in these pages issues from the active abrasion of clauses and image clusters; conclusions and meanings feel, at best, provisional.

Zagajewski's longer persona poems—like "Late Beethoven" and "Franz Schubert: A Press Conference"—warrant more discussion than I have space for. Each in its own way dissolves our imagining of the nineteenth century in the cataract of the twentieth. The measured movement of clock hands speeds up until there is nothing but a dizzying blur. But it is the penultimate long poem, "A View of Cracow," that finds the words for the true terror.

Before me, Cracow in a grayish dale.
Swallows carry it on long braids
woven of air. Rooks in black
frock coats watch over it.

Adam Zagajewski

The poem begins with an easy mingling of perspectives. Glimpsed in its natural setting, the city exudes an enchanted timelessness. But before long, the past and present are delineated: "Of the more recent architecture,/the Palace of Police stands out" and "What was, what is, meticulously/separated." This troubling fact—that the extrusions of different epochs, different zones of being, can coexist in space—then triggers the first shift. We are moved from exterior, synoptic vantage to the human and inward:

> A lonely woman lived here
> and not long ago she died of old age
> or loneliness. Who remembers
> what pastry she used to bake
> or how much anger was stored in her eyes?

A commonplace reflection, but it yields immediately to a more strident indictment:

> Before me, character actors
> hidden in their apartments,
> hidden under their costumes. Oppressors
> pretend they are oppressed, women perform
> the roles of women, old people impersonate
> old people.

The litany goes on, builds, until at last the question is thrust under our noses: "Is it/a divine comedy or is it a divine/tragedy borrowed from the city library?" The poet does not answer. Instead, he slips a new panel into place:

> Through the park, through a dense tunnel,
> a young girl hurries, late for her lectures.
> Petals of peonies grow in her hair,
> the tenderness of time weaves a nest
> in her hair. She is running fast but
> she doesn't move, she is still
> in the same place, under the chestnut branches
> which fling off greenery
> and put on new greenery.

Zagajewski has summoned up the image of duration, that privileged mode of being that belongs to youth—and, in this poetry, to
the historical past—and that is a form of timelessness. In the condition
of duration, things are exactly themselves, seeming is banished,
plunged in the plenitude of the moment, and meaning inheres in actions if only because they are unquestioned. The girl does not move
because she is an anomaly in a world turned false. After a dozen more
lines, Zagajewski concludes:

> Airy smoke drifts from the chimneys
> as if a conclave were still going on,
> as if the tenements wanted
> a turn to play at existence.
> Before me, Cracow, a gray planet,
> the charcoal of bliss and expectation (life played the part
> of life, joy was joy, and suffering was suffering).

Difficult as it is to present a poem through episodic cuttings like
these, the idea is central to the work and demands our attention. The
final parenthetic statement—primerlike in its simplicity—sums up
Zagajewski's vision of our posthistorical condition. We are no longer
connected to meaningful time, to that sustaining taproot; every atom
of our human cosmos is now merely impersonating itself. History has
been succeeded by a stage act. To me, this is more than just an assessment of life under totalitarian rule—it is news about the collective life
of our times. We do not have to be in Cracow, or in exile from it, to
get the shudder of recognition. Our common exile from a comprehen-
sible reality bound to tradition, natural process, and a living sense of
the spiritual suffices. Zagajewski may be looking at Eastern Europe, but
his gaze wraps itself around the whole globe.

Adam Zagajewski

Octavio Paz

"**P**oetry," proclaims Octavio Paz at the opening of his study *The Bow and the Lyre,* "is knowledge, salvation, power, abandonment. . . . Poetry reveals this world; it creates another. Bread of the chosen; accursed food. It isolates; it unites. Invitation to the journey; return to the homeland." He goes on in this vein for some time. But even this short citation maps the sensibility: Paz is at once dialectical and poetical; his conceptual oppositions vie at every turn with the imperatives of metaphoric formulation. The mind is always pushing its way forward by way of assertion and negation, plying among theses and antitheses in order to reach some still point of synthesis. Any arrival, however, is but a preparation for the next depar-

---

Octavio Paz

ture. An inspection of Paz's poetry, or his myriad writings on literature, art, Tantrism, and Mexican culture, will convince anyone that the man whose name means "peace" never has any.

Born in a suburb of Mexico City in 1914, Paz has been his country's busiest thinker and man of letters for the better part of our century. If Mexico is, as is often asserted, the land that the European Enlightenment bypassed (it experienced the reaction of the Counter-reformation instead), then Paz can be seen as one of the bearers of lost light. He has grappled with the historical and artistic legacies of both hemispheres, he has directed the concentrated rays of international modernism upon the dark mythic strata of pre- and postcolonial Mexico, and he has successfully combined the implicitly political role of the public intellectual with the solitary gestations required by the poetic Muse—no small task.

Assembling between covers the poetic output of this dynamo is a bit like trying to hang a stationary frame around a catherine wheel. Poem by poem, of course, the centrifugal bursts of his talent are arrested within lines and stanzas. But the cumulative effect of any larger sequence is of a motion very much at odds with the customarily tranquil development of a poet's career.

Readers, then, should be alerted. The beautifully designed, classic-looking *Collected Poems of Octavio Paz, 1957–1987* is not a memorial slab—Paz in his mid-seventies is creating valorously. But neither is the book's enormous heft a token of uncontested greatness. The contents manifest a profusion that becomes at times unruly: Poems of great distinction are set out side by side with less engaging exploratory exercises. Only on the plane of translation is the uniformity of excellence certain—Paul Blackburn, Elizabeth Bishop, Charles Tomlinson, Mark Strand, Lysander Kemp, Denise Levertov, John Frederick Nims, and Eliot Weinberger, who has rendered the bulk of the poetry, are as fine a team of translators as any writer could dream of having. (This is not to say that there will not be quibbles. My favorite is with Weinberger's translation of the lines "Un grito/en un cráter extinto/en otra galaxia/¿cómo so dice ataraxia?" into "A shout/in a dead crater:/in another galaxy/how does one say pathetic fallacy?" My English dictionary has "ataraxia"—"a state of tranquility"—but try as I may I cannot figure out how "pathetic fallacy" fits in its place. This is a rare lapse, however. Weinberger has done a heroic job of bringing Paz into a lucid and quick-moving idiom.)

The assertion implicit in Weinberger's editing of the volume—which will not be contested here—is that Paz first came into his own with the publication of his *tour de force* long poem "Sunstone" (1957), which is the opening selection. He had been writing poems for decades already (an *Early Poems, 1935–1955* was published some years ago), but with this performance he is ready to start making his mark on international literature. Indeed, in its ambitiously synthetic momentum, "Sunstone" can be viewed as an important precursor of the innovative work of Carlos Fuentes, Gabriel García Márquez, Julio Cortázar, and other writers of the celebrated boom of the 1960's.

"Sunstone" is written as a single circular sentence—its end joining its beginning—of 584 eleven-syllable lines. Its structural basis is the circular Aztec calendar, which measures the synodic period of the planet Venus (I take this from the helpful "Author's Notes" at the back). But the reader need not be alarmed by this esoteric correlative design. While it organizes the work, it does not circumscribe its subject. "Sunstone" is, like so many of Paz's longer poems, a lyrically discursive exploration of time and memory, of erotic love, of art and writing, of myth and mysticism. The axis is the urgently ruminating "I"; the links between one flight and the next, often between one line and the next, are forged by the relentless alchemical transformations of metaphor:

> I search for an instant alive as a bird,
> for the sun of five in the afternoon
> tempered by walls of porous stone:
> the hour ripened by its cluster of grapes,
> and bursting, girls spilled out from the fruit,
> scattering in the cobblestone patios of the school,
> one was tall as autumn and walked
> through the arcades enveloped in light,
> and space encircled, dressed her in a skin
> even more golden and more transparent,
>
> —trans. Weinberger

Octavio Paz

Paz's procedure allows him to create a vast and fluid-feeling panorama of the psyche in intensified motion, with all of its dilations and shifts. The hazard is that which threatens all such inclusive (and, yes, baroque) undertakings: that the pressure of necessity will be vitiated by the too-bountiful imaginings, that the progress on the page will at times resemble a free-for-all of competing ideas and images. Stunning as Paz's cadenzas can be, the reader may long at times for a clearer sense of directional development. (Paz's polymorphous tendency is encouraged, I suspect, by the vowel-rich sonorities of the Spanish language; it would be difficult to generate so hypnotic a flow of sounds in our Anglo-Saxon-based tongue.)

Though Paz's reigning structural conceit in "Sunstone" harks back to the indigenous Aztecs, his poetic art strongly reflects the influence of André Breton and the French surrealists as well as the deep symbolist heritage running back through Eliot to Rimbaud. It's hard to miss the Rimbaldian echo in a passage like this:

—when was life ever truly ours?
when are we ever what we are?
we are ill-reputed, nothing more
than vertigo and emptiness, a frown in the mirror,
horror and vomit, life is never
truly ours, it is always belonging to the others,
life is no one's, we are all life—
bread of the sun for the others,
the others that we all are—

Paz is clearly less interested in subject matter than he is in re-creating the momentum of psychic—and spiritual—processes. "Sunstone" is as much about the porosity of boundaries and the frailty of the ego as it is about the solar mythologies of the Aztecs.

One does not have to read far to discover a rather striking artistic split at the core of Paz's endeavor. Throughout the compendium, long, all-embracing poems of the "Sunstone" variety alternate with short, stripped-down lyrics. The latter are often lyrically superior—cleaner, more mysterious, less didactic—but they bear no freight of ideas. It is almost as if these were the two warring sides of the poet's nature—a will to proliferation and a will to asceticism. Compare the passages already cited with the swift and tremulous "Dawn," also from the 1950's:

Cold rapid hands
draw back one by one
the bandages of dark
I open my eyes
        still
I am living
       at the center
of a wound still fresh

                        —trans. Tomlinson

The cool economy of strokes does not sort easily with the expressive prolixity found in the longer poems.

In 1962, when he was forty-eight, Paz was appointed to the post of Mexican ambassador to India. Out of the six-year period that he served—the key years of poetic maturity—came the collection *Ladera Este,* or *Eastern Slope.* The impact of Indian religious creeds upon a sensibility avid for spiritual syntheses was, predictably, immense. Paz already suspected the fortified boundaries of the ego. Now, for a time, he would seek to tear asunder the veil of *maya* (or "illusion"). Here, for instance, are some lines from "Reading John Cage," a remarkable fusion of Paz's avant-garde inclinations and his more mystical probings:

        It is not the same,
hearing the footsteps of the afternoon
among the trees and houses,
        and
seeing this same afternoon
among the same trees and houses now
           after reading
Silence:
      Nirvana is Samsara,
         silence is music.

                    —trans. Weinberger

Octavio Paz

Even more ethereally pitched is Paz's long fugal poem "Blanco,"
which reads in places like some Eastern holy text:

No and Yes
together
        two syllables in love
If the world is real
            the word is unreal
If the word is real
        the world
is the cleft the splendor the whirl
No
    disappearances and appearances
                            Yes
the tree of names
        Real unreal
are words
        they are air nothing

—trans. Weinberger

Paz is not the first Occidental poet to have embraced Oriental
ways. The great Swedish poet Gunnar Ekelöf put himself through similar sea change; and both Gary Snyder and Allen Ginsberg have, for
periods, brought their aesthetics in line with the practice of Eastern
religious disciplines. The marriage of strains has often resulted, as it did
in some of Paz's poetry of the time, in a haunting, if peculiar, music.

But the Indian period was not to last. The 1968 massacre of student demonstrators by government troops at the Mexico City Olym-
piad stunned Paz. He resigned his post in protest and returned home.
Though he had long since broken with the leftist orthodoxy of the
Latin American intelligentsia, he had no tolerance for the repressions
of the state's pretend democracy, either. His gesture marked him as a
radical without an ideological portfolio—a status that continues to irk
many of his countrymen.

The poetry from this turbulent epoch (1969–1975) was collected
in *Vuelta,* or *Return* (*Vuelta* is also the name of the cultural journal that
Paz began to edit at this time). The poet appeared to be turning from

the quietistic meditations of his Indian years. A poem like the title piece, "Return," reveals a preoccupation with the crises of the day, and sequences of sharply surrealistic imagery expose a distinctly non-transcendental point of vantage:

> We have dug up Rage
> The amphitheater of the genital sun is a dungheap
> The fountain of lunar water is a dungheap
> The lovers' park is a dungheap
> The library is a nest of killer rats
> The university is a muck full of frogs
> The altar is Chanfalla's swindle
> The eggheads are stained with ink
> The doctors dispute in a den of thieves
>
> —trans. Weinberger

Once again, Ginsberg comes to mind, this time the Ginsberg of *Howl* (1956). We see the same effort in both writers to find a declamatory idiom adequate to the outrageous character of contemporary events.

Rage is not the only thing that Paz disinterred upon his return. He also became fascinated with the myth of the self and of the past (a fascination that might have signaled the return of the repressed ego). In 1974, Paz published his long poem *A Draft of Shadows*. The epigraph is drawn from Wordsworth's *Prelude:* "Fair seed-time had my soul, and I grew up / Fostered alike by beauty and by fear. . . ." Throughout the poem, Paz attempts through repeated elisions of memory to come to terms with his family history, his own emotional and spiritual experience, and his poetic vocation. He begins with an Eliotic evocation of the mysteries of memory:

> Heard by the soul, footsteps
> in the mind more than shadows,
> shadows of thought more than footsteps
> through the path of echoes
> that memory invents and erases:
> without walking they walk
> over this present, bridge
> slung from one letter to the next.

Octavio Paz

carries on through hundreds of lines figuring phases in his autobiography:

> Child among taciturn adults
> and their terrifying childishness,
> child in passageways with tall doors,
> rooms with portraits,
> dim brotherhoods of the departed,
> child survivor
> of mirrors with no memory
> and their people of wind:
> time and its incarnations
> broken into travesties of reflections.

and finally concludes with these enigmatically symbolist lines:

> I am where I was:
> I walk behind the murmur,
> footsteps within me, heard with my eyes,
> the murmur is in the mind, I am my footsteps,
> I hear the voices that I think,
> the voices that think me as I think them.
> I am the shadow my words cast.
>
> —trans. Weinberger

If Paz had earlier, in "Blanco," opposed the reality of the world to that of the word, he appears here to have cast his lot with the latter. He is hardly the first poet to have looked to language as the seat of the real—Rimbaud, Mallarmé, Eliot, and Stevens all did—but few poets have subjected their readers at such length to the to-and-fro of the preliminary meditations. Indeed, this might well be the main complaint against this grand *oeuvre:* that it asks us to track what are often just the reflex actions of a soul bent upon transcending the here and now. When Paz is at his best, we can feel the struggle pressurizing the verse. But there are too many instances of the mind milling abstract nouns, and too many patches of "sublime" musing that come across more as a conjuring with verbal counters than as a pitched battle with necessity. This unevenness keeps Paz from being a poet of the very first order—

the ore keeps disappearing inside the bedrock. Take this short passage from *A Draft of Shadows:*

> Amazed at the moment's peak,
> flesh became word—and the word fell.
> To know exile on earth, being earth,
> is to know mortality. An open secret,
> an empty secret with nothing inside:
> there are no dead, there is only death, our mother.
> The Aztecs knew it, the Greeks divined it:
> water is fire, and in its passage
> we are only flashes of flame.
> Death is the mother of forms . . .

The switches and equivalences are just too deft: flesh becoming word, exile opening upon mortality, the assertion that there are no dead, that water is fire . . . One starts to wonder if the nouns could not be interchanged—with flesh becoming fire, word water—without great loss.

The volume concludes with the hitherto uncollected poems of *Árbol Adentro* (*A Tree Within,* 1976–1987). Paz's spiritual battles continue unabated. It may be tempting to read the more recent poems as episodes in an elderly poet's confrontation with mortality. And the evidence can be found for such a tack. In the long poem "Preparatory Exercise (Diptych with votive tablet)," for instance, the speaker laments: "The Buddha did not teach me how to die." But an open-eyed assessment shows a contrary development as well. Many of these poems give us Paz at his most celebratory—and most youthful. He sounded older at forty when he was tormenting himself with metaphysics. Now, in places, we heed a sprightlier voice, a vision that looks to the earthly as well as to the ineffable:

> The One
> is the prisoner of itself,
> it is,
> it only is,
> it has no memory,

Octavio Paz

it has no scars:
>to love is two,
always two,
>embrace and struggle,
two is the longing to be one,
and to be the other, male or female,
>>two knows no rest,
it is never complete,
>it whirls
around its own shadow,
>>searching
for what we lost at birth,
the scar opens:
>fountain of visions,
two: arch over the void,
bridge of vertigoes,
>two:
mirror of mutations.

>—from "Letter of Testimony: Cantata"

Fountain, arch, and bridge—all three are curving emblems of reconciliation and, in this context, human love. Paz's career may yet have room for a poetry of earth.

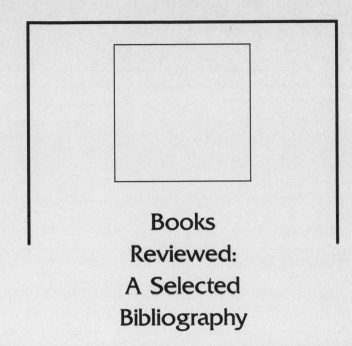

Books
Reviewed:
A Selected
Bibliography

Ashbery, John. *Selected Poems*. New York: Viking, 1985.

Bidart, Frank. *The Sacrifice*. New York: Random House, 1983.

Blackburn, Paul. *The Collected Poems of Paul Blackburn,* ed. Edith Jarolim. New York: Persea, 1985.

Blumenthal, Michael. *Laps*. Amherst, Mass.: University of Massachusetts Press, 1984.

Clampitt, Amy. *What the Light Was Like*. New York: Alfred A. Knopf, 1985.

Corkery, Christopher Jane. *Blessing*. Princeton, N.J.: Princeton University Press, 1985.

Corn, Alfred. *Notes from a Child of Paradise*. New York: Viking, 1984.

Ekelöf, Gunnar. *Songs of Something Else,* trans. Leonard Nathan and James Larson. Princeton, N.J.: Princeton University Press, 1982.

Fulton, Alice. *Palladium*. Champaign, Ill.: University of Illinois Press, 1986.

Graham, Jorie. *The End of Beauty*. New York: Ecco Press, 1987.

———. *Erosion*. Princeton, N.J.: Princeton University Press, 1983.

Green, Melissa. *The Squanicook Eclogues.* New York: Norton, 1987.

Harrison, Tony. *Selected Poems.* New York: Random House, 1987.

Herbert, Zbigniew. *Report from the Besieged City,* trans. John and Bogdana Carpenter. New York: Ecco Press, 1985.

Kinsella, Thomas, ed. *The New Oxford Book of Irish Verse.* New York: Oxford University Press, 1986.

Klappert, Peter. *The Idiot Princess of the Last Dynasty.* New York: Alfred A. Knopf, 1984.

Leithauser, Brad. *Hundreds of Fireflies.* New York: Alfred A. Knopf, 1982.

Leppmann, Wolfgang. *Rilke: A Life,* trans. with the author by Russell M. Stockman. New York: Fromm International, 1984.

Logue, Christopher. *War Music: An Account of Books 16 to 19 of Homer's "Iliad."* New York: Farrar, Straus & Giroux, 1987.

Lowell, Robert. *Collected Prose.* New York: Farrar, Straus & Giroux. 1987.

Menashe, Samuel. *Collected Poems.* Orono, Me.: National Poetry Foundation, 1986.

Meyers, Jeffrey. *Manic Power: Robert Lowell and His Circle.* New York: Arbor House, 1987.

Middleton, Christopher. *Two Horse Wagon Going By.* New York: Carcanet, 1986.

Milosz, Czeslaw. *The Witness of Poetry.* Cambridge, Mass.: Harvard University Press, 1982.

Muldoon, Paul. *Selected Poems, 1968–1986.* New York: Ecco Press, 1987.

————. ed. *The Faber Book of Contemporary Irish Poetry.* London: Faber & Faber, 1986.

Pasternak, Boris. *Boris Pasternak: "My Sister—Life" and "A Sublime Malady,"* trans. Mark Rudman and Bohdan Boychuck. Ann Arbor, Mich.: Ardis, 1983.

————. *Pasternak: Selected Poems,* trans. Jon Stallworthy and Peter France. New York: Viking, 1982.

————. *Poems of Boris Pasternak,* trans. Lydia Pasternak Slater. London: Unwin, 1984.

Pasternak, Yevgeny, et al., eds. *Letters/Summer 1926: Pasternak/Tsvetaeva/Rilke.* New York: Harcourt Brace Jovanovich, 1985.

Paz, Octavio. *The Collected Poems of Octavio Paz: 1957–1987,* ed. Eliot Weinberger. New York: New Directions, 1987.

Prater, Donald. *A Ringing Glass: The Life of Rainer Maria Rilke.* New York: Oxford University Press, 1986.

Rich, Adrienne. *Your Native Land, Your Life: Poems.* New York: Norton, 1986.

Rilke, Rainer Maria. *The Complete French Poems of Rainer Maria Rilke,* trans. A. Poulin, Jr. St. Paul, Minn.: Graywolf Press, 1986.

————. *The Duino Elegies and the Sonnets to Orpheus,* trans. A. Poulin, Jr. Boston: Houghton Mifflin, 1977.

————. *Letters on Cézanne,* trans. Joel Agee. New York: Fromm International, 1985.

Books Reviewed: A Selected Bibliography

————. *New Poems* (1907), trans. Edward Snow. San Francisco: North Point Press, 1984.

————. *The Notebooks of Malte Laurids Brigge,* trans. Stephen Mitchell. New York: Random House, 1983.

————. *Rilke: Between Roots,* trans. Rika Lesser. Princeton, N.J.: Princeton University Press, 1986.

————. *The Selected Poetry of Rainer Maria Rilke,* trans. Stephen Mitchell. New York: Random House, 1982.

Rosenthal, M. L., and Sally M. Gall. *The Modern Poetic Sequence: The Genius of Modern Poetry.* New York: Oxford University Press, 1983.

Snyder, Gary. *Left Out in the Rain: New Poems, 1947–1985.* San Francisco: North Point Press, 1986.

Storace, Patricia. *Heredity.* Boston: Beacon Press, 1987.

Swenson, May. *New and Selected Things Taking Place.* Boston: Atlantic–Little Brown, 1978.

Tranströmer, Tomas. *Selected Poems,* trans. Robin Fulton. Ann Arbor, Mich.: Ardis, 1981.

Walcott, Derek. *Midsummer.* New York: Farrar, Straus & Giroux, 1984.

Wormser, Baron. *Good Trembling.* Boston: Houghton Mifflin, 1985.

Zagajewski, Adam. *Tremor: Selected Poems.* New York: Farrar, Straus & Giroux, 1985.

Books Reviewed: A Selected Bibliography

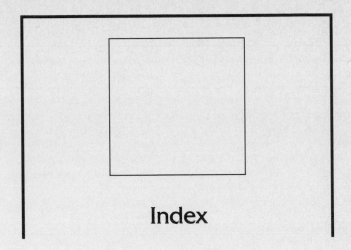

Index

Index

Index

Index

Index

A
Note
About
the
Author . . .

Sven Birkerts grew up in Michigan and received his B.A. in English from the University of Michigan, where he won first prize in the Hopwood Writing Awards. His essays have been published in *The Boston Review, The Nation, The New Republic, The New York Review of Books,* among others. His first collection of essays, entitled *An Artificial Wilderness,* was published by Morrow in 1986. He teaches writing at Harvard University and lives in Arlington, Massachusetts, with his wife, Lynn Focht.